D0872174

HOLDING UP MORE THAN HALF THE SKY

The Asian American Experience

Series Editor
Roger Daniels, University of Cincinnati

A list of books in the series appears at the end of this book.

Holding Up More Than Half the Sky

Chinese Women Garment Workers

in New York City, 1948–92

XIAOLAN BAO

Foreword by Roger Daniels

UNIVERSITY OF ILLINOIS PRESS
URBANA AND CHICAGO

Library of Congress Cataloging-in-Publication Data
Bao, Xiaolan.
Holding up more than half the sky : Chinese women garment workers in
New York City, 1948–92 / Xiaolan Bao ; foreword by Roger Daniels.
p.   cm. — (The Asian American experience)
Includes bibliographical references and index.
ISBN 0-252-02631-4 (cloth : alk. paper)
1. Women clothing workers—New York (State)—New York.
2. Chinese American women—Employment—New York (State)—New York.
3. Chinatown (New York, N.Y.) I. Title. II. Series.
HD6073.C6U533   2001
331.4'887'08995107471—dc21   00-010607

Women Sewing

In the garment shops,
The sound of the machines, "za za,"
The point of the needle jumping.
It stitches line after line,
    Wrinkling the corners of her eyes,
    Blurring her eyesight.
Long lines, straight lines, and short lines,
    Turned over, circling corners, circling in lines.
The point of the needle endlessly jumping,
    All for earning a few dimes.

The needle jumps,
The machine wheels run like wind,
Rough fingers push forward the strips of cloth,
    Pushing forward the family,
    Pushing forward the giant wheel of society.

Hands powerful,
Yet still cannot push away the threat of unemployment.
It comes like a ghost, knocking at the door
In the slow season.
Endless worry,
Like the endless circling of the needle.

In the garment shops, the dust of the cloth flies.
In the dust, their children play,
    Raising their innocent faces,
    Calling again and again, "Mama, Mama."
She looks at her child wordlessly,
She sews at the garment wordlessly,
Her thoughts silently pushing forward with the lines she sews—
    Should the steps of our lives
    Be like the points of our needles,
    Endlessly jumping and circling?
She raises her head and looks at her child,
    Looking into the future.

Wordless but determined, she thinks—
    No, no,
    The day will come,
    When even the strident sound of the machines
    Cannot drown our voices.
Unite!
Our protest will be the storm of spring,
    Releasing loud crashes of thunderbolts.

        —A Jing (*China Daily News,* December 25, 1976)
          Translated by Xiaolan Bao and edited by Marilyn S. Johnson

CONTENTS

Illustrations follow page 142

FOREWORD
Roger Daniels

While the labor of Chinese men in America has often been chronicled, analyzed, and celebrated in scholarship and fiction, little has been written about the labor of Chinese American women. Xiaolan Bao's *Holding Up More Than Half the Sky* begins to fill that void. Her poetic title rings a change on a saying attributed to Mao Zedong: "women hold up half the sky." Bao's addition of "more" does not represent a kind of hyperfeminism but the crucial fact that, although the Chinese women garment workers are exploited, often under sweatshop-like conditions redolent of an earlier era, they work in shops that have a union contract. Therefore they have benefits including health insurance, so their labor is often more vital to family survival than that of their husbands, who tend to be employed in nonunionized restaurants and laundries.

Born in Southeast Asia and educated at Beijing and New York universities, Bao has not only done intensive research in the scholarly literature and the ethnic press but has also been a participant-observer of the garment industry and the Chinese American community. She actually worked in a New York garment shop and lived in garment workers' households. Her ability to conduct interviews not only in Cantonese and Mandarin but also in other Chinese dialects gives her book a richness and earthiness rarely found in works of scholarship. It combines a focus on the Chinese women workers themselves with a deep understanding of the complex nature of the garment industry in an era of globalization. In addition it places the experiences of contemporary Chinese American women workers within the tradition of their Jewish American and Italian American sisters of an earlier era. All were members of the same union: the International Ladies' Garment Workers' Union (ILGWU). But the ILGWU the Chinese women joined, Bao shows, was often the passive and sometimes even active supporter of the bosses rather than the workers. She recounts the uphill struggle of Chinese American women activists for at least a measure of control over what should have been their own union.

This is not a neutral work. The author is a committed supporter of the activists whose lives she recreates, but she manages in spite of this to have a realistic view of their accomplishments and, unusual in a work of labor history, an understanding of the problems of the entrepreneurs, who are also Chinese. This book's greatest attraction for many readers will be the human interest in the dozens of stories, many of them quite dramatic, that Bao has gleaned from her extensive interviews with workers and others in the Chinese community, interviews that are punctuated by the earthy language of the recent immigrants. Bao's work shows us a Chinese America too often lost in the mindless celebrations of "model minorities." These women and their families are a part of that other immigrant America: an exploited immigrant America struggling, as American immigrants have always struggled, not only to survive but also to provide their children a place in a better America than they themselves inhabit. A century ago a Polish immigrant leader in Chicago told Jane Addams that "my people don't live in America, they live under America." The story that Xiaolan Bao tells shows that, at least in some ways, the same can be said about many of today's immigrants.

ACKNOWLEDGMENTS

In the almost ten years between the completion of my doctoral dissertation and the completion of this manuscript I have accumulated countless debts to numerous people. Thanks first go to Shun Nan Young, Ying Yi Deng, Agnes Wong, Tang Wei, and many other Chinese immigrant women garment workers and labor activists who have ungrudgingly spared me their precious time and shared with me their life stories. Out of respect for their wishes I am unable to name most of them here, but their stories will remain with me forever. This study would not have been possible without their support. It is therefore dedicated to them.

Many friends and colleagues have provided me with crucial support through the long and difficult period of revising my work. I would like to express my heartfelt thanks to Annelise Orleck, Alex Jetter, Wendy Locks, Gail Hershatter, Linda Gail Arrigo, Donna Boutelle, Kaye Briegel, Sherna Berger Gluck, Marilyn Johnson, Eugene Odell, and Sharon Sievers for reading part or all of the manuscript and offering insightful suggestions to improve my work. I also want to thank Renqiu Yu for suggesting the topic; Ping-Chun Hsiung, Ming-ling Yu, Linda Gail Arrigo, and Esther Chow for deepening my understanding of Hong Kong and Taiwan; Mimi Cho for her insights into Asian immigrant labor in the United States; Ellen Chen and Rebecca Rittgers for offering me a home in New York; Yi Hsiao-Ye, Nancy Quam-Wickham, and Wayne Knutson for technical assistance; John Sanchez and Chen Weimei for making the maps possible; and Xiaodan Zhang, Bing Chen, Zhao Lihua, Guo Xiaobo, Jennifer J. Y. Chen, Mike Augustine, and John Jung for their friendship and various forms of support.

I have benefited greatly from the comments and suggestions of the faculty of New York University, in particular Tom Grunfeld, Mary Nollan, David Reimans, Susan Ware, and especially Marilyn B. Young, who has gone out of her way to offer me support. For the completion of this study, my special thanks go to Roger Daniels, who has read many drafts of the manuscript, offered valuable ideas to improve it, supported me in many ways, and never lost faith in my ability xii

Acknowledgments

to complete this study. Thanks also go to Sue Fawn Chung for her thoughtful suggestions; to an anonymous reader; to Karen M. Hewitt (former executive editor) and Michele May at the University of Illinois Press for their helpful editorial suggestions; and to Matt Mitchell for preparing the copyedited manuscript.

Many individuals at various institutions have offered me essential support: Yu Ding Bang at Guangdong Zhongshan University; Huang Song Zan and Zhou Yi Er at Guangzhou Jinan University; Mei Wei Qiang at Jiangmen Wuyi University; Liu Zhong Min at the Taishan County Association for Overseas Chinese Studies; Guan Ze Feng at the Overseas Chinese Affairs Office of the Taishan People's Government; Qu Ning at the Guangdong Provincial Women Cadres' School; Wu Xing Ci, Li Ping, and Huang Ling at the Overseas Chinese Affairs Office of the Guangdong Provincial People's Government; Susan Cowell, David Melman, Carl Proper, and Walter Mankoff at the International Ladies' Garment Workers' Union (ILGWU, now the Union of Needle Industry and Textile Employees [UNITE!]); Stanley Leung, Liang Huan Ru, and Richard Chu at ILGWU/UNITE! Local 23-25; Wing Lam, Rhoda Wong, and JoAnn Lum at the Chinese Staff and Workers Association in New York; Fay Chew, Charlie Lai, and Dorothy Rony at the New York Chinatown History Project (now the Museum of Chinese in the Americas); Tom Corban at the Division of Research and Statistics of the New York State Department of Labor; and I-Der Jeng at the China Press. Special thanks go to May Ying Chen, Lily Moy, Connie Ling, Shui Mak Ka, Alice Ip, Wing Fong Chin, Katie Quan, Sherry Kane, and Betty Leung at ILGWU/UNITE! Local 23-25 and Danyun Feng at ILGWU/UNITE!, whose years of struggle, enthusiastic support, and willingness to share their experiences were among my most valuable assets while pursuing this project.

I am grateful for the generous support of various institutions. I thank the history and Asian studies departments at New York University for jointly granting me a teaching fellowship in the fall of 1994, California State University at Long Beach, my home institution, for the many faculty awards I have received in the forms of teaching relief and financial assistance, without which I would not have been able to complete this study. As the writing drew to a close, I was granted a Residential Fellowship with the Sweatshop Project in New York, a Rockefeller Humanities Institute cosponsored by the New York Lower East Side Tenement Museum and UNITE!. It allowed me to reexamine historical issues within the contemporary context and broadened my perspective by offering me an opportunity to share research findings with scholars of other ethnic groups in the New York City garment industry. I thank Nancy Carnevale, Steve Fraser, Virginia Yans-McLaughlin, Daniel Soyer, and Carmen Teresa Whalen for what I have learned from them.

Thanks also go to the librarians and archival staff at the following institutions for their kind assistance: the Tamiment Library at New York University; the Oriental and Research Divisions of the New York Public Library; the New York

Chatham Square Public Library; the East Asian Library of Columbia University; the Labor Archives and Research Center of San Francisco State University; the Special Collections Division of the University of California at Los Angeles; the East Asian Collection of the Hoover Institution at Stanford University; the Asian American Studies Library at the University of California at Berkeley; the Library of Congress; the Sun Zhongshan Archival Section of the Guangdong Provincial Library; and the Taishan County Archival Library. In particular I want to thank Barbara Morley at the Kheel Center for Labor-Management Documentation and Archives in the M. P. Catherwood Library of the New York State School of Industrial and Labor Relations at Cornell University; Vicky Munda and Catherine Lews-Ida at the Interlibrary Loan Services at California State University at Long Beach, whose witty humor and magic power for attaining rare materials made research for this project a joyful adventure.

Most of all, thanks should go to my late father, Pau Keit, and my mother, Shun Shut Yiu, for planting the seeds of appreciating social equality in me at an early age; to my siblings and their families: Shiu Lan, Mei Lan, David Wei, Sukie, Fok Wai, Micheal Lap, Andrew, and Nicky for their inexhaustible love and support; to Uncle Phoy Waing Lec for witnessing me growing up in Burma (now Myanmar), picking me up at the airport the first day I arrived in the United States, and getting me started by introducing me to the close-knit New York Chinese community; and to his family, particularly his daughter and my childhood friend Margaret and her family, Emily and Henry, for their love and hospitality and for always being there for me. Without them this project would not have been conceivable.

A NOTE ON INTERVIEWS
AND TRANSLITERATIONS

This study has drawn substantially on interviews with 176 individuals. Except for eleven oral histories conducted by the New York Chinatown History Project (now the Museum of Chinese in the Americas), one by the Oral History Program at California State University at Long Beach, and five by the Oral History Project of the Tamiment Library at New York University, and a few in the Margaret Mead Papers at the Library of Congress, all of the interviews were conducted by the author between 1986 and 1998. Nineteen took place in China, one in Poughkeepsie, and the rest in various boroughs of New York City. Twenty individuals were interviewed more than once, and I have maintained close contact with about ten garment workers and concerned individuals over the years.

The persons interviewed for this project include members of emigrant families in the former Si Yi District in China, the source of most early Chinese immigrants to New York City, employers and labor activists in the Chinese garment industry of New York City, and officials and staff members of various social organizations of the Chinese community and institutions related to the city's garment industry. Most of the persons interviewed, however, were Chinese immigrant women who were working or had worked in garment shops in Chinatown or other parts of New York City. These workers came to New York in various historical periods from different parts of China and Asia, and represent a range of ages and socioeconomic and educational backgrounds. Two among them were widowed, three were single, five were divorced, and the rest were married with children and lived with their families.

I used a recording device or took handwritten notes when the interviewee gave me permission to do so. I did, however try to record the most relevant information based on my memory within a few hours if I could not do so during the interview; I did this with the full knowledge of the interviewee. I have approximately seventy-five hours of recordings and have transcribed most of them. Most of these interviews were conducted in Cantonese; others were conducted in Mandarin, Taishanese, Burmese, English, or a mixture of these languages.

I respect the privacy of the persons I interviewed and use pseudonyms in identifying them in this study, unless I have been given permission to use their names. I address many of them according to the ways in which they were introduced to me when we met, which reflect our age and generation differences.

* * *

Following standard transliteration practice, I use the pinyin romanization system for Chinese names and phrases and the Yale system for common words and phrases in the Cantonese dialect or direct quotations from Cantonese-speaking persons.[1] For immigrants from Hong Kong I apply the 1982 Hong Kong telephone directory to transliterate their names to comply with the rules to which they were accustomed. For the few common words in the particular Taishan dialect of the Province of Guangdong or other Chinese dialects and languages of other countries, I follow the ways in which they have most frequently appeared in English-language texts.

When using a person's Chinese name, I follow Chinese practice by giving the surname (family name) first and then the given name, except for those who have adopted a Western first name or have transcribed their Chinese names but followed the Western name sequence (their last name after their first name).

The English titles of Chinese-language newspapers—the *China Daily News,* the *Central Daily News,* the *World Journal,* and *Sing Tao Daily*—are given as they appear(ed) in print.

HOLDING UP MORE THAN HALF THE SKY

INTRODUCTION

New Yorkers who take the B, D, E, F, N, and number 6 trains through the Chinatown area between 7:30 and 9:00 P.M. are met by a familiar scene. No matter how empty the trains are, they instantly fill with crowds of passengers once they pull into the station. Most of these are Chinese women in their thirties and forties who have just ended a day's work in the Chinatown garment shops and are anxious to return home. Carrying heavy bags of groceries, they scramble for seats. Many doze off once seated. Others seize this precious moment to share their joys and frustrations with their fellow workers. Competing with the clatter of the train, they raise their voices often to such a high pitch that it is likely to invite frowns and glowering from other passengers.

What unsympathetic passengers do not realize is that these Chinese women are part of a mainstay of the city's economy. Since 1975 their labor in Chinatown garment shops not only has helped anchor the garment industry to the city and maintain its leading position in the nation's garment production, it has also been central to the economy of the Chinese community in the city.[1] With the majority of Chinatown garment shops unionized since the 1970s, these workers have emerged as the largest group of organized Asian working women in the United States.[2]

It is not surprising that their important role is largely ignored by the public, however, because few major studies have been written about them. Apart from sensational media coverage, which labeled their workplaces "sweatshops" and portrayed them as eroding wages and working conditions across the United States, there is no systematic study about their lives. Chinese American working-class immigrant women are not only missing in the literature on American women's history, but they are only dimly visible in most literature on Chinese Americans.[3] The lack of a systematic study of their experience has hindered the development of an adequate understanding of Chinese American history and that of ethnic women workers in the United States.

This study is a step toward filling that gap. Focusing on the lives of the New

York Chinese women garment workers in the post–World War II era, it addresses major issues in Chinese American history and U.S. labor history. The location, subject, and time chosen for this study provide an important venue to achieve this goal. Since 1970 New York City has replaced San Francisco as the city with the largest Chinese community in the United States, and the garment industry has also replaced the traditional hand-laundry business as one of the two major sources of income for working-class Chinese families in the city. By the late 1970s, four out of ten Chinese families in New York had members working in the Chinatown garment shops, and about 85 percent of the city's Chinese adult female population who worked in the ethnic economic sector were garment workers.[4]

Given the fact that in 1980 almost 90 percent of the Chinese women garment workers were married and 70 percent of the new immigrants in the Chinese community were members of the working class, this high rate of married women participating in wage-earning labor outside the home has not only significantly contributed to the growth of the family economy but has also profoundly transformed its culture.[5]

This study examines women workers' experience in the historical context of the Chinese community in the city; its central subjects are working-class women and their important contributions. The purpose of this study, however, is not simply to recognize their important role in the community. Rather it intends to advance new interpretations of Chinese American experience in New York City. By recovering an important part of history and by asking how and why the invisibility of working-class women has taken place, this study reveals the differing significance of the changing cultural, economic, and political structures of the community for various social groups.

This study also provides a powerful lens through which to inspect major issues in the development of organized labor in the United States. As the center of women's garment production since its beginning, the industry in New York City has long been an important site for scholars to investigate the intricate interrelationship between class, gender, and ethnicity in the lives of U.S. workers. Although many studies have explored the experiences of ethnic women workers in the industry, none has focused on the Chinese.[6]

The Chinese workers' experience is similar in many ways to that of their counterparts in the history of the city's garment industry. From the beginning of the Chinatown garment industry, women formed more than 80 percent of its workforce. Most of the workers were recent immigrants. Driven by family need and the lack of English and marketable skills in the United States, they found in the garment industry an opportunity to earn a living. The International Ladies' Garment Workers' Union (ILGWU) began to organize the Chinatown garment industry in the 1950s.[7] Women workers' experience at their workplace, intersecting with their changing role in the family and the community, has nurtured labor militancy in the Chinatown garment shops. This labor militancy culminated in the historic Chinese garment workers' strike in 1982, the largest labor strike in the history of New York's Chinatown.

However, the Chinese women workers' experience in many ways differs from that of their predecessors. They came from a different culture and entered the garment industry at a time when it had already been significantly impaired by the global economy.

Although this is not a comparative study of women's historical experience in New York's garment industry, it places the Chinese experience within the context of garment industry labor history. By so doing, it asks how the Chinese experience can enrich our understanding of women's experience in U.S. labor history. In this era of capital globalization, when most literature on women workers focuses on the Third World, this study will contribute to our understanding of the conditions of workers in the First World by focusing on a single group of ethnic women workers in the United States.

Concentrating on the period from about 1948, the putative beginning of the Chinatown garment shops, to 1992, a decade after the historic Chinese garment workers' strike, this study is divided into three parts.[8] Part 1 provides a historical context for understanding issues to be discussed in this study. Part 2 explores the important role of working-class women in the history of New York's Chinese community and how the intersection of the garment workers' experience in the family and the workplace fostered their labor militancy. Part 3 discusses the historic 1982 strike and its impact on the workers.

* * *

A major focus of this study is the multiple intersecting forces that have shaped the lives and perceptions of Chinese women garment workers in New York City. Gender, race/ethnicity, and class are the three major categories of analysis that will be employed. Recent scholars have persuasively argued that the meaning of any analytical category is relational, discursive, and historically constructed; subjects must be situated within their particular cultural and historical contexts.[9] The complexity of these categories is heightened by the realities of the New York Chinese American community.

Scholars engaging in the study of Chinese Americans are cognizant of the difficulty in defining class in the community. Historically, there have been striking social differences between students, scholars, businessmen, professionals, and other members of the community. But there has also been a high degree of fluidity among various social groups, particularly small business owners and workers. This was true especially after the 1870s, when anti-Chinese agitation began to mount in New York City. The U.S. working class has historically been characterized by its whiteness, its industrial work setting, and its masculine identity based not only on its members' biology but also on their gendered behavior, work culture, and occupational identities. To be a member of such a social group was beyond the reach of the Chinese American laborers. Relegated to the

service sector, many early Chinese American male laborers had to content themselves with self-employment in small laundry and restaurant businesses, traditionally women's work. Although their unique experience can contribute to our
understanding of the nature of American society, it has made it difficult to apply any classical definition of class to them.

Renqiu Yu's outstanding study of the Chinese Hand Laundry Alliance of New
York (CHLA) illustrates this difficulty. He shows that many Chinese small laundry owners worked in the stores themselves. Many worked an average of fifteen
to seventeen hours a day, six to seven days a week, and were subjected to extortion by larger interests in and outside their community. Their status as small
business owners might assist them in applying for immigration status for their
families, but their lives differed only slightly from those of their employees.

The ambiguity in their social status was fully demonstrated by the dilemma
Chinese leftists faced in the 1930s when they attempted to apply orthodox Marxist theory to define social class. It was difficult to identify owners of the one- or
two-manned Chinese hand laundries with the proletarians in an industrial setting, but it was also difficult not to recognize the laboring nature of their lives.
The term "poor laboring class" that the Chinese leftists finally created and applied to the Chinese laundrymen is not a far cry from "working class."[10]

Things have changed greatly since the 1960s, after the massive Chinese immigration to the city began. However, most Chinese immigrants continue to be
segregated in the ethnic economic sector. Characterized by its small-capital
enterprises with a high turnover rate, the line between small business owners
and workers in the Chinese ethnic enterprises, including those of the manufacturing sector, remains blurred.

Some scholars have employed the concepts of "uptown" and "downtown"
Chinese to highlight social differences in New York's Chinese community. As
early as 1953 two geographically defined groups with "almost no sense of common interest" but "definite antagonism" were identified by Virginia Heyer. The
Mandarin-speaking, better educated, professional, and wealthy uptown Chinese
elite, who resided in upper Manhattan, considered the Cantonese-speaking,
poorly educated, lower-class downtown Chinese, who lived and worked in
Chinatown, to be the source of "American animosity against Chinese in general." Anxious to distinguish themselves from the downtown Chinese, the uptown
Chinese even wrote articles to justify the Americans' resentment against those
in Chinatown.[11] Some scholars have resumed the use of these terms in the study
of the New York Chinese community.[12]

Although the use of "uptown Chinese" and "downtown Chinese" demonstrates an awareness of social differences in the community, it lacks historical and
geographical accuracy. The Mandarin-speaking community of uptown Chinese
in the area around Columbia University was in fact a relatively recent phenomenon. The earliest Chinese students sent by the Chinese court to study in the
United States in the late nineteenth century were overwhelmingly Cantonese-

speaking and from poor families.[13] They studied in New England, and there is no record of problems with the men in New York's Chinatown when they visited.[14] Students from various parts of China began to study at Columbia University in the early twentieth century, but their number remained small, and few sought residence in the United States after completion of their studies.

The "uptown Chinese," as a group of better-educated and Mandarin-speaking professional Chinese, did not emerge until the end of the Second World War, when American universities began to recruit students from China in response to President Truman's decision to extend postwar recovery assistance to China. They became noticeably visible only after the Communist success in China in 1949, when the U.S. government passed a series of refugee acts. Although the Chinese population in New York City has subsequently increased, this group has had little to do with Chinatown, except for occasionally dining and shopping there. They developed their own elite culture in the uptown area.

Furthermore, even when the uptown Chinese community began to grow, not all Chinese residing in Chinatown were poor, nor were all those who lived in upper Manhattan members of the Chinese elite.[15] To complicate the matter further, as Cheng Tsu Wu has pointed out, as early as 1950 members of the Chinese elite who had taken up permanent residence in the United States began moving out of Manhattan and into Flushing and Long Island City in the borough of Queens.[16] The Chinese distribution in the city became even more complicated in the 1970s and 1980s, with the rise of high-income buildings along Park Row Drive in Chinatown and the increased movement of the Chinese to other boroughs.

Considering the complexity of class stratification and historical changes in the community, I prefer to use the more inclusive term "working class" to refer to the working people in the Chinese community. It primarily refers to workers in the factories and various forms of ethnic enterprises after the end of World War II, but it is also used to include all those Chinese laborers, employed or self-employed, in the prewar era. In its broadest possible sense this term can be used to include all working members of the community except for big business owners, full-time students, scholars, and professionals. Although this broad definition does not seem to comply with the orthodox Marxist theory of class, it is based on an understanding of the complex reality of the Chinese community and on the belief that members of this group did not and still do not have the same opportunity for betterment as did their compatriots with wealth and professional skills in the highly stratified and racialized society of the United States.

Complications also exist in the racial/ethnic identity of the Chinese community in the city. Like its counterparts elsewhere, New York's Chinese community has been historically fractured not only by gender and class but by regionalism and other political and cultural differences. Although regionalism, for instance, is nominally based on immigrants' identification with their native place in China, it is more than a concept of geographical identity. This was true especially during the Exclusion era. To seek protection from discrimination in the larger society and violent conflicts within their own community, Chinese immigrants tended to pledge their loyalty to different social and political organizations in the community, which claimed their roots in the immigrants' kin or lineage organizations in their native land. As a result, the self-proclaimed regional identity of an immigrant man often also indicated his social and political position in the community. The influence of this aspect of the Chinese experience remains to this date.

One way to understand the complexity of the political and cultural differences within the community is to look at the various dialects its members spoke. Compared with the contemporary New York Chinese community, the early Chinese population was much more homogeneous. Since almost all of them were Han, the majority Chinese ethnic group, and most came from the county of Taishan (Xinning before 1914) in the Si Yi District of Guangdong Province, the Taishan dialect became the lingua franca of the community.[17] Differences already existed, however, as there were some who came from other Si Yi counties, the San Yi District, the Hakka community in Guangdong, and other parts of China. They spoke different dialects.[18]

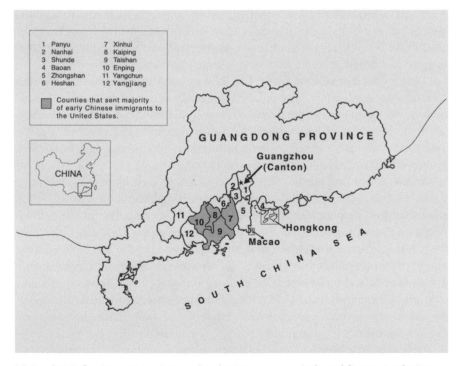

Map 1. Guangdong counties mentioned in the text, pre-1949. (Adapted from a map by Huang Jinghu and Lu Huaiyuan, edited by Jin Qingyu, published by Ya Guang Yu Di Xue She, Shanghai, 1950; available in the Sun Zhongshan Archival Library, Gangzhou, China.)

Although the early Chinese community was generally defined as a "Cantonese" community by many outsiders, the dialects of San Yi and Si Yi, particularly the latter, are not only distinctly different from the dialect generally defined as "Cantonese" and taught as such in many Chinese programs in the contemporary Western world; they are also different from each other. Even the dialects of the counties in each of these two districts differ slightly.[19] Linguistic and cultural differences were particularly evident between the Hakka and the rest of the immigrants from the same province. Speaking a dialect that belongs to another major linguistic family, the Hakka people, as descendants of early migrants to the province, tended to maintain their ethnic culture, which was significantly different from that of the Guangdong locals. The bloody confrontations between the Hakka and the locals at the turn of the twentieth century, which lasted for almost fifty years, further planted the seeds of dislike and even animosity between them.[20]

Adding to the complication is the fact that while many Chinatown social and political organizations claimed to have their roots in the lineage or kinship systems of the immigrants' native villages, many villages in Guangdong Province were under the influence of more than one lineage or kinship organization. Hence, immigrants from the same geographical area who spoke the same dialect did not necessarily share the same political loyalty. Local politics festering under the cloak of differences originating from the immigrants' native land did significantly undermine the solidarity of New York's early Chinese community.

The diversity among the New York Chinese has become even more salient in the past few decades, when increasingly large numbers of Chinese have come not only from China, Hong Kong, and Taiwan but also from Southeast Asian countries and with different social, cultural, and political backgrounds. Nevertheless, the umbrella Chinese ethnic identity still weighs heavily with most Chinese Americans.[21] This study will further explore the significance of Chinese identity for various social groups in the community and differences among these groups within the particular historical contexts.

Like class, race, and ethnicity, gender, as a central category of analysis in this study, is by no means monolithic and stable. Although the subject of this study is pursued with clear gender, class, and other social specificities, the Chinatown women garment workers have never been a monolithic group, especially after the massive Chinese immigration of the late 1960s. Like the rest of the female population in the community, these workers were and still are different not only in age, time of and reason for immigration, and prior educational, social, and cultural backgrounds but also in political inclination. Influenced by the political system of their native place as well as their social status there, these workers did not necessarily see things alike.

The historical differences among these workers demonstrate that like that of any other member of a society, the identity of a woman is multidimensional and relational. Gender is not the only principle of social organization. Nevertheless, constantly intersecting with other principles of social organization, it defines a major aspect of one's social identity. Recent feminist scholarship has demonstrated that however contingent and unstable their foundations, gender roles in a culture, once constructed, shape the subjectivity and behavior of men and women, define social relationships, and justify social stratification. In this sense, the study of gender is not simply about women. Rather it aims to unearth the power relationships embedded in the historical process that have constantly constructed various forms of gender relations in a society. It is along this line of thinking that I pursue gender analysis in this study.

Although class, gender, and race/ethnicity are the three major categories of analysis in this study, they are not the only ones. The continual contestations between concerned social groups and institutions within constantly changing social and political milieus determine that the meanings of these categories cannot be unitary and static, nor can human experience be neatly compartmentalized into categories of scholarly analysis. Nevertheless, by examining how the multiple meanings of class, gender, and race/ethnicity have been constituted over time and the intersections between them as well as their intersections with other analytical categories, this study endeavors to reveal the myriad power relations that have shaped the lives of Chinese Americans in New York City.

Methodology

Due to the dearth of historical records about Chinese American working-class women, this study is substantially based on interviews with them and my own observation over a period of more than a decade. More than a hundred individuals were interviewed for this study, including labor activists, longtime residents of New York's Chinatown, members of various social organizations in the Chinese community, and officials and staff members of the former ILGWU Local 23-25 and other garment-related institutions in the city. However, the majority of those interviewed were Chinese women garment workers and their family members.

Except for eleven oral histories conducted by and preserved in the New York Chinatown History Project (now the museum of Chinese in the Americas), five by the Oral History Project of the Tamiment Library at New York University, a few in the Margaret Mead Papers at the Library of Congress, and one in the collection of the Oral History Program at California State University at Long Beach, all the interviews were conducted by the author in 1986, 1989, the summer of 1992, the fall of 1994, and the academic year 1997–98. All but one of the interviews conducted in the United States took place in New York City. I was introduced to more than half of the interviewees by the union and various organizations in the city's Chinese community, but the institutional influence diminished as my relationship with them continued over the years. I came to know the rest of them primarily through my family connections, friends, and the social network I established through my involvement in the community. To attain a better understanding of women's lives in the emigrant families in China, I also conducted a number of interviews in Guangzhou, Jiangmen, and the two former Si Yi counties of Taishan and Xinhui in the summer of 1997. Most of the individuals I interviewed were wives and other family members of early Chinese emigrants to the United States.

My contact with the New York Chinese women workers did not begin with this project, nor was it limited to interviews or something that might be described as an ethnographic "field trip." It began as early as 1984, the second week after I arrived in New York City as a foreign student. Thanks to a family connection and the close-knit nature of the New York Chinese community, I was introduced to a garment worker's family and became their tenant. When this family wanted to occupy the room I rented, I moved into the home of my first landlady's closest friend, who was also a garment worker. Hence, my living experience with workers' families spanned a period of about five years.

I began this study in 1989, when I started working on my dissertation, and I carried on research after the completion of my graduate program. For more than ten years I interviewed workers and other concerned individuals whenever circumstances permitted. I also taught in a Chinatown Sunday English school for more than two years, volunteered services to a number of garment workers, worked briefly in a Chinatown garment shop, participated in workers' activities on various occasions, and maintained close contact with a number of garment workers over these years.[22]

Among my friends are longtime Chinatown garment workers as well as recent immigrant garment workers employed in the new center of Chinese garment production in the Sunset Park area of Brooklyn, documented as well as undocumented, unionized as well as nonunionized, homeworkers as well as factory workers. In addition, as this project was ending I was fortunately granted an opportunity to be a resident fellow with a Sweatshop Project in New York City, which allowed me to explore further the historical significance of my work in the contemporary context.

My longtime relationship with many workers and my constantly enlarging network of contacts, created by workers and their friends and family members as well as my own family connections and other social networks, provided me with easy entry into the workers' community and helped reduce the problems researchers tend to encounter in short-term interviews.[23] My long-term contact with the workers and other individuals in the community offered me important opportunities to observe their lives and understand the meanings they attached to their life stories. It also enabled me to detect and decode significant discrepancies in the narratives before I decided on the most typical ones to present in my work. In addition, this long-term contact allowed me to rectify any inappropriate methods and attitudes that I happened to adopt.

I do not intend to imply, however, that a long-term relationship can eliminate all potential problems embedded in the interaction of two subjectivities in interviews, nor would I deny the subjective nature of either the life histories and historical realities presented here or my way of representing them.[24] However, as the U.S. immigration historian Virginia Yans-McLaughlin argues, "Even when these oral interviews do not describe an objective past, they bear its unmistakable imprint."[25] It is the task of a historian to reveal the "unmistakable imprint" of history in these personal accounts, and this is precisely what I have endeavored to do in this study. By examining the social and historical contexts from which the personal accounts emerged and the meanings the individuals attached to them, I intend to expose a historical process that has important implications for understanding the meanings of Chinese American as well as women's and U.S. labor history.

I have also drawn substantially on other historical sources, including U.S. government documents and publications, union archives, and community newspapers and other publications. Although all these sources were helpful in reconstructing the historical process, they are by no means objective, as some historians and social scientists would like to believe. Not only are they slanted by the positions of their publishers, but they are often limited by the scope of their coverage and by the period during which they were published.[26] Even statistics provided by the U.S. Census Bureau and U.S. Immigration and Naturalization Service reveal the "hidden" subjectivities of their compilers. The inconsistent and insufficient categories under which they collected and compiled their data demonstrate their social biases and inadequate understanding of their times.

By weaving together information from these historical sources and deciphering the open subjectivities (in the case of oral interviews) and "hidden" subjectivities (in the case of the conventional written historical records) embedded in them, I have struggled to unearth a part of history that I believe is too important to be ignored.

Given the diverse backgrounds of the Chinese women garment workers in New York City, the multilayered and multidimensional structure of the garment industry, and the complex realities of the Chinese community, this study is by no means exhaustive. Nor does it represent an "insider's perspective," as there is hardly one unitary perspective of any social group in the community studied here. Although I have tried to understand the historical context from the perspectives of those who lived through it, I am fully aware of my limitations.

My experience living in an overseas Chinese community at an early age and my command of various Chinese dialects spoken in most major overseas Chinese communities perhaps places me in a better position than those who do not have this background. My training in women's history and feminist studies might also sharpen my understanding of the lives of women workers. However, this does not guarantee that I will be able to understand fully those from social groups different from mine, particularly workers who have been toiling in the Chinese garment shops and labor activists who have been in the forefront of the Chinese American labor movement.

Those who toiled in the shops and who persevered in carrying on the struggle for workers' rights in the community have taught me a great deal. Their wisdom in constructing psychological fronts to fend off the assaults generated by the exploitative labor system and social institutions without losing essential elements of their identity and human dignity and their courage in initiating change under adversity not only made sense of what I had learned from feminist programs in an academic setting but also pointed to their weaknesses. I have been working on this study for so long that it has become a part of my life. It has taught me the importance of understanding differences among women and of learning from those whose life experiences are different from mine. All this has greatly influenced my other feminist pursuits in the last ten years and will continue to do so in the years to come.

I rewrote this introduction after I completed this study. In doing so, many unforgettable episodes in the long course of my research surfaced.[27] I do not think I can ever adequately thank the individuals, particularly the workers and labor activists who have so generously extended their support, for what they have taught me. If there is a way for me to pay back their kindness and support, it is with this study. What is presented here may not be exactly as they would like to see it. However, I believe that they would appreciate my effort to disclose the multiple forces that have shaped the lives in the community and to recover an important part of its history. I present this study also in the hope that it can initiate dialogue among concerned scholars and community labor activists and generate more studies on similar subjects in the future.

PART 1

The Milieu

Since the late 1960s the Chinatown garment industry has had a strong transforming impact on many aspects of the Chinese community in New York City. However, like most of what has happened in Chinatown, the growth of the industry was not shaped only by factors in the community. Although contemporaneous with the decline of the Chinese laundry business, it was an aspect of the development of the city's garment industry and the demographic changes in the Chinese community since 1965. The history of the city's garment industry provided the context for and helped shape the growth of the garment industry in Chinatown. This part is therefore devoted to long-standing issues in the city's garment industry as well as the impact of the Chinatown garment industry on the community.

CHAPTER 1

The Vicissitudes of New York City's Garment Industry: A Brief History

To this date, almost all Chinatown garment shops are contract shops. Their organizational structure and the nature of their products have been shaped by the development of the city's garment industry over the last century. Although the New York City garment industry has undergone various forms of transformation since the mid-nineteenth century, when it became the center of garment production in the United States, many major aspects remain largely unchanged. By constantly adjusting to the changing economic and political climates, these major aspects not only managed to anchor the garment industry to the city but will continue to influence its future. A brief history of the city's garment industry will lead us to better understand this influence.

The ready-made clothing trade was insignificant in New York City before 1820, as most New Yorkers wore homemade clothing. Journeymen and custom tailors designed and made clothes that only affluent classes could afford. An article of tailored clothing was considered so valuable that a person kept it for a lifetime, and families passed clothes down from generation to generation. Those who did not have the material to make their own clothing or could not afford custom-made clothing had to content themselves with second-hand clothing.[1]

Before 1820 the only ready-made clothing was worn by sailors who had no time to wait for clothes to be made. The shops making such clothing in New York City were located first on Water and Front Streets and then on Cherry Street and Maiden Lane. Made of cheap materials and requiring little care and fitting, this type of clothing was defined as "slop work" and was shunned by custom tailors who feared degrading their craftsmanship.[2]

Several factors contributed to the growth of New York's ready-made clothing trade in the 1820s. Among them were the development of the textile indus-

try in the northeastern part of the United States, which provided the city's industry with less expensive fabrics; the high tariff imposed on imported goods
after 1816, which significantly undermined the competition from British imports;[3] and the completion of the Erie Canal and the beginning of a railroad
network in the 1830s, which led to the further expansion of New York City's
clothing trade into the western market.[4] By the mid-nineteenth century, clothing made in New York served not only the plantations in the South and the
markets in the Midwest but also the gold mines on the Pacific Coast.[5]

Three interrelated factors account for the growth of the city's clothing trade
in subsequent decades: the use of the sewing machine, the outbreak of the
American Civil War, and the presence of a European immigrant workforce. The
use of the sewing machine, allegedly invented by the New Englander Elias Howe
in 1846 and improved upon and marketed by Isaac Singer, another New Englander, five years later, made clothing manufacturing much quicker, better, and
cheaper. This was especially true after the invention of a series of labor-saving
devices, such as the power drive, which replaced the original foot treadle, the
button-hole machine, the machine cutter, which supplanted hand shears, and
the mechanical presser, which replaced the hand iron.[6]

The Civil War proved the importance of the sewing machine for mass production in the garment industry. Since orders for military uniforms were large
and often placed on short notice, wartime demand not only ensured a market
for the city's ready-made clothing industry but also highlighted the importance
of large-scale production in the city's industry and the use of the sewing machines in this production.

The most important factor for the growth of the city's industry in this period, however, was the presence of a European immigrant workforce. Beginning
with English and Scots in the early nineteenth century and Irish and Germans
in the 1840s and 1850s, immigrants furnished the city's clothing industry with
inexpensive skilled and unskilled labor. This was particularly important for the
garment industry because labor costs formed a major and invariable part of its
production cost. The importance of immigrant labor to the city's garment industry can be seen in the 1855 New York State Census. Of the 12,609 tailors and
9,819 dressmakers and seamstresses in New York State that year, 12,109 tailors
and 6,606 dressmakers and seamstresses were foreign-born, and most of them
were believed to be in New York City.[7]

Bolstered by this ample supply of immigrant labor, the city's clothing industry began to grow. Between 1860 and 1880, the numbers of clothing manufacturing establishments and employees doubled, growing from 303 and 21,568 to
736 and 47,647, respectively. As early as 1850, the clothing industry became the
third most important manufacturing enterprise in New York State, and New
York City became the leading production center for ready-made clothing in the
nation. By 1855 the clothing industry was already the largest in New York City.

A number of scholars have pointed out that the contracting system, which remains the basic organizational system of the city's industry, was established at its beginning.[8] Even technological improvement could not alter this system. Although sewing machines increased productivity, they had their limits. Initially, an operator could only join the straight seams of the front, sides, and back of a coat by machine and still had to sew the rest by hand. To expedite production and reduce labor costs, shop owners began to separate hand sewing from machine-operated work and to replace a number of skilled workers with unskilled and semiskilled ones for the sewing that could be done by machines. This began the segmentation of work and the reduction of craftsmanship in garment production.

Starting from the early years of the industry, two types of shop, the "inside shop" and the "outside shop," laid the foundation for the contracting system. Manufacturers ran inside shops, where the entire manufacturing process was completed under one roof, though many sent out the sewing to be done elsewhere.[9] Contractors ran outside shops, accepting cut garments either directly from manufacturers or from other contractors and sewing them according to their specifications. However, as Nancy Green has pointed out, "the terms ['inside shop' and 'outside shop'] are misleading."[10] Before 1892 most outside shops were actually inside the homes of contractors or workers. There were several levels of contracting, but profit at each level was made from the margin between the fixed payment received from manufacturers and the costs paid out for labor and overhead. Hence, despite some variations between them, both the inside and outside shops employed the contracting system.

Before 1860 all ready-made clothing was for men, and coats and suits were the staple items of the city's garment business until 1910.[11] The only women's ready-made clothing before 1860 was a limited number of cloaks, mantillas, and hoop skirts. The women's garment industry, which became the major component of the city's garment industry in the early twentieth century, did not grow until the late nineteenth century.[12] Its growth can be largely attributed to the changing patterns of women's clothing, which reflected the transformation in women's social status, and the massive entrance of immigrants from eastern and southern Europe, particularly Russia, Poland, Hungary, Romania, and Italy. It was estimated that by 1920 some 460,000 Eastern European Jews and 390,000 Italians had settled in New York.[13] They provided human resources for the growth of the industry.

The women's garment industry began to take off in the late nineteenth century. Manufacturers produced almost all the lines—shirtwaists, skirts, undergarments, dresses, suits, cloaks, and coats—and the product value of the women's garment industry in New York began to increase steadily. From 64 percent in 1899, its share of the national market grew to 74 percent in 1921 and 78 percent in 1925.[14] The position of New York City as the women's garment production center of the nation was thus well established by the end of the nineteenth century.

The contracting system also underwent significant development during this period. Owners of inside shops began to face a severe challenge from the outside shops run by recently arrived Eastern European Jews. Speaking little if any English and unfamiliar with the new environment, as well as adhering to religious practices different from those of German Jews, the Eastern European workers preferred to work in shops run by persons from their region. Although these shops were much smaller, they were located in Eastern European neighborhoods and followed the same religious practice as their workers. This gave the Eastern European Jewish contractors a competitive edge in the industry. As Roger Waldinger has put it, so long as their labor force was formed by newly arrived immigrants "too bewildered and dependent to look for jobs elsewhere," the Eastern European Jewish contractors could "drive their workers to the peak of their productivity" and "hold on to them during the wild seasonal fluctuations of the industry."[15] Acknowledging their inability to compete with the contract shops owned by Eastern European Jewish immigrants, more and more German Jewish inside shops, particularly those manufacturing women's garments, began to farm out their cut garments.

This new development in the contracting system marked the beginning of an increasingly clear separation of production from the rest of the operations in the city's garment industry. By farming out their cut garments to contractors, owners of the inside shops were able to shift most production risks to contractors and bring down prices by pitting one contractor against another. Under this new system, contractors became the overseers of labor in the industry. They arranged for workers to follow the specifications set by the manufacturers. Although a contractor might subcontract his work, the line between contractor and manufacturer was distinctly drawn.

The new system resulted in cutthroat competition among the contractors. As Louis Levine observed, competition was so severe that contractors went to manufacturers in search of work, "hat in hand like a beggar."[16] The system, however, offered some entrepreneurial Jewish male immigrants a path from employment to proprietorship. Since sewing machines were cheap and could be bought on credit and a shop could be set up in a room of a tenement building, one needed very little capital to start a business.[17] As long as a contractor was adept at maximizing profit, undercutting the prices of other contractors by offering his compatriot workers the lowest possible wages, and cutting overhead costs to the bone, he too could climb up the economic ladder and become a proprietor. It was therefore not unusual during this period for "the labor crusader of yesterday" to become "the unconscionable sweatshop boss of today."[18] Clustered in the Lower East Side and on Division, East Broadway, and Wooster Street, the Eastern European contractors became known as "moths of Division Street," in comparison with the German Jewish "Broadway giants."

As had been the case with the former "Broadway giants," for these "moths of Division Street" to grow fat and turn into new giants someone had to suffer.

The high turnover rate caused by intense competition among contractors resulted in even more unscrupulous practices by the new contractors in their search for profit.[19] As a result, sweatshops proliferated in tenement buildings on the Lower East Side in the late nineteenth century, and with living and working spaces packed together the area became immensely crowded.[20] Elizabeth Ewen describes working conditions in the shops as follows:

> A twelve- to fourteen-hour day was common. Workers were often cheated out of their full wages—clocks were slowed down during working hours or sped up at lunchtime. Workers were charged for needles, thread, mistakes, and even electrical power (if there was any). They were fined for being late, talking, singing, and taking too much time in the bathroom. The sanitary conditions were deplorable, the working conditions unsafe; floors collapsed in small lofts incapable of carrying the weight of machines and people, the doors were locked when work began, and shop fires were common. The speed of the work was intense.[21]

Infectious diseases spread easily in the crowded tenements. The New York State Health Department reported that "The death rate of children under 5 years of age in tenements ran up as high as 204 per thousand" and that "homeworkers living in the Italian district of New York City were 14 times more likely to die from tuberculosis than people living in the upper-income neighborhoods across from Central Park."[22] In 1892, alarmed by the high rate of tuberculosis on the Lower East Side, New York State passed the first of a series of laws to regulate manufacturing outside of factories, which stipulated that no work was allowed to be done in any room used for eating or sleeping, except that by immediate members of the family residing in a tenement and with a permit from the Board of Health.

Although shops were said to have consequently moved out of homes to the factories after 1892, Nancy Green shows that homework and tenement production were not completely abolished.[23] Jesse E. Pope's visit to the district in 1902 also revealed that the majority of shops were still in buildings "unfit for factory purposes," where "even reasonably fair conditions as to ventilation and light are out of the question."[24]

Nevertheless, as the contracting system continued to develop and smaller production units increased, there was a relative shift to larger concentration of production at the turn of the century. Many factors contributed to this shift: the outcome of attempts to regulate homework, the growing standardization of production, and the metamorphosis of "moths" into "giants." Roger Waldinger, however, claims that the most important reason was the change in buying and selling practices in the industry.[25] Direct purchases from manufacturers, the rapid development of department stores, and the growth of mail-order houses undercut the role of wholesalers and distributors in the previous period. This trend reduced the importance of contract shops and increased the size of the inside shop. In response, the number of workers employed in licensed tenement shops dropped from twenty-one thousand to fifty-seven hundred between 1900 and 1915.[26] In 1913, 56 percent of the dress and waist workers worked in factories of seventy-five or more employees, and 27 percent were in establishments of one to two hundred workers.[27] Organized labor made significant gains during this period of relative concentration.

Unlike other industries in the United States, the increased size of the garment factories in New York City does not necessarily indicate a higher degree of mechanization. Instead, the "task system," a new form of contracting that emerged in the late-nineteenth-century inside shops, increased segmentation in garment production and built the contracting system into shop-floor operation. Some scholars believe that this new system relates to the skill levels of the new male immigrant workers; since there were so many unskilled or semiskilled among them who were not able to make up an entire piece of clothing, they formed teams to complete the task.[28]

Under this task system, the work formerly done by a skilled tailor was divided into three main parts—basting, machine operating, and sewing—each headed by a tailor who supervised the rest. The team assembled a number of garments and received payment based on completed work. According to Pope, this division of labor was more widely used in the production of lower- or middle-grade clothing up to 1895. The majority of Jewish male workers were thus able to get a foothold in the clothing industry and eliminate women from most of the higher-skilled jobs, such as cutting in the women's garment industry and machine operating in the men's clothing industry.

Waldinger and other scholars consider the 1920s to be the heyday of the New York garment industry. A major reason for the boom of the industry, they argue, was the change in women's fashion. The interest of relatively affluent female consumers in dressing up spurred the production of the high-fashion, highly priced garment in New York, lines in which the city's garment producers were traditionally the strongest. The emphasis on fashion, which implies differences and rapid changes, increased the importance of varying products and marketing and selling capabilities. It also led to organizational change in the city's garment production.

The older manufacturers, saddled with sizable single-line production facilities, could not meet the challenge of volatile market demands. In response, a number of wholesale manufacturing firms began to phase out part of their production and concentrate on designing and selling. At the same time, a new type of garment firm with multiple operations began to grow. These firms needed more space than was available in the old lofts in the Lower East Side. Expedited by new transportation facilities, which effectively linked its workforce to the production sites, the city's garment production began to crawl slowly uptown and finally reached the location of the present garment district, "bounded by Thirtieth and Forty-Second Streets and from Tenth to Fifth Avenue."[29]

Buildings in the new garment center were specifically designed for clothing manufacturing and marketing and were able to house most manufacturing and contracting as well as design and administrative activities. Concentration of garment firms also attracted other garment-related businesses to the area, such as textiles, stores supplying thread, trimming, and embroidery, belt factories, machine repair shops, and machinery and trucking companies. With the clustering of garment firms and related businesses in a central location, the "spot market" for garment production was established in New York City.

The spot market not only significantly reduced the time and cost of communication and transportation for almost all garment-related businesses but was able to capture the largest market for the city's garment industry as well. Since many highly specialized apparel firms were located in the same area, often in the same building, buyers could easily gain virtually all the information they needed about style and fashion in New York City. This was particularly convenient for out-of-town buyers. No wonder so many owners of plants that had sprung up in other boroughs felt an urge to relocate to the center during this time.

However, growth and concentration does not give the entire picture of the city's garment industry. As Nancy Green has observed, the transformation of the New York garment industry in the early twentieth century was characterized by "a centrifugal motion and a constant redefinition of an inner core of urban production."[30] Although the city's garment industry continued to grow, and its upward movement finally created the present-day garment district on Seventh Avenue in the 1920s, these changes took place in the context of relative decline and decentralization of the industry.

The shift to greater concentration at the turn of the century was brief and relative. With the stagnation of the economy after 1915 and the need for shops with great flexibility to produce short-run clothing, stimulated by the growing importance of style, manufacturers became cautious about too great a fixed investment and reverted to the new jobber-contractor system. In response, small contract shops specializing in different lines proliferated in the city.

Driven by their concern for space, rent, and, most importantly, labor costs, some contract shops, particularly those manufacturing relatively low-cost clothing, began to explore new production sites in the outlying boroughs. To ship precut as well as finished goods to and from the contractors, manufacturers had to increasingly rely on trucking companies, giving rise to the importance of trucking in the city's industry. Although the consolidation of the garment district on Seventh Avenue temporarily checked the centrifugal movement of garment shops in the 1920s, the trend soon resumed. The impact was obvious. For example, Brooklyn's share in the city's garment industry was less than 6 percent in 1899 but grew to 14.6 percent in 1937.[31] This trend of centrifugation intensified in the postwar years.

Although the city's industry continued to grow in absolute numbers in the 1920s, it suffered relative decline. Garment production fled the city, not only

Manhattan, particularly after the 1910s, when unions made unprecedented gains in the industry. With labor constituting almost a third of the total cost and the major variable cost in clothing production, manufacturers were determined to explore alternative locations outside the city.

Two major factors facilitated this transfer in the first three decades of the twentieth century: the availability of inexpensive labor in nearby states, particularly southern Massachusetts and northeastern Pennsylvania following the almost simultaneous collapse of the cotton textile and mining industries, and the construction of new highways in the 1920s and 1930s. Improvements in transportation reduced significantly the shipping time between New York and neighboring areas. Taking advantage of the situation, big firms began to relocate production outside New York City, leaving only the more complicated work of designing and merchandising in the city. While New York employed almost 58 percent of the nation's garment workers in 1919, only 39 percent were found there in 1941.[32]

The erosion of New York's share of the nation's industry was temporarily arrested during the Second World War, when a higher percentage of money was spent on garments as a result of the shortage of durable goods. Wartime prosperity was short-lived, however, and the city's garment industry continued to decline after the end of the war as a result of the availability of a wider range of durable consumer goods and changes in fashion. As more people enjoyed greater leisure in their suburban lifestyle and an increasing number of women participated in the labor force after the war, women's fashion became more casual and less distinctive from men's.

The increasingly casual style of women's garments encouraged standardization of garment production, which was less susceptible to the whims of style, allowing longer production runs and a higher degree of segmentation in manufacturing. Longer production runs justified investment in specialized, single-purpose equipment and provided manufacturers with more flexibility in relocating their production. An operation could be enlarged and labor costs reduced by adopting assembly-line production and substituting less-skilled or unskilled workers for those with skills. Since large firms needed a great volume of materials, suppliers were likely to offer them more favorable terms.

The advantages of large garment firms became even more evident during the "retail revolution" of the 1960s and 1970s, when department store chains mushroomed in the cities. Large firms found themselves with more leverage in dealing with larger retailers. Interested in reducing uncertainty in their operations, they were likely to buy from the more established manufacturing firms. As a result, firms with the capacity for multiunit large-scale production began to grow.

These developments had a devastating impact on New York City's garment industry. They significantly reduced the market for contract shops, which specialized in highly skilled, expensive products. The industrial facilities in New York also found it difficult to enlarge their production. Even in the garment district's multistory structures, the average manufacturing space was only two to four thousand square feet, while a modern assembly-line factory, with its elaborate division of sewing operations, required at least six thousand square feet. Although more spacious production sites could be found in the outlying boroughs, such as Queens and Brooklyn, they lacked the unparalleled advantages that only the garment district could offer.[33]

The major reason for the decline, transcending almost every other factor, was high labor costs. In 1956, for example, when the national averages were only $2.01 per hour in coats, suits, and skirts and $1.32 in undergarments, the average New York wages were $2.54 and $1.56, respectively. In short, New York City simply could not compete in labor costs with any other city in the country, not to mention foreign production, where wages could be many times lower.[34]

The impact of these combined factors is clearly reflected in a comparison of garment production in New York and Los Angeles in the postwar years. From 1947 to 1954, when the garment workforce of the New York–New Jersey metropolitan area increased only 1.8 percent and that of the nation increased by 7.8 percent, the Los Angeles area experienced a spectacular gain of 30.5 percent, largely thanks to the growth of its women's casual wear industry.[35]

Once begun, the outflow of garment production from New York City snowballed. Starting with the relocation of some garment production to the northeastern United States and Puerto Rico in the 1930s and the South in the 1950s and 1960s, U.S. garment production was soon internationalized, moving chiefly to Asia, Mexico, and Central America. Although the ILGWU strove to organize labor wherever relocation took place, there was little it could do beyond U.S. borders.

Imported garments have entered the U.S. market since the late 1950s. They were first imported from areas with low labor costs, mainly in Asia. Imports from Japan first penetrated the U.S. market by the 1950s, followed by products from Hong Kong, South Korea, Taiwan, and China. In 1959 imports constituted only 6.9 percent of domestic production of all women's and men's clothing. By 1980 the share of imports had risen to 51 percent.[36]

In addition to imports from Asia, offshore production began to take place in the Caribbean region, including Mexico and the five countries linked by a common market in Central America—Guatemala, El Salvador, Honduras, Nicaragua, and Costa Rica. Big firms took advantage of a loophole in the U.S. tariff codes, Item 807, to ship materials made in the United States for assembly abroad, paying only on the value added. Although the cost of transportation was always a major consideration in offshore transactions, costs from the Caribbean area were reduced because of its proximity to the United States.

Viewing U.S. offshore production as an important means to stimulate their economy, the Caribbean countries also offered U.S. firms favorable financial terms and labor conditions. It is therefore no surprise that U.S. firms found a

more congenial reception in these countries than in their own. This was especially true after the Reagan administration expanded the pool of sourcing countries through the creation of the Caribbean Basin Initiative (CBI) in 1983.[37] From
1965 to 1983 the dollar volume of Item 807 imports from these countries went
up 1,600 percent, growing from $578 million to $9.226 billion, and the percentage of all garment imports under Item 807 increased from 0.3 percent in 1965
to 6.7 percent in 1983.[38]

Offshore production had a retarding impact on the domestic labor market.
New York, as the nation's traditional center of garment production, was hit hard.
Employment in women's outerwear dropped by nineteen thousand between
1948 and 1959, and twenty thousand more jobs were lost in the following decade.[39] The industry tumbled in 1969 when a nationwide recession occurred and
continued to decline after the economy recovered. As the city's garment industry was facing an irreversible decline, it was also plagued by many other problems, including the increasing influence of organized crime, racketeering unions,
the revival of homework, and the increasing number of nonunion shops.[40]

Of all the problems, perhaps the most serious was the shrinking of the workforce. The decline in the number of Jewish and Italian workers began as early
as the late 1940s, when the labor force began to age and recruitment among the
second generation was unsuccessful, particularly among Jews. To replace them,
employers intensified their recruitment among African American workers, who
had been in the industry since the early twentieth century, and Puerto Rican
workers, who had just begun to migrate to the city in large numbers. The entrance of African American and, in particular, Puerto Rican workers from the
late 1940s through the 1960s was crucial to the survival of the garment industry
in this period.

New York City's garment industry faced new challenges in the 1960s. As the
city was gradually transformed from an economy based on manufacturing industries to one based on the provision of services, minority workers, assisted
by civil rights protests and equal opportunity legislation, had more job opportunities than before, and the welfare system also began to develop. With a growing range of alternative employment and income-generating opportunities for
minority workers, the garment industry found itself handicapped by a steadily
sinking wage position and limited economic opportunities for its minority
workers.[41]

Changes in the city's labor market during this period coincided with the dis-
persed settlement of Puerto Ricans throughout the nation. Although New York
City continued to have the nation's largest concentration of Puerto Ricans, its
share dropped from 95 percent to 65 percent between 1946 and 1956. Between
1950 and 1970, New York's share of the national Puerto Rican population decreased from 88 to 58 percent.[42]

Employment instability and sinking wages in the industry, coupled with the
outward movement of their communities, led many African American and Puer-

to Rican women workers to depart from the mostly unionized garment shops in the center of the city. Many, however, remained in the industry. An increasing number of those who remained chose to work in their neighborhoods either in garment shops or as homeworkers. Since many of the garment shops in the African American and Puerto Rican neighborhoods in Harlem, Brooklyn, and the East and South Bronx had been relocated there as early as the 1950s to avoid unionization, and since most were nonunion shops in the 1970s, they offered the lowest possible wages. To make a living, workers had to work off the books and supplement their meager income with government assistance programs.

Because many of these women workers engaged in the so-called underground industry, they were ignored in union and government records. Union census records show that membership of the dressmakers' Local 22, in which most of the African Americans and Puerto Ricans were found, dropped from 27,252 in 1950 to 14,886 in 1965 to a low of 7,849 in 1977—only slightly more than one-fourth of the 1950 level. U.S. Census publications also report that between 1960 and 1970 the percentage of Puerto Rican women in the workforce declined from 38 percent to 29 percent. The largest proportion of this decline was among women between the ages of twenty-five and forty-four, who had been the backbone of the workforce in the city's garment industry. No wonder that by 1970 New York firms found themselves "tied into an aging and increasingly uncommitted labor force whose ability to work rapidly and under pressure was declining."[43]

Nevertheless, after a thirty-year decline, New York City's garment industry miraculously regained its share of employment in 1975. As Waldinger puts it, even "after the nation's economy faltered in 1979 and again in 1981 and 1982," the city's industry managed to hold on to its position as the leading production center in the nation.[44] Several studies attribute this success to the merits of the spot market in the city.[45]

Although large multiunit firms had many advantages, they lacked the flexibility needed to tackle the uncertainty and unpredictability inherent in the industry. One major problem lay in the long period required for mass production at home and abroad. The lead time required to import clothes from Asia ranged from six to twelve months, and goods in most of the key exporting countries had to be ordered a year in advance of expected sale to ensure that they would enter the United States before the country's import quota was filled. The long production runs not only undermined the ability of many U.S. firms to cope with transient consumer demand but also increased their vulnerability to competition of imported garments from countries that could produce standardized products at much lower costs. It is not surprising that by 1970 many large firms that had left New York began to return.[46]

The spot market had failed to meet the challenges of the 1950s and 1960s but proved to have many structural advantages over the large firms in the 1970s. Conveniently located though smaller in size, the firms in New York could produce highly specified items to meet the demand of last-minute orders and fill shortages in mass-produced imported goods. They were therefore able to carve a special niche for the city's garment manufacturers in the highly competitive world of garment production. The advantages of the spot market became even more important in the late 1960s and 1970s, when women's fashion began to change. As Waldinger observes, the aging of the baby-boom generation and the proliferation of double-income families shifted clothing expenditures once again to higher-priced and more fashion-sensitive goods, which reinforced the importance of the variety of lines the city's industry produced.

Shaped by the trend of standardization in the nation's garment production and the kind of garments the city's manufacturers finally secured to produce, the women's garment industry in New York City underwent significant changes. Between 1969 and 1980, although New York held on to only about a quarter of the more standardized blouse industry, it retained almost 60 percent of the less standardized sportswear production. As its number of employees increased from twelve thousand in 1969 to more than sixteen thousand in 1980, the women's sportswear industry has anchored the garment industry to New York City.[47] It has also been the major line of garment production in Chinatown.

The key factor leading to the resurgence of New York City's garment industry was the ample labor force furnished by recent immigrants. Since 1965, with the ending of the discriminatory nationality quotas, large numbers of immigrants have entered the United States; New York received a great portion of them. In 1980 the recorded foreign-born population living in New York City reached 1.67 million, 56 percent of whom had arrived after 1965. The largest portion of new immigrants were Hispanics and Asians, mostly Dominicans and Chinese.[48] Handicapped by the lack of skills needed in the U.S. labor market, many had to accept whatever jobs were available to them. Employment opportunities in the garment industry provided them with a means of survival. These immigrants have supplied vitality and hope to ensure the future of the city's garment industry.

The rise of the garment industry in Chinatown was central to the revitalization of the city's garment industry. By 1980 there were twenty-five thousand Chinese garment workers in New York; their entry marked the beginning of a new chapter in the history of the city's garment industry. However, the fervent striving of management at every level to make profit by reducing labor costs, a central theme throughout the industry's history, has continued to shape the course of the Chinatown industry.

CHAPTER 2

The Garment Workers: Gender, Race, and Class in the City's Garment Industry

Like its counterparts in most parts of the world, the garment industry in New York City has historically been stratified by gender, race, and class. In her study of Jewish women garment workers, Susan Glenn cautions against making simplistic generalizations concerning gender issues in the industry. Mediated by "ethnic group culture, local conditions, and variations in shop size and production methods," gender boundaries in the garment industry have remained "somewhat permeable," and the particular features of the industry have "created a situation of fluidity and ambiguity rather than a fixed and dead-end place for female wage earners."[1] In truth, despite the generally adverse conditions in the workplace, the garment industry in the late nineteenth and early twentieth centuries provided some opportunities for upward mobility for immigrant women.

Glenn's study, along with many others on the garment industry, also demonstrates that despite the variations and unstable boundaries of gender and other categories, the basic organization of the industry has been characterized by a gender hierarchy. Although employment opportunities were provided to both genders, the work done by men and women and the skill levels and wage scales were largely defined by gender. Men were always given the better positions and employment priorities, and the bottom layer of the garment workforce was invariably formed by women.

The gender division of labor in the sewing trade was discernible even before the birth of the ready-made clothing industry.[2] Before there was an industry, women—wives, daughters, and female servants—made clothing at home. People called upon the services of tailors only for clothing that required more skill and fitting. In most cases, male artisans, custom tailors, and journeymen only dealt with men's clothing. They worked at home and in their shops, assisted by women and sometimes children. Women artisans went out to assist other women who sewed at home. Master tailors would not turn to "slop work" until the slack season for custom orders; they would contract journeymen to perform slop work, who would then seek the assistance of women, and the plain part of the work was simply done by poor women at home. This gender hierarchy had important ramifications for the development of New York City's garment industry.

From the outset of the ready-made clothing industry, women formed the majority of the workforce in the lowest-paid sectors. Before 1905, when men's clothing was the staple of the city's industry and the industry was still organized around inside and outside shops, men predominated in the inside shop, where clothing of better quality was produced and working conditions were better. Women formed the majority of the workforce in the outside shops, which produced lower-grade clothing and were situated mainly in workers' or contractors' homes.[3]

In the outside shop women workers performed piecework. They had to pay overhead, which severely reduced their meager earnings. Under the relentless piecework system, women were under severe pressure to make ends meet. They worked unusually long hours, using almost every minute of the day, transforming the living areas of their flats into workshops and converting every member of their families into garment laborers. Working conditions in the outside shop were so poor that only the new immigrant women would work there. American-born women were replaced by Irish and German immigrant women after 1860, who in turn were replaced by Eastern European Jewish and Italian women by 1890.

Most of the women garment workers in the inside shop were young and single. According to a 1908 survey by the U.S. Bureau of Labor, 60 percent of the women workers in the men's clothing industry were under twenty-five, and the majority were between the ages of seventeen and eighteen. The Joint Board of Sanitary Control also estimated that 50 percent of the women in the dress and shirtwaist industry were under twenty.[4] However, their working conditions in the shops were not much better than at home.

Opportunities for women workers varied in different branches of the clothing industry. Compared with other cities, the men's clothing industry in New York, shaped by the ethnic components of its workforce, offered "the smallest range of opportunities for women."[5] Starting around the mid-nineteenth century, women were able to venture into this domain of men, but they were employed in a much smaller proportion than in the women's clothing industry and worked primarily as poorly paid finishers or hand-sewing workers. They did work that was eschewed by male workers and considered to be below the dignity of any American tailor. Chances for them to be promoted to a higher-skilled and better-paying position were slim. Unlike in other parts of the country, an unwritten law in the men's clothing industry in New York prohibited women from operating machines, reserving it exclusively for men. However, the New York men's clothing industry was in decline by the 1920s.[6]

Women had more and better opportunities in what was collectively known as the "ladies' garment industry," which included shirtwaists, women's and children's dresses, undergarments, kimonos, and wrappers. From the outset women predominated in the workforce, comprising between 85 and 95 percent in the first decades of the twentieth century. They monopolized not only the machine-operating jobs but also almost every other task. Although cutting and pressing remained the domain of male workers, women worked as sewing-machine operators, designers, sample makers, and drapers and even assisted the cutters as slippers and markers. They were also able to rise to positions of authority and prestige in shirtwaist, dress, and undergarment factories.

However, even in the women's garment industry gender differences could be perceived. Women workers held almost all positions except cutters in branches such as dresses and shirtwaists, which were defined as less tailored. Nevertheless, in the branches that required more tailoring, such as coats, cloaks, and suits, more skilled and better-paid jobs were more likely men's.

In addition, in almost all branches of the women's garment industry men were given priority in employment. A revealing period was the late nineteenth century, after large numbers of Eastern European male immigrants entered the industry. Alice Kessler-Harris has pointed out that shortly after the sewing machine was introduced in the second half of the nineteenth century, the number of men employed in the men's clothing industry increased from 35,051 to 41,173 between 1850 and 1860, while the number of women workers decreased from 61,500 to 57,730.[7] Women workers were not only edged out but also replaced by men in the higher-skilled and better-paid jobs. Unlike the men's clothing industry, which traditionally followed the British model, the U.S. women's garment industry traditionally followed the French model, with women as cutters. This tradition was also changed with men replacing women as cutters.

The practical outcome of the gender-defined skills and men's and women's work was fully reflected in the differentiation of their earnings in the industry. Stanley Vittoz's account of the late-nineteenth-century inside shop makes this discrepancy clear:

> The subcontractors and their few favorites would earn fair and even high wages, while the majority of the workers would be condemned to "starvation" wages. There were sub-contracting pressers, for instance, who made $100 and $150 a week, while the "helpers" who worked for them would "go home" at the end of a week's work with $6 or $8. . . . [Moreover, with the general proliferation of subcontracting after the turn of the century], wages seem to have remained stationary and in some cases even to have fallen. In 1900 the [U.S.] Industrial Relations Commission reported that during the busy season the average operator could earn from

$15 to $20 a week, a baster could make $9 to $15 a week, while a presser could earn $12 to $15. An expert operator would earn during the busy season as much as $40 a week. In 1910 the average wage in the busy season was estimated between $15 and $18 a week for operators and at $14 a week for pressers. The wages of cutters had been $24 a week as far back as 1890, while in 1910 the number of cutters who were earning that wage was but a small portion of the total numbers engaged in the trade.[8]

However, as some scholars have pointed out, gender roles in the garment industry were never fixed. While there was a constant redistribution of gender roles in the industry, there was also a persistent effort to justify them based on pseudoscientific theories about physical strength or biological differences between men and women, no matter how inconsistent and self-contradictory they were. The use of the sewing machine was an example. When the machine was first introduced in the 1840s, custom tailors resented it as a labor-saving device, a menace to the craftsmanship of sewing. As a result, most machine operators were women. However, in the late nineteenth century, when men entered the industry in large numbers, sewing machines became a men's tool and were allegedly too skill- and labor-demanding for women. They resumed their status as a women's tool in the early twentieth century, however, when the men's clothing industry was in decline and sewing machine operators were once again predominantly women. The operation of these machines was again considered as less skilled than cutting and other male-dominated work in the garment industry.[9]

The gender hierarchy in the organization of garment production inevitably led to unequal relations between men and women workers on the floor. This was especially obvious in the small contract shops and the male-dominated shops of the men's clothing industry. Young female workers felt particularly insecure and socially isolated in the overwhelmingly male environment. Many of them had to endure the men's joking, storytelling, and banter, which were "heavily spiced with sexual innuendo or outright obscenity," and some women workers faced outright sexual harassment.[10]

Major changes in the industry did not seem to have a positive impact on women. Take the introduction of the sewing machine as an example. Although initially intended to reduce labor as its inventors claimed, it did not improve the lot of its operators, most of whom were women. Women workers in most of the outside shops had to buy or rent their own machines. Even in the inside shops and some outside shops that furnished machines, operators usually were responsible for their maintenance, the cost of various accessories, and an additional charge for use of electricity.

Greater productivity created by the use of machines was not necessarily a blessing for women. As prices fell with the higher degree of mechanization, women workers had to work longer hours to make ends meet. The division of work in the industry resulting from technological advancements also put women in a more vulnerable position in competition with men. The large number of women being temporarily replaced by men in the late nineteenth century also took place after sewing machines were widely used in the industry.

In addition, the use of sewing machines was often a health hazard. As Virginia Penny pointed out as early as 1863, machine sewing could be as taxing as hand sewing. By shifting the strain from "the muscles of the lower limbs and the weaker parts of the system" to the hips, it produced chronic pain in the hips, nervous disorders from the jarring of the mechanism, and eyestrain from following the long lines of stitching. Her assessment still holds today.[11]

Similarly adverse consequences also arose from new developments in the contracting system. Although the new system led to a further division of labor between male employers and benefited them in different ways, it did not help improve the conditions of women workers at all. As a union publication noted in 1910, it meant only that "the girls' bosses, the inspection and criticism of her work, the incessant supervision of her every move were all doubled."[12]

This was particularly true when subcontracting was built into the operation of the larger inside shops after 1900. Women had to work for the skilled male workers in the shops, who in turn worked as subcontractors for the shop owners. Women workers were classified as either workers with some experience or as "green hands," who served as apprentices and earned the lowest wages.

To redress their adverse conditions in the shops, women garment workers in New York began organizing as early as 1825. The most spectacular event in New York's labor history was the 1909 "Uprising of 20,000" shirtwaist makers, who were mostly women. The young women strikers were described by observers as committed, self-sacrificing, and courageous. Their spirit captured the hearts of the public, and their dedication to the cause of labor and their actions in the historic strike of 1909 led to an unprecedented growth of the ILGWU. Before 1909 the union's membership fluctuated around two thousand. It jumped to fifty-eight thousand in 1909. From 1910 through the 1930s, the ILGWU had "more women workers than any other single union in the country."[13] A young garment worker at the time, Yetta Burshy, did not exaggerate when she said, "Kids like me made the union."[14]

The founding of the ILGWU did not mark the end of the struggle, however. Women workers continued to wage battles "on two fronts: inside and outside the unions," as Joan M. Jensen has described it.[15] Soon after the two major garment workers' strikes in U.S. history, the 1909 Uprising of 20,000 and the 1910 "Great Upheaval" of the (predominantly male) cloakmakers, the ILGWU signed agreements with the majority of the city's manufacturers, which came to be known collectively as the "Protocol of Peace."[16]

The Protocol of Peace proved to be a mixed blessing for union members. It provided workers with benefits that they would not have otherwise had, including a fifty-hour week, bonus pay for any limitations on overtime, ten legal holidays, and free electricity for machines.[17] The price of these gains, however, was high. The agreement prohibited strikes and lockouts. Minor labor disputes had to be taken before a Committee on Grievances, and major ones had to be de-

cided by a permanent Board of Arbitration, formed by three nominees representing the employee, the union, and the public, respectively. By signing the
agreement, the union forfeited the right to strike, which was the workers' only
power. From that time on, if a strike was to be called, everything, even the length
of the strike, had to be preset. Strikes became a mere "demonstration of unity," a performance, at this stage in the garment industry.[18]

Manufacturers established their role as the major players in the future of the
industry. In the negotiation process they made it clear that their main purpose
in assisting the union to expand its organizational reach throughout the industry
was to "protect the legitimate manufacturers from the small fry who are cutting into their trade."[19] Their acceptance of the arrangement was not unconditional. Both sides understood that "the agreement between the association and
the union would become effective only if the union succeeded in bringing into
its membership the majority of the workers in the trade."[20] To gain recognition
in the industry the union had to enlarge its membership and maintain the stability of labor conditions.

The Protocol of Peace was the first agreement of its kind signed by a U.S. labor union to use outside arbitrators to settle a dispute with management. Although the terms of the protocol were never fully enforced, protocolism had a
strong influence on redefining allies and enemies in the industry. Green is accurate in pointing out that the Protocol of Peace was more than a truce. By
heralding "a new philosophy of common interest between employers and employees to end class warfare," it transformed the debate and dispute from a struggle of workers against employers into "an alliance of the organized employers'
associations and labor unions against unorganized employers and their nonunion workers."[21] This new philosophy of partnership between labor and management, led by the garment-industry unions, reshaped the culture of American organized labor in the following years.

Given its heroic tradition of collective bargaining, it is ironic to see that a labor
union like the ILGWU would readily bargain away the power of the workers by
signing such an agreement. Many individuals and scholars have commented on
this concession on the part of the ILGWU's leadership. Helen Marot claimed
that the male leaders of the union lacked confidence in its rank-and-file women members, even though it was their struggle that had brought them to power.[22] Annelise Orleck comments that the male union's leaders "were caught in a
bind." Although their power depended on their ability to organize an industry
of unskilled women, they continued to subscribe to the masculine AFL-type
vision of unionism, "a fraternity unity of skilled male workers."[23] Obviously,
gender was very much at work at this juncture.

* * *

I would like to take these arguments a step further in pointing out that factors
that shaped the attitude of union leaders were not simply ideological but also

structural. Given the elite status of male skilled workers in the organizational structure of the industry, there was in fact only a fine line between them and the "moths" who ran the shops. It is therefore no surprise that the male-dominated union leadership was more inclined to deal with management than with its own members, who were overwhelmingly women workers.

The Protocol of Peace reshaped the relations of the ILGWU's leaders with its members and management in the garment industry. Rather than empowering their members and strengthening the organization, after signing the agreement the union's leaders began to increasingly rely on the goodwill of management to enforce peace and order in the industry. Organizing efforts became a means of gaining recognition from the employers rather than a struggle to defend workers' interests. To avoid jeopardizing its newfound relations with the employers, the ILGWU sought to control conditions within the union and put a tight lid on opposition forces among its own ranks.

However, the organizational principles of the protocol were not carried out without resistance. The strongest resistance came from Local 25, which had a predominantly female membership. In January 1913, to demonstrate its organizing ability and, as it told the workers, to give them a chance to express "their protest against the bad conditions in the trade," the leadership of the union decided to stage a general strike.[24] Instead of letting the strikers set their own terms, the leadership had negotiated a deal with the employers and agreed to end the strike once employers consented to extend the benefits stipulated in the protocol to the dress trade. They called off the strike after only three days of negotiation.

Outraged at not having been consulted in the decision-making process, four thousand Italian women strikers revolted. They called the protocol a "frame up" and protested by sitting down on Third Avenue and stopping traffic. Nearly half of the women cast a vote of no-confidence in the leadership, and although the union finally managed to get a majority to support the deal, as Louis Levine has pointed out, it was "a bare majority," and members supported the pact "without much animation."[25]

Women workers in Local 25 continued their struggle to reform the ILGWU.[26] In 1917 members who attended the Education Program conducted by Fannia Cohn formed a permanent Current Events Committee and began to publicly criticize leaders of the local and the international. As Louis Levine remarked, they wanted to "rejuvenate" the local by imparting a "soul" to it and by getting rid of "old" leaders and officers, who they considered to be "too practical" and "conservative."[27] Having gained confidence from the education program, they began to question women's underrepresentation in the union leadership. Their local, with more than 75 percent female membership, did not have a single woman officer!

In 1919 women workers formed a Shop Delegates' League (SDL), calling for reform in governing the union. Until this point, under the union's election system only established national leaders were recognized and won unionwide office. The SDL proposed that each shop elect two delegates to a unionwide assembly, which would then select the executive board and standing committees. Since the chairs of almost every shop in Local 25 and many other union locals were women, this proposal would dramatically increase women's position in the union's leadership and diminish that of men.

Deeply threatened by the proposal and fearing that the shop-floor movement would spread to other locals, the ILGWU president Benjamin Schlesinger accused the waistmakers of trying to bring about the union's "destruction." To thwart what he called a "Bolshevik" threat, he split Local 25 into three locals and placed them under the administration of the male cloakmakers' union. The leadership's effort failed. The democratization movement soon spread to other locals, but, as Annelise Orleck has noted, "what had begun as a campaign by militant women workers for a greater voice in their union" was quickly taken over by a group of male organizers involved in the union's internal battle between "left" and "right." Women's issues were overshadowed.[28]

In the early 1920s, Communist Party organizers in the ILGWU were able to attract discontented unionists of both genders to William Z. Foster's Trade Union Educational League (TUEL). Accusing TUEL members of dual unionism and organizing for two competing unions simultaneously, the ILGWU's executive board ordered all of its members to resign from the TUEL. Robert Laurentz shows that those workers who refused to resign were hauled before the union tribunal in New York.[29] These trials resulted in the expulsion of many of the union's most militant shop-floor leaders. Many were in fact trained by the ILGWU Education Department, as Annelise Orleck notes. The political infighting significantly weakened the union. Between 1920 and 1924, the union lost 45 percent of its membership. During the same period, its female membership dropped from 75 percent to only 38.7 percent, as twenty thousand men joined the union while forty-five thousand women left.[30]

In the midst of this political infighting, the women on the ILGWU staff, most of whom had previously been garment workers, were in the most difficult position. Their dilemma, as portrayed by Alice Kessler-Harris, was "being part of, and yet not part of" the union.[31] Like most women members of the ILGWU, they treasured the success of their years of struggle. Many of them were committed to unionism, which, for all its flaws, held out the best hope for them. They considered the union to be their "family."[32] However, these women often found themselves caught between their affiliation with the union and their commitment to the workers.

Their dedication did not seem to be appreciated by many male union leaders. Biographical studies reveal that their lives in the union were not easy.[33] Differences in gendered perspectives erected an invisible wall between them and their male colleagues. Despite their dedication and indispensable contributions to the union, their abilities were constantly doubted and their efforts were ignored, discounted, and misunderstood. In addition, they had to endure routine

Table 1. International Ladies' Garment Workers' Union
Membership Census, 1902–95

	Census			Census
Year	(December 31)		Year	(December 31)
1902	3,846		1949	423,010
1903	1,802		1950	431,200
1904	1,605		1951	423,321
1905	1,949		1952	430,830
1906	2,513		1953	439,277
1907	1,609		1954	440,650
1908	7,830		1955	445,093
1909	58,226		1956	450,802
1910	69,945		1957	446,880
1911	74,378		1958	442,901
1912	84,637		1959	452,017
1913	77,559		1960	446,554
1914	74,518		1961	443,122
1915	72,707		1962	441,138
1916	85,351		1963	439,899
1917	78,585		1964	442,318
1918	129,311		1965	446,856
1919	107,693		1966	455,164
1920	88,555		1967	451,192
1921	73,717		1968	455,022
1922	76,645		1969	457,517
1923	54,740		1970	442,333
1924	48,754		1971	432,331
1925	48,451		1972	427,568
1926	32,300		1973	428,734
1927	28,416		1974	404,737
1928	31,672		1975	376,750
1929	39,148		1976	365,346
1930	34,793		1977	351,794
1931	23,876		1978	348,380
1932	40,422		1979	340,951
1933	198,141		1980	322,505
1934	216,801		1981	308,056
1935	222,369		1982	282,559
1936	242,290		1983	264,227
1937	253,646		1984	247,570
1938	234,825		1985	219,001
1939	239,346		1986	196,445
1940	247,937		1987	181,517
1941	298,669		1988	165,710
1942	300,550		1989	156,273
1943	305,075		1990	146,506
1944	304,002		1991	137,315
1945	320,772		1992	130,473
1946	379,197		1993	120,999
1947	385,802		1994	n.a.
1948	400,342		1995	108,057

Sources: ILGWU membership census records, courtesy of Susan Cowell (for
1905–92) and the ILGWU Research Department (1993–95).

feuds with male union leaders over tactics, equal pay, and sexual harassment, as well as the men's crude jokes over their gender and lifestyle. Many male leaders of the union could not understand women workers and accused the women unionists of "seeking publicity" when they stood up and spoke for the interests of the workers against the will of these male leaders. The insincerity of the union's male-dominated leadership in organizing women workers destroyed the confidence and trust of the rank and file not only in them but also in the women officers of the union. That kind of trust was what these women unionists cherished most.[34]

Many women unionists, however, persevered, sustained by their vision of unionism. Based on their experience as garment workers and inspired by memories of those who had perished in the nightmarish Triangle Fire, their vision differed from that of many male leaders. While many of the union's male leaders saw unionism as an important vehicle for labor organizations to gain recognition in the industry, the women unionists believed that unionism stood for "the reconstruction of society."[35]

Their different visions led to different attitudes toward organizing efforts and the union rank and file. For many male leaders, the purpose of organizing was to increase the union's leverage in bargaining with management. They thought of organizing campaigns only when the situation required. They were more concerned about the size of union membership than its quality. For many women unionists, however, union membership was "an invitation to struggle for equal pay and access to good jobs," and the purpose of organizing was to mobilize workers for this struggle.[36] They believed that the strength of the union stemmed from empowering its rank and file and that membership education should be the union's long-term commitment.

It should therefore come as no surprise that despite their diverse approaches to the cause of labor, many women unionists stressed the importance of educating the workers and creating alternative social institutions; Fannia Cohn's important contribution in creating the first nationwide Education Department for garment workers is a good example.[37] The program successfully trained a significant number of women leaders in the union, regardless of their racial and ethnic backgrounds. Among the graduates of this program were Rose Pesotta, vice president of the ILGWU from 1934 to 1942, and Maida Springer, the first African American woman to serve as the union's business agent. Considering the prevalence of racism in U.S. organized labor during the time, the degree of cross-racial labor activism fostered by the program is remarkable. The economist Jack Barbash did not exaggerate in his appraisal of Fannia Cohn's contribution to the union movement when he wrote, "'For many people the fine reputation of the ILGWU was represented through Fannia Cohn.'"[38] Many other women unionists in the ILGWU also deserve similar praise.

In truth, not all women unionists were idealistic. They were not a homogeneous group, nor were women workers in the New York City garment industry. Jewish and Italian workers constituted the two largest groups of shirtwaist makers from 1909 to 1910.[39] There were differences in language, culture, and experience between them. While many Jewish workers had been exposed to radical ideas in their homelands and had some preparation for urban life, most Italian immigrants came from rural areas. Most Jewish and Italian women workers in the shops were young and single, but Jewish workers tended to leave the industry after marriage. Married Italian women continued to sew at home due to the low incomes of their husbands and thus constituted the most exploited segment of the workforce.[40] Employers played on these differences and pitted one group against the other. However, during the Uprising of 20,000, through the efforts of Clara Lemlich Shavelson and other women labor activists, Italian women and women of other ethnic groups banded together with the Jewish workers, who formed the majority of the strikers, and continued until the final victory.

Problems related to the interplay between gender and race/ethnicity in the city's garment industry became more obvious after African American and Puerto Rican women entered the garment industry in the 1920s. "Pushed" by poverty and persecution in the South and "pulled" by the prospect of work in the North, the early wave of African American migrants entered New York City during World War I. Between 1910 and 1920, the African American population of New York City increased by more than sixty thousand.[41] It was during this period that African American women made their first inroads into the city's clothing industry. Their numbers significantly increased after World War II.[42]

Closely following African Americans were workers from Puerto Rico. Driven by the deterioration of their local economy caused by U.S. economic and political domination, a small group of Puerto Ricans began to seek opportunities for advancement in the United States after 1917. The number of Puerto Ricans in the United States increased from 1,513 in 1910 to 11,811 in 1920 and to 52,774 in 1930.[43] The overwhelming majority of the migrants settled in New York City, and in 1930 the New York Health Department reported that there were nearly forty-five thousand Puerto Ricans in the city, forming more than 85 percent of the mainland Puerto Rican population.[44]

Among the reasons for this concentration was the commercial linkage between San Juan and New York, facilitated by the relatively inexpensive transportation through steamships and, after 1945, airlines as well as the existence of an early Puerto Rican nationalist exile community in the city, who had fled the country under Spanish control and could now provide assistance to these immigrants. The principal reason, however, was the availability of employment opportunities in New York City.[45]

In 1930 women constituted almost half of the Puerto Rican migrants in New York City.[46] Prior to migration, many of them had experience working in the garment factories owned by New York jobbers and manufacturers based in Puerto Rico. Drawn by job opportunities and higher wages and benefits in New

York, they came to seek a better life. Between 1930 and 1936 about 40 percent of the gainfully employed Puerto Rican female workers were either garment, needle, or hand-sewing workers. However, most of them worked at home until the late 1940s and early 1950s, when they began entering the garment shops in great numbers.[47]

Despite differences in the time and causes of their migration, their prior experience, and their ethnic cultures, African American and Puerto Rican women workers shared similar experiences in the garment industry. Like the Jewish and Italian women workers in the late nineteenth and early twentieth centuries, they were relegated to the lowest-paid, unskilled or semiskilled jobs. Most of them worked in the dress, waist, blouse, skirt, and garment-related accessories industries, with most African American women employed as finishers and drapers and Puerto Rican women as operators. They received much lower pay than their Jewish and Italian counterparts on the same jobs, however. In 1929, for example, African American dressmakers received as little as eight to twelve dollars per week, while white dressmakers were earning between twenty-six and forty-four dollars per week.[48]

The time during which African American and Puerto Rican workers entered the city's garment industry was an important factor in causing this disparity. New York's garment industry was already on its way from being one of the highest-paid to one of the lowest-paid industries. Between 1946 and 1949 the average hourly wage in the dress industry, which employed large numbers of African American and Puerto Rican women, decreased from $1.44 to $1.37, in contrast to all manufacturing industries, where wages increased from $1.08 to $1.40. By 1961 the disparity was even greater, $1.84 in the dress industry as compared with $3.32 in manufacturing.[49]

The ILGWU made little effort to redress the situation. Instead, in 1962, preoccupied with the industry's survival in the city, the ILGWU supported wage entrenchment and refused to endorse the increase in New York City and New York State's minimum wage. The union's attitude greatly affected those in the lowest-paid sectors, who were by this time primarily African American and Puerto Rican. Jewish and Italian workers already occupied better-paying jobs that required more skill, and they were not willing to insist on equality for the newcomers.

African American and Puerto Rican women workers were not the only ones who suffered from the racial/ethnic stratification in the industry; the men had to face the same reality. Sharing similar status with their male counterparts in the industry, African American and Puerto Rican women workers found it easier to identify with the interest of their communities than with their white fellow women workers. Such an alliance, however, did not always counteract the injustice imposed on them. In a labor market stratified by gender, they were also vulnerable to competition from their male allies.

For example, during the National Recovery Administration's organizing drive from 1933 to 1935, employers began to use African American women pressers to minimize labor costs. Seven hundred of them were members of Dress Pressers' Local in 1936, and they were considered to be "the best paid women in Harlem." However, in the 1940s, when an increasing number of African American and Puerto Rican men accepted the same wages for working as pressers, the women lost their jobs. Pressing once again became an all-male trade, mostly white but with a small number of black and Puerto Rican men.[50]

As was always the case for newcomers in the garment industry, African American and Puerto Rican women workers were economically and politically exploited. Employers brought them in not only to replace the white workers in the lowest-paid labor sector but also as a counterweight to the earlier workers' labor militancy, perceiving them to be "loyal and less subject to extremist propaganda."[51] Although no case has thus far been found in New York City in which African American workers served as strikebreakers, as occurred in Chicago and Philadelphia, the union was wary about accepting them. The union's attitude in turn made African American workers even more vulnerable to exploitation by their employers.

Compared with other trade unions, the ILGWU appeared to be at the fore of the American labor movement in its acceptance of workers of color, its defense of immigration, and its special programs for immigrant workers. However, as some scholars have pointed out, this relatively progressive attitude was more a reflection of how rampant racism was among U.S. organized labor than an indication of the adequacy of ILGWU policies.[52] An analysis of the actual situation reveals that most of the ILGWU's organizing efforts among workers of color were not self-initiated, nor did the union accept these workers on entirely equal terms. As late as 1929, while there were approximately four thousand African American women in New York dress shops, no more than two hundred were ILGWU members.[53] The union's large-scale organizing drive among African American workers did not begin until 1928, when the Communist Needle Trades Workers' Industrial Union (NTWIU) had made strong inroads among them and posed a direct challenge to the ILGWU. Likewise, the union's organizing efforts among Puerto Rican workers did not begin until 1933, when the National Recovery codes became law and inexpensive Puerto Rican labor posed a dire threat to union work in the city's garment industry.[54] Nevertheless, the union's organizing efforts among these workers in the early 1930s were successful. Between 1932 and 1935 the union organized some five thousand black and two thousand Puerto Rican workers, which contributed to the rapid increase in its membership during this period.[55]

However, like their Jewish and Italian counterparts in the early period, union membership did not guarantee African American and Puerto Rican women workers participation in the organization and sufficient labor protection in the industry. "Being a part, yet not a part of" was still an accurate description of their experience in the union. Although special programs were set up and union benefits were extended to them, union leaders made little effort to understand them and address their particular problems. They did not try to redress the low-

paid status of their African American and Puerto Rican members in the industry.[56] Nor did they make any effort to rectify the racial segregation in the union's
locals until the ILGWU came under a congressional investigation in 1962. Up
to 1958, union meetings were conducted in either English, Yiddish, or Italian,
which could not be understood by most Puerto Rican members.[57]

Like their earlier counterparts in the industry, African American and Puerto
Rican women workers could not expect any meaningful protection from the
male-dominated leadership of the union on issues regarding gender. The union
leaders' attitude toward sexual harassment at the workplace is a case in point.
Like their predecessors, African American and Puerto Rican women workers were
often coerced by their foremen and male employers into providing sexual favors
in return for employment security. However, when they brought complaints of
this nature to the union, they were either told that they should feel "flattered"
by the interest of their employers or resolve the matter quietly through monetary settlement.[58]

Like their predecessors, African American and Puerto Rican women workers were excluded from decision-making positions in the union. As late as 1964
no African American workers and only one Puerto Rican woman worker had
been chosen to serve on the executive board. What differentiated their experience from that of the Jewish and Italian women workers was the increased control over them by the union. Although there had been an Italian local in the
ILGWU, Latino workers' request for a separate local, with their own elected
leaders, was turned down twice by the ILGWU general executive board in 1937
and the early 1950s. To dampen community-based militancy among Puerto
Rican workers, the union continued to appoint organizers who did not speak
Spanish to the Harlem area, where a good number of workers were Spanish-
speaking Puerto Ricans.[59]

Considering the institutional development of the union in the first few decades of the twentieth century, it is not difficult to understand why the problematic attitude of the leadership has remained unchanged and its control over
its rank and file has increased in recent years. The problems resulted primarily
from the lack of rank-and-file democracy within the union. Since the 1920s,
especially after its crackdown on the six-months-long left-wing cloakmakers'
strike in 1926 and its purge of the "communists," the union's leadership moved
to the right politically. It implemented a series of institutional reforms to tighten
its grip on its discontented members. The most effective of these was perhaps
its effort to eliminate democratic elements in its election system by requiring a
candidate to have served a number of years as a paid officer in the union.

By so doing, its election system not only guaranteed the long-term leading
position of the "old boys" in the union but also closed possible channels for
dissident voices and the active participation of the rank and file in union politics. To further prevent the growth of militancy in its ranks, local elections were
closely monitored and members were not allowed to form clubs or groups within the union until three months prior to the election. The leadership even re-

quired officers to sign an undated letter of resignation at the beginning of their employment so that they could be discharged any time.[60]

Even as the ILGWU became more and more bureaucratic, its status as a major labor union in national politics began to grow. With the rapid expansion of its membership after the end of World War II, its financial stability and political influence in the nation were greatly enhanced. By the late 1950s it had become one of the most influential unions in the American labor movement, exerting its influence on municipal, state, and national political affairs. The growth of the ILGWU's financial and political status, however, did not necessarily translate into improving the status of its African American and Puerto Rican members.[61]

The growing political influence of the ILGWU made it even harder for its members to challenge the wrongdoing of its leadership, but many African American and Puerto Rican women workers did not remain resigned to the status quo. They fought on two fronts: on the floor they countered their employers; in the union they had to fight for their rights as members. In 1933, when a general strike took place and the owner of the Weinberg Dress shop attempted to pacify his workers by offering them money to buy ice cream and sodas, the workers, many of whom were African American and Puerto Rican, accepted the money but contributed it to the general strike fund. As they put it, "'He wanted we shouldn't go out on strike, so he gave us the money to make himself a nice fellow, a "big shot." Like this he never paid us any wages. Well, we'll use the money to fight him.'"[62]

Starting in the late 1950s, with the support of their communities, African American and Puerto Rican garment workers began to challenge their union. In 1957, four hundred of them who were working in the Bronx picketed the local office of the ILGWU and filed a petition with the National Labor Relations Board (NLRB) calling for the decertification of the ILGWU as their bargaining agent. Two similar events occurred in the following year. Puerto Rican workers in Local 62, one of the ILGWU's largest locals, held a major demonstration. One of their signs read, "We're Tired of Industrial Peace. We Want Industry Justice." A *New York Herald Tribune* reporter made it clear that the protest was staged not only against their employer but "more important, against the workers' own union." In another incident, two hundred members of ILGWU Local 132 demonstrated in front of the union's headquarters with signs reading: "80% of our members speak Spanish. A meeting conducted in English is a farce." The demonstrators were also reported to have shouted: "Mr. Dubinsky, we don't want your contract!"[63]

The African American and Puerto Rican women workers were courageous in their fight to improve their status in the city's garment industry. Florence Rice, an African American garment factory chair from 1957 to 1961, was one of them. In 1962, after workers filed charges of racial discrimination with the New York State Commission for Human Rights against the ILGWU, and the House Committee on Labor, Education, and Welfare decided to launch an investigation, she was one of three rank-and-file workers who stood up to testify against the union, despite the union's warning that she would suffer if she bore witness to union racial discrimination.[64]

Although the congressional subcommittee did not find the union legally guilty of racial discrimination in the end, the leadership of the ILGWU, under the workers' pressure, was forced to make a visible though not substantive shift in policy toward its African American and Puerto Rican members. Between 1964 and 1980, the first Spanish-speaking local managers were selected and, after the union modified its election system in 1972, the first Latino and African American members were elected to the general executive board. A significant number of Puerto Ricans and a smaller number of African Americans were also given positions as business agents and union organizers.

The change was more quantitative than qualitative, however, as Robert Laurentz has observed. With the increasing number of African American and Puerto Rican workers on the staff, there was racial tension not only between the union officials and the rank and file but also between them and the lower ranking officials. Like their Jewish and Italian predecessors, African American and Puerto Rican women unionists found themselves in a difficult position. While militant women officers were, as a rule, passed over for promotion in the union, those promoted were either faithful to the male Jewish leaders or ready to retire. Angered by such treatment, many Puerto Rican women officers chose to identify first and foremost with their community rather than the union.[65]

While African American and Puerto Rican women unionists faced racial tension in the union, ethnic workers in the unionized garment shops could receive little institutional support in relation to their wages and employment security. This was particularly the situation in the 1960s, when the low-wage sector of the city's garment industry was most affected by changes. No wonder that as more job opportunities were open to minority workers and the welfare system began to develop, many African American and Puerto Rican workers left the garment industry, and an increasing number of Puerto Rican workers worked for the nonunion garment shops in their own community, where they could supplement their meager income with government programs and as shopworkers and/ or homeworkers.[66] The decrease of African American and Puerto Rican women workers in the organized segment of the city's industry, coupled with the aging and exodus of the senior skilled Jewish and Italian workers, effectively sapped the vitality of the city's garment industry.

It was at this time that Chinese, Dominican, and other groups of immigrant workers entered the city's garment industry. Although times had changed, and in many respects the industrial organization and culture of the Chinese, Dominican, and other ethnic garment shops differed from those of the earlier ones, the legacy of history continued to have important implications for newcomers in the industry.

The Growth of the Chinatown Garment Industry

Since the second half of the nineteenth century the garment industry has been a major industry in some Chinese communities on the West Coast.[1] However, it did not enjoy the same status in the New York Chinese community because the number of New York Chinese clothes makers remained negligibly small.[2] Census data show that as late as 1930 there were only nine Chinese tailors and eight men and one woman sewing-machine operators in all of New York State. Considering that there were 7,674 Chinese men and 116 women gainfully employed in the state and nearly 90 percent of the state's Chinese population were in New York City, the clothing trade was not a major source of income for the early Chinese community in the city.[3]

A principal reason for the absence of a Chinese garment industry in New York City was the scarcity of women. Although the male-to-female ratio was out of balance in almost all Chinese American communities before the Second World War, it was more pronounced in New York City. By 1940, when the Chinese male-to-female ratio dropped to about three to one nationally and two to one in California, it remained more than six to one in New York City. The gender imbalance in New York City was even more striking among those fifteen years of age and over: more than nine Chinese men to every one Chinese woman.[4]

Leong Gor Yun did not exaggerate when he concluded in the 1930s that "Chinatown is a man's town."[5] Guo Zhengzhi also might not have overdramatized the situation when he reported that before the end of the Second World War the sight of Chinese women was such a rarity that they were treasured by Chinese men as "pearls." For a mere glance at a Chinese woman, a Chinese man was said to have waited on the corner of Mott Street from morning till night for two days in a row.[6] Since the overwhelming majority of the Chinese

Table 2. Chinese Population of the United States, the States of California and New York, and the Cities of San Francisco and New York by Sex, 1900–1990

Year	Total	Males	Females	Males per 100 Females
United States				
1900	89,863	85,341	4,522	1,887.2
1910	71,531	66,856	4,675	1,430.1
1920	61,639	53,891	7,748	695.5
1930	74,954	59,802	15,152	394.7
1940	77,504	57,389	20,115	285.3
1950	117,629	77,008	40,621	189.6
1960	237,292	135,549	101,743	133.2
1970	431,583	226,733	204,850	110.7
1980	806,040	407,544	398,496	102.3
1990	1,648,696	821,542	827,154	99.3
California				
1900	45,753	42,297	3,456	1,223.9
1910	36,248	33,003	3,245	1,017.0
1920	28,812	24,230	4,582	528.8
1930	37,361	27,988	9,373	298.6
1940	39,556	27,331	12,225	223.6
1950	58,324	36,051	22,273	161.9
1960	95,600	53,627	41,973	127.8
1970	170,131	87,835	82,296	106.7
1980	325,882	163,060	162,822	100.1
1990	704,850	346,928	357,922	96.9
San Francisco				
1900	13,954	11,818	2,136	553.3
1910	10,582	9,235	1,347	685.6
1920	7,744	6,020	1,724	349.2
1930	16,303	12,033	4,270	281.8
1940	17,782	12,264	5,518	222.3
1950	24,813	15,595	9,218	169.2
1960	36,445	20,624	15,821	130.4
1970	58,696	30,084	28,612	105.1
1980	82,480	40,668	41,812	97.1
1990	127,140	61,475	65,665	93.6
New York State				
1900	7,170	7,028	142	4,949.3
1910	5,266	5,065	201	2,519.9
1920	5,793	5,240	553	947.6
1930	9,665	8,649	1,016	851.3
1940	13,731	11,777	1,954	602.7
1950	20,171	14,875	5,296	280.9
1960	37,573	23,406	14,167	165.2
1970	81,378	43,919	37,459	117.2
1980	147,250	75,885	71,365	106.3
1990	284,144	143,083	141,061	101.4

Table 2. Con't.

Year	Total	Males	Females	Males per 100 Females
New York City				
1900	6,321	6,189	132	4,688.6
1910	4,614	4,419	195	2,266.1
1920	5,042	4,527	515	879.0
1930	8,414	7,549	865	872.7
1940	12,753	10,967	1,786	614.1
1950	18,329	13,627	4,702	289.8
1960	32,831	20,658	12,173	169.7
1970	69,324	37,504	31,820	117.9
1980	124,372	64,018	60,354	106.1
1990	238,919	119,837	119,082	100.6

Sources: U.S. Department of Commerce, Bureau of the Census, U.S. Census of Population, 1900, 1910, 1920, 1930, 1940, 1950, 1960, 1970, 1980, 1990 (Washington, D.C.: G.P.O).

Table 3. Chinese Population Fifteen Years and Older in the United States, New York State, and New York City by Sex, 1900–1940

	1900	1910	1920	1930	1940
United States					
Males	83,633	64,394	49,818	51,519	48,633
Females	3,204	2,955	4,407	8,109	12,463
Males per 100 females	2,610	2,179	1,130	635	390
New York State					
Males	6,961	4,958	4,948	8,127	10,872
Females	96	113	297	592	1,213
Males per 100 females	7,251	4,388	1,666	1,373	896
New York City					
Males	6,129	4,318	4,249	7,122	10,153
Females	91	109	272	508	1,103
Males per 100 females	6,735	3,961	1,562	1,402	920

Sources: U.S. Department of Commerce, Bureau of the Census, Fourteenth Census of the United States Taken in the Year 1920 (Washington, D.C.: G.P.O., 1922), vol. 2, chap. 4, tables 1, 11, 16; Fifteenth Census of the United States: 1930, Population (Washington, D.C.: G.P.O., 1933), vol. 2, chap. 11, tables 4, 16, 27; Sixteenth Census of the United States: 1940, Population: Characteristics of the Nonwhite Population by Race (Washington, D.C.: G.P.O., 1943), table 28.

concentrated in Chinatown, the situation there reflected that of the city's early Chinese community.[7] Given the garment industry's long tradition of relying on female immigrant labor and the scarcity of women in the Chinese community, it is not difficult to understand why the industry did not grow in New York's Chinese community.

For decades, restaurants and laundries remained the two major Chinese businesses in New York City. By 1930 they employed more than 70 percent of the Chinese male blue-collar workers in New York City.[8] Most of the laundry businesses were staffed by only one or two people. Wielding an eight-pound iron and working from twelve to sixteen and sometimes twenty hours a day, the Chinese laundrymen called their lives "the blood and tears eight-pound livelihood."[9]

Restaurants and laundries were male businesses. Although many family-owned businesses demanded the unpaid labor of female family members, they employed mostly men.[10] With these two businesses dominating the economy of New York's Chinese community, there were few opportunities for women to be employed outside the home. Like their counterparts in other ethnic groups, women in Chinese American families always worked, but most of them worked at home. While fulfilling their household responsibilities, they helped out with their family businesses or engaged in various forms of wage-earning labor at home.[11]

It is therefore not surprising that the percentage of New York's Chinese women who participated in the labor force tended to be low. New York State Census manuscripts show that between 1905 and 1925, except for two women who registered their occupations as "actress" in 1905 and one as "cook" and one as "waitress" in 1925, almost all the adult Chinese women in New York's Chinatown identified themselves as houseworkers.

Hua Liang's study of the U.S. census manuscripts, however, reveals a more varied picture. It shows that in 1900 a fifteen-year-old daughter of a merchant living on Mott Street assisted the family income by doing needlework, and a twenty-eight-year-old widow of a Chinese American dry-goods merchant supported three children as well as her Chinese father and Caucasian mother by running the store on her own. Based on these data and a Chinese woman's lawsuit against an American businessman, as well as other sources, Liang argues that a number of Chinese women began to be involved in investment and other businesses around that time.[12]

Table 4. Chinese Population of New York City by Borough, 1870–1920

	1870	1880	1890	1900	1910	1920
New York City	20	853	2,559	6,321	4,614	5,042
Bronx	—	—	—	208	175	146
Percent	—	—	—	3.3	3.8	2.0
Kings/Brooklyn	7	121	549	1,206	799	811
Percent	35.0	14.2	21.5	19.1	17.3	16.1
New York/Manhattan	12	731	1,970	4,686	3,476	3,862
Percent	60.0	85.7	77.0	74.1	75.3	76.6
Queens	1	—	23	146	115	160
Percent	5.0	—	0.9	2.3	2.5	3.2
Richmond	—	1	17	75	49	63
Percent	—	0.1	0.7	1.2	1.0	1.2

Sources: U.S. Department of Commerce, Bureau of the Census, *U.S. Census of Population,* 1890, 1900, 1910, 1920 (Washington, D.C.: G.P.O.).

Note: Except for individual cases, number of Chinese men and women, respectively, by borough are not available prior to 1930.

Compared with their immigrant mothers, second-generation Chinese American women seemed to fare better. In 1920 many of them took after-school jobs and engaged in a wider range of wage-earning activities.[13] The personal account of a Chinese American woman, who was born in New York's Chinatown in 1907 and lived there until 1947, suggests that some of them worked full-time outside the home upon completion of their high school education. According to the narrator, whose name was concealed by the interviewer, she first worked at an import and export company as a bookkeeper, then went into show business and traveled around the country singing and dancing. She continued to work after her marriage. Shortly before and during the Depression she even posed for sculptors and painters and went on the road with a Japanese acrobat and a Filipino comedian.[14]

Arthur Bonner also reports that in 1915 a young Chinese American woman named Alice Lee, born on Mott Street and educated at Washington Irving High School, was hired to be in charge of the lounge and thus became the first Chinese woman to be employed by a New York hotel. Although their work might not have been typical among their peers, and second-generation Chinese American women were also subjected to racial discrimination, the experiences of these two women indicate that they enjoyed a much wider spectrum of life than did their immigrant mothers.[15]

The opportunities enjoyed by second-generation Chinese American women were not extended to their immigrant sisters. Despite the scarcity of women in the early Chinese community, there were a number of women in Chinatown who remained single and stayed with their parents. In 1925, for example, there were sixteen of them. Except for one forty-four-year-old, all of them were between the ages of eighteen and thirty-two. Twelve were Chinese-born, and ten were elder daughters of widow-headed households engaged in laundry or restaurant businesses. Except for the forty-four-year-old Chinese-born woman and a second-generation daughter, who registered as "cook" and "waitress," respectively, all of them identified their occupations as "housework." The fact that these marriageable daughters in working-class families remained with their parents and that most of them were Chinese-born demonstrates not only how indispensable their labor was to their families but also the limited economic alternatives they had.[16]

Guo Zhengzi suggests that things began to change gradually in the 1930s. During the Depression a number of immigrant women literally began to unbind their feet and work outside the home to supplement their family incomes. Some even began to run family businesses on their own.[17] Prominent businesswomen such as Mrs. Pon Sue Louie and Mrs. Jessie Young began to emerge. As described in the *New York Times*, Pon Sue Louie was the "manager of the Yick Quon Company in Chinatown and was also widely known for her services to needy families," and Jessie Young took over her husband's business after his death, successfully ran the business, and managed to put three of her sons through college.[18]

Although the achievements of these Chinese women entrepreneurs are impressive, their number remained small. Even up to 1940, Chinese women business owners and professionals constituted fewer than 20 percent of all the gainfully employed Chinese women and fewer than 4 percent of all the Chinese women fourteen years of age and over in the city. Up to 1950, fewer than one-fourth of the adult Chinese female population was in the labor force, with an even smaller percentage among the foreign-born. In 1940, for example, only 16 percent were gainfully employed and nearly 70 percent worked in laboring or service sectors.[19]

The census data have obviously understated women's important economic role in the community. Unpaid family workers contributed significantly to their family economy. A few accounts left by early Chinatown residents have indicated that a number of Chinese women sewed or engaged in other forms of wage-earning labor at home.[20] Except for these few accounts, however, there is no hard evidence detailing this aspect of women's lives in the prewar Chinese community.

The gender ratio of the city's Chinese community began to change after the Second World War, when Chinese immigrant women entered the city in significant numbers. This increase largely resulted from a series of changes in U.S. immigration law during and after the Second World War: the 1943 repeal of all Chinese Exclusion Acts and the granting of the right of naturalization and a limited annual immigration quota of 105; and the 1945 War Bride Acts and the act passed in 1946 that placed the entry of wives and minor children of Chinese American servicemen and Chinese American citizens on a nonquota basis.

The opportunities for Chinese immigration were further increased by a series of Displaced Persons and Refugee Relief Acts passed between the late 1940s and 1950s, which reserved a special quota for Chinese officials, professionals, and students who were "stranded" in the United States when the Communists took over China in 1949. Between 1962 and 1978 the Presidential Directory admitted more than fifteen thousand Chinese, primarily from Hong Kong.[21] The *New York Times* reported as early as 1964 that the number of the Chinese grew so significantly that the city's Board of Education began to create a specific category for their children.[22]

Women outnumbered men among the Chinese immigrants after the end of the war. Ninety percent of the Chinese immigrants who entered the United States between 1947 and 1952 were women.[23] Of the 7,892 Chinese women who immigrated from 1946 to 1950, 5,132 were wives of Chinese American men, and 4,875 of these were war brides.[24] After the War Bride Act expired in 1952, many others continued to enter the United States as nonquota immigrants under the act passed in 1946, which allowed the wives of all Chinese American citizens to enter the country on a nonquota basis.[25] Others came under the Displaced Persons Acts and other Refugee Relief Acts. As a result, between 1940 and 1980, while the nation's Chinese population increased over tenfold, the number of Chinese women increased almost twentyfold.[26]

The increase in Chinese women's immigration effectively redressed the gender imbalance of the Chinese population in the United States, dropping the ratio of men to women from almost 3 to 1 in 1940 to 1.3 to 1 in 1960. Since many of these new immigrant women settled in New York City, the gender ratio of New York's Chinese population also dropped significantly, from more than 6 men to 1 woman in 1940 to almost 3 to 1 in 1950 and 1.7 to 1 in 1960.[27]

Table 5. Chinese Immigrants Admitted to the United States by Country or Region of Birth and by Sex, 1945–95

Year[a]	Total	China/ Taiwan	Hong Kong	Males	Females	Percent Female
1945	109			45	64	58.7
1946	233			71	162	69.5
1947	1,128			142	986	87.4
1948	3,574			257	3,317	92.8
1949	2,490			242	2,248	90.3
1950	1,289			110	1,179	91.5
1951	1,081			126	957	88.5
1952	1,152			118	1,034	89.8
1953	1,093			203	890	81.4
1954	2,747			1,511	1,236	45.0
1955	2,628			1,261	1,367	52.0
1956	4,450			2,007	2,443	54.0
1957	5,123			2,487	2,636	51.5
1958	3,555			1,520	2,035	56.0
1959	6,566	5,722	844	3,044	3,522	53.6
1960	4,156	3,681	475	2,075	2,081	50.1
1961	3,838	3,213	625	1,565	2,273	59.2
1962	4,669	4,017	652	1,916	2,753	59.1
1963	5,370	4,658	712	2,297	3,073	57.2
1964	5,648	5,009	639	2,597	3,051	54.1
1965	4,769	4,057	712	2,242	2,527	53.0
1966	17,608	13,736	3,872	8,613	8,995	51.1
1967	25,096	19,741	5,355	12,811	12,285	49.0
1968	16,434	12,738	3,696	7,862	8,572	52.2
1969	20,893	15,440	5,453	10,001	10,892	52.1
1970	17,956	14,093	3,863	8,586	9,370	52.2
1971	17,622	14,417	3,205	8,287	9,335	53.0
1972	21,730	17,339	4,391	10,437	11,293	52.0
1973	21,656	17,297	4,359	9,937	11,719	54.1
1974	22,685	18,056	4,629	10,724	11,961	52.7
1975	23,427	18,536	4,891	11,179	12,248	52.3
1976[b]	31,116	23,857	7,259	14,928	16,188	52.0
1977	25,396	19,764	5,632	12,176	13,220	52.1
1978	26,472	21,315	5,158	12,507	13,966	52.3
1979	28,383	24,264	4,119	13,242	15,141	53.3
1980	31,511	n.a.	n.a.	n.a.	n.a.	n.a.
1981	29,858	n.a.	n.a.	n.a.	n.a.	n.a.

Table 5. Con't.

Year[a]	Total	Country or Region of Birth			Males	Females	Percent Female
		China	Taiwan	Hong Kong			
1982	41,955	27,100	9,884	4,971	19,250	21,041	50.2
1983	46,144	25,777	16,696	3,671	21,966	24,178	52.4
1984	41,306	23,363	12,478	5,465	19,715	21,591	52.3
1985	44,853	24,787	14,895	5,171	21,209	23,644	52.7
1986	43,551	25,106	13,424	5,021	n.a.	n.a.	n.a.[c]
1987	42,478	25,841	11,931	4,706	20,244	22,234	52.3
1988	46,933	28,717	9,670	8,546	22,460	24,473	52.1
1989	55,986	32,272	13,974	9,740	27,941	28,039	50.1
1990	56,259	31,815	15,151	9,393	n.a.	n.a.	n.a.[c]
1991	56,726	33,025	13,274	10,427	26,481	30,219	53.3
1992	65,703	38,907	16,344	10,452	29,904	35,724	54.4
1993	89,066	65,576	14,329	9,161	43,684	45,371	50.9
1994	71,748	53,985	10,032	7,731	34,319	37,422	52.2
1995	52,089	35,463	9,377	7,249	23,592	28,492	54.7

Sources: U.S. Department of Justice, Immigration and Naturalization Service, *Annual Report* (Washington, D.C.: G.P.O., 1945–78) and *Statistical Yearbook* (Washington, D.C.: G.P.O., 1979–95).

a. Fiscal years ending on June 30 prior to 1977 and on September 30 from 1977 to 1995.

b. Including the transitional period from July 1 to September 30.

c. In 1986, 11,812 males and 13,294 females came from China and the female percentage of the total immigration was 53; there were also 6,282 males and 7,142 females from Taiwan and the female percentage was 53.2. In 1990, 15,573 males and 16,220 females came from China and the female percentage was 51; there were also 7,056 males and 8,080 females from Taiwan and the female percentage was 53.3. What is not known is the numbers and gender ratios of the immigrants from Hong Kong in both years. Hence, it is impossible to provide statistics in these columns.

The arrival of women immigrants in this period had a tremendous impact on the Chinese community. Although a significant number of Chinese male laborers were continuously separated from their wives and children, the change in U.S. immigration law held out hope for the entire community. Concerns about the quality of family life began to surface in the community newspapers. For example, in late 1948 the *China Daily News* began to run a biweekly column on "Women and the Family." Most of the issues raised in this column, ranging from "What is miscarriage?" and "How to deal with the first tooth of your infant child" to "The danger of having sex right after delivering a baby," were addressed to the younger immigrant women.

Stories about how "married bachelors" yearned for a family reunion were also common. More than ten major stories about family life were covered in the issues of the *China Daily News* in the first three months of 1949, and an even larger number of such articles appeared in the following years, a great improvement over the prewar years, when there were almost no such stories.[28] The prevailing concern about and interest in family life left little room to perpetuate the sojourner's mentality in the community.

As the Chinese American journalist Zhu Xia observed, the new immigrant women's economic contributions revitalized not only families but also the

Table 6. Chinese Immigrants Admitted to New York City by Country or Region of Birth, 1957–95

Year[a]	Total	Country or Region of Birth	
		China/Taiwan	Hong Kong
1957	n.a.	1,439	n.a.
1958	n.a.	810	n.a.
1959	n.a.	1,412	n.a.
1960	1,098	980	118
1961	886	731	155
1962	1,133	971	162
1963	1,157	980	177
1964	1,080	922	158
1965	977	800	177
1966	4,231	3,271	960
1967	5,846	4,518	1,328
1968	3,861	2,949	912
1969	4,561	3,209	1,352
1970	3,658	2,699	959
1971	3,856	2,938	918
1972	5,279	4,190	1,089
1973	5,210	4,129	1,081
1974	4,958	3,810	1,148
1975	5,233	3,872	1,361
1976[b]	6,123	4,332	1,791
1977	4,034	2,873	1,161
1978	4,922	3,607	1,315
1979	6,112	5,163	949
1980	n.a.	n.a.	n.a.
1981	n.a.	n.a.	n.a.
		China	Taiwan	Hong Kong
1982	n.a.	5,808	913	n.a.
1983	n.a.	n.a.	n.a.	n.a.
1984	n.a.	6,019	1,170	n.a.
1985	n.a.	6,488	1,442	n.a.
1986	9,689	7,186	1,435	1,068
1987	n.a.	7,042	1,202	n.a.
1988	9,624	7,101	853	1,670
1989	13,716	9,983	1,734	1,999
1990	12,389	9,030	1,434	1,925
1991	12,295	8,964	1,200	2,131
1992	12,861	9,871	1,223	1,767
1993	14,315	11,998	879	1,438
1994	11,975	10,163	653	1,159
1995	11,930	10,281	536	1,113

Sources: U.S. Department of Justice, Immigration and Naturalization Service, *Annual Report* (Washington, D.C.: G.P.O., 1957–78) and *Statistical Yearbook* (Washington, D.C.: G.P.O., 1979–95).

a. Fiscal years ending on June 30 prior to 1977 and on September 30 from 1977 to 1995.

b. Including the transitional period from July 1 to September 30.

traditional Chinese laundry and restaurant businesses in the city, which had suffered during the war due to the labor shortage caused by the drafting of Chinese men into the military forces.[29] With most of the one- and two-person Chinese laundries transformed into family businesses, the trade soon regained its status as a major source of income for New York's Chinese working families.[30]

The *China Daily News* noted that new enterprises run by women also began to emerge in New York's Chinatown. In 1951, for example, a beauty salon on Mott Street and a dress store in another part of Chinatown were established.[31] Among the few entrepreneurial Chinese working-class immigrant women, the most well known beyond the community was Lan Gu (Aunt Lan). Lan Gu emigrated from Hong Kong in 1952. She had been the breadwinner of her family there, supporting her son and her elderly mother by working as a maid from 1929, when she was only seventeen and was abandoned by her gambler husband. After immigrating to the United States, she managed to save three thousand dollars through hard work and frugal living. With this small capital, she opened a tofu store on the corner of Catherine Street and Chatham Square in 1957. Working seven days a week and eighteen hours a day, her hard labor finally paid off. The stuffed tofu and wide rice noodles that she made became so popular in Chinatown that she even caught the attention of the *New York Daily News* in 1979, when her story was first told.[32]

Family life, however, engendered new problems in the Chinese community, including the high divorce rate among recently reunited or newlywed couples and the relatively high suicide rate among women. These problems have to be understood in the context of the social and cultural backgrounds of the Chinese women who immigrated during this period, the particular forms of marriage in the Chinese community, and the situation in the community at the time.

Rose Hum Lee, a sociologist who made a detailed study of Chinese immigrant families in the postwar period, observed that most of the women who arrived after the end of the Second World War fell into two categories, "separated wives" and "war wives." The first refers to women who had been separated from their husbands from one to two decades; the second stands for those who had been married to Chinese American servicemen.[33] Separated wives tended to be much older, between thirty and fifty years of age; they tended to come from rural areas and were less educated. Steeped in their native culture and handicapped by the lack of English language skills, this group of Chinese women immigrants had a difficult time adjusting to the new land. They were more restricted in their social lives than the second group.

The war wives married young Chinese American servicemen after the end of the Second World War and entered the United States as nonquota immigrants in the immediate postwar years. Much younger than the separated wives, the majority were between twenty and twenty-two years of age. A few came from urban areas, but most were from rural areas and families of former emigrants who received financial support from relatives in the United States. They were better educated than the separated wives and had not experienced long separations from their husbands. However, they faced a higher demand for accultur-

ation from their husbands, who had experienced a rapid and intensive acculturation in the army.

Among the Chinese women I interviewed in New York City there were separated wives and war wives, but their backgrounds and lives were much more
diverse than Lee described. Since the majority of Chinese women immigrants,
older or younger, entered this country under the act passed in 1946, younger
Chinese immigrant women in the postwar era were not all war brides, and wives
of American citizens could also be newly wed, since many male citizens went
back to China to get married after the war.

In addition, it should be noted that although most China-born immigrant
women came directly from China before 1949, many of those who immigrated
in the 1950s and 1960s had resided in Hong Kong or places outside China for
varying lengths of time before immigrating to the United States. Given the fact
that kinship networks and sometimes even nuclear families spanned both sides
of the Hong Kong–China border before 1949, the massive emigration from
China to Hong Kong after 1949, and the ending of diplomatic relations between
China and the United States after the Communist success in China, it is no surprise that most of the Chinese-born did not come directly from China.[34]

Chinese immigrant women in the postwar era were differentiated by their
ages, their social and educational backgrounds, and, most importantly, the status of their husbands in the United States. Although cases varied individually,
the social and demographic profiles of the older immigrant women in the Chinese working-class families in many ways resemble Lee's description of the separated wives. Most of them had been separated from their husbands from one
to more than two decades, and many had virtually no urban experience or education prior to immigration. However, they were under less pressure to accul-
turate, as many of their husbands also lived in a world segregated from the larger
American society. In addition, since many of their husbands had their own restaurants or laundries, which required their assistance, these women spent most
of their time taking care of their families and their family businesses. They were
largely confined to the domestic sphere but were more financially secure than
the younger women.

The backgrounds and lives of the younger working-class women were much
more diverse. Most were related to the families in rural Guangdong who received
financial support from relatives in the United States. Depending on their time
of immigration, some of them came directly from rural Guangdong, while others had either spent part of their adult lives there or had grown up in the working-class families in Hong Kong that had migrated from Guangdong. Thus their
urban experience and educational backgrounds varied. While those from Hong
Kong might be more urbanized than their counterparts from rural China, they
might be less educated than the latter due to the relatively high level of education daughters of many emigrant families could receive in the Si Yi District in
Guangdong Province.[35]

Despite their different backgrounds, many young immigrant women in working-class families who married Chinese men of their ages shared similar experiences in the United States. Loneliness and isolation were their two major problems. Many of their husbands worked in Chinese restaurants, since they were either too young to have their own business or did not have the resources to start a business after military service. Restaurant employment required long hours, and wives of restaurant workers were left at home most of the time. Without friends and with no place to go, immigrant wives of restaurant workers found their lives like "being detained in jail."[36] One young wife of a restaurant worker, constantly panicked by her inexperience and lack of assistance in caring for her newborn baby, expressed regret for emigrating from her homeland. She said that she would rather toil in the fields of China than live as she did in America.[37]

Some of the younger immigrant women who came from urban China were not necessarily related to emigrant families in rural Guangdong. They were better educated; some had even studied English before coming to the United States. Most were married to upwardly mobile Chinese Americans. This latter group of women drew most of the attention from the press in and outside the Chinese community. The community newspapers and major newspapers in the city noted that the young Chinese immigrant women who came in the immediate postwar era were modern in dress and thought. Not only did they dress in "the increasingly skimpy dresses of the period," but they also shopped in supermarkets, attended classes run by churches to brush up on the English they had learned in Canton and Hong Kong, and befriended their American neighbors. They did all this in an attempt to reach out to the world beyond their own community.[38]

Their efforts, however, did not seem to get them far. The experience of a Mrs. Yu, reported in the *China Daily News,* is enlightening in this regard. She had come as a war bride in 1948 with an education in English and experience in a Red Cross organization in China. She had romanticized the West and was happy to emigrate, expecting to be treated equally in her new land. The reality shattered her dream. After her husband left the army, the couple hunted for an apartment and were consistently turned down by white homeowners. They had to settle in Chinatown. "I knew people had different thoughts," she said in despair, "but I did not expect that I would be discriminated against just because of the color of my skin."[39]

However, my interviews suggest that not all young immigrant women were married to men their own age. Rather, many of them married men much older, even twice their age. Since quite a few Chinese men who searched for wives in the postwar era were already in their waning years and had sent to families of their prospective brides pictures that they took when they were in their mid- or late twenties, their young wives would not realize their actual age until the couples met in New York.[40] There were also cases in which couples of disparate ages had met before being married, but the decision to marry was often made by the brides' parents rather than the women themselves. Some of these women were better educated than their husbands, but their lives were more like those of the older immigrant women than their cohorts of their own age who married younger men.

Although a number of the new immigrant women lived in other boroughs of the city where their husbands had their own businesses, most lived in Chinatown. As a result, the Chinese population in Chinatown began to grow rapidly.[41] Chinatown was, however, not an ideal place for immigrant families to live. Housing was a major problem. The tenement buildings were built to be dormitories for the single men who spent most of the day at their workplace and expected only a bed to sleep in at night. Many lacked cooking facilities, heat, and adequate lighting and ventilation. Bathtubs were in the living rooms, and shared toilets were in the halls. According to the Chinese American journalist Zhu Xia, it was not unusual in the 1950s and 1960s for several families to live on the same floor, sharing a common bath and kitchen, in buildings without heat or ventilation, and for a family of five to nine persons to be housed in a one-bedroom apartment.[42]

Table 7. Chinese Population of New York City by Borough and by Sex, 1930–50

	1930	Percent[a]	1940	Percent[a]	1950	Percent[a]
New York City	8,414		12,753		18,329	
Males	7,549		10,967		13,627	
Females	865		1,786		4,702	
Males per 100 females	872.7		614.0		289.8	
Bronx	287	3.4	597	4.7	996	5.4
Males	244		490		666	
Females	43		107		330	
Males per 100 females	567.4		457.9		201.8	
Kings/Brooklyn	1,405	16.7	1,251	9.8	2,268	12.4
Males	1,222		1,039		1,555	
Females	183		212		713	
Males per 100 females	667.8		490.1		218.1	
New York/Manhattan	6,268	74.5	10,370	81.3	13,687	74.7
Males	5,680		9,027		10,560	
Females	588		1,343		3,127	
Males per 100 females	966.0		672.2		337.7	
Queens	399	4.7	465	3.6	1,255	6.8
Males	354		351		754	
Females	45		114		501	
Males per 100 females	786.7		307.9		150.5	
Richmond	55	0.7	70	0.5	123	0.7
Males	49		60		92	
Females	6		10		31	
Males per 100 females	816.7		600.0		296.8	

Sources: U.S. Department of Commerce, Bureau of the Census, *U.S. Census of Population,* 1930, 1940, 1950 (Washington, D.C.: G.P.O.).

a. Percentage of New York City's Chinese population.

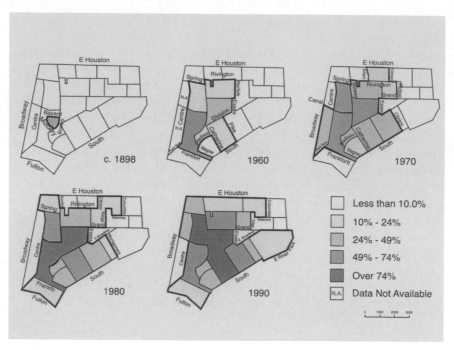

Map 2. Chinese population growth in New York's Chinatown (percent Chinese by census tract), c. 1898–1990. (Adapted from Louis J. Beck, *New York's Chinatown: An Historical Presentation of Its People and Places* [New York: Bohemia Publishing Co., 1898], and U.S. Census records, 1960–90).

In addition to the crowded living conditions, many Chinese immigrant women were harassed frequently by police and immigration officers, who were anxious to combat "Chinese illegal immigration," and simultaneously victimized by crime in Chinatown.[43] The suffering of the immigrant women intensified when their marital relations went sour. Marital problems stemmed primarily from the type of marriage they had undergone, which often did not allow the couples to develop any emotional bond. For many if not most Chinese men and women in the United States and China, marriage was more a matter of family obligation and necessity than of love. Most Chinese men in the United States had married in haste. Many either could not afford the time or simply did not see the need to spend time developing intimate relationships with their spouses before and even after marriage. A widely circulated story in the Rocky Mountain region, reported by Rose Hum Lee, told of a serviceman who managed to complete all stages of courtship and marriage within his one month's leave of absence from work—travel to and from China, the selection of a spouse, the courtship, and the wedding.[44] This story did not sound so unusual to the Chinese veterans in New York's Chinatown whom I interviewed.

Although many recently reunited or newlywed couples managed to develop interdependent relationships, mutual understanding and respect, and sometimes even love in their efforts to build their family life in the United States, many did not. Money constituted a major source of tension. Financial problems were mainly caused by insufficient employment opportunities for the Chinese in the city after the end of the war. As Arthur Bonner has put it, in the postwar era "exclusion had ended, but racism was still strong." Except for a few who chose to take advantage of the GI Bill to pursue an education, most Chinese war veterans returned to the old trades of their community, the restaurant and laundry businesses.[45] With an increasing number of these small businesses run by their owners and their recently arrived relatives, many Chinese men found it difficult to locate a job, not to mention any employment opportunity for their wives. As a result, many newly formed or recently reunited families faced severe financial problems.

Three stories covered on the same day in the *China Daily News* give difficult case histories of couples living in Chinatown hotels because they could not find an apartment.[46] One story tells about an unemployed Chinese ex-serviceman who was so financially drained by staying in the hotel and eating out all the time with his newlywed pregnant wife from China that he abandoned her when it was close to her expected date of childbirth. The second story also tells of a financially strained new couple, who, after the wife became pregnant, posted a for-sale note in a garment shop to sell their future baby—five hundred dollars for a girl and a thousand dollars for a boy. The third story, reportedly well circulated in Chinatown, tells how two ex-servicemen forced their wives into prostitution to pay their bills. Although such accounts may have been tainted with journalistic hyperbole, their timing and increasing frequency in the newspaper does reveal community problems.

Most Chinese men enjoyed having a family life, but many had not been prepared to assume financial responsibility to support a family after so many years of bachelorhood. The shrinking job market also made it difficult for them to do so. This failure to assume their traditional gender role as the breadwinner of the family generated great psychological pressures on them. Many vented their frustration and anger on their spouses. Cases of family breakup, domestic violence, and wife abuse thus began to grow.[47]

Regrettably, newspaper coverage of domestic violence and wife abuse usually did not stem from a concern for the abused women. For example, a May 1950 issue of the *China Daily News* describes how the president of the Chinese Consolidated Benevolent Association (CCBA), Chen Zhonghai, had severely battered his wife. The pro-Beijing community newspaper presented this case as a political issue to demonstrate problems with those affiliated with the Chinese conservative political party rather than a reflection on the serious domestic violence in the community.[48] Nevertheless, the fact that a public figure as influential as Chen Zhonghai recklessly battered his wife in a community in which one cared for one's reputation above everything else suggests how widespread the problem was at the time.

While most of these incidents occurred among younger women immigrants, the older separated wives faced another problem. After being separated from their husbands for decades, some of them came to the United States only to discover that their husbands had formed a new family. Virginia Heyer recorded two such cases in her study. In one case, a young war bride found that her husband had been living with an American woman, and he refused to recognize her as wife after she immigrated to the city. In the other case, the woman arrived only to find herself in the middle of an intense family feud over the property of her deceased husband with his other family in the United States, of whose existence she had no previous knowledge. Devastated by the painful reality, both women turned to their family associations and the authoritative CCBA for help. Although seemingly trying to help, these male-dominated organizations offered neither a satisfactory solution to the cases nor justice for the women.[49]

Despite variations in their lives in their new land, the situation of the new immigrant women in the postwar era was later succinctly summarized by a Chinese woman psychiatrist in the Chinatown branch of the Community Service Society. As she pointed out, all these women had to undergo two kinds of adjustment, "adjustment to culture, and adjustment to a husband."[50] The anguish and frustration caused by these two major aspects of life had driven a number of new immigrant women either to the verge of nervous breakdown or to commit suicide. One source estimated that the suicide rate among New York's Chinese American women remained twice that of the city average until the 1970s.[51]

Chinese immigrant women's difficulties in adapting to their lives in the new land aroused concern from a number of community service agencies. For instance, beginning in the 1950s, Beekman Hospital, the medical facility most frequently used by Chinese American families, for the first time allowed family members of young Chinese mothers to bring ethnic food to the maternity ward. Similarly, the City Community Service Society also decided to shift the focus of its work in Chinatown from the problem of tuberculosis to the problems of the "young mothers living away from their kin in an environment totally new to them."[52] Although their efforts helped ease some of the pains of new Chinese women immigrants, the assistance these agencies could provide was still very limited, given the volume of the problems many Chinese women faced at that time.

The rising number of Chinatown garment shops in the late 1940s, with their expanded employment opportunities, offered one solution to the problems faced by many new immigrant women. Stories about Chinese women garment workers first appeared in the *China Daily News* in May 1952, and help-wanted ads from the garment shops first appeared on June 27, 1952.[53] Guo Zhengzhi documents three Chinese-owned garment shops in 1952. According to Guo, women who worked in the garment shops tended to be young. Even the floor workers, who were traditionally much older than the rest of the workforce, were in their thirties. The reason given by Guo is that while the employers preferred to hire younger women, whom they believed could work much faster than the older ones, the younger women also most needed to work, because their husbands tended not to have their own businesses.[54]

Working in the garment shops brought meaning into the lives of the immigrant women in various ways. For a small number of women workers in comfortable circumstances, garment shops provided an important place to socialize with others in the community and to apply their talents to their lives in the United States. Nancy Ng, whom I interviewed in 1989, when she was seventy-three years old, told me such a story. In 1948, when she came to join her husband in New York, she had a high school education, some knowledge of English, and some teaching experience in Guangzhou (Canton). She first worked in a white-owned shop making artificial flowers, but, disenchanted by the working environment there, she decided to work in a Chinese garment shop. After two years she started her own shop with a relative, but when business slowed down, she sold her garment shop and once again became a worker. When asked whether there was any economic motivation for her to work in the garment shops, her answer was a definite "no!" Supported by her husband, who was an engineer, she insisted that her only reasons were to kill time and to test her managerial and other skills.[55]

Employment in the garment shops was, however, indispensable for another group of women, who were also from families with a relatively high social status. They were wives of the "stranded" students or others who left China before 1949 and decided to stay in the United States after the Communists took over. Since they could no longer receive any financial support from the new government, their wives had to work in the garment shops to support their families and, in many cases, their husband's education. Old-timers in the Chinatown garment industry recalled that the number of these workers remained small and that they were "a lonely group in the shops." Their different language, cultural, and class backgrounds built an invisible wall between them and the rest of the workers.[56] Ostracized by their fellow workers in the shops and feeling no incentive to stay, this group of workers left the industry and became uptown Chinese once their husbands completed their education and landed well-paying professional jobs. For them, working in the garment shops was a temporary expedient to make ends meet. The fact that they too had to work in the garment industry illustrates the limited nature of Chinese female employment in postwar New York.

For the majority of women workers, however, income from working in the garment shops was crucial for their family's survival in the United States. The following dialogue recorded in a community newspaper demonstrates the importance of their financial contribution:

"Old Aunt Ma, where are you going and why are you in such a hurry at such an early hour?"

"I am in a hurry to go to work."

"Then, what about the kids? Who takes care of them?"

"Well, to make a long story short, with two kids to care for, I really shouldn't have left home to work. But things are not always as good as you wish. As you know, Old Ma works only three to four days a week. The thirty something dollars he earns every week is hardly enough to pay for our food and rent. It really gets us if some-one in the family is ill. Take the past two months for example. Old Ma was ill for several days and we had to borrow money from friends to cover our daily expenses. So, I decided to come out to work."

"Isn't it too hard on you?"

"Well, I ask a woman to take care of the kids and pay her fifteen dollars a week. I myself work in a garment shop and earn more than thirty dollars a week. After paying the baby-sitter, I still have some money left for family expenses. I feel much better now."[57]

Like the Ma family, many Chinese immigrant families faced serious financial problems. Women's wage-earning labor in the garment industry was so impor-tant to these families that, as one worker I interviewed stated, "without the gar-ment industry, I really can't imagine how my family could survive to this day."[58]

If the income from the garment industry was crucial for the family survival of most married women workers in the few Chinatown garment shops, it was the only means of survival for some women who had chosen to remain single. Shun Nan Young, who was seventy-seven years old when I interviewed her in 1994, is a good example. She was born and raised in a village of Shunde County in Guangdong Province, a county well known for its unique culture of wom-en's resistance to marriage before 1949.[59] She was the daughter of a concubine in a wealthy and influential family in a Shunde village. Her mother was a maid in the family before being married to her father, and her mother's obscure or-igin and low status in the family made Young an underdog among her father's offspring. The injustice imposed on her and her mother nurtured her strong will of resistance to the family institution in general and marriage in particu-lar. In 1936, at the age of nineteen, she decided to break with the family and start her own life. With her mother's unconditional support and the resourceful plan-ning of her *kaih ma* (Cantonese: sworn mother), who had also vowed not to marry, she managed to escape from the village and landed at Hong Kong.[60]

For the first time in her life she lived on her own. She first worked in a knit-ting factory and began working as a housekeeper or cook for wealthy families in Hong Kong, Guangdong, and Guangxi after the Sino-Japanese War broke out in 1937 and the subsequent decline of the knitting industry in Hong Kong. She remembered that she could not even cook well for herself, not to mention for an entire family, when she first embarked on her career as a cook for wealthy families.[61] However, the reputation of *Shunde nu* (Shunde women) as good cooks helped. Taking advantage of this special reputation of her place of birth and with the unfailing assistance of her girlfriends from Shunde, she not only managed to stay on the job but soon became a well-known cook. Her excellent performance finally earned her an offer from an internationally acclaimed physicist of Chinese descent, a professor in an American university.

Under the sponsorship of a friend of this professor, Shun Nan Young, at the age of forty-four, came to New Jersey in 1961 and began working for the professor. However, she did not have good luck with her first employment in the United States, as she put it. Shortly after she began working for the family, she found the wife of her employer difficult to deal with. Furthermore, for a person who appreciated good food, the family's diet of hamburgers for three meals a day was also too difficult to swallow. She thereupon decided to leave.

Her employer, however, refused to return her immigration documents in an attempt to keep her. "Nothing can stop me once I make up my mind," Young told me at the top of her voice as she recalled this moment. Shrewdly, she had asked her friends in Hong Kong to prepare a list of her former Shunde girlfriends' Chinatown addresses for her in English before she immigrated. By showing this small piece of paper all the way from the professor's home to the train station in Jersey City and then to New York's Chinatown, the strong-willed Young outwitted the world-acclaimed physicist and joined her friends in New York City.

With the recommendation of a Shunde friend, she became a machine operator in a Chinatown garment shop. From that time on, she managed not only to support herself but also to accumulate some savings. She retired at the age of sixty-nine. When I first met her in the fall of 1994, almost ten years after her retirement, she lived comfortably near her friends in a one-bedroom apartment in Queens, which she bought with her savings from her income in the Chinatown garment shops. "I did not need a husband to survive, but I needed a job. . . . It was the Chinatown garment industry that saved my life," she said emphatically at the conclusion of our interview.

Although the Chinatown garment industry was crucial for many women, the number of the Chinese-owned shops remained small: about three in 1952, eight in 1960, and thirty-five in 1965.[62] They employed only a small number of workers. Census data show that up to 1960, restaurants and laundries remained the two major sources of income for working-class Chinese families in the Northeast.[63]

Ironically, before the mid-1960s, when the Chinese garment industry was almost invisible, there was a midtown garment district, well known for its low-priced merchandise, called "Chinatown" in midtown Manhattan, located on Thirty-fifth Street between Lexington and Eighth Avenue.[64] Staffed by Jews, Italians, blacks, and Puerto Ricans, this garment marketplace had virtually nothing to do with the Chinatown in the Lower East Side of Manhattan, but the use of "Chinatown" in association with low-priced merchandise reflects the lingering discrimination against Chinese Americans in the city.

Dramatic changes did not take place in New York's Chinatown until after 1965, when Congress passed an amendment to the 1952 McCarran-Walter Act abolishing the discriminatory national quota system, introducing new preferences for family reunification, establishing a labor certification program, and imposing a ceiling on immigration from the western hemisphere. Although the new act enabled the immigration of a large number of highly trained Asian professionals in the early 1970s, the four-family reunification preferences and the repeal of the discriminatory national quota had a larger impact on Asian American communities. As a result of "chain immigration," immigrants from Asian countries under these preferences constituted almost a third of the total number of quota immigrants.[65]

The number of Chinese immigrants also began to rise rapidly after 1965, an annual average of nineteen thousand from 1966 to 1970. Between 1976 and 1980 the number soared to more than twenty-eight thousand. By 1982 more than four hundred thousand Chinese immigrants had entered the United States each year.[66] Unlike the early waves of Chinese immigrants, the new wave came from various countries and regions with their families. Although the relaxed U.S. immigration policy enabled Asians to enter the country, it was the political and economic instability in their native land that had pushed them out.

Until the late 1970s Hong Kong and Taiwan remained the main sources of Chinese immigration to the United States. Although emigrants from these two places shared the same apprehension about the impending Communist takeover of their native places, the immediate forces that pushed them out were somewhat different. The massive emigration from Hong Kong in the late 1960s and 1970s was mainly caused by the political turmoil there. The riot that took place in Hong Kong in 1967 was considered to be the most violent in its modern history. It is estimated that fifty-one persons were killed, nearly a hundred injured, and five thousand arrested, not to mention those who were secretly deported by the colonial government.[67] The event, believed by many in Hong Kong to be controlled by the Communists in the mainland, seemed to confirm their apprehensions over what might happen after 1997, when the colony was to be returned to China. As a result, those with the means to emigrate began to leave Hong Kong in large numbers.

U.S. immigration statistics show that between 1966 and 1979, 172,848 immigrants came from Hong Kong. About 50 percent had been blue-collar workers, and the majority were women and children who reported no prior occupation.[68] In terms of their social and educational backgrounds, the new immigrants from Hong Kong resembled their predecessors in the United States, because of the family-oriented nature of the new U.S. immigration law.

Like Hong Kong, Taiwan experienced a wave of emigration in the 1970s and the early 1980s. As revealed in the interviews done by Chen Hsiang-shui , the Taiwanese left their homeland for economic and political reasons. Although

Taiwan's economy began to take off in the early 1960s, its unemployment rate remained high, and many college graduates could not obtain jobs related to their field of study. In addition, the repressive political climate before the lifting of martial law in 1987 made it a less desirable place to live. People's confidence in their government was further undermined when the People's Republic of China replaced the Taiwanese government as China's official representative in the United Nations in 1971 and by the normalization of diplomatic relations between China and the United States in 1979. To ensure a better future for themselves and their families, residents of Taiwan began to search for a way to leave the island. The number of emigrants greatly increased after 1979, when the Taiwanese government agreed to issue its people tourist passports. Many Taiwanese entered the United States with tourist or student visas and never returned.[69]

The massive wave of immigrants from the People's Republic of China did not begin until the late 1970s, after Richard Nixon's visit to Beijing in early 1972 and the normalization of diplomatic relations between the two countries in 1979. Like those from Hong Kong and Taiwan, immigrants from China sought to escape political and economic instability at home. Although many positive changes took place after the Communist success in China, people were frustrated by the instability in state policies caused by the ongoing power struggle within the leadership of the ruling party. Especially after the ten most chaotic years of the Cultural Revolution (1966–76), many people lost confidence in the leadership. Like an unlocking of the floodgates, the Chinese government's "open door" policy in 1979 led to massive waves of emigration from the country.

Unlike their predecessors in the United States, the new immigrants from China came not only from the Si Yi District in Guangdong Province but from almost all parts of the country. Many immigrated to the United States under categories of family reunion. Others came with student and other nonimmigrant visas and, like their Taiwanese counterparts, remained in the United States after their documents expired.

In addition, ethnic Chinese also came in significant numbers from various countries in Southeast Asia. Before the late 1970s they primarily came from countries like Indonesia and Myanmar (named Burma before 1996), where anti-Chinese sentiment was ignited by the government and ethnic Chinese were persecuted in the 1960s. Many immigrated as family members and relatives of U.S. citizens or permanent residents. After 1975 their numbers increased dramatically. Most, however, entered as refugees from Vietnam, Kampuchea (named Cambodia before 1975), and Laos. There are no statistics recording the exact number of persons in this group because of the lack of ethnic specificity in the U.S. census and other statistical surveys. However, it is estimated that 70 to 80 percent of the "boat people" from Vietnam after the Communist takeover in 1975 were ethnic Chinese. A similar proportion of ethnic Chinese was also found among refugees from Kampuchea and Laos, even though they might be of somewhat different social backgrounds.[70] With new immigrants from many countries and regions of the world, the Chinese community in the United States became one of the most culturally diverse Chinese concentrations in the world.

As the "port of immigrants," New York City received the largest number of Chinese immigrants among all cities in the nation in the postwar era, especially after 1965.[71] Over one-fifth of the 229,696 Chinese immigrants who entered the United States between 1966 and 1976 registered New York City as their place of intended residence. One source estimates that of the 48,364 Chinese who came to New York between 1970 and 1980, 45,846 remained in the city.[72] With the fourfold increase of the city's Chinese population from 32,831 to 124,764 between 1960 and 1980, Chinese began to account for about 1.8 percent of the city's population. Although the Chinese population in California remains the largest in the nation, since 1970 New York City has begun to replace San Francisco as the city with the largest Chinese population.[73]

Like their predecessors, many immigrants who came in the 1970s and early 1980s settled in Chinatown. As a result, New York's Chinatown expanded greatly. From an area bounded in the 1960s by Grand and Canal Streets in the north, Essex Street in the east, Center Street in the west, and Division Street in the south, in 1980 it reached Rivington Street in the north, Norfolk and Clinton Streets in the east, Park Row in the west, and Wagner Place and South Street in the south. As early as 1964, journalists outside the community noticed that Chinese signs had replaced those in Spanish in the Lower East Side.[74]

The linguistic makeup of the community also changed. With immigrants coming from various parts of China and Asia in different periods, the Taishan dialect, once the lingua franca of the community, lost its predominant position. Replacing it were not only the varied fashions of Cantonese spoken in Guangzhou and the regions of Hong Kong and Macao in the late 1960s and 1970s but the forms of Mandarin spoken in Taiwan and China; Shanghai, Fujian, Zhejiang, and other major dialects of China as well as Burmese, Vietnamese, Laos, and Kampuchean surfaced in the late 1970s and early 1980s.

The rapid increase of Chinese families in the city coupled with the aging of its earlier population also had a transforming impact on the nature of social organizations in the community. As the demand for social services grew, the inwardly drawn social organizations in the community proved to be unable to meet new challenges. New types of social organizations began to grow that received funds from the larger society and had strong ties with the outside world. In providing recent immigrants with the assistance they most needed, these organizations had an impact not only by linking the Chinese community to the larger society but also by posing a challenge to the old conservative political institutions and forces in the community.[75]

However, shaped by the availability of low-skilled jobs in New York City, the Chinese immigrants in this period also had fewer marketable skills. The 1979

Table 8. Chinese Immigrants Admitted to the States of California and New York and the Cities of San Francisco, Los Angeles, and New York, 1957–95

Year[a]	California	Los Angeles	San Francisco	New York State	New York City
1957	1,591	310	679	1,664	1,439
1958	980	164	475	910	810
1959	2,005	301	939	1,574	1,412
1960	1,430	202	699	1,040	980
1961	1,168	113	612	818	731
1962	1,562	208	720	1,058	971
1963	1,695	254	750	1,132	980
1964	1,571	231	640	1,106	922
1965	1,597	257	706	926	800
1966	6,316	852	3,181	3,526	3,271
1967	6,700	1,282	2,883	5,150	4,518
1968	4,193	765	1,653	3,323	2,949
1969	5,584	919	2,205	3,845	3,209
1970	4,460	732	1,605	3,290	2,699
1971	3,079	786	820	3,602	2,938
1972	4,340	903	1,434	4,919	4,190
1973	4,648	889	1,483	4,782	4,129
1974	5,449	1,237	1,447	4,548	3,810
1975	5,654	1,068	1,681	4,536	3,872
1976[b]	7,713	1,153	2,338	5,069	4,332
1977	7,027	1,060	1,760	3,546	2,873
1978	7,046	977	1,475	4,172	3,607
1979	9,173	1,124	2,715	5,740	5,163
1982	13,618	1,618	2,828	7,241	6,721
1983	15,167	n.a.	n.a.	9,162	n.a.
1984	n.a.	4,084	3,947	n.a.	7,189
1985	n.a.	5,262	3,800	n.a.	7,930
1986	15,528	5,820	8,117	9,235	8,621
1987	15,236	5,427	4,324	9,022	8,244
1988	15,573	5,948	3,711	8,806	7,954
1989	17,074	6,863	3,948	12,647	11,717
1990	18,300	6,909	4,154	11,504	10,464
1991	18,105	6,374	4,419	11,248	10,164
1992	19,249	6,967	3,523	12,561	11,094
1993	20,857	8,056	3,998	15,093	12,877
1994	22,309	8,525	4,251	12,596	10,816
1995	14,906	5,677	3,171	11,957	10,817

Sources: U.S. Department of Justice, Immigration and Naturalization Service, *Annual Report* (Washington, D.C.: G.P.O., 1957–78), and *Statistical Yearbook* (Washington, D.C.: G.P.O., 1979–95).

Note: The Chinese immigrants in this table do not include those from Hong Kong because their statistics are not consistently available for the purpose of this table. This table also does not include 1980 and 1981 because the statistics are not available for these two years.

a. Fiscal years ending on June 30 prior to 1977 and on September 30 from 1977 to 1995.

b. Including the transitional period from July to September.

unpublished data of the U.S. Immigration and Naturalization Service show that 70 percent of the Chinese immigrants who had reported their occupation had been blue-collar workers. Of the 14.6 percent of Chinese immigrants to the United States who reported prior professional and technical occupations, only 3.2 percent chose to settle in New York City.[76]

Because of their low skills and inability to speak English, many new Chinese immigrants were relegated to the most labor-intensive and lowest-paying sectors in the city. Census data show that in 1980, while only 16.5 percent of the foreign-born non-Hispanic white population in the city were laborers, of whom 67 percent worked over forty hours per week, over 30 percent of the foreign-born Chinese population were blue-collar workers, and 73.5 percent worked over forty hours per week.[77]

The problems of low skills and the inability to speak English were even more pronounced among the new Chinese immigrant women. U.S. immigration data for 1979 show that only 28 percent of Chinese immigrant women reported any previous employment experience, of whom only 30 percent had worked in a factory and about 8 percent had experience in white-collar positions.[78] Although my interviews suggest that the category of "housewife," with a connotation of having no wage-earning experience at all, was highly misleading for Chinese women immigrants in this period, a large proportion of them were from blue-collar working families.[79]

Despite their disadvantageous position in the U.S. labor market, the economic contribution of most recent adult Chinese immigrant women was indispensable to their families. Many of their families had borrowed money to travel to the United States, and most of their husbands worked in restaurants and other low-paid labor sectors after immigration.[80] Fortunately, the majority of them were of working age with more than 45 percent in the prime working ages of twenty to forty. To sustain their families, they had to enter the labor market and take whatever jobs were available shortly after their arrival in New York City. Like their counterparts on the Lower East Side at the turn of the century, these Chinese immigrant women were hardworking and determined to build a better life for themselves and their families. They thus became a much-needed labor reservoir for the city's garment industry.[81]

The new Chinese immigration brought not only a large proportion of low-skilled immigrants but also a significant number of entrepreneurs who came with managerial skills and capital. Although 70 percent of the new immigrants reporting prior occupations had been blue-collar workers, almost 15 percent of male and 5 percent of female immigrants had been proprietors and/or had managerial experience before immigrating.[82] These new immigrants readily joined members of the community who had already accumulated moderate capital in establishing businesses. Like the early Eastern European Jewish immigrant men, this group of new and old Chinese immigrant entrepreneurs was anxious to climb the ladder of proprietorship in New York City. Together they provided the capital and managerial force needed for the development of the garment industry in the Chinese community.

The increased availability of inexpensive loft space and tenement housing in the Chinatown area also significantly aided the growth of the garment industry there.[83] Starting in the early twentieth century, when New York City's garment manufacturing began to crawl slowly uptown, other garment-related industries began to relocate in other parts of or outside the city. Since the number of industrial properties in Manhattan decreased from 9,231 to 7,442 between 1952 and 1961, the supply of manufacturing spaces continued to exceed the market demand in subsequent years. Especially in 1969, when the nation was hit hard by a recession, the vacancy rate of the city's industrial lofts soared to almost 35 percent, and rents plunged to the rates of the 1940s and even 1930s.[84] One area where industrial space became vacant was the lower Manhattan industrial district that bordered on Chinatown. A study reports that as late as 1980, the factory space in Manhattan cost only $1.50 per square foot.[85] At the same time, the tenement residential quarters in proximity to the manufacturing lofts in this area became accessible to its workforce.

The four most important ingredients for the growth of the garment industry—the availability of an inexpensive low-skilled labor force, the capital, the managerial skills, and the space—were thus present in or near Chinatown. Midtown manufacturers and jobbers, who had been anxious to explore new resources to anchor the industry to the city, were more than willing to provide Chinese contractors with favorable financial terms. Between the late 1960s and early 1980s, Chinese contractors could purchase a factory of twenty-five to thirty sewing machines, complete with a boiler and electrical and gas hookups, for as little as twenty-five thousand dollars by making a down payment of six to seven thousand dollars, with the remainder to be paid in installments over a period of eighteen to twenty-four months at below-market interest rates.[86]

As a result, the garment industry began to grow rapidly in Chinatown. From 1965 to 1975, the number of Chinese-owned Chinatown unionized garment shops grew from 34 to 247; by 1980 the number of such shops peaked at 430.[87] Lining Canal Street and Broadway, these Chinese-owned garment factories began to reach into Little Italy along Mulberry and Elizabeth Streets and extended into the Lower East Side along East Broadway and Allen Street.[88] By 1983 the Chinese garment shops had contributed at least $125 million annually in the form of wages and profits to the city's economy. Chinatown thus incontestably became the city's largest garment production center.[89]

Although downtown employment shrank from fifty-eight thousand to forty-five thousand between 1969 and 1980, total jobs in the apparel manufacturing industrial district south of Houston Street and east of Broadway rose from twenty thousand to twenty-three thousand, largely due to the growth of the garment industry in Chinatown.[90] Although the growth of Chinatown garment manufacturing was unable to curb the continuing decline of the city's garment industry, it did manage to moderate it, helping to save the city's remaining industrial area and anchoring the garment industry to the city.[91]

The most significant impact of the Chinatown garment industry was on the Chinese community. In the 1960s, as the laundry business was edged out by laundromats and in-home washers and dryers, the economy of the community went downhill. The Chinatown garment industry provided the city's Chinese immigrant families with a new source of income. By 1979 garment workers constituted 85 percent of the city's Chinese women working in the ethnic industries.[92] Providing income to 60 percent of the families in Chinatown and 40 percent of the Chinese families in the city, the Chinatown garment industry was central to the family economy of the New York City Chinese community.[93]

The growth of the garment industry also boosted other lines of business in Chinatown. As Peter Kwong has pointed out, many owners of real estate and

Table 9. Local 23-25 Contractors in the Chinatown Area, 1960–85

Year	Chinese	Non-Chinese	Total
1960	8	1	9
1961	16	2	18
1962	18	2	20
1963	15	3	18
1964	22	2	24
1965	34	2	36
1966	40	4	44
1967	49	4	53
1968	59	5	64
1969	73	6	79
1970	102	8	110
1971	118	5	123
1972	146	4	150
1973	185	5	190
1974	209	7	216
1975	247	10	257
1976	269	9	278
1977	316	9	325
1978	370	6	376
1979	388	5	393
1980	430	6	436
1981	429	3	432
1982	420	0	420
1983	429	0	429
1984	450	0	450
1985	480	0	480

Sources: Numbers for 1960–82 are quoted from *The Chinatown Garment Industry Study* (1983), 42, table 8. Those for 1983–85 are from Roger Waldinger, *Through the Eye of the Needle: Immigrants and Enterprise in New York's Garment Trades* (1986), 117, table 4.5.

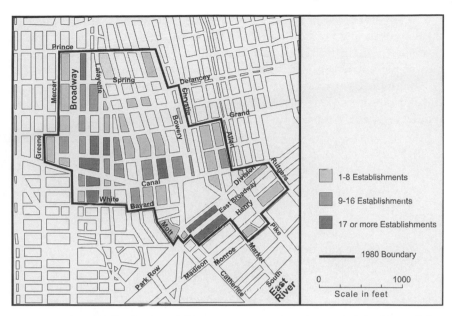

Map 3. Location and distribution of Chinatown garment shops in 1981. (Adapted from Abeles, Schwartz, Haeckel, and Silverblatt, Inc., *The Chinatown Garment Industry Study* [New York: ILGWU Local 23-25 and the New York Skirt and Sportswear Association, 1983]).

import-export companies in Chinatown began as garment industry entrepreneurs. The grocery and restaurant businesses benefited tremendously from the growth of the Chinatown garment industry. Since work hours in the garment shops were flexible, most women garment workers would take advantage of working in the Chinatown area and squeeze time in between their shifts to do their families shopping. In addition, as they tended to work long hours in the shops and had little time left for eating meals during the day and cooking for their families after work, many relied on inexpensive take-out food services. In response, grocery stores and small restaurants offering fast, inexpensive, but decent food mushroomed in Chinatown. Many owners of these small businesses would use their profits to expand their businesses or to invest in other lines of business, thus boosting the growth of the grocery and restaurant businesses as well as other lines of ethnic enterprise in the area.[94]

The rise of the garment industry also transformed the political structure of the community. As a vital part of the city's garment industry and the only industry in the Chinese community that was unionized by a major labor union, the Chinatown garment industry not only could serve as an important link between the Chinese community and the larger society but also had the potential to greatly strengthen the influence of the working class and challenge the conservative political powers in the community.[95]

The impact of the Chinatown garment industry, however, was not limited to the economic and political aspects of the community. As the percentage of Chinese women in the labor force rose from less than 25 percent in 1950 to more than 50 percent in 1980, and over 70 percent of these workers were married, the growth of the garment industry in Chinatown also had a profound impact on transforming its working-class family culture. Since this aspect was so profound, it deserves special treatment in the following chapters.

PART 2

Chinese Women Workers before 1982

Women have played an important role in working-class families throughout the history of Chinese Americans in New York City. From the inception of the Chinatown garment industry they formed more than 85 percent of its workforce, and they have contributed greatly to the industry. However, in various areas of their lives gender was constructed so that their important roles tended to be ignored not only by society at large but also by their own community.

Nevertheless, as in the case of other ethnic women workers in the history of the city's garment industry, changes in their lives after immigrating to the United States, particularly their changing roles in the family and their experience in the workplace, had a strong impact on reshaping their perception of life. This changing perception fostered labor activism among them and prepared them for the historic Chinese garment workers' strike in 1982, the largest labor strike ever to take place in New York's Chinatown.[1]

CHAPTER 4

New York's Chinese Working-Class Families during the Exclusion Era

Unlike most European women workers in the early years of the city's garment industry, more than 85 percent of the Chinese women garment workers in New York City were married.[1] Their families constituted an important part of their lives. With women garment workers playing an increasingly important role in their families, the growth of the Chinese garment industry has helped to transform the culture of Chinese American working-class families in New York City.

Scholarship on Chinese American families in the United States has developed rapidly in the last three decades. Many earlier studies tended to attribute the strength of Chinese American families to the family-centered values of traditional Chinese culture.[2] This approach was strongly challenged by a number of scholars in the 1980s, who argued that changes in the Chinese American family over the last century or more were primarily a result of "the interplay between shifting institutional constraints and the efforts of Chinese Americans to maintain family life in the face of these restrictions."[3] Their structural approach pointed to the weakness of the previous cultural approach and challenged any attempt to attribute problems experienced by "unsuccessful" ethnic groups to their own cultures rather than to the social and institutional forces that caused these problems.

Scholarship on Chinese American families in the 1980s also introduced a new dimension to feminist theories on the family. Based on her comparative study of women's experience in various ethnic groups, Evelyn Nakano Glenn calls into question the theory that focuses on unequal gender division of labor in the family and projects it as simply a locus of gender conflicts. She emphasizes the hostile and oppressive social attitude toward ethnic groups in the United States and argues that for members of the ethnic groups, the family was "a source of resistance to oppression from outside institutions" rather than "a form of exploitation by men." According to Glenn, conflicts over gender division of labor in the racial/ethnic family are "muted by the fact that institutions outside the family are hostile to it."[4]

Although her study successfully demonstrates the diverse experience of women in the United States and the racial/ethnic and class bias in feminist scholarship, it inadvertently falls in with traditional approaches that treat the family as an entity with a unitary interest and ignores the potential tension within the institution. This tendency has been amended in her recent collaborative study with Stacey G. H. Yap on Chinese American families, which holds that the family is "a differentiated institution" in that power "is not equally distributed" and each member "has a different position in the division of labor."[5]

The discussion in this chapter owes much to previous studies on Chinese American families, particularly those by Glenn, who has endeavored to integrate feminist perspectives into Asian American studies and the class and racial/ethnic perspective into feminist studies for almost two decades. Previous scholarship, however, has also raised important issues for this study to address. Although the cultural approach, as it was used by many scholars in the past, was cognizant of the potential influence of native culture, it failed to acknowledge Chinese American culture as a culture in its own right that was changing and was shaped by various factors. The structural approach, though politically powerful in combating the attempt to blame the victims for the consequences of the institutional forces that victimize them, has slighted or simply ignored the interaction of the past and present experiences of ethnic groups and the interplay between their native cultures and the culture of their receiving land in shaping their perceptions of life over their years in the United States. The two approaches, however, have something in common: a focus on Chinese American families in the United States while ignoring their transnational nature.

To understand some of the internal dynamics of Chinese immigrant garment workers' families, I would like to begin by analyzing the experience of one specific family, whom I came to know in 1984. It was with the joys and sorrows of this family in mind that I have pursued my study of the transformation of Chinese American working-class families in New York City.

The Tale of a Chinese Immigrant Family

The Yeungs resided behind their laundry in the Bensonhurst section of Brooklyn. With its eye-catching red sign, "Moy's Laundry," in the front and the family living quarters situated behind, the Yeung's laundry was typical of Chinese laundries, which had a history of almost a century in New York City.

Mr. Yeung, a skinny, cheerful man with a good sense of humor, had just turned sixty when I first met him in 1984. He came to the United States at the age of fourteen as the "paper son" of his father's business partner. Although Mr. Yeung's father jointly owned a laundry, he was foreign-born and had not acquired the status of a small business owner when he began applying for his son's immigration.[6] He therefore had to turn to his business partner, Mr. Moy, for help. Mr. Moy was a single Chinese man who happened to have a U.S. birth certificate but had never managed to save enough money to return to China to form a family. Following the common paper son practice in the community, the senior Yeung offered him a decent sum of money in exchange for his collaboration in claiming to have acquired a son after an alleged visit to China, thus creating a slot of entry for Mr. Yeung. In 1939, registered under the name Moy, Mr. Yeung immigrated to New York City. He was the Moys' son on paper, but everyone in the Chinese community called him *Yeung jai* (Cantonese: little Yeung or Yeung junior), and he continued to live with his father.

In 1946, at the age of twenty-two, Mr. Yeung, like many young men in the Chinese community, returned to his family village in China to marry a young woman handpicked by his mother. Six months later he returned to New York, leaving his pregnant wife behind to take care of the family. In the first two years after he returned, like most married Chinese men in the United States, he initially kept his promise to send remittances home. However, as he resumed the costly habits that he acquired in the community before marriage—drinking, gambling, and whoring—his remittances became sporadic and finally ended. His young wife, who was left behind, had to bear the consequences.

Like many Chinese women who married the *gam saan haak* (Cantonese: guests from the Gold Mountain) during that time, Mrs. Yeung was born and raised in Kaiping, a county in the Si Yi District. Left with the responsibility of taking care of her son and her husband's entire family, Mrs. Yeung toiled endlessly. As she recalled, "The Yeungs were not rich enough to buy a slave, but they got the labor of a slave by letting their son marry me . . . . Who cared about me at that time? No one. Really, no one."

When Mr. Yeung stopped sending money home, Mrs. Yeung had to leave her son in the care of her husband's family and cross the border to work in Hong Kong as a maid.[7] When her son turned fifteen, she followed the community's old practice and found him a "paper father" through her connections in Hong Kong, putting him on the same path as his father. However, due to insufficient cooperation on Mr. Yeung's part and confusion caused by the complicated legal procedure, her son was able to leave China but was stranded in Hong Kong and registered under yet another name, Lee.

In 1971, thanks to the 1965 amendment to U.S. immigration law, like many Chinese immigrant women of the time, Mrs. Yeung was able to join her husband in the United States, more than twenty years after their marriage. She was greatly disappointed, however, by what she found in the new land: "I would have rather died than lived to see that. . . . After all those years of suffering, I came to this country to find that your Uncle Yeung was literally a threefold addict— an alcoholic, a gambler, and a john. The laundry business he had inherited from his father was almost bankrupt. . . . No wonder that I could not get a single penny from him! I was so sad that I even thought of jumping into the East River when he took me to Chinatown by train from our home in Brooklyn."

Mrs. Yeung, however, was not the kind of person to give up easily. She continued:

> After crying several days, I realized that I could not live like that. I had endured so much suffering and overcome so many difficulties in the past, why shouldn't I try one more time? . . .
>
> At first, I forced my old man to rebuild the shop. I helped him with the laundry business, washing and ironing in the back, and let him take care of things in the front. . . . But, unfortunately, before our business could get any better we had a baby—one more mouth to feed. In addition, don't forget, we still had a son to raise in Taiwan. Remember?—He was the son we had left behind in Hong Kong with a different last name. This son could not join me when I came to New York because his last name was different from mine. In addition, at that time he did not want to come because he was just admitted to a university in Taiwan after failing to pass the university entrance exam in Hong Kong for so many times. . . . We didn't want him to suffer from being away from us, so my old man and I tried our best to provide him with a good life there . . . . It was very hard on us at that time, you know, but the saddest part of our life was, no matter how hard we tried, things just did not get any better. The laundry business was slow everywhere and we finally realized that we just could not rely on it to make a living.
>
> It was exactly at this time that I heard someone saying that there were plenty of sewing jobs in Chinatown and it was very easy for women to get a job out there. . . . I said to myself, why don't you try? I tried and I got a job. . . . Life was indeed very hard for both of us at that time. During the day, I went to work in the shop and let your Uncle Yeung take care of the baby and the laundry business at home. I came home from work about 7:00 in the evening, then your Uncle Yeung left. He took the subway to Chinatown to wash dishes in a restaurant and did not come home until very late at night. . . .
>
> Can you young people imagine how hard we worked in those days? . . . Take me for example. When I got to the shop, I would drive myself crazy to make as much money as possible. Once I got home, I was, again, as busy as a bee. I tried to do as much as I could for the baby and the family. . . . To be fair, I must admit that your Uncle Yeung also changed a lot after I came to join him. He is by nature a very good person . . . . He cares very much about the family. . . . He too worked very hard at that time. . . .
>
> Life was, indeed, rewarding. With our sweat and blood, we managed to save enough money to move out of the previous unsafe neighborhood in the other part of Brooklyn and came to this better one. Now we don't have to worry about our safety any more. . . . Look at this place, we bought it five years ago. . . . Yes, I am still working in a Chinatown garment shop and your Uncle Yeung is still a laundryman but our life is much better now.

Our conversation was once interrupted by a call from her son, a student at MIT, following which she shifted her focus:

> Don't laugh at me if I tell you my son is a good boy. . . . This boy of mine is a real good one. Every week he calls me at least once from school—see, never his father. . . . He would tell me what food he ate and what interesting things he saw at school. . . . You saw that, didn't you—we talked on the phone a minute ago? Do you know what he told me? . . . He told me that he had just returned from grocery shopping for the week. I asked him, "son, what food did you buy?" He said, "I bought some pork chops." I said, "why didn't you buy some steaks?" I know he is very crazy about steaks. He said, "they are not on sale this week, too expensive to buy." I said, "son, why are you so stingy? Didn't you suffer enough in the past?" . . . Saying this, those days came back to my mind, my heart ached and tears gathered in my eyes. You don't know how much this boy has suffered. . . .
>
> When he was only six months old, I left him at home with his dad and worked in a garment shop in Chinatown. Almost every evening when I came home, he was exhausted from crying, his bottom was red, soaked with his urine, . . . Seeing this, my heart ached and I cried. I tended to have a big fight with your Uncle Yeung every night because of this. . . . I felt guilty because I could not take good care of my son. But what could I do? The family needed money. . . . Who was to blame? Your Uncle Yeung? Yes, I did yell at him a lot, but deep in my heart I also knew that it was not his fault. It was also very hard on him to take care of the business in the front and the baby in the back, all at the same time . . . .
>
> This boy of mine is really a thoughtful boy, a very good boy. . . . When he was about twelve, not much taller than the counter of our shop, he began looking for a job to help the family. He went to apply for a job as a newspaper boy. People said "no, you are too young." But he said, "I am old enough for the job." Chinese tend to be shorter, you know? . . . So he got the job. . . .
>
> Life was really hard on him. At that time, he got up at 5:00 every morning to deliver the newspapers. Then he had his breakfast and went to school. After school, he would either help his father in the storefront with the language or do the laundry and take care of his baby sister in the back—yes, we had another baby girl by that time. He was already learning to share with me some of the household chores when he was only ten. He used the electric rice-cooker to cook the rice so that the family could have dinner once I got home with all those ready-made dishes from Chinatown. . . . Usually he did not have time to do his homework until I came home in the evening. . . .
>
> I always told him, "son, you have to *jaang hei* [Cantonese: 'bring credit to' or 'don't let people down']. I, your mother, don't expect you to help me so much. If you do well at school, it will be the greatest comfort to me. . . . I, your mother, really don't want to see you suffer in the same way as we did—and still do." . . . Every time, he would say, "Mom, take it easy, I won't let you down." . . .
>
> True, he never let me down. . . . His life was hard but he did extremely well at school. He managed to get a kind of money called scholarship from his school,

scholarship, do you know that? The kind of money the school would give to its best students. I didn't know how he got it and how much he got but I know that we never had to pay for his education. . . . Now he is in a university, I cannot recall the name, perhaps his father does. . . . Anyway, I never had to worry about his study. What I always worry about, even to this day, is that my son may not have enough to eat. . . . You know, he is somewhat shorter than his friends of his age. . . . Perhaps, it was because he was not properly fed when he was a baby and did not have enough good food to eat when he was growing up. Whenever I think about this, I feel very sorry and very sad. . . .

Deeply impressed by the strong emotional tie between the mother and son, I once talked with the son, David Yeung, on the phone:

You are asking me why I am so attached to my Mom? The reason is simply: Mom has sacrificed too much for this family. . . . When I was a kid, I thought my mom was a superwoman. Every day I woke up, she was already there cooking, washing, cleaning. . . . When I went to bed, she was still there washing, cleaning. . . . The last to go to bed and the first to get up. . . . Thinking about her always reminds me of what the Chinese say about the greatness of cows, "they eat grasses but produce milk." Mom did everything for the family but never asked for a single thing in return. Even today, you know what she has for her lunch in the shop? The leftover of the family's meals a day before. Can you imagine? What a life! . . . I am not saying that every one should live like that. No, not at all! I don't want to see this happen to anyone in the world. In fact, I think life is very unfair to my mom. What I am trying to say is, I will never forget what my mom has done for us. . . . Dad is not bad, he is okay, but he needs to be pushed. . . . Without Mom, I just can't imagine how our family would be like.

His father also credits his wife a great deal:

No matter how reluctant I am to admit this, I must say that I have learned a lot since your Aunt Yeung came. Without her, I simply don't know what kind of life the family and I would be leading now. . . . True, she is too quick and bad-tempered, sometimes just intolerable, . . . but just think about the kind of stressful life she has gone through, it is indeed not difficult to understand why she is like that. . . . All that she has been doing was for the family. I feel ashamed for my life in the past. . . . Never before did I come to see so clearly that I have married the best woman in my life. . . . To tell you the truth, deep in my heart, I have a lot of respect for her but I don't want to admit this in front of her. . . . You, too, don't tell her what I have told you.

The family was obviously in crisis when I visited them in 1989 before I left New York. Mrs. Yeung was wailing and crying, and Mr. Yeung was sitting with his head buried in his arms on the dining table. It turned out that their eldest son, who had recently joined the family after being separated for more than two decades, had asked to return to Taiwan. With a master's degree in classical music and having led a comfortable life as a "golden bachelor" in Taiwan, he found it difficult to adjust to the simple and hard life in the living quarters behind the family laundry in the United States. Although he was given the best room and received special love and respect from his parents and siblings as the eldest son and brother, he did not feel comfortable with the family. Instead, facing a family with a name different from his own, he felt even more keenly the psychological pain he had endured since he was separated from them. Finding it difficult to identify himself with the family and its lifestyle, he asked to leave only three months after his parents finally managed to get him to immigrate to the United States.

Mr. and Mrs. Yeung were equally distressed to see how deeply their youngest child and only daughter had become enmeshed into what the young woman herself considered "the true American culture." She had recently traveled in Europe with her Caucasian boyfriend. Not only had she spent the entire credit line in her parents' credit card but also almost all the cash her parents had accumulated over the years, hidden under the mattress. The old couple did not discover this until shortly before my visit. The discovery had triggered a brawl between them. Mrs. Yeung yelled at Mr. Yeung for having spoiled the girl by giving her free access to their credit card. Mr. Yeung snapped back and charged Mrs. Yeung with being too old-fashioned, distrusting the modern banking system and piling part of their savings under the mattress.

What made things look even worse was that their younger son, their favorite good boy, also asked to leave. Having recently graduated from the university, he wanted to lead a life of his own. Although he promised to visit the family regularly, his decision to leave was regarded by the old couple as yet another heartbreaking sign of "family disintegration." Holding to a traditional culture that glorified multiple generations living under the same roof as a sign of family unity and prosperity, Mrs. Yeung was greatly confounded by the recent actions of her children: "What wrong did I do in my previous life to deserve this punishment?" She wailed and wailed inconsolably.

In many ways, the hardships and cultural conflicts that the Yeung family has endured over the last few decades capture the experience of Chinese American working-class families in New York City in the three major historical periods: the Chinese Exclusion era, the immediate post–World War II years, and the post-1965 period.

New York's Chinese Working-Class Families, 1882–1943

Most of the literature on New York City Chinese Americans in the pre–World War II period focuses on men.[8] The city's early Chinese population was overwhelmingly male, and the proportion of married Chinese men living with their families was historically small. Even in 1940, when the gender ratio among Chinese fifteen and older in the nation was redressed to four to one, that of New York City remained more than nine to one.[9] Although more than 50 percent of all adult Chinese men in the city were married by then, about 80 percent lived without their families.[10]

A number of studies have noted that New York City had a higher rate of interracial marriage among Chinese men than any other part of the United States due to the absence of antimiscegenation laws.[11] This relatively liberal atmosphere in the cosmopolitan port city of New York gave the impression that Chinese men had a better chance to enjoy a family life in New York City. However, this phenomenon did not last long. It began to decline significantly in the 1920s.[12]

While chances of living with their family were slim for New York's Chinese men in general, this was especially true for male laborers. Although class lines were not as clearly drawn as they were in later years, and married men represented a wide range of the social spectrum in the early New York City Chinese community, the more financially secure Chinese men had a better chance at both inter- and intraracial marriages.[13] Up to 1940 about 80 percent of the 5,245 married Chinese men in New York City were still separated from their families.[14] Forced bachelorhood had a devastating impact on the Chinese men. Having come from a family-centered culture that defined manhood by their ability to perform their traditional role as the provider and discipliner of the family and that stressed the paramount importance for men to carry on their family lines through marriage, Chinese men who were forced to lead a bachelor's life in the early New York Chinese community felt enormous pressure to live up to these expectations.

Conventional wisdom would have it that single Chinese men could return to China to form a family, while married men could fulfill their family obligation by visiting their families as frequently as possible. Not many, however, could afford to do so. A journey back home, with its spending on travel and gifts, could cost a laundryman ten to twenty years of savings.[15]

Like their counterparts elsewhere in the country, New York's Chinese men developed their own ways of offsetting the loss caused by their prolonged absence from home. Sending money to their families in China was one of them. Following the practice of the paper son, common to major Chinese settlements in the United States after the 1906 fire at the San Francisco immigration building, was another way to cope with the situation. Like the Yeung family, many would try to create a slot for their sons to come to work in the United States. By so doing, they were able to guarantee an uninterrupted succession of providers for the family and to continue patriarchal control over its resources in the United States.[16] It is therefore not surprising to find that some families in New York City had successive generations of men working in the United States, but none of them was born in the United States before the late 1960s.

However, sponsoring the immigration of a son to the United States could be expensive, and not every one could afford it or succeeded in doing so. Added to the high costs was the complicated legal procedure. As illustrated in the case of Mr. Yeung's son, it required the concerted efforts of all parties involved, and any lapse by one party could result in the failure of the endeavor.[17]

The prolonged absence of married Chinese men from their families inevitably undermined their control, which was demonstrated in part by their strained relations with their children. Children in the early immigrant families felt alienated from their fathers due to their lack of daily contact with them. Their sense of alienation was so strong that years after they joined their fathers in the United States, they often could not recover from this psychological wound. The vacuum caused by the father's absence was likely to be filled by the mother, thus strengthening the children's ties with their mother and further undermining the father's dominant position in the family.[18]

The pain the Chinese male laborers were likely to feel from being emasculated in their own culture was intensified by their experience in the United States. Like their counterparts in other major Chinese settlements in the country, most Chinese men in New York were relegated to the laundry and restaurant businesses, which employed more than 70 percent of the city's gainful Chinese male workers by 1930. Cooking and doing laundry were traditionally women's work, and men in China did not "step into it for fear of losing their social standing."[19] The onerous working conditions associated with the laundry trade, in addition to its low-paid status, made it unappealing to even immigrant women or women of color under straitened economic circumstances.[20] Relegated to a traditionally feminine labor sector, it is not difficult to imagine the profound psychological pains many Chinese male laborers had to endure.[21]

The Chinese laborers' longing for a family life in New York City could not be assuaged by the companionship they could seek from their countrymen and the limited healthy recreational resources available in Chinatown. Some sought emotional outlets in gambling, opium smoking, and whoring, vices common to almost all male-dominated societies. Facilities in Chinatown, such as opium joints, gambling dens, and brothels, were ready to exploit their situation. As Mr. Yeung's experience shows, indulgence in these vices could be costly. They not only undermined the health of the men but also drained them financially.[22] Given the Chinese laborers' meager incomes, the consequences of these vices could be catastrophic, undermining significantly their ability to visit their homeland and financially support their families. They also provided racists in the city with ammunition with which to attack them and portray Chinatown as a den of iniquity.

While the Chinese Exclusion Acts deprived the majority of Chinese men of an important part of their lives, they had an even more severe impact on women. Most of the wives of Chinese American laborers were left in China. The lives of women in many, perhaps most, of the emigrant families were similar to that of Aunt Yeung before she immigrated to the United States. As a professor at Zhongshan University aptly described it, "women in the former Si Yi Chinese American emigrant communities held up the entire sky."[23]

My interviews suggested that the number of families in the Si Yi District who were able to hire maids and extra hands to help out with household chores and to farm their land were in fact very small. An average emigrant family in Taishan, the major source of Chinese immigrants to New York City, owned a limited amount of land.[24] Except for the busiest seasons, when the family might hire some help, the land was primarily farmed by women, daughters-in-law who sometimes worked with their teenage children or their husband's younger siblings.

During my visit to the town of Gu Jing in Xinghui County in 1997, Wu Zhenze, a seventy-eight-year-old son of a Chinese American emigrant family there, still remembered clearly how his mother used to drag him out of bed and take him to the field when he was only five. The slow season for farm work differed from the harvest season only in that his mother would not wake him until the roosters began to crow, and he could eat breakfast at home with his mother.[25] Other interviews showed that Wu's experience was not unusual. Since women formed the majority of farm workers who were left behind in the Si Yi District labor market and women in many emigrant families also worked, it was not surprising that visitors and researchers to the area were struck by the high rate of women farming in the fields.[26]

In addition to farming, women in the emigrant families were the major family caregivers. Life in rural Guangdong was never easy. The mere preparation of food for a family could sometimes consume a woman's entire day.[27] Many also engaged in sideline production to supplement their family income. Above all this, they still had to play their traditional roles as mothers and daughters-in-law in the family. As the only parent, they were both nurturers and disciplinarians of their children. Being daughters-in-law, they were also expected to meet all the demands of their husbands' parents and siblings, which could be more emotionally and physically taxing than any other task. A ballad, "Xifu Yao" (The song of daughters-in-law), well circulated in the Si Yi District, vividly describes their plight:

> Curled is the tail of the rooster,
> Difficult is the life of a daughter-in-law.
> No matter how early she gets up,
> They [the in-laws] always say "Too late."
> There stands a watermelon in the kitchen,
> She asks the mother-in-law,
> "Boil or steam?"
> She says, "boil."
> He [the father-in-law] says, "steam."
> Boil or steam,
> No way to please both.
> Three sticks break in three days for beating her,
> Five skirts ruined in five days for punishing her by making her kneel on
>   the floor.[28]

Although women in other parts of China held similar responsibilities and positions in their families, what is unusual about women's lives in emigrant families was that they sometimes had to take up arms to protect their family. Starting from the early twentieth century, the Si Yi District was plagued by robbery and banditry. Especially after 1913, when the warlord Yuan Shikai came to power in China and Guangdong Province was ruled by a series of warlords and coalitions of their military commanders, *bing fei yat ga* (Cantonese: government officials and bandits are the same family) became a gruesome reality in the Si Yi District, and the families of *gam saan haak* were their prime targets.[29] Many overseas Chinese sent remittances home to build "fortress-type" houses and watchtowers to protect their families and their communities.[30] These watchtowers and fortress-type houses, with their windows well above the ground and barred with strong iron rods, stand to this day.

In those emigrant families who could not afford to employ armed protectors or receive protection from the local militia, women had to play a major role in protecting the family. A popular ballad in Taishan, "Que Zei Yao" (Song of driving out the thieves), describes their situation well:

> The night is pitch dark.
> The wind is blowing hard.
> Hearing the dogs barking wildly,
>   Everyone is palpitated with fear.
> Suddenly, up there on the tiles,
> There is some mysterious rustling
> —The thieves are on the roof!
> Having hurried up from the bed,
> Mother guards the skylight with a revolver in hand.
> She shoots first to the left then to the right,
>   Until the thieves cry for mercy.[31]

One can hardly find a single trace of the stereotypical Oriental woman in the Guangdong reality of the Chinese mother woman warrior.

Despite the differences in their lives, there were several commonalities among women in almost all emigrant families. Loneliness was one of them, a reality for which they had prepared themselves from the day they were betrothed to the families. Most experienced decades of separation from their husbands after marriage. In an extreme but not rare case, Gao Ying, a woman from the town of Sha Dui in Xinhui County, was married at the age of nineteen by proxy, with a live rooster symbolizing the bridegroom. She then spent the rest of her life taking care of her husband's family. She died in 1992 at the age of ninety without ever meeting her husband.[32] People in the area described the lonely life of an emigrant's wife as *sau wuht gwo* or *sau sang gwo* (Cantonese: leading a widow's life when the husband is still alive). There was a well-known ballad in the Si Yi District, "Qiaufu Yuan" (The lament of an emigrant's wife), which records their suffering:

I am leading a widow's life at such a young age,
      When my husband is still alive.
Thousands of *li* apart,
It is difficult for us to communicate.
The more I think about him,
The more my mind is like a tangled skein.
He is on the other end of the world,
And I am still thinking of him and longing for his return
      Even at this small hour of yet another day.[33]

Although remittances from abroad could not cover all expenses of most emigrant families, they constituted a significant proportion of their income. Most emigrant families were therefore vulnerable to any bad turn in the lives of their overseas providers even in peaceful times, which is well illustrated by the experience of the Yeung family before it reunited in the United States.[34] The most nightmarish for almost all people in the Si Yi District, however, was the total disruption of remittances after Pearl Harbor. Any savings soon disappeared and dependents of the *gam saan haak* began to face the biggest challenge of their lives. Things worsened in 1943, when Si Yi was hard hit by a drought that produced widespread famine. Within that year, in Taishan County alone it is estimated that more than a hundred thousand died of starvation. Similar situations occurred in other Si Yi counties.[35]

As the only caretakers at home, women had to bear the brunt of these disastrous years. According to local accounts during this period, many women brought their families with them and fled to the nearby counties, such as Yang Chun and Yang Jiang. For family survival, they begged in the streets or even sold themselves to brothels or rich families there as maids or concubines. A number of elderly people in Taishan still remember clearly what was written on the signs widely posted in Yang Jiang and Yang Chun during the time: "Today there are XX [a number] *gam saan poh* [Cantonese: wives of the guests from the Gold Mountain] on sale. Those good-looking and between the ages of 20 and 25 will be sold for XX yuans and those with average looks and between the ages of 25 and 35 will be sold for XX."[36]

The wives of Chinese Americans also had to endure many other consequences of their husbands' prolonged absence. They were taken advantage of by local hooligans in various forms; they were cheated out of money by local charlatans claiming to predict their husbands' dates of return; and they were psychologically tormented by those who were at odds with them and retaliated by spreading rumors about the deaths of their husbands abroad or their "unchaste" behavior.[37]

To redress the negative consequences of their long-term separation from their husbands and protect themselves from their vulnerable position in the communities, many childless women adopted a son with their husbands' consent and in the name of continuing their husbands' family lines. Although adoption was looked upon as an unsatisfactory way to perpetuate the patrilineal family in traditional Chinese culture, this was not the case with the Si Yi emigrant families. The husbands' prolonged absence, the long gaps between their visits, and their aged conditions when they finally returned made it difficult for many emigrant families to produce children. Adoption therefore was common in the Si Yi emigrant communities. It could occur in more than one generation in a family. It is therefore no surprise that different generations of males in some Si Yi emigrant families were not related by blood.[38]

Adoption helped to meet the family's need for male descendants. However, it also created new problems. Adopted sons were reported to have deserted adoptive families when they grew up, and a number of them were said to have simply taken money and run away with their wives and children after they had their own families. In 1935 the problems reportedly became so severe that to guarantee the sons' loyalty to their adoptive families and to protect the interests of these families, the local government issued an edict to prohibit adopting children over the age of thirteen.[39] There is no denying that these stories were tainted with social contempt for the adopted sons, but they indicate how widespread the practice of adoption was in the area.[40]

Another aspect of life that affected almost all women was the powerful patriarchal control and women's subordinate position in the community. Studies of south and southeast China have noted the strong influence of patrilineal and kinship organizations in the area. These influences were particularly strong in the Si Yi emigrant communities.[41]

There were formal and informal institutional forces that intersected in regulating people's behavior in the area. Public opinion in the form of gossip, a favorite pastime among villagers, was one of the informal forces. Although both men and women were subjected to the scrutiny of their fellow villagers, public opinion was particularly harsh on the alleged immoral conduct of women and could have devastating results.[42]

What happened to the Chen family in the village of Sanxi near the city of Taishan is illustrative. The wife was said to have been faithful to her husband during the years he was away from home. The husband in the United States, however, chose to believe the anonymous letter he had received from a fellow villager, which informed him that his wife had broken the moral codes. He quickly returned and, without a word, started to kick and beat her the moment he set foot in the house. Although he was finally stopped by members of his wife's family and fellow villagers and apologized, his wife was seriously injured.[43]

An extreme case involved a Chinese laundryman in New York City, who had been away for more than twenty years. When he returned to the village in 1934 and was told that his wife, who was living in Guangzhou, had not only been unfaithful but had also become pregnant in his absence, he went to Guangzhou and shot her to death.[44]

The family was another informal institutional force in the community to exert patriarchal control over women. With few exceptions, an emigrant's wife resided either with or close to the residence of her in-laws. She was under their close surveillance. To ensure their control over their wives, many married Chinese men in the United States sent money to their male kin in China, often a brother or the head of their local lineage, and entrusted them as well as their parents with the responsibility of checking on the loyalty and chastity of their wives and the well-being of other members of their families before they handed over the money.[45]

There were also formal institutional forces to impose moral codes on people in the villages: local security forces were led by the heads of the local patrilineage and formed by the remaining single and able-bodied men in the village, who worked for the local heads and were called *saan jai* (Cantonese: the unattached males) by the villagers. Although these security forces were supposed to regulate both men's and women's conduct, the punishments meted out to women were much more severe. A number of studies and personal accounts mention the punishment of *jam jyu luhng* (Cantonese: drowning the pig cage), as the local people called it.[46] Under this punishment, the alleged adulteress was put in a cage, weighted with a big piece of stone, and drowned in the river.[47] Although I could not find any substantiation of this practice since the first decade of the twentieth century either in interviews with the elderly in the community or from the coverage in local newspapers or publications, the threat of such punishment always loomed large and it could be as fatal as if it was actually meted out.

The following is an account of an alleged adulteress. The seriously ill mother of a young emigrant man named Chen Xue, a native of the village of Gaosha in the Hengshui area of Xinghui County who had left home at an early age, decided to form a family for her son to inherit the family property, for fear that the family property would be taken away by her husband's kin after she died. She took the liberty to choose the daughter of the Huang family to be her son's future wife and urged him to return to marry. Fully occupied by his business abroad, Chen Xue could not make the trip. The Chen family decided to follow the local custom and have the Huang's daughter marry a proxy, a rooster representing the bridegroom.

After the marriage the young woman met a young man in the village, and the two soon fell in love. The affair was discovered by the village security force, who threatened to execute the punishment of "drowning the pig cage." The young couple managed to placate the security force by paying a fine, but word soon spread to the county security force, which believed that the problem had not been handled properly and decided to hold a town meeting to settle it. Upon hearing the sound of the gong announcing the meeting, the young woman, ashamed and frightened by the prospect of being drowned in the pig cage, committed suicide.[48]

Under this strong patriarchal control women had no formal rights. Although many of them were the de facto heads of their family, and some virtually ran the businesses owned by their husbands, they did not have the right to buy or sell family property. Likewise, even though women prepared and made decisions for every detail of the ancestor worshipping ceremony in the village, those families headed by women that did not have sons could not receive a share of the sacrificial roast pork after the ceremony, a symbol of a recognized place in the patrilineage of the village.

The strong patriarchal control led to a number of paradoxical phenomena. One would be impressed by the relatively high degree of westernization in the area, with the returned Chinese Americans wearing flannel suits and speaking a language exoticized by English words and phrases and, occasionally, democratic ideas. One would also be struck by the degree of savagery involved in the social treatment of women. Especially since the late 1920s, daughters in the Si Yi emigrant families, especially those in Taishan, enjoyed a literacy rate higher than young women in the adjacent rural areas. However, they were taught primarily how to read and write as well as some accounting to prepare them for life as an emigrant's wife. As the Chinese scholar Fang Di has pointed out, women's education was so well controlled in conformity to the need of the patriarchal family that girls' schools in emigrant communities did not necessarily nurture political agitation as did their counterparts elsewhere in China in the early twentieth century.[49] Obviously, the returned Chinese Americans' translation of the new, democratic values to their homeland was conditional and bounded by gender.[50]

However, like their counterparts elsewhere in the world, women in the emigrant communities did not passively accept their lot. Despite severe punishments, a number of women continued to try various means to cast off the shackles imposed on them. Some simply committed suicide to protest the injustice.[51] Most, however, developed support networks to assist one another. *Neuih nguk* (Cantonese: girls' houses) were a major form of such female support networks in the San Yi and Si Yi Districts. Teenage girls would join other women, older or of similar ages, to form a girls' house, and members of a girls' house would spend the night together in the same house, donated by local people, and return to their families during the day. It was an important socialization process for young women in the two districts.

Unlike those in the county of Shunde, however, girls' houses in Si Yi District did not necessarily nurture a culture of resistance to marriage. My interviews and local literature indicate that the influence of this socialization process on women was mixed. On the one hand, it had the effect of handing down traditional values and moral codes from one generation of women to another with young women of various ages getting together at night, sharing rumors, hearsay, actual or merely fantasized sexual experiences, gossip, and weighing together the gains and losses of various behavior. On the other hand, it also helped to foster the bond between them, which became the most enduring friendship in their lives. Various studies have shown that, especially in times of woe, most continued to turn to their "sisters" in the girls' house for condolence and assistance even after they were married.[52]

The most important period in which a significant number of women actively participated in political activities in the Si Yi emigrant communities was during the Sino-Japanese War (1937–45), especially after the Japanese invaded Taishan in 1939. Women in Taishan, like their counterparts in New York City, actively participated in the antiwar efforts. Many donated jewelry, food, clothing, and even guns and ammunition, which they had kept for protecting their families, to finance and support the Chinese troops fighting against the Japanese. Some of them even joined local militias and fought side by side with men. It was also during this period that a number of young women were drawn to the radical ideas of Communism. Some joined the Communist Party and laid down their lives in defending their homeland. Many others used this opportunity to challenge various forms of traditional practices and patriarchal control.[53]

The lives of women in the Chinese emigrant communities during the Exclusion era, therefore, were not stagnant. Nor were the communities homogenous or one-dimensional throughout the years. Although being married to emigrants to the United States might provide women with an economically better life, and their husbands' prolonged absence from the family might also strengthen their relations with their children, these were not without cost. No wonder that popular local ballads and writings often conveyed conflicting reactions to their lives. While a ballad, addressed to the parents, says, "be sure to marry your daughter to a *gam saan haak,* who would return with hundreds and hundreds of money," lines in a poem, speaking on behalf of the women themselves, admonish, "let it be known to all my sisters: Don't ever marry a young man going overseas!"[54]

A number of studies have documented the extraordinary fortitude with which Chinese Americans and their communities on both sides of the Pacific collaborated to maintain the ebb and flow of their families during the Exclusion era.[55] The mechanism that allowed these families to survive surprisingly well, even under the pressure of long-term separation, was not based on equal terms among their members. To maintain male control over the communities, not only were women's important contributions largely ignored, but they were also subjected to even stronger patriarchal control. In this context, one can surely say that the gender implications of the Chinese Exclusion Acts for Chinese American working-class families were, indeed, transnational.

The Transformation of New York's Chinese Working-Class Families after World War II

If family life became the norm in other major Chinese settlements in the United States during the 1920s, this was not the case in New York's Chinatown, at least not until the end of World War II.[1] The most significant changes occurred only after 1965, when the discriminatory U.S. immigration law was amended, and the Chinese garment industry began to grow in New York City.

The Turning Point, 1945–65

The patterns of Chinese working-class families in New York City varied during the postwar years. A number of Chinese men continued to live in the absence of their families. Others worked in restaurants and other Chinese enterprises and left their recently reunited family or newly married wives at home to engage in paid or unpaid labor. Nevertheless, with a growing number of Chinese groceries, restaurants, and laundries owned and run by family members as a result of women's immigration in the postwar era, the "small producer family" became common.

The small producer family was characterized by the lack of clear demarcation between family and work life, especially among the Chinese laundries scattered throughout the city.[2] Living quarters were usually situated behind or above the store for the sake of convenience and economy or simply for the lack of options. Women, like Aunt Yeung, usually worked in the back, doing housekeeping and child care while providing all kinds of assistance to the family business. Men worked in the front, taking care of the customers and dealing with the outside world. By pooling the labor of all family members, many newly reunited Chinese working-class families managed to survive in their new land.

As the number of families began to grow, there was the potential for traditional Chinese values to be reestablished in New York's Chinese community after the end of World War II. The former Chinese laborers, now with their family businesses and their wives' and children's free labor at their disposal, appeared to have regained their power in the family. A careful examination, however, reveals that this was not the case. As their wives' and children's labor became indispensable to the family business, many Chinese men found it difficult to play their traditional role as the sole breadwinner of the family. In addition, handicapped by their limited English and knowledge of the larger American society, they often had to rely on the assistance of their U.S.-educated children in dealing with the outside world. All this significantly undermined their traditional roles as *wai zi* (the person who takes care of the affairs outside the home) and *yan fu* (stern father) in the family.

In contrast, many immigrant women, like Aunt Yeung, played an increasingly important role in the family after reuniting with their husbands in the United States. Not only did they continue to shoulder a major proportion of the family responsibilities, they also contributed significantly to the family business by working in the living quarters, either by themselves or side by side with their children. In the course of working together in the closed environment behind or above the store, women strengthened their ties with their children by playing the role not only of nurturer and disciplinarian but also advisor, providing them with strategies and instilling them with courage to deal with the often unfriendly environment outside the home.

Although their lives after reuniting with their husbands were not always easier than in China, many enjoyed their lives in the United States. In addition to the pleasure of having the entire family living and working together to build a new life in a new land, they appreciated the degree of autonomy they could enjoy in the family. Due to financial constraints and the nature of the War Bride Acts and other immediate postwar changes in U.S. immigration law, which benefited only wives and children of ex-GIs and other U.S. citizens, most of the Chinese American immigrant families in this period lived as nuclear families. Women therefore did not have to be subjugated to the control of their mothers-in-law, as did their counterparts in China. Instead, contributing significantly to almost every aspect of their families' lives, they had the chance to gain a higher degree of respect and appreciation from their husbands and children.

However, this higher degree of respect and autonomy was not without a price. In addition to the profound loneliness they had to endure in the new land, they had to meet all kinds of challenge, some of which were simply beyond their imagination prior to their immigration to the city. The sixty-five-year-old Mrs. Tang, whom I interviewed in 1998, provides a telling example.

She came to the United States in 1957 to join her husband, a U.S. citizen twenty-six years her senior. She was introduced to the man by friends of her family and was married to him based on her parents' decision. She began working in the laundry he owned the day after she arrived in New York City. She describes her life as the wife of a small Chinese laundry owner:

Nowadays, young people who work in a garment shop tend to complain about their hard lives in the shop. Whenever I hear their whining, I tell them to stop it. It is nothing compared with what I went through in those days. . . .

At that time, my husband and I literally worked from morning till morning. Our store was in Long Island. We usually got up at 7:00 in the morning. Before we opened the store at about 9:00, we had to finish separating different kinds of laundry we received a day before, sort out those bigger pieces, such as bed sheets, to be picked up by the laundrymat delivery men. We also had to make sure that all the finished work to be picked up by customers on that day had been numbered correctly and tagged with right prices, all this had to be done before we opened the door. . . . It was an intense battle. . . .

Then we opened the store. . . . Yes, most of the time, my husband dealt with the customers in the front, and I worked in the back, hand-washing those smaller pieces, such as socks, and those pieces that required special care, such as ladies' blouses. I also had to put starch on the collars and cuffs of the shirts, iron, and attach numbers and price tags to the washed laundry from the laundrymat. Once in a while I would also help out with the business at the front desk, if there were too many customers for my husband to handle at a time. Of course, my husband would also help me to do the washing, ironing, and starching in the back, if he did not have much to do in the front. . . .

I, however, was the one who did the cooking. Our meals were very simple: we usually had rice, salted eggs, and some vegetables. . . . No, no Chinese vegetables, usually broccoli, cauliflower, or whatever we could get from the American supermarket. Even for those simple meals, it was still difficult for me to find time to cook. We did not have regular hours for our meals. We ate only when no customer set his or her feet in our store. Most of the time, we ate while we worked. . . . Since I ate so irregularly and worked under so much pressure, I began having stomach problems only a year after I came to this country.

We closed our store at about 8:00 P.M. every day, but my husband and I continued to work late into the night. We usually did not go to bed until 1:00 or 1:30 in the morning. Yes, we closed the store on Sunday but not until afternoon, when we finished most of what we had left over from Saturday. My husband and I would then take a good rest at home or go to Chinatown to do the grocery shopping.

In those days, going to Chinatown was the best time in my life. Sometimes, my husband and I would go to a Chinese restaurant there to enjoy a meal. Food in Chinatown at that time was not like what we have now. The wrappings of the dumplings were so thick that you would feel like chewing a piece of dough when you ate them. I could not help throwing them out when I first tried, but I soon learned to like them. . . .

The most unbearable for me at that time was the feel of enormous loneliness. I barely knew my husband before I came. We did not talk much even after we lived together. He did not seem to have anything else to say to me, except for teaching me how to say the numbers on the tags in English so that I could take care of the customers when he was too busy. . . . I had no friend, no relative, and there were also very few Chinese laundries in Long Island in those days, to say the most, one in every many, many blocks, maybe. . . . In addition, most of those serving at the storefront were men.

When I first came, every minute in my life seemed to be testing my will. Language was, and is still, a big problem for me. I remember very well one day my husband and I ran out of rice before we realized it. It was well past noon and both of us were very hungry. My husband was too busy to leave the business to go to the store, so he sent me out. He told me that the supermarket was three blocks away on the right-hand side of our laundry, and he also taught me how to say "rice" in English. After practicing several times and making sure that I could say it, I was on my way to the store. . . . I kept practicing the word all my way there, but I was so nervous when I got there that I forgot everything. People there asked me again and again what I needed but I could not reply. I felt myself such a damned fool that I left the store. I walked, and walked, and walked, but could not return to the store. I was so scared that I cried all the way until I finally saw a Chinese laundry. The Chinese men there called my husband to pick me up. . . . It turned out that I walked in the wrong direction when I left the store! . . .

For almost twenty years after I came to this country, I did not get a chance to visit Hong Kong. I also did not have much contact with my family because I could not read and write, and there were no Chinese providing letter-writing services in Long Island City. In order to send a letter home, I had to wait for my husband to take me to Chinatown. Sunday was the busiest day for letter-writing men in Chinatown and, very often, when we went there, by the time we finished shopping and other businesses, it was already dark and we needed to rush back. So, I did not send letters home very often. Once a year, *bou go pihng ngon* [Cantonese: reporting that I was safe and sound], perhaps. . . .

At that time, long distance calls were too expensive. A round-trip ticket to Hong Kong could cost several thousand dollars and we made only about two hundred dollars a month. . . . All those years, I was so homesick that whenever there was a plane flying in the sky, I would look up and ask, "When can you take me home?"[3]

My interviews reveal that the heavy workload and extreme loneliness Mrs. Tang had to endure were not uncommon among many Chinese immigrant women whose husbands were small laundry owners. However, her experience is unique in that she did not have children, which allowed her to help out at the storefront and leave home occasionally.

The majority of women in the newly formed or reunited Chinese American families were mothers of young children. Their lives were even harder. Separated from their female friends and kin in China, they were deprived of the female companionship they relied on for emotional comfort and practical assistance in their homeland. In a land completely alien to them, they had to shoulder all the household responsibilities on their own while providing indispensable labor to their family businesses. Attending to their family needs could consume all their time. Their lives were therefore largely confined to their living quarters. Some of them did not leave their homes for years.[4] Aunt Chen of Brooklyn is one such case.[5]

Like many Chinese immigrants in the postwar era, she was born and raised in Taishan County but had resided in Hong Kong prior to immigrating to the United States. She came to join her ex-GI husband in 1952 and began working in the family laundry the second day after she arrived in the city. For more than thirty years, she barely ventured two or three blocks from her family's apartment in the Bensonhurst area of Brooklyn and never visited Chinatown without the company of her husband or children. Her mission in life was clear: to provide all kinds of service to the family and the store. Giving birth to one child after another and raising her three children all alone, she had little time to explore the world beyond the horizon of her family's living quarters. Talking about this aspect of her experience, she said, "I was blind with a pair of seeing eyes."

When I interviewed her in the spring of 1986, her husband had died not long before, and her married sons and daughter lived with their own families in other parts of the city. Left alone, she had to rely on her Chinese friends in the neighborhood for almost every detail in her life. Frustrated by the difficulties she faced, she lamented that if she had known what her life would be like when her husband died, "I would have followed him in death."

Although the traditional Chinese family culture did not have a sufficient material base to sustain itself in the new land, the unique structure of the small producer family had the effect of confining women to the domestic sphere. Many new Chinese immigrant women displayed heroic fortitude in order to survive in their new land. However, as demonstrated by the life of Aunt Chen, separation from the outside world took a severe toll. This situation continued in many working-class families until the 1960s, when the number of Chinese laundries and other small family businesses in the city significantly declined.

What has to be kept in mind is that the lives of the immigrant women discussed above do not form the entire picture of women's lives in the Chinese American working-class families in the immediate postwar era. Many women in these families continued to be separated from their husbands. Although there are no statistics accurately documenting this aspect of life in New York City before 1970, census data show that as late as 1960 there were still 3,344 married Chinese men living with their spouses absent in New York State.[6] Most of these men lived in New York City. Given our understanding that few Chinese immigrants were able to come to the United States directly from China after 1949 without first emigrating to Hong Kong or elsewhere due to the termination of diplomatic relations between the two countries, many if not most of their wives were likely to be left in China.[7]

The ordeals of the wives of Chinese Americans who remained in China continued after the end of World War II. Shortly after the Japanese surrendered, the

Chinese Communist Party (CCP) and the National Party (GMD) resumed their military confrontations. To finance its losing battle against the Communists, the GMD government proceeded to print billions of dollars in unbacked currency, leading to skyrocketing inflation. Lives in the emigrant communities were seriously affected. To maintain the value of their money, many Chinese in the United States sent their remittances to Hong Kong and relied on their relatives and friends there to exchange the money into Hong Kong dollars and bring them back to their homeland. As a result, the amount of remittances sent to Hong Kong from the United States grew from $100,000 in 1945 to $24.6 million in 1946.[8] By 1948 the GMD had lost much of its support among the Chinese Americans and their families at home and abroad.[9]

My interviews revealed that lives in the emigrant communities began to change significantly after the Communist success in China. Owing to the determined efforts of the new government, people were no longer subjected to banditry. The agricultural production of the Si Yi District also greatly increased as a result of the large number of irrigation and other public construction projects undertaken by the new government. By the 1950s the economy of the district was able to stand on its own, regardless of the fluctuation of remittances from abroad.

The greatest changes, however, took place in the status of women in the country. The new government pledged its commitment to gender equality. Like their counterparts in other parts of China, women in San Yi and Si Yi for the first time in history enjoyed equal constitutional rights with men. The new marriage law passed in 1950 defined marriage as a voluntary union between a man and a woman based on love and outlawed all forms of mercenary marriage and other traditional practices in relation to marriage. The official rhetoric of "women holding up half of the sky" also accorded unprecedented importance to gender equality and women's roles. To enable women to play an active part in society, the new government held literacy classes in many parts of the district not only to improve literacy among women but also to educate them in socialist values and principles of gender equality.

Despite the discrepancy between the official rhetoric and actual practice and the fact that traditional influences persisted in many aspects of life, changes in the country held out hope for women.[10] Many wives and daughters of Chinese American emigrants, including those who had already migrated to the city of Guangzhou, gave up their opportunities to leave the country and chose to stay. The eighty-six-year-old Wu Peixuan in Taishan, who is fondly known by her fellow villagers as Aunt Xuan and whom I interviewed in the summer of 1997, was one of them. Having had a hard time after her husband emigrated to the United States, as did most of her counterparts in the emigrant families, she was particularly drawn to the new government's policy toward women. She turned down her in-laws' offer to sponsor her and her entire family's emigration to the United States after the Communist takeover and chose to remain in Taishan.

Especially in the 1950s, she took an active part in almost every campaign undertaken by the new government. When asked why she did so, she said, "I don't know. I just felt very, very excited. All the opportunities were too good for me to miss!"[11]

The excitement generated by these changes in the communities was communicated across the Pacific and reached New York's Chinatown. The following is a dialogue between a newspaper reporter and a Chinatown man whose wife was still in China:

> "Well, in the past, my *jyu faahn poh* [Cantonese: the one who cooks for me] did not know how to read and write. She had to ask someone to read her the letters I sent home. But now she had someone to write me and tell that she already knew how to read simple letters. She also said that in a year or so, she could even write to me herself."
>
> "How old is your wife?"
>
> "Over fifty, over fifty."
>
> "She did not go to school before. How come she can read your letters now?"
>
> "Ha, look, I forgot to tell you about this. My *jyu faahn poh,* together with a group of grannies and aunts in the village, went to attend the women's literacy classes organized by the Women's Federation. She has attended the classes for only one year or so. Look, what great progress she has made! What great progress she has made!"
>
> "Had it not been the new society, she wouldn't had been able to read!"[12]

Although saturated with the sexist language prevailing in the community during the time, the remarks of the Chinatown men unmistakably display the excitement shared by members of the community in response to the changes in their native land.

This excitement, however, was soon overshadowed by the retarding impact of other state policies in China, particularly those toward overseas Chinese and their families. Chinese government policies between 1949 and 1979 toward emigrants abroad and their dependents at home vacillated, to say the least. They demonstrated a lack of understanding of the particular experiences of Chinese American emigrant families. The impact of land reform is an example of this insufficient understanding. Since many emigrant families learned to purchase a certain amount of land to protect themselves for a rainy day after the famine in 1943, they were most often classified as the "landlord class" during the land reform, a "scarlet letter" that was to affect all family members for the rest of their lives.[13] The irony is that while members of many Chinese American emigrant families in China were labeled as "class enemies," their male relatives or family heads in New York City were suspected for their "pro-Communist activities" in the United States and harassed by the FBI, police, and immigration officials.[14]

There were periods of political relaxation, but the relatively generous gestures were inadequate for many emigrant families to overcome the anger, confusion, and frustration they felt toward the ways in which they and their families had been treated in the past.[15] This bitterness escalated during the Cultural Revolution (1966–76), when ultraleftist ideologies prevailed throughout the country, and many emigrant families were persecuted. By this time, even many of those women who had been greatly inspired by the state's radical gender policies in the 1950s were disenchanted and began to resign from their political activism.

As in the past, wives of emigrants in China bore the brunt. As the head of the family, they had to swallow their own pain and help their children and other members of the family to cope with the difficult situation. The life of a Mrs. Jian in Baoan County prior to her immigration to the United States in 1983 sheds light on the lives of many women during this period.[16] She was married to Mr. Jian in 1949, shortly after the Communist success in China. Unable to endure the hard labor and low returns at home, Mr. Jian, the only son of an emigrant family, decided to join the exodus of illegal emigration to Hong Kong in 1958. Mrs. Jian was left behind with three young children and three elder women, who were the wife and concubines of Mr. Jian's deceased father, and all of whom she had to consider as her mothers-in-law.[17] As she recounts:

> In the fifties, things in Baoan were not as good as in other places. Since Baoan was close to Hong Kong, many young men fled there, leaving women and children behind. He [her husband] was gone too. Before he left, the production team assigned only two to three *mu* for us to farm. But since more and more men left the village, we had to farm nearly ten *mu* instead. No one could help me at that time. His three mothers watched the cows for the production team and each earned two work points a day—only enough to buy the grains to feed themselves.[18] Well, it was good enough, because after all, that was all what they could do. I had to feed the three kids and myself. . . .
>
> We did not have a man in the family, so I worked like a man. My family did not have cattle to plough the land, so I was the one who drew the plough and ploughed the land. . . . In the summer, when the storms came, everyone ran home, fearing that they would be hit by the lightning, but not me. No, not me. . . . Not that I did not want to, but because I could not afford to do that. At moments like this, I could only comfort myself by saying, "No, Renyi, don't be afraid. You did not mistreat anyone, you did not beat your parents, and you did not do any harm to anyone. The God of Thunder can tell good from bad. . . . He would not wrong you."
>
> After twenty years of hard working, I became so skinny and in such a bad shape that your Uncle Jian simply could not recognize me when he came to pick me up at Kennedy Airport in 1983 . . . . I could not join him earlier because, as you know, he did not get his legal status in the United States until 1982.

However, as in the past, women and members of the emigrant families did not passively accept the injustices imposed on them. Many fought to resist the labels meted out by their local authorities, but there were always limitations on what they could do under the highly centralized political system in the country. Their bitter feelings, pent up like the surging water behind a floodgate, were yet to be discharged.

A Period of Significant Change, 1965–82

The most significant change in New York's Chinese working-class families occurred after the late 1960s, when Chinese immigrants came to the city in unprecedentedly large numbers and the economic structure of the community underwent drastic change. Women continued to form a majority of the new immigrants. While most came with their families, many came to join their husbands from whom they had been separated for decades. As a result, in 1970, only four years after the change in immigration law, the percentage of married bachelors among all married Chinese men in the state dropped from about 30 percent in 1960 to 12 percent.[19] Family life indisputably became the norm in the New York Chinese community.

While significant changes occurred in the demographic profile of the Chinese community, its economic structure also underwent significant transformation. In the 1940s, the importance of Chinese laundries for the community's economy began to decline.[20] By 1970 they employed less than 15 percent of the city's Chinese adult male population. Crippled by their limited marketable skills, many Chinese men gravitated toward the Chinese restaurant business either in Chinatown, in other parts of the city, or in the greater New York area. As a result, in 1970 about one-third of the city's gainfully employed Chinese men worked in this trade.[21] Since employment in the Chinese restaurant business was low-paid, highly competitive, and unstable, the Chinese working-class family in New York City badly needed a second income.

It was at this juncture that the garment industry stepped into the economic center of the community. By 1983, six out of ten families in New York's Chinatown and four out of ten Chinese families in the city had members employed in the garment industry.[22] Women in the New York Chinese community had always worked, but never before did they work outside the home in such large numbers. Nor did their wage-earning labor ever become so crucial to their families, particularly in those families whose male heads were unemployed. In addition, their work in the garment industry was indispensable for their families because the garment industry was the only industry in the community that was unionized by a major American labor organization and could offer the Chinese working-class families health insurance, which they badly needed but could not have otherwise afforded. The Chinatown garment industry has thus effectively transformed Chinese working-class families in New York City from the small producer family into the modern dual-income family.

The rise of the Chinatown garment industry also helped to transform the culture of many Chinese working-class families in the city. Since most of the men worked long hours in restaurants, usually from ten or eleven in the morning to around twelve at night, home for them was but a place to sleep, a "hotel," as one women garment worker put it in an interview. This was particularly true for those who worked outside the city. They could only visit their families two days every other week or four days per month. Exhausted by their long workdays and heavy workload, many could not play any significant role even when they were home.

Consequently, almost all the household responsibilities were shifted to the female head of the family. Many worked in the garment industry, as work hours there were believed to be flexible. Men's frequent absence from the family coupled with the decline of their economic role in the family often made them almost dispensable. Christine Lin, a sixteen-year-old daughter of a garment worker and a waiter in New York's Chinatown, related her situation: "We hardly see our Dad during the week. Every night he comes home, we are in bed; when we are up, he is in bed. On his day off, he is so tired that he often loses his patience to talk to us. . . . I don't know what to talk to him about either. . . . I love my Mom. She is always there. . . . Whenever we are hungry, we have problems, we go to Mom. . . . We can do without Dad, but we can't do without Mom."[23] Hence, a new mother-centered culture began to take shape among some dual-income Chinese working-class families in the city. The traditional Chinese family structure simply had no place.

What impact did this family transformation have on transforming gender and other power relations in the family? To what extent did the immigrants' past experience influence this transformation of family culture? How did men and women in the family react to this change? In what ways did women's wage-earning labor outside the home contribute to this change? Several patterns emerged in my interviews with the women immigrant workers and their families.

As illustrated by the experience of the Yeung family, women's wage-earning labor outside the home was likely to have some positive impact on gaining respect for them and thereby gradually transforming gender relations between husbands and wives in those earlier Chinese immigrant families that improved their conditions after women's immigration to this country. Similar situations also occurred among recent immigrant families who entered the United States after 1965. This is exemplified by changes in the Chen family, with whom I had close contact between 1984 and 1987.[24] Mark Chen, the male head of the household, came to New York City in 1970 under the sponsorship of his sister, who had married an ex-GI in 1961 at the age of eighteen, for the family was too poor to keep her home. This set off a "chain immigration." Mark, the only son in the family, was the first to follow. However, as a daughter-in-law, his sister could not offer him a place to stay with her husband's family. Mark therefore had to begin his life in the Gold Mountain by renting a bed in a Chinatown *gong si fang* (public dormitory). After changing jobs several times, he, like most of his compatriots, worked as a waiter in a Chinatown restaurant.

Mark Chen was anxious to make his fortune in the new land. After saving enough money, he started a small restaurant with a friend. The business, however, failed, and the friend embezzled the remainder of the money and ran away, forcing Mark to resume work as a waiter. Greatly disheartened by his first entrepreneurial endeavor, he realized that he needed a wife, a more reliable partner. At his mother's advice, he took a three-month leave from work and went wife-hunting in Hong Kong.

A Ying was the last woman he met in the third month of his visit to Hong Kong. Although Mark was greatly disappointed by her sunburned complexion and "rustic" manner, he was impressed by her strong build and deftness at work, which indicated her industrious nature and her potential to become a great help for a labor-intensive business. More importantly, as he put it, time was running out when he met her and he had no better choice. With the approval of his mother, who was in turn assured by a fortune-teller that the couple was a perfect match after reading their "eight characters," Mark married A Ying three weeks after they met and returned to the United States.[25] One year later, A Ying came to join him in New York City.

In retrospect, Mark once jokingly told me that the most successful venture he had ever had was his marriage with a woman whom he barely knew at the time of marriage, but who proved her worth. After immigrating to the United States, A Ying quickly became one of the fastest sewing-machine operators in a Chinatown shop. Her earnings contributed substantially to the family income. Although Mark did not realize his American dream of owning a Chinese take-out restaurant in New York City, the Chens bought their own house in 1983, three years after A Ying came to the United States. When I saw them again in the fall of 1990, the family had already taken out mortgages on another two houses and turned them into rentals. Mr. Chen had modified his American dream: he now wanted to become a real estate broker in the New York Chinese community. When I chatted with him, Mark, grinning from ear to ear, said with great satisfaction, "You women are really great! . . . True, without A Ying, this family can't be like this. . . . Now, I'm one hundred percent happy with her. Look, even her skin color is getting lighter after all these years in the United States—ha, ha, ha." In truth, his remarks do not demonstrate a fundamental cultural change on his part. Nevertheless, changes in his family conditions did force him to begin acknowledging A Ying's important role in the family.

More cooperative and interdependent relationships between husbands and wives took place in those immigrant families where husbands worked relatively regular hours and had been exposed to a higher degree of gender equality in their native land. Tang Mei's relationship with her husband is an example. The family came from Shenzhen, China. In order to qualify for immigration status under the U.S. immigration preference for skilled workers, Tang Mei's husband Wang Weijun had learned to make *dim sum* in China.[26] Although the family was able to immigrate to the United States in early 1982, they were in heavy debt. To pay back the money they had borrowed from their relatives in the United States to cover their travel expenses, Tang's husband began working in a Chinatown restaurant the second day after their arrival in New York City, and she went to work in a Chinatown garment shop on the following day.

Since dim sum was served in many Chinatown restaurants in the early morning and the serving ended around 2:00 P.M., Tang's husband had to go to work before 6:00 A.M. but returned home much earlier than she did, usually between 4:00 and 5:00 P.M. He was therefore able to share a significant number of family responsibilities with Tang Mei, picking up their daughter after school, helping her with her homework, and cooking dinner. Tang Mei was therefore able to attend the English night school run by the union twice a week after work. When asked how he felt about his life in the United States, Wang responded frankly and unreservedly to me, whom he saw as sharing the same native place and past experience as he did:

> You know, the double-income family is nothing new to us who came from China. We, husbands and wives, all worked in China, right? What is different is, our wages in China were low but our life there was guaranteed. We ate out of "the iron bowl."[27] In addition, Tang Mei and I lived with my parents. They were both retired and had time to help us to take care of everything. We had a baby girl when we were in China, but we had no problem at all. My parents took care of her. . . . Life was very easy for me at that time. I didn't have to work very hard at my workplace because, as the saying goes, "do it or not, you will get thirty-eight yuan."[28] After work at home, I would sit back on my armchair, cross my leg on the stool, read the newspapers and let my mom wait on me—you know, she loved to do that and I was her only son. . . .
>
> But now, everything is so different, I can't have such a good time any more. . . . In this country, we have no one to help out, and the system is so competitive. You simply can't survive if you have poor health or are unskilled, not to mention if you don't work hard. . . . I had a hard time getting used to life in this country. Both Tang Mei and I have been working very hard because we know we need to face reality. . . .
>
> Having children is indeed a burden now. We had another girl after we came to the United States. We could not afford the time and money to raise her. So, last year, Tang Mei took her back to China to be taken care of by my parents. We love our children but we have no choice. . . . In China, people resist the single-child policy and want to have more children. But here, in this county, even if we are encouraged to have more children, we have to think twice before we act. . . .
>
> In order to get a better job in this country, we need to learn English. I tried very hard when I first came here, but I simply did not have the brains for it. Tang Mei is much better. . . . In addition, it is easier for a woman than a man to get out of Chinatown. Knowing a little bit of English, they can find a job in a midtown American garment shop, but we men can't do that. Especially me, how can I make dim sum in an American restaurant? Forget it! . . . Tang Mei and I had talked about

this and we decided that she should attend the English night school to learn English and I would stay home after work to take care of our daughter and other household responsibilities. . . .

I did not feel good at first, but Tang Mei and I knew very well that this was the only way for us to survive and improve our lives in this country. . . . Well, after all, we belong to the generation who grew up with the teaching of "our great leader Chairman Mao": "Men and women are the same. Women can do whatever men can." Remember? Sound familiar? Ha, ha, ha. . . . Now, look at my family: women can do even what men can't. Well, let it be like that. I don't mind. It is all for the family. In any case, I would say life in this country is much more hopeful than in China. We have confidence in our future. . . . Yes, looking back to our lives in China, I also began to question how really equal we had been there.[29]

His response also suggests how immigrants' lives after immigration could lead them to reevaluate their past experiences and change their perceptions of life.

A cooperative and interdependent relationship could also develop between couples who had gone through thick and thin before and after immigrating to the United States. Shui Mak Ka and Sun Fook Ka were such a couple. Both were medical school graduates in China in the 1950s. Before they emigrated Ka was the acting director of a major kindergarten, and Jia was the chief physician of a major hospital in the city of Zhengzhou in Henan Province.

In 1966 Shui Mak Ka left China to meet with her father in Hong Kong, who earlier had emigrated to the United States.[30] She decided to stay in Hong Kong after the meeting because, as she explained, China at that time was in turmoil due to the outbreak of the Cultural Revolution (1966–76) and could not provide her with the medical facilities to treat the illness she had contracted. In 1973, under the sponsorship of her cousin, who had already immigrated, she came to the United States with her three young children, an eight-year-old girl and six-year-old twin boys, to seek a better life. She first arrived in Boston and worked at a restaurant owned by her cousin. Since her income from the restaurant was not sufficient to support a family with three children, she came to New York to look for a better-paying job.

Life was extremely difficult for Ka in the first two years after she came to New York. As she recalled, the family did not have their own house and had no furniture for the apartment they rented. Her days began at five in the morning and would not end until 11:00 at night. She worked at two jobs, sewing during the day in a Chinatown garment shop owned by a relative and serving in the evening at a restaurant in the Bedford section of Brooklyn owned by another relative.

Like most working mothers in New York's Chinatown, Ka had to rely on the cooperation of her young children to run her family life. Her children would either play at her side or work side by side with her at odd jobs in the shop when they did not have any homework after school; if they had homework they had to stay home by themselves. Every day she would assign each of her children a certain household responsibility, such as mopping the floor or washing the dishes, and if her children were at home, she would call them and check up on their homework, household assignments, baths, and bedtime, from work.

At night when she came home after a day's work, she had to cook for the children so that they could have meals to heat up the next day. With her irregularly long work hours, the family could have only one evening each week to sit down and have dinner together. Yet her children were bound to her and looked up to her as their hero. As they put it in an interview, they understood that she had tried her best to give them the best possible life, and she was their "great mother."

Sun Fook Ka did not join the family until 1974, after bearing the political stigma of allowing his family to live under the capitalist system for almost ten years. Life was not easy for him when he first arrived. His own children, having been separated from him for almost ten years, refused to accept him as their father. The youngest, who was only one year old when he left China, called him "uncle" and tried to stop his mother from sleeping with him at night. Equally painful for him was the downward social mobility he underwent after immigrating to the United States. Speaking no English and with no time to study, he could not take the examination for a doctor's license in the United States and had to give up his career as a doctor, an occupation he had held for almost twenty years in China.

Mr. Ka first worked in a Chinese restaurant as a waiter but soon decided to quit after running into a former colleague at the restaurant who had been invited to visit a prestigious university in New York City as a distinguished scholar. He found it difficult to swallow the pain caused by such reminders of his past. To avoid more such encounters, he chose to work in the closed environment of the Chinatown garment shops. He began working as a sorter, responsible for sorting the bundles of cut-up textiles according to the quality of the material and the specifications set by the manufacturers before sending them out to different sections.

The couple never worked at the same shop, but they never failed to discuss their experiences and to encourage each other to fight for justice on the floor. As Ka has put it, "Almost every one of us was working to raise a family. How could we afford to accept any unfair treatment by the bosses?" Both had been workers' representatives in their shops. As Ka recalled, when she played the role as a major organizer of the historic Chinese garment workers' strike in 1982, Mr. Ka provided her with all kinds of support: washing dishes, cooking and doing laundry at home, and accompanying her to the subway stations to distribute flyers in the early morning before the strike. They are a couple who understand and support each other.

Changing gender roles in the family, however, could also aggravate potential tensions between husbands and wives, particularly in families where the husband had difficulty locating a regular job and found it hard to accept his changing position in the family and society. Such men tended to vent their anger at their wives through physical or sexual abuse. Although there are no relevant statistics before 1982, my interviews with women workers suggest that domestic violence was not uncommon in the community.[31] A union staff member, well informed about the community, believed that the problem of domestic violence was more common among working-class families due to the pressure in their lives.[32]

While the example of Tang Mei and Shui Mak Ka may suggest that the higher degree of gender equality in China had a positive influence on the immigrant families, this was not necessarily the case. Chen Donglu, the offender in an extreme case of domestic violence among New York's Chinese immigrant families that drew substantial social attention to the problem of domestic violence in the Chinese community for the first time, was actually from post-1949 China. This case can shed important light on how tensions between men and women could be aggravated by the changing gender roles in the new immigrant working-class families.[33]

Chen Donglu came from Taishan with his family in 1986. Lacking a job and language ability, he could not find employment in New York City and ended up working in a Chinese restaurant in Maryland. By contrast, his wife, Chen Jianwan, had no difficulty getting a job in a Chinatown garment shop and was able to establish a household for the family in a Brooklyn apartment. As Chen Jianwan's fellow workers have noted, Chen Donglu was unable to adjust to this change of position in the family, which he regarded as inferior to that of his wife. He habitually vented his anger and frustration on her either in the form of physical violence or excessive sexual demands. On September 7, 1987, frustrated by his harassment, Jianwan allegedly admitted to having an affair with another man. Greatly humiliated, he beat her to death with a claw hammer.

Chinese women's participation in work outside the home also influenced their relationships with their mothers-in-law. Since the late 1960s, shaped by the nature of immigration law, which emphasized the importance of family reunification, many older immigrants also came to join their sons and daughters in the United States. Of the 273,770 Chinese immigrants who entered the United States from 1968 to 1979, more than 8 percent were parents of U.S. citizens.[34] Most lived with their children, so the number of extended Chinese immigrant families began to grow.

The relationship between mothers-in-law and daughters-in-law took on new meaning in the lives of immigrant families in New York City. In some families, the younger woman's participation in work outside the home helped improve her relations with her mother-in-law. Since most working-class Chinese immigrant families could not survive without pooling the labor of all its members, older women in many of these families had to undertake more household chores than usual in their native land in order to free the younger women to work outside the home. In this context, a feeling of partnership might develop between the mother-in-law and daughter-in-law in some immigrant families, which would help ease the potential tension between them.

Take Wang Ying's relationship with her mother-in-law for example.[35] Wang Ying and her family immigrated to the United States from Jiangmen, in Xinhui County, China, in 1982, under the sponsorship of her in-laws, whom she had never met. For their first two years in New York City, mainly for economic reasons, Wang Ying, her husband, and her two children, aged five and three, lived with her in-laws in their Chinatown apartment in a tenement building. Like most new immigrants, Wang and her husband had to start working a few days after they arrived in the city. Her mother-in-law took care of the children, did the shopping, and cooked for the three generations of the family. Even after Wang Ying and her husband found a place to live in Brooklyn, they continued to have dinner at her in-laws after work during the week.

Wang Ying told me that her family owed every improvement in their life to her mother-in-law. As she put it, "without Ma's help, I don't know whether we could have survived to this day." The mother-in-law and daughter-in-law were so close that they were always the first to share each other's happiness and sorrow. "Chen Mingxin [her husband] is lucky to have such a good mother. The kids are lucky to have such a good grandma. But I am the luckiest one to have such a good mother-in-law," Wang Ying said emotionally. "We are closer than mother and daughter."

When asked what motivated her to do so much for her son's family, Wang Ying's mother-in-law said,

> Well, as a woman I know what life is like for A Ying. . . . I cannot forget the days when I was left all by myself in China, raising two kids and serving my in-laws. . . . I know how a mother-in-law can make her daughter-in-law's life miserable. Have you heard about the "Song of Daughters-in-Law" in my hometown? [I recited this ballad].[36] Yes, exactly. . . . Of course, I also cannot forget what kind of difficult life their father and I went through when we first came. A Ming and A Ying are all my children, how can I let my own children suffer? My old man said that I was silly enough to not know how to enjoy an easy life and to have taken on all these responsibilities at this age. I said, "you stupid old man, don't you feel your heart ache whenever your own children suffer? Well, I don't even know whether you have a heart or not!"

Not every immigrant family was on such harmonious terms. My interviews suggest that with the gender division of labor unchallenged and the authority of mother-in-law in the family unchecked, the extended family pattern in the United States did not necessarily ease the burden in the lives of the younger women. In some cases the redistribution of household labor would aggravate tensions between mother-in-law and daughter-in-law. What happened to the Chen family in recent years is a good example. Mark Chen's mother had long been the breadwinner of the family when they were in Hong Kong, because his father could not keep a regular job. The livelihood of the family was dependent on the mother's income from assembling plastic flowers, wigs, or toys at home. Mark began helping his mother with her work at home at an early age, and the ties between the mother and son were strong before Mark got married. He first immigrated to the United States, and then returned to Hong Kong to form a family at his mother's advice. To maintain her son's bond with her, the mother played an important role in choosing his mate and had tried hard to maintain a good relationship with her daughter-in-law after the son's marriage.

Circumstances changed, however, after the two generations of women reunited in New York City. Like Wang Ying's mother-in-law, Mark's mother had to shoulder a larger share of household chores and child-care responsibility than she had expected, to free A Ying to work in the shop. The older woman found it difficult to adjust to her new role in the family. Tensions soon mounted between her and her daughter-in-law, finally leading to the split of the two generations. The old couple moved out and lived separately from the younger couple, leaving them to take care of their family on their own. Not surprisingly, some women workers found that living with in-laws added a third burden to their lives.

Many of the women workers whom I interviewed felt that the most encouraging change in their lives was the tightening of their relationship with their children. Working day and night and dedicating almost all they had to their families, many women workers, like Aunt Yeung, gained increasing respect from their children. Many women workers sought comfort in this respect. Particularly for those who had difficult relations with their husbands or other members of the family, their relationship with their children was "the only ray of light in their lives," as one of them put it. Regrettably, women did not always gain credit for their contributions to the family. Since the community continued to define a woman's place to be at home and children's education as women's responsibility, women who worked outside the home were often blamed for the rise of juvenile delinquency in the community.[37]

How did the women perceive these changes, and how did they interpret the meaning of their work outside their homes? My interviews reveal that their past experience and culture did influence their perceptions. For those women workers who had been housewives or homeworkers in Hong Kong and other parts of Asia, engaging in wage-earning labor outside the home and being able to contribute significantly to their family was an entirely new experience. When asked what they thought about it, many would enthusiastically list the following changes as the most significant in their lives: they had an increased say in their family expenses due to their economic contributions, and they gained a degree of freedom in spending money on the items that they considered important, such as remittances to their natal families or relatives left in their native places, gifts for their children or friends on special occasions, and their own clothing and necessities to improve the quality of their lives. To gain and maintain control over the spending of their incomes, some women even opened personal bank accounts without the knowledge of their husbands or other family members.

Women workers from China, whose numbers began to grow sharply in the late 1970s, responded differently. For most of them, working outside the home, with all its joys and pains, was nothing new. After 1949 more than 70 percent of the women in China worked outside the family. Employment was guaranteed because the official ideology considered it to be an essential step for women to gain equality with men in society. The generally low wages in the country also made it necessary for a family to have two incomes.

Used to lifetime employment in their native land, many new immigrants from China found it difficult to adjust to the highly competitive labor market in the United States and were constantly haunted by a sense of insecurity. Nevertheless, many women workers from China appreciated the relatively stable political situation in the United States and the better educational opportunities it could offer to their children. Life in New York held out hope, especially when it was not difficult to get a job in the Chinatown garment industry after they came to the city.

Despite differences in the past experience of the workers, there was a kind of consensus among them. Most women workers believed that their work outside the home was rewarding. The most rewarding aspect, as they saw it, was its financial contribution to their children's education. In truth, "shirt collars put a lot of second-generation Chinese through college" in Chinatown, as the *New York Times Magazine* reported.[38] Limited by the opportunities available to them in the United States, they pinned their hopes on the future of their children. Coming from a culture that emphasized education as an important channel of upward social mobility, many believed that a better education could guarantee a brighter future for their children; it was in this belief that they had invested their hopes for a better life in the new land.

The responses of many married Chinese women workers demonstrate a strong family orientation. This could not be more obvious than when they were asked about their goals in life. Almost without exception they said they hoped for a better future for their families. How are we to understand this? Was this simply a demonstration of how tenacious the influence of their ethnic culture was? To what extent and in what ways did their experience in the United States help shape their perceptions of life? What impact did their labor participation outside the home have on changing their perceptions of life?

My interviews suggest that while native cultures and past experiences strongly influenced their language and reactions, the family orientation of their responses should also be understood in the context of their lives in the United States. Relegated to a disadvantageous position in the labor market and facing a society that alienated them, women in Chinese immigrant working-class families had to rely on their families for economic and emotional support. The family therefore constituted the most important part of their lives in the new land.

The impact of this family orientation on the women workers was double-edged, however. Although it gave them emotional comfort and material support that they could not attain in the larger society, it also had the effect of reinforcing their traditional gender roles in the family, when their actual situation in the new land already provided them with opportunities to challenge these roles. Not only did their family orientation lead to double burdens, but the overconcern about family reputation also prevented many of those who suffered abusive relationships from seeking public assistance.

However, while the strong family orientation in the workers' responses could be a reflection of the constraints in their lives, it could also be a strategy used to legitimize and justify their ways of living and their resistance to injustice in their new land. In the particular context of New York's Chinese community, while the dominant culture still did not readily accept women working outside the home, women workers not only had to work but also had to fight to protect their rights under the adverse working conditions in the garment shops. The rhetoric of family importance and family survival has thus become a powerful way to justify their deeds.

What should not be ignored is the workers' growing sense of self and self-confidence behind their family orientation in life or rhetorical strategy. In a society that attaches value only to wage-earning labor outside the family, it is not surprising that many workers whom I interviewed, particularly those who did not have prior wage-earning experience outside the home, noted that they had come to see their worth in their family only after immigrating to the United States and engaging in paid labor in the garment shops. The increased respect many women workers gained in their families, coupled with their experience in the shops, could generate in them the strength to subvert the traditional norms and reshape their destinies.

The experience of Alice Ip, a major organizer of the 1982 strike, is a case in point.[39] She grew up in a working-class family with six children in Hong Kong. She married her ex-husband at the age of seventeen, even before completing her high school education. Her husband emigrated to Holland in 1968, two months after their first daughter was born, leaving Alice alone to take care of the baby and her mother-in-law in Hong Kong.

From the outset, Alice Ip's marital life had not been a happy one. She did not realize that she had met a "Mr. Wrong," who was a gambler and a womanizer, until after the marriage was consummated. Her husband showed no sign of improvement, even after the family reunited in the Netherlands. For Alice Ip, every day in the Netherlands was a struggle. The couple already had three children by that time, but her husband continuously refused to share any responsibility for the family. Alice Ip shouldered the entire household and child-care responsibilities in the family and had to fight for every penny from her husband to raise her children. Fully occupied by her family responsibilities, she could not engage in any form of wage-earning labor. Without any income of her own and with three young children to raise, she could not entertain any thought of ending her relationship with her husband.

Under her sister's sponsorship, Alice Ip immigrated to the United States with her family in 1976. She began working in a garment shop the day after she arrived in New York City. She first worked alongside her mother-in-law in the finishing section and then as a machine operator, after her mother-in-law retired. For the first time in her life she was able to support herself and three children with her own income. As she recalled, being a working mother of three young children, life was indeed hard on her. She had to send her children to school and the day-care center in the morning before she began working. She also had to pick them up after school and make special arrangements for them between her hours of work in the shop. For example, during the summer she would place a mattress in the hallway and let her children nap on it; in winter she would put the younger children in the care of the older one at home. When her children were older, she followed the example of her fellow workers, preparing enough food at home, letting the eldest take charge of everything at home after school, and checking on them by phone frequently from her workplace.

Despite all the difficulties in her life, Alice Ip did not hesitate to defend workers' interests in the shop, which she said she saw as an effort to protect the interests of her own family. Knowing a little English herself, she was always ready to help her fellow workers with the language whenever needed. Like Shui Mak Ka, she was elected chairperson in every shop in which she worked. When the historic Chinese garment workers' strike took place in the summer of 1982, she became one of its major organizers. After the strike, she was recruited to become one of the business agents of ILGWU Local 23-25.

Indeed, it was not easy being both a union activist and a mother. As she recalled,

> At first there were certainly some conflicts. My children didn't want me to work in the union. They want me to spend more time with them. It was very difficult especially when they were young. I tried my best to explain to them the significance of my work, helping them to understand me. My mother-in-law didn't want me to work in the union either. She was afraid that I would become too good for her son.[40]

However, in retrospect she saw a reciprocal relationship between her union involvement, her previous work at the garment shop, and her stronger ties with her children. "The greatest reward was my children's increased respect for me," she said. "I gained tremendous condolence from what they have said." A few lines from her daughter Amy Tse's essay, "Life's Greatest Gift," fully convey the young woman's love and respect for her mother:

> This is an essay about someone that has greatly influenced my life: my Mother. . . . She is an everlasting symbol of hope, determination and love. . . . Even though her English is limited, it's never stopped her from achieving her goals. My

mother began working in New York City the day she got off the plane. She started off as a seamstress, now she is a business agent with the nation's renowned International Ladies' Garment Workers' Union. In the few years that she's been employed with them, she has earned a reputation that makes me proud just to say she's my Mom.[41]

From housewife to garment worker and union official, Alice Ip has experienced great changes in her life. The growing respect she gained from her children at home, her fellow workers in the shops, and her colleagues in the union helped build her self-confidence, which led her to see how inane her relationship with her husband was. In 1989, when her husband again beat their children, she, with the support of her three children, finally ended her agonizing relationship with her husband after more than twenty years of marriage. Regardless of the foreseeable prejudice for a woman divorcee in the community, she began a new chapter in her life.

Although the experiences of women workers in the New York Chinatown garment industry varied individually, labor participation outside the home, in various degrees, helped to transform the culture of their families and their own perceptions of life in the new land.

CHAPTER 6

Women in the Chinatown Garment Industry

From its outset, women constituted more than 85 percent of the workforce and have greatly contributed to the growth of the Chinatown garment industry. Their working conditions, however, drew social concerns almost as soon as the industry began to take off. In 1965 the *New York Herald Tribune* reported that numerous Chinatown garment shops, run by Chinese who clung to their traditional business practices, did not name their shops, falsified records, and paid workers nowhere near the minimum under conditions that were characterized by "dusty steps to a toilet that does not work."[1] Other reports related to the Chinatown garment industry appeared in the city's newspapers around the same time and continued in the following years.[2]

The term "sweatshop" began to be used by the media to describe the conditions of the Chinatown shops in 1972, after the U.S. Department of Labor vowed to step in and "clear up" the "sweatshop exploitation" there.[3] Such newspaper coverage reached its height in 1979, when almost half of the Chinese garment shops investigated by the U.S. Labor Department were charged with labor law violations.[4] Describing the Chinatown shops as "crawling with rats, cockroaches," Frank B. Mercurio, the regional administrator of the Employment Standards Administration of the U.S. Department of Labor, concluded that the situation was "reminiscent of a time we thought was long gone."[5] Many seem to have agreed with him.[6] Even Joe Denahy of the ILGWU chimed in and said, "There's going to be another Triangle fire down here. I know it."[7]

Not everyone related to the industry conceded that the Chinatown shops in the 1970s and early 1980s could be called sweatshops, however. Frederick Siems, the executive vice president of the ILGWU, who was leading the union campaign against the shops in 1979, rejected the notion. "The buildings are old there," he said. "It's crowded. . . . But there is a union in Chinatown and I think we're 75 to 80 percent organized. And that helps."[8]

Although most of the longtime Chinatown workers whom I interviewed in the late 1980s and 1990s recalled clearly the unpleasant working conditions in the early Chinatown shops, not all would define their labor as "sweating." Apart from their repugnance to being associated with a term that defames their labor, as they perceive it, times also made a difference. With their appraisal of the past revised and their historical memory weakened by comparison with the further deteriorating present, some of them even called the early years the "golden age" of the Chinatown garment industry.

Although government agencies vowed to clean up Chinatown as early as 1972, things did not seem to have improved. The Chinese sweatshops have continued to make headlines in the city's newspapers and other media coverage.[9] What accounts for this perpetuation? Some scholars believe that it is because there has never been any "hard and fast" definition of what actually constitutes a sweatshop. In truth, over the last century many writers have given their interpretations of the term. For example, Louis Levine defined it as an example of "insanitary conditions, excessively long hours, and extremely low wages."[10] Leon Stein argues that "the sweatshop is a state of mind as well as a physical fact. . . . It demeans the spirit by denying to workers any part in determining the conditions of or the pay for their work."[11] However, as Mark Levitan has argued, even today, when sweatshops are generally believed to have once again become a serious problem in New York's garment industry, the official definition of the term remains too broad to have any specific criteria.[12]

However, despite its lack of a hard-and-fast definition, "sweatshop" is a highly charged term, as Nancy Green observes. It conjures up the turn-of-the-century image of extremely exploitative working conditions that trapped immigrant workers.[13] The intended power of this imagery is complicated. Although it has often been used to combat labor abuse and defend workers' interests, it has also been used in political infighting, which sometimes simply strips workers of their only opportunity to work. Instead of joining the fray and investigating the users' political or emotional vested interests, I will examine six major aspects of life inside the shops: physical conditions, the division of labor in garment production, hours of work, relations among workers, relations between workers and their employers, and the issue of homework. The purpose is to present a complex and multifaceted picture of the life in the Chinatown garment industry.

Physical Conditions in the Shops

Chinatown garment shops in the 1970s and early 1980s had many things in common, but the homogeneously dilapidated picture presented in the city's newspapers does not fully reflect the reality. The physical conditions of the Chinatown garment shops varied according to the location, the age and size of the building, and the managerial pattern of the shop. In the 1950s, the few Chinese-owned garment shops were scattered in the core area of Chinatown, bounded by Mulberry, Bowery, and Canal Streets. This core soon expanded with the growth of the Chinese garment industry in the late 1960s. By 1981 shops had spread up Canal Street and Broadway, reached into Little Italy, and extended into the Lower East Side along East Broadway and Allen Street.[14] However, as a study of the Chinatown garment industry has pointed out, no matter where they were located, all the Chinese garment shops were housed in the oldest remaining industrial buildings in the Lower East Side of Manhattan.[15]

Comparatively speaking, shops in Soho, one of Manhattan's major remaining industrial areas, were larger, newer, and had better conditions, and those in the area of East Broadway and Division Street and along Canal Street were the smallest, oldest, and most neglected. Since most of the buildings that housed the Chinese garment shops had been designed for producing the traditional fashion-sensitive lines of the city's garment industry, such as dresses and coats, they could hardly meet the need for larger space in manufacturing sportswear, the major line of the Chinatown garment industry in the 1970s and 1980s.

The problem of insufficient space was even more noticeable if one looked closer into the space distribution among the shops. In 1981 five hundred Chinatown garment shops were housed in 130 lofts, with as many as fourteen shops per building, and occupied 2.4 million square feet. Individual shops ranged from two to eight thousand square feet. Those in Soho had the largest average size, about 6,070 square feet, while those on the Lower East Side averaged only 3,200 square feet.[16]

Employers made intensive use of the space available in the shops. Sewing machines were placed as close to one another as possible; piles of materials in different stages of production were strewn around; and racks of finished garments lined the aisles and filled the spaces between sewing machines. There was hardly enough room for the flow of production, not to mention any space left for the workers.[17] Workers' personal belongings, usually including a lunch box, a mug, and a roll of toilet paper, were either put in a box beside their chairs, which was meant to hold materials or finished garments, or packed in a plastic bag and hung on the racks erected on one side of their sewing machines. Some were fortunate enough to have an extra space to hang their coat or jacket if they were seated next to a wall.

Most workers ate lunch in the shops, but there was no space for a dining table. Since the late 1970s, when a growing number of workers commuted to work in Chinatown from their homes in other boroughs, employers began to provide their employees with free rice for lunch. Some workers ate out, and others bought ready-made dishes in nearby restaurants and ate them with the free rice in the shops. Most, however, brought leftovers from their family dinner the night before to save money. They warmed them up on the top of the pressers' steam boiler and ate them with the free rice. In any case, they had to eat at their machines and "swallow their food with the lint and dust floating everywhere in the air," as a worker described it in a community newspaper.[18]

In addition to crowding, two other major problems existed in almost all the loft buildings: aging and neglect. Since the late 1960s, as a result of a nationwide recession, the demand for industrial space plunged. In response, landlords began to cut back sharply on building maintenance. Any incentive to maintain the conditions of their properties for a low-paying industry was further eroded by the rising value of Chinatown real estate, which provided them with opportunities to profit through selling the buildings or converting them to more lucrative commercial or residential properties. Garment industry employers, anxious to grab as much immediate profit as possible, were not motivated to pressure landlords to maintain the buildings for a long-term investment. As a result, the old industrial buildings in the Chinatown area deteriorated rapidly.[19]

Symptoms of this deterioration included a lack of heating in winter and air-conditioning in summer, which literally turned many shops into a place of torture. According to the workers, in winter many had to wear thick cotton-padded coats in the shops because they felt like *bing xiang* (refrigerators). In summer they were so hot that they felt like *zheng long* (bamboo food steamers). To combat the heat, many had to work in shorts, despite a cultural reluctance to wear them.[20]

Other problems included insufficient ventilation as well as plumbing, elevator, and fire safety problems in all seasons. The stagnant air in most shops, caused by the severe lack of ventilation, was always thick with dust and lint. Steam from the pressers made the shops abominably humid in winter and oppressively hot in summer. The constant use of electric fans, which provided the only air circulation, "decorated" the workers' hair with thread and dust. Workers had to develop their own strategy to cope with their working environment. Some wore surgical masks and hats. Others, holding on to the Cantonese folklore belief that *faat choi* (Cantonese: a very expensive form of dry seaweed used in special dishes) has the power to absorb accumulated dust and lint in one's lungs, devoutly added it to their diet.[21]

The plumbing problems included leaks, a lack of hot water, and, most seriously, insufficient or broken toilets.[22] A staff member at the Chinatown Health Center speculated that the stench resulting from overused or broken toilets might have prevented workers from using the toilets as frequently as they should, thus causing widespread kidney ailments among them.

Other safety problems were evident as well. Although most buildings were equipped with sprinklers and fire alarm systems, often these were not maintained and did not work. Fire exits were sometimes blocked by piles of garments, and some gates were simply locked to prevent burglaries, which had been a growing problem since the late 1960s. In addition, freight and customer elevator breakdowns were so common that workers were often forced to use ill-lit and neglected stairways. The dimly lit hallways and broken elevators, which sometimes were only a big piece of wood hung horizontally and pulled up and down by a barely functioning shaft, led to a number of accidents, including at least one fatality.[23]

The physical conditions of the shops seriously endangered workers' health. Several illnesses were common among the workers: tuberculosis induced by poor ventilation and heavy layers of dust in the shops; dermatitis and eye infection caused by dyes; gastric disease occasioned by the workers delaying eating meals and working under severe stress; kidney problems resulting from the workers' reluctance to drink sufficient fluids and use the bathroom. Additionally, poor eyesight was produced by long periods of eye strain after working closely on striped and printed fabrics under glaring fluorescent lighting; joint pain resulted from the repeated manual tasks at the sewing machine; and circulatory problems often resulted from sitting or standing for extended periods.

Advanced sewing machines, such as the automatic thread-cutting machine that had long been a part of garment production in many parts of the world, were not used in New York's Chinatown garment shops prior to the mid-1980s. Most shops continued to use the nineteenth-century type of sewing machines. The equipment was so outmoded that even the most experienced immigrant workers needed to be trained to operate them when they first began working in a Chinatown shop. As a worker once complained, "When I first worked in the shop, the boss thought that I lied because I told him that I had worked in a garment shop in Hong Kong for many years, but I didn't know how to operate the machines in his shop."[24]

Two phenomena in the shops demonstrated the employers' single-mindedness in pursuing immediate profits. One was the omnipresent piles of debris and filth, an accumulation that illustrated the key characteristic of Chinatown garment production: nothing matters but production. The other was the important space that many employers saved for the God of Wealth. As precious as space was, the God of Wealth always occupied the best and the most prominent place facing the entrance. Either on the wall or on the floor, flanked by red scrolls with auspicious Chinese sayings written in golden characters on the walls, he was always smiling in his shrine, greeting every visitor to the shop: *Gung Hei Faat Choih!* (Cantonese: congratulations on making a good fortune!), *Choih Yuhn Gwong Jeun!* (Cantonese: may wealth come from all directions!), *Yat Bun Maahn Leih!* (Cantonese: may a single capital bring ten thousand units of profit!), *Fo Yuhn Leuhn Jyun!* (Cantonese: may the wheel of sending work never stop!).[25] A visit to the shops would always set one wondering how Wealth could manage to make its way into the shops with mounds of garments and filth blocking its way.

Division of Labor

From the outset, Chinatown garment shops were contract shops, contracting work from midtown manufacturers. According to the recollection of veteran workers, Chinatown garment shops before 1970 produced primarily dresses, coats, and jackets, the traditional lines of the garment industry in the area. Work was not divided into sections, and workers in the shops were expected to assemble an entire garment on their own.

Beginning in the early 1970s, influenced by changes in the city's garment industry, the Chinatown garment industry began to manufacture sportswear and other low-priced lines of women's apparel. Although most shops continued to accept whatever work they could get from manufacturers, by the late 1970s two kinds of shop emerged: those producing skirts and pants and those producing dresses and coats. There was also a third type of shop that produced evening dresses. Their numbers, however, decreased so rapidly that they were of little importance by the late 1980s.

Starting in the late 1970s, production in many Chinatown shops became increasingly segmented, particularly those producing shirts and pants and those producing dresses and coats. The division of work and production procedure in these two kinds of shop remains largely unchanged today. Generally speaking, there are six kinds of workers in the shops: the sorter; the foreperson; pressers; operators of sewing machines with different functions; the floor workers, who do not operate machines; and finishers, including the quality inspector and workers who prepare the finished garment for shipping.

The work of sewing garments on the floor starts with the sorter, who sorts the cut-up fabrics according to the qualities of the materials and the specifications set by the manufacturers and turns out the work schedule. The sorter decides where the work should begin. It goes either to the single machine operators to be sewed or to the hemmers to have the seams bound on the automatic overstitch (or long needle) machines before being sewn. The foreperson, who is responsible for maintaining the smooth operation of production on the floor, checks the sewn and hemmed garments before the operation goes any further. After a garment is sewn according to the manufacturer's specifications, it is sent to buttoners to have buttons attached and buttonholes sewn on the bottonhole machines and then to the floor workers to have extra threads trimmed. The garment is then sent to the quality inspector. Once approved by the quality inspector, it is sent to the drapers to be labeled, put in a transparent plastic bag, and shipped.

It has always been a spectacular scene to see finished garments shipped from the Chinatown shops located on the second floor or higher in the buildings. They are not delivered by workers via the stairs or elevators. Rather, they are slid to the ground along a strong rope, with one end fastened to the shop's windowsill and the other to a lamppost on the street or the door of the truck.[26]

The division of labor is more specific in shops producing dresses and coats than in those producing skirts and pants. For example, although they both have a special section for turning out belts or attaching zippers and pockets, shops that produce dresses and coats have additional sections for attaching shoulder pads, attaching elastic tape or thread, or working on other parts of the garment.

However, there is little division of work in the few shops that produce evening dresses. Except for hemming, workers continue to assemble the entire garment.

Like their counterparts elsewhere, gender division of labor was evident in the Chinatown garment industry from the outset. Sorters and pressers, the two highest-paid jobs, were invariably men, while trimmers, the lowest-paid work, were all women. This gender division of labor, as has always been the case in the garment industry, was rationalized by traditional gender roles or pseudo-scientific assumptions about mental and physical differences, and the rationale shifted over time. For example, men were hired to be sorters because management claimed that women lacked the mental capacity and overall vision to lay out work plans as well as the physical strength to move around bundles of cut-up materials. Women were not hired as pressers because their "delicate" bodies were believed to be unable to bear the heat and to handle the heavy irons. What had been ignored was the fact that the constant speed and exertion of force, termed by workers *yam lihk* (Cantonese: female exertion), and the extraordinary skill required to figure out how best to sew garments that were ever-changing in style could be as taxing and demanding as any other type of work on the floor.[27]

Women were mostly employed as single machine operators. Management argued, and many in the industry came to believe, that this position well suited their needs, because household responsibilities were their primarily responsibility, and they needed more flexible work hours to balance their family and work lives. Since almost all Chinatown garment shops operated on a piecework basis, and there were many more machine operators than any other section in a shop, workers were believed to be under less pressure to complete work in a limited time and could enjoy more flexibility in their work schedule. This presumed flexibility, however, was a myth. Since the rates were so low, work was so seasonal, and there were so many of them in the same section, single machine operators had to stretch almost every minute in the shops to compete with each other and to make ends meet. Such working conditions left women workers with little flexibility but great stress.

However irrational these assumptions were, they determined the gendered earnings in the shops. Chinese men and women garment workers were both relegated to the low-skilled, low-paying garment production sectors; both operated under the piecework system and sweated in the shops. In addition, actual earnings varied greatly according to the work season, the nature of the work, and the piece rate offered by manufacturers, and there was also no gender preference in the union's wages for work mostly done by either men or women. However, men earned more than women did. According to longtime Chinatown workers, the average weekly earnings of the pressers ranged from three to four hundred dollars in the 1970s and four to five hundred dollars in the 1980s, but highly skilled single machine operators earned from two to three hundred dollars per week in the 1970s and a little more than three hundred dollars in the

1980s. Trimmers earned the least. One source reported that they earned as little as sixty dollars a week in the late 1980s.[28]

Earnings in the garment shops were based not only on the piece rates and the speed of work but also on the nature of the work itself. The more mechanical and simple the job, the faster a worker could work, and thus the more he or she could earn. Most pressers worked under great stress because their number was small, usually only two or three and not more than four in a shop, with an average of thirty machine operators. They had to press all the garments sewn in the shop within the given time. Their work, however, was more mechanical and simpler than that of the machine operators. They could easily speed up their work once they were used to the specifications and thus increase their incomes. In addition, the small number of pressers also insulated them from the frenetic competition prevalent among machine operators and enabled them to earn a more stable and regular income.

Unlike the pressers, the income of the machine operators fluctuated a great deal because of the transient and unpredictable nature of their work. As styles changed frequently, so did the specifications set by manufacturers. It took much more time for a machine operator to get familiar with her work before she could speed up. The unpredictable nature of their work also allowed employers to keep their wages low. Single-needle machine operators found it difficult to keep up with their employers' constantly changing ways of calculating piece rates. For example, the rate for work on a collar could be fifteen cents one day and drop to ten cents the next with a line or so less of sewing, before rising back to twelve cents a few days later with the original specifications. Even among workers who would like to calculate reasonable rates for their work, few managed to do so. The seasonal nature of the garment industry and the highly competitive climate in the shops also left them with no time to calculate or negotiate the fairness of the piece rates. Employers could thus increase their profits by manipulating piece rates.

The concept of family wages was often evoked to justify gender differences in earnings. Although workers knew that pressers generally earned higher wages than machine operators, few seem to have questioned it. Typically, men were believed to be the only "legitimate" breadwinners in their families. The notion of family wages helped justify not only wage differentials between pressers and operators but also the gender division and particular forms of payment in other sections of garment production. Take buttoners in the 1970s and early 1980s for example. There were usually only one or two of them in an average shop, and they were always men. These men were allowed to bring in their family members to help out if they could not finish their work alone. They were paid according to the entire workload rather than pieces. For this, the Chinese shop owners argued that since piece rates for buttoning were low and the work was often done in large quantities, it would save time on both sides if finished work was paid according to the entire workload. More importantly, men should be allowed to bring in their family members to maximize their income, because they were expected to feed the entire family. Interestingly, the issue of family wages was no longer raised in later years, when more and more male buttoners left the industry for higher-paying jobs, and women took over the position.

Management applied similarly inconsistent and contradictory rationales wherever skills were concerned, as in the case of the foreperson. In theory this position was open to both men and women, and the worker who held this position was supposed to be the highest-skilled machine operator. In most cases, however, it was filled by women because, as employers argued, women were the majority of machine operators. Ironically, this high-skilled position did not necessarily entail a higher income. Although her average hourly wage might be higher than the rest of the workers, she did not have the opportunity to increase her income, as did most of the skilled workers working under the piecework system, because a foreperson earned a regular income. No wonder few skilled workers in the prime of their lives would take this position. While skilled women workers were reluctant to take this position, women who were either too old, too young, or too inexperienced to operate the machines had to be content with the lowest-skilled and lowest-paid jobs, such as trimmers and cleaners, the other domain of women in the Chinatown shops.

Gender hierarchy existed not only in the labor force but also in management. Most Chinatown shops in the 1970s and early 1980s were essentially family businesses. The employers tended to be men, and they were assisted by their wives and relatives. There was a clear line between the responsibilities of the husbands and their wives and relatives in the shops. The wife and other female relatives of the shop owner supervised production, hiring and firing workers. The husband or other male family members were primarily responsible for dealing with the outside world, negotiating with manufacturers, seeking market information, and maintaining good relations with other Chinese employers. In many shops, men retained the final say on every major aspect of production on the floor and were the real bosses.

This division of labor was often ascribed to the English-speaking ability of the men. However, one male employer's statement in an interview is revealing. With outright contempt, he said, "How can you expect me to deal with them [the workers]? They are all women!"[29] This prejudice against women was shared by many men in the shops. It helped narrow the gap between them and their employers, but it also isolated them in the shops, where women were the overwhelming majority.

As Nancy Green and Susan Glenn have argued, gender roles have never been fixed in the city's garment industry. Structural flexibility generated a degree of fluidity between classes and genders in the shops.[30] This was also true for the Chinatown garment shops, where many Chinese employers had been workers themselves, and there were always a number of women among them. Speaking from fair to good English, these Chinese women employers could run their shops successfully on their own.[31]

The experience of being a woman employer, as described by a number of Chinese women shop owners, was mixed. Some bitterly recalled being bullied or taken advantage of by midtown manufacturers and jobbers because they were Chinese women. Others were more amused by the patronizing and hypocritical cavalier attitude of some in dealing with an "Oriental" woman. Nevertheless, without exception all agreed that the tough bargaining Chinese contractors were subjected to in dealing with manufacturers was made even more difficult for them because of their gender.

In addition, like women workers in the shops, women employers were torn by their traditional roles in the family and their career pursuits as entrepreneurs. Most felt overwhelmed by the double burden. Bound by their culture, even those who were financially able to employ other women to help reduce their household responsibilities said that they could not help feeling guilty for not being able to play their traditional role in the family. "It is hard to be a boss, and it is even harder for a woman to be a boss," many of them commented in interviews.

Gender, however, did not guarantee that women would be benevolent bosses. Sam Wong, the union business agent, could have been correct when he told the press that women ran the shops more efficiently than men in Chinatown because they "may have worked their way up from the bottom and do a better job communicating with the women workers."[32] However, my interviews suggest that, situated in a marginal position in the highly competitive garment industry, some female employers could be as unscrupulous as their male counterparts when driven by the cutthroat competition among the contractors.

Hours of Work

Most women entered the garment industry out of economic necessity. Driven by the piecework system, almost all of them tried to maximize the number of hours they worked. There were, however, variations in the hours worked due to age, marital status, household composition, ages of children, and the load of household responsibilities. To understand why some women selected the hours of work they did, we need to differentiate between mothers of young children, middle-aged women with adolescent children, elderly women with no household responsibilities, and single women and students.[33]

Mothers of young children formed a significant part of the labor force. Constrained by their child-care responsibilities, they worked the shortest, most irregular hours under the greatest stress. Strictly scheduled according to their children's activities, their lives constantly circled around a center beyond their control. The changing work hours of A Ying in the early 1980s provide a glimpse of the lives of women workers with young children.[34]

A Ying was a young mother with a nine-month-old son when we first met in 1984. She lived with her in-laws, who had come from Hong Kong shortly before her son was born. Her fellow workers considered her to be lucky to have in-laws to help out at home. In fact, living with the in-laws did not make her life any easier. Her position in the family as a daughter-in-law required her not only to do all the household chores as before but also to take every precaution to avoid any negligent behavior and manners, so as to maintain good relations with her in-laws at home.

Like most of the men in Chinese working-class families in New York City, A Ying's husband worked in a Chinatown restaurant as a waiter and did not come home until late at the night or early in the morning. To show her affection for him and to fulfill her role as a good wife, she usually stayed up late and waited for his return. She would cook homemade soup boiled with traditional Chinese herb medicines for him, the kind of soup that the Cantonese believe to be very nutritious and indispensable for one's health. They would have a chat about the events of the day before they went to bed. She therefore seldom went to bed before one or two o'clock in the morning.

When A Ying's first son was still a baby, she had to get up whenever he awoke, no matter how late she went to bed the night before. She had to feed the baby, dress in a hurry, and then discuss the family shopping list with her mother-in-law to demonstrate her sense of family responsibility. She would not leave home until she was sure that her mother-in-law was in a good mood and willing to take care of the baby. All this took at least a couple of hours before she could be on her way to work. She then spent almost another hour on the train from Brooklyn to Chinatown. By the time she arrived at the shop, it was around noon.

For A Ying the shop was another battlefield. As she put it, she would work as fast as a "headless fly" once she got there. She would waste no time for snacks and spend the least possible time for lunch or in the restroom. The deadline for her to end a day's work was 7:00 P.M. Once the clock struck she would hurry out of the shop, scurrying through the vegetable and food stands on her way to the subway station to finish shopping for the family. She had to be home before 8:30 P.M. because any delay in getting home would upset her mother-in-law and lead to the suspension of her child-care assistance.

When A Ying's first son was three, she had another baby son. She then worked out a new schedule with her mother-in-law. In order to continuously work in the shops, she sent her older son to a day-care center in the neighborhood and put her newborn baby under the care of her mother-in-law. She went to bed as late as before but had to get up around 7:00 in the morning. She dressed, prepared breakfast for her older son, packed lunch for herself, and then started her arduous effort to wake up her older son. After he was up, she helped him wash, pushed him to finish his breakfast as quickly as he could, and took him to day care. All this had to be done before the newborn woke up. To begin her workday earlier in the garment shop, she had to increase the monthly allowance to her mother-in-law so that the older woman would help feed the baby.

With all these new arrangements, A Ying was able to start working in the shop around 10:00 A.M. However, she had to leave the shop at around 3:30 P.M. because her son's day-care center closed at 5:00 P.M. and levied a five-dollar-per-hour penalty on parents who came late to pick up their children. After she left the shop, she had to do the family shopping as before. She usually managed to get to the day-care center before 5:00 P.M. Her work hours were therefore much shorter than before. To make up for the lost hours at work, she began to sew at home after her children went to bed, while she was waiting for her husband to return. Hectic as her schedule was, it was not uncommon among the Chinese women garment workers with young children whom I interviewed.

Middle-aged women who lived with their husbands and adolescent children were under less pressure. They did not have younger children to care for, and their household responsibilities were further reduced by sharing them with their children. Hence they could work longer and much more regular hours. Many who lived in the Chinatown area worked from 8:30 A.M. to 8:00 P.M., while those who lived in Queens, Brooklyn, or other boroughs of the city or the greater New York area often worked from 9:00 A.M. to 6:00 or 7:00 P.M.

The elderly workers spent the longest hours in the shops. Although their number was relatively small, it has grown since the late 1970s. Many were older immigrants who lived alone in New York City, since their sons and daughters were already married, lived separately from them, and did not need their child-care assistance. Realizing that they could no longer count on their children's support for their old age in the United States, they tried to work as long as they could. They arrived at the shop before the door opened and stayed until it closed. Most of them were trimmers and worked more than ten hours a day, six or seven days a week, or as long as the shop was open. Although they worked the longest hours, they earned the least. These workers stayed in the shops to combat loneliness and to earn money for security as they grew older.

The young single women workers were the most carefree in the shops. As daughters, they had fewer household responsibilities and less financial pressure. They usually worked the most regular hours, from 9:00 A.M. to 6:00 P.M., five or six days a week, and took an hour or more for lunch every day. Once in a while they would even take time off to travel and enjoy life. Many were regular participants in union activities or trips organized by the union or the Chinatown travel agencies. They were a minority among the workers.

High school and college students were the most transient workers. They worked in the Chinatown garment shops to earn their tuition or for other expenses. The college students were usually foreign students or members of newly immigrated families. They sewed in the Chinatown shops before gaining proficiency in English. They scheduled their work hours according to their schoolwork and worked the most irregular hours. They left the Chinatown shops whenever they had too much work at school or found a better job elsewhere. Most worked on weekends. Those who worked on weekdays were mainly high school students, who worked from 3:00 to 6:00 P.M. after school.

Although hours of work varied among workers, there were occasions when most of them worked long hours. These were the occasions when work was *sih yauh gai* (Cantonese: "soy sauce chicken," Chinatown garment industry slang for easy work) and had to be rushed out.[35] Except for mothers with younger children or students swamped by their schoolwork, most workers would work as long as they could on such occasions.

In the 1970s two more factors began to influence workers' hours in the Chinatown shops. One was their immigration status. In all categories, new immigrant workers tended to work longer hours than those who came to this country in earlier years, which tended to generate resentment in the shops. There were also tensions between documented and undocumented workers. To pay back their debts, the undocumented workers were anxious to gain as much immediate earnings as possible. Their readiness to work under whatever conditions they were offered and as long as they could was considered a major threat to the rest of the workers. Although their number did not grow visibly until the late 1980s, tensions between them and the rest of the workers had already existed.

Another factor that influenced work hours was where the workers lived. Although until 1970 more than half of the Chinese population in New York City continued to live in Manhattan, mainly in the extended Chinatown area, census data show that the percentage of Chinese in Manhattan began to decline as early as the 1950s. From almost 75 percent in 1950 it dropped to 63 percent in 1960, 57 percent in 1970, and 42 percent in 1980. In contrast, the percentage of Chinese in Brooklyn and Queens grew rapidly between 1970 and 1980 from 17 and 18 percent to 21 and 32 percent, respectively.[36] Most of the Chinese garment shops, however, remained in or around Chinatown. Union data show that by the early 1980s, half of the Chinese garment workers in unionized shops commuted to Chinatown from other boroughs.[37] With their time reduced by travel, workers who lived outside Chinatown tended to work fewer hours.

On average, most workers in the Chinatown shops worked more than eight hours a day and at least six days a week. Those who worked fewer hours tended to work under greater pressure. The long work hours, coupled with the stress generated by competition, seriously endangered workers' health. The most frequent injuries in the shops, as many workers recalled, resulted from sewing-machine needles piercing the operators' fingers. Employers blamed the workers for not operating their machines properly. However, workers attributed it to fatigue resulting from overwork. These wounds were easily infected, and infected wounds often forced workers to stay home for weeks without pay.

An Extension of the Workplace

Like their counterparts in other ethnic groups, many Chinese women workers assembled garments at home. As they told me in interviews, few would have chosen to sew at home if piece rates had been higher and child-care facilities more accessible. Their reasons for working at home were not the same, howev-

Table 10. Chinese Population of New York City by Borough and by Sex, 1960–1990

	1960	Percent[a]	1970	Percent[a]	1980	Percent[a]	1990	Percent[a]
New York City	32,831		69,324		124,372		238,919	
Males	20,658		37,504		64,018		119,837	
Females	12,173		31,820		60,354		119,082	
Males per 100 females	169.7		117.9		106.1		100.6	
Bronx	2,667	8.1	4,785	6.9	5,081	0.1	7,015	2.9
Males	1,532		2,560		n.a.		3,611	
Females	1,135		2,225		n.a.		3,404	
Males per 100 females	135.0		115.1		n.a.	1	06.1	
Kings/Brooklyn	4,636	14.1	11,779	17.0	26,067	21.0	68,191	28.5
Males	2,742		6,236		13,348		34,381	
Females	1,894		5,543		12,719		33,810	
Males per 100 females	144.8		112.5		104.9		101.69	
New York/Manhattan	20,761	63.2	39,366	56.8	52,165	41.9	71,723	30.0
Males	13,824		21,970		27,225		35,983	
Females	6,937		17,396		24,940		35,740	
Males per 100 females	199.3		126.3		109.2		100.7	
Queens	4,585	14.0	12,855	18.5	39,526	31.8	86,885	36.4
Males	2,447		6,449		13,348		43,330	
Females	2,138		6,406		12,710		43,555	
Males per 100 females	114.5		100.7		105.0		99.5	
Richmond	182	0.6	539	0.8	1,822	0.2	5,105	2.1
Males	113		289		n.a.		2,532	
Females	69		250		n.a.		2,573	
Males per 100 females	163.8		115.6		n.a.		98.4	

Sources: U.S. Department of Commerce, Bureau of the Census, *U.S. Census of Population,* 1960, 1970, 1980, 1990 (Washington, D.C.: G.P.O.).

a. Percentage of New York City's Chinese population.

er. For some, sewing at home after work was a way to supplement their family income. Living in a close-knit community that emphasized family and social relations and leading a life that could not avoid unexpected hazards, Chinese immigrant families had many expenses in addition to their daily necessities. For instance, they had to buy presents for friends, children, and family members on special occasions; send remittances to relatives in their homeland; and pay for their family members' medical bills that were not covered by union health insurance. Since their meager income did not allow them to cover all these expenses, they had to increase their wages by extending their work hours at home. This part of their income allowed some not only to set aside savings in preparation for a rainy day but also to help them realize their American dreams of owning a car and a house.

For most homeworkers who had young children but no access to child care, working at home was the only kind of work that was feasible.[38] Lack of child-care facilities was a common problem among many working women in New

York City, but it had an even greater effect on the lives of Chinese women garment workers. This had a lot to do with their particular childbearing pattern. One study shows that between the 1970s and early 1980s, despite the massive Chinese immigration and the entrance of a large number of married Chinese women into the city, the birthrate of New York's Chinese community dropped from 22.4 per thousand people in 1970 to 13.1 in 1980. Although the Chinese population was 19 percent more fertile than that of the city's entire population in 1970, and the average birthrate of New York's Chinese community was 24 percent higher than that of all Chinese in the United States, by 1980 the New York Chinese fertility rate was 13 percent less than that of the city's entire population and 18 percent lower than that of all American Chinese.[39]

Betty Lee Sung has noted that new Chinese immigrant women who arrived in New York State after 1965 tended to marry later, postpone their childbearing longer, and have fewer children than women in other ethnic groups. In 1970, when 14 percent of those sixty-five or older had seven or more children, 16 percent of Chinese women forty-five to forty-nine years old had five or six children, and twenty-five- to forty-five-year-olds had only one or two children.[40] This decline in the Chinese birthrate, according to Betty Lee Sung, was influenced by the situation in the immigrants' places of origin.[41] Although this observation might be accurate for immigrants from other places, it seems unlikely for those from China. The single-child policy did not become compulsory until 1979 and, in some places, the early 1980s. The fact that the policy's implementation met tremendous resistance in China demonstrates people's strong determination to produce a male heir, regardless of family size.[42]

The preference of New York Chinese immigrants for smaller-sized families should be understood in the context of their lives in the city. Since most of the new Chinese working-class immigrants, men as well as women, could find only low-skilled, low-paying jobs after immigrating, and the cost of living in New York City, especially housing, was extremely high, many had to postpone childbearing until they could afford a more spacious apartment. This can be understood by comparing the birthrate in Manhattan with other boroughs. The 1983 study shows that in 1970 and 1980 the birthrate among Chinese immigrants in Manhattan, with Chinatown as their core residential area, was significantly lower than that of those in Queens and Brooklyn. The study finds high rents in Chinatown to be the major cause.[43]

Family needs also helped shape childbearing patterns. Chinese immigrant families in New York City not only postponed childbearing and chose to have fewer children, they also preferred shorter intervals between the births of their children. A number of women workers have noted that raising more than one child at a time would add only a little more work to raising one, and longer intervals between children would only shorten their work lives. Since men could only get low-paying jobs, and childbearing years coincided with the prime of women's work lives, Chinese working-class immigrant families could not afford to have women absent from their workplaces for too long.

This childbearing pattern of new Chinese immigrants coupled with their families' economic status accentuated their need for child-care facilities. Unfortunately, such facilities were few in New York City, and those that did exist were expensive and difficult to find. As many workers reported in interviews, even if they managed to find such a facility, the fees usually amounted to 50 to 80 percent of their income from working in a Chinatown shop. Many young mothers therefore chose to work at home.

Such work was not difficult to find. Sometimes help-wanted advertisements for homeworkers would appear in community newspapers, or notices would be posted on the doors of Chinatown shops. But most often, workers who worked at home found out about opportunities for work by word of mouth. A Chinatown employer would ask people he knew in the community or workers in his shop to spread the word when he needed homeworkers to help out with production. Since Chinese immigrants tended to live in the same neighborhood as their friends and relatives, they would pass the information around. If there was too much work for one person to handle, friends and neighbors would also share work among themselves. It was therefore not difficult for those who wanted to work at home to get work.

Chinese homeworkers, like their counterparts elsewhere in the city, were often paid off the books. Except for a few homeworkers who were either highly skilled or related to the employers, most received no benefits and no overtime pay, nor would their employers pay any Social Security tax on their earnings. For those few who received benefits, most did not come out of their employers' pockets. Employers would secure benefits for them at the union's expense by entering the workers' names and partial incomes in their books and registering them as union members.

Employers who benefited from homework argued that the system had a number of advantages. According to them, it offered homeworkers the kind of freedom and flexibility that workers in the shops were denied. Homeworkers, they argued, were free from supervision and had complete control over the time they chose to work. They did not have to clock in and out, they did not have to ask permission to take a vacation or other time away from their jobs, and they could work at any time and in any way they wanted. Above all, they contended that the system allowed workers to engage in wage-earning labor without disrupting the schedules of other family members and neglecting their needs. To this list Chinatown employers had one more reason to add. Since many workers had worked at home before immigrating to the United States, they argued, "it was but an old practice in a new land."

The experience of Ms. Lee gives us an idea of what the lives of the homeworkers was like and what they thought about working at home:

> I worked at home years ago, because at that time the father of my kids made only $300 to $350 a week in a restaurant, and we had to pay $700 a month for rent. I had two kids, a baby girl and a five-year-old boy, and I did not have anyone to help

me take care of them. . . . If I sent the kids to a baby-sitter, I would have to pay at least $20 a day. With my time taken off to send the kids to the baby-sitter and to pick them up, I could only make $30 to $40 a day in a shop. After paying the baby-sitter, I had only a little more than $10 left. What could one do with $10 in those days? Nothing! . . . So, why should I be so stupid to put my children in other people's care, let them suffer from traveling back and forth while I couldn't make enough money in the shop. It didn't make sense to do that, right? So, I decided to work at home. . . . Of course, working at home was very frustrating. The work I could get was all *jyu tauh gwat* [Cantonese: "pork neck bones," Chinatown garment industry slang for difficult work]. Who, working in the shops, would like to do this kind of work? No one. But what could I say? I didn't dare to say no, because I was afraid that the boss would be angry and would not give me any work next time. . . .

When I sewed at home, I didn't have any time of my own. My daughter woke at 6:00 every morning. After I fed her, she would sleep again. Then I washed her diapers, woke up and got the older one ready for school. If the little one was still sleeping, I was lucky. I would leave her at home and take the older one to school. But, if she was awake, I had to take her with me. . . . That would be very difficult, especially if the weather was bad. . . . The bad weather was really a curse to me. . . . Especially when it snowed, I would really get into trouble. It was so cold that the plastic cover over the stroller couldn't help much in keeping the girl warm, and she would cry all the way. If I put her in a stroller, the wheels were often "sucked" by the snow, but if I carried her on my back, the road was so slippery that who knows what would have happened if I fell! The kids' father never helped; he came home after midnight every day, never woke up until 10:00 and left at 10:30 in the morning. Home was but a hotel to him. What help can you expect from this kind of person? . . .

If the baby was awake, I could only do auxiliary work not involving the use of the sewing machine, such as turning corners and trimming. But when she slept, it was my turn. I would drive myself at full speed. All at once, I would finish my household chores and the part of sewing that would do harm to my baby. I would not turn off my machine for lunch. I couldn't afford the time, you know! For lunch, I usually ate fast food, a slice of pizza, a bowl of Chinese instant noodles, or whatever I could grab . . . I ate while I was working. . . .

The most frustrating moments were when the work had to be rushed out. The boss would drive me crazy. At moments like this, if the kids cried or made a fuss, which was most likely to happen, I simply wanted to choke them to death. . . . I never drank coffee in Hong Kong but now I am a coffee addict, because I can't stay up late and work without coffee. . . .

When I had to rush out the work, I tried to finish cooking and eating dinner in forty-five minutes. After washing the rice, cleaning the vegetables, and cutting the meat, I turned on my electric rice pot and the four burners of my gas stove, cooking dishes and the soup all at the same time. . . . When the meal was ready, I could only take care of myself. I would flush down the food and start working immediately, leaving my son playing and eating all by himself. My baby daughter would cry in her bed and my son would take forever to finish his dinner, but I had no time for them. . . . Life was so hard and frustrating that sometimes, to vent my frustration, I beat my kids without any reason. I felt regret for what I had done every time after the beating, but I couldn't help doing it again and again. . . .

Once I almost broke my daughter's fingers with my sewing machine when I rushed to beat a deadline. I didn't pay enough attention to her when she was crawling on the floor. What happened was, she was going to put her fingers into the wheel when I was about to start the machine! Luckily, I was quick enough to stop myself. Otherwise, oh, I can't imagine what would have happened to my little girl. . . . From that time on, whenever I had to sew when she was awake, I circle my machine and myself with an iron screen wrapped with bumper pads to keep her from getting dangerously close to the machine.[44]

Almost none of the homeworkers I interviewed would have chosen to work at home if better options were available. Homeworkers theoretically could work at any time they wanted, but the deadline set by the employers allowed no such flexibility. They often had to fill every possible minute with work and enlist every possible family member to be their helper to meet their employers' deadlines. Completely cut off from the workforce in the shops, they lacked the leverage of collective bargaining in dealing with employers. Not only did they have to accept the hardest and lowest-paid jobs that workers in the shops would refuse, they also had to pay for their machines, the use of electricity, and sometimes even thread and other overheads as well. Homework, in a worker's own words, was just like "a vampire, endlessly sucking up and draining our blood."

Employers benefited the most from this type of labor. It enabled them to cut costs to the bone by shifting overhead costs to their homeworkers and forcing them to accept the lowest possible wages by mobilizing additional family members to work at no cost to their employers. The system also provided employers with a powerful tool to increase their leverage in dealing with their workers in the shops. By cultivating a labor surplus outside the shops, employers could hold down wages by taking on and letting go homeworkers according to the amount of work they had to do and the seasons of the industry. Although employers seemed to have no control over their homeworkers' work schedules, they could compel them to produce at a rate that tested their limits by allowing them the shortest possible time to complete their work. What differentiated the late-twentieth-century Chinese contractors from their nineteenth-century counterparts was that they also exploited the union. Not only did they manage to shift the cost of benefits for their homeworkers to the union, they also dodged contributing to the union's health and security funds for doing nonunion work by placing some homeworkers on the books and the rest off the books.

Homework was certainly not an issue unique to the Chinese women garment workers in New York City, nor was it only a contemporary one. From the outset, homework was integrated into the city's garment industry. It was a bone of contention between organized labor and sympathizers of the system as early as the first decade of the twentieth century, when workers began to organize. Periodically homework was proclaimed eradicated, for example, after the passage of the federal Fair Labor Standards Act in 1938, but it was "just as frequently (re)discovered," as Nancy Green has concluded.[45]

Although homework allowed women workers to solve the conflict between their traditional role in the family and the family's needs, it reinforced the separation of the domestic and public spheres. By diminishing homeworkers' opportunities to develop their sense of identity as workers and attaching lesser value to work at home, it reinforced women's subordination in the family and in society. However, despite its exploitative nature, homework remained the only viable way for some Chinese women garment workers to cope. As Eileen Boris and Cynthia R. Daniels have argued, both the conditions and the concepts of the workplace and the home must be transformed.[46] Without such a transformation, women workers who could not work in the shops for various reasons would have to continuously rely on homework for an income and hold a subordinate position in society.

"Blood Thicker Than Water"?

In analyzing the success of their businesses, Chinatown garment employers tend to stress the importance of their ethnic commonality with their workers. They describe it as "blood thicker than water." The seemingly harmonious atmosphere in the Chinatown shops was so impressive to outsiders that even Edgar Romney, the executive vice president of ILGWU Local 23-25, once singled out the Chinese-owned shops as exceptional among all garment shops in the city. "You look around and cannot necessarily pick out who's the boss because she's often working along with the workers," he said. "The office is often somewhere in a corner," he continued, "sometimes just a desk with a phone—no secretary, clerical, or accounting facilities. The structure of supervision and management is not formal and obvious. It's very different from an American company."[47]

In truth, the Chinatown garment shops were very different from the giants in midtown or the multiethnic garment shops in the city. They were not much different from other ethnic garment shops in the history of the city's garment industry, however.[48] Like their counterparts elsewhere in the city, most Chinatown garment employers were immigrants. Except for a few, most shop owners did not arrive with capital. For them, the Chinatown garment industry was an American phenomenon. They did not have the know-how of the industry, nor had they accumulated enough capital to open their own shops until they immigrated to the United States and actually worked in the garment shops for years.

In addition, most Chinatown garment shops in the 1970s and early 1980s were family businesses. Employers of these shops managed to start their own businesses by pooling savings and sharing production and managerial responsibilities with their family members. Since most of the shops were started with a small amount of capital, the owners could not afford to hire a large number of workers and had to do a significant part of the work in the shops themselves. This situation continued into the 1990s, especially among owners of small and medium shops.

The experience of one shop owner with whom I am acquainted follows the general pattern of Chinatown employers. She was a sample maker before she was able to save enough money to start her own business. Limited by her financial resources, she hired only about ten workers and had to work alongside them twelve to thirteen hours a day, seven days a week. Like this shop owner, many Chinatown employers were handicapped by limited financial and human resources and continued to work in their shops. It is therefore no surprise that an outsider would see no difference between management and workers when they first visited a Chinatown garment shop.

The fact that most Chinatown garment employers were originally workers themselves allows scholars to assign double meaning to their management in the industry. Their past experience enabled them to understand their workers better and assist them if they wished to do so. It could, however, also lead them to exploit their employees more effectively. Situated in a marginalized position in the highly competitive structure of the city's garment industry, Chinatown employers, like their counterparts elsewhere in the city, exploited communal ties by developing a particular type of management in their shops.

Creating a familial atmosphere in their shops and developing a paternalistic relationship with their employees based on *gam chihng* (Cantonese: emotional ties) constituted a major part of their managerial scheme. People in most Chinatown shops addressed each other by attaching kinship terminology, such as *a je, a sam, a mui, a mouh, a sou, a suk, a baak* (Cantonese: elder sister, aunt, younger sister, granny, sister-in-law, younger brother of one's father, older brother of one's father) to first or last names, based on the individual's age and marital status. Working together with his or her workers and helping them to solve problems in their lives and work, the Chinese employer acted like a family patriarch who tried to meet everyone's needs. This familial atmosphere continues in many shops today, even though workers in the shops are not actually related.

Employers began cultivating gam chihng with their employees when they were first recruited. Like many ethnic enterprises, recruitment in most Chinatown shops was based on strong ties between newcomers and those already employed, who often came from the same areas in China. Help-wanted advertisements for garment workers began to appear in the community newspapers as early as 1952, but most recruitment actually took place within the orbit of kinship and friendship connections.[49] Since Chinatown employers tended to recruit workers from their home towns, workers and their employers in many Chinatown shops shared a common geographical origin.

This particular recruitment pattern helped Chinese employers to reinforce their bonds with the settled workforce in their shops and to foster new workers' loyalty toward them through their friends and relatives already working in the shop. This cultivating strategy was most effective if the new recruits were "green hands" in the trade. Employers offered them opportunities to try their hand in the trade and even "hands-on" training, which they could not find elsewhere. Since workers were paid on a piecework basis, slow-learning workers had to bear the loss, but employers could always enjoy their trust and loyalty by training them.

The Chinatown employers also cultivated gam chihng among their workers by providing them with additional services, such as assistance in filling out documents that required English as well as immigration advice on how to sponsor other family members to come to the United States. Chinese immigrant workers would not have been able to obtain this kind of help if they worked in a garment shop run by members of another ethnic group.

Flexibility was another key managerial tactic in the Chinatown shops. In most shops the work rules, especially those governing work hours, were particularly flexible. Workers could set their own hours so long as they met the demands of production, and they were even allowed to cook their lunches in the shops. Mothers of young children could bring their children to work if they could not secure child care elsewhere. They could put their babies in the garment baskets or cardboard boxes next to them while they were working. Grade school children or preschoolers were tolerated on the floor, and high school students could receive part-time jobs and work along with their mothers. In addition, workers could work at home after work or simply at home if they wished.

Equally flexible were the forms of payment. Claiming that they did all this at workers' requests, employers would pay their workers either partially off the books or in more than one name. The person whose name was placed in the book alongside the worker's tended to be her mother-in-law, who helped take care of her children at home. As justification for this practice, employers argued that the older women were entitled to enjoy union benefits because no garment-related institutions were thus far able to solve the child-care problem of workers in the shops. The various forms of off-the-book payment left workers with little Social Security in their old age and would only hurt them in the long run.

Special occasions, such as shop anniversaries and Chinese festivals, were also important opportunities for employers to cultivate gam chihng in the shop. On these occasions, shop owners would hold banquets or luncheons and invite their employees and sometimes even their families to attend. Chinese New Year was the most important occasion for this purpose. Employers held elaborate parties, passing out gifts and the traditional *huhng baau* (Cantonese: lucky money wrapped in a small piece of red paper or stuffed in a red envelope). They would often hold raffles to stimulate the festive atmosphere.[50]

However, as many workers have pointed out, shop owners did not offer favors and accommodations indiscriminately. In most cases, only highly skilled workers were plied with easy work, special meals, and expensive gifts. The majority of the workers, especially those who were new, inexperienced, or elderly, were not cultivated. They were, as one worker recounted with a touch of humor, cast in "a corner that love has forgotten."

Employers also did not grant generosity unconditionally. Workers were expected to yield to their employers in every regard. Even highly skilled workers would be fired if they dared display any degree of militancy. Some employers could retaliate ferociously. Workers who chose to have an open confrontation with their employers faced not only the loss of their job but also being blacklisted in the community and sometimes even physical abuse in the streets, as some shop owners had connections with gangs or secret organizations in the community. Assaults in the streets were launched so skillfully that they would leave no trace that could be used against the offenders.

Fully aware of their vulnerable position in the industry, many workers developed their own forms of resistance to mistreatment. Resourcefully turning the informal rules of management to their advantage was one of these. Taking advantage of the "flexibility" offered by piecework, they ran family errands in between their work hours, brought their children to the floor, and cooked lunch in the shops. When piece rates were high and work was plentiful and easy, they worked as many hours as they could. However, when business was slack, piece rates were low, and work was difficult, they took advantage of the organizational flexibility to concern themselves with tasks that they considered more valuable than their work in the shops.

The most taxing moment for workers in the shops, as for those working at home, was when the work had to be completed within a limited time. This was also when the employer tried to make as much profit as possible at the workers' expense. In such moments, workers would develop particular measures to protect their interests. For example, when work had to be rushed out and back-stitch sewing was required on the inside sewed lines before covering them with the front layer, they would simply cover them with the front layer to reduce their workload. Similarly, when work was returned by the quality inspector on the floor, they would send it out again without redoing it to save time and energy. If the technically defective workmanship was not discovered until it reached the manufacturer, the employers had to bear the consequence.

Workers also used the rhetoric of ethnicity in their collective bargaining with their employers. For example, when the boss said, "Blood is thicker than water. We are of the same family. Don't be too hard on me," workers would reply, "Yes, we are of the same family. Members of the same family should take care of each other. You are the boss, the head of the family, and we count on you. Now the prices are so low that we don't have enough to feed our families. You have to take care of us." This play on the importance of ethnic solidarity would go on for a while, and sometimes it did work in the workers' favor.

Many workers also saw the election of the shop representative as an opportunity to defend their rights. Although most workers did not want to serve in that capacity, they were careful to ensure that the candidates were not the employers' sycophants or relatives. As one Mandarin-speaking worker explained, "we don't want to make the employer *ru hu tian yi* [like tigers with wings, adding power to something already very powerful]."

The workers' political consciousness was also demonstrated by some skilled workers' resistance to their employers' favoritism. As one skilled worker noted, "My boss once offered to make me the forelady in the shop. He said he would offer me the highest hourly wage he had ever given to any worker in the shop. He thought he could buy my loyalty like this. . . . Come on. I am not a fool! I said, 'Thank you very much. If you really want to help me to earn more, why don't you raise the piece rates? Then I could earn more without having to ask you for favor.'"[51] Another skilled worker who had been showered with gifts by her employer responded in a similar manner: "I said to my boss, 'Thank you very much for all your gifts, but I need higher piece rates. If you raise the piece rates a little higher, I can buy the gifts myself and don't have to bother you to go through all this trouble.'"[52]

Chinatown employers, however, were not a monolithic group. Not all of them shared the same social background prior to immigrating to the United States, nor did they have the same financial resources in their new land. Some came with sufficient capital to start their businesses and employed more than a hundred workers in their shops, while others managed to increase the number of their shops to as many as seven or eight after they began their businesses in the industry. Most, however, worked their way up through laboring in the shops and had only one shop of small to medium size with thirty to forty workers. There were also gender differences among them. In addition to their different personalities, these factors interacted to define their attitudes toward their workers. The diverse backgrounds of Chinatown employers makes it difficult to generalize about their attitudes toward workers.

In any event, workers would react when working conditions were beyond tolerance. Changing jobs, a historically important strategy used by women workers in the city's garment industry, was not only applied by the Chinese workers but also proved to be more effective in the Chinatown area.[53] Since most Chinese shops sewed similar types of garments and were situated close to each other, it was easy for workers to exchange information about the conditions in each shop and locate a better one. In fact, this was such a common practice among Chinatown workers that a majority had changed their jobs at least once after working in the industry for two to three years, which they jestingly called "firing their bosses." The degree of autonomy workers had in choosing their workplace not only gave them a sense of contentment but also, to some extent, helped curb employers' unscrupulous practices on the shop floor.

Workers usually tried to avoid direct confrontations with employers, but these did occur when piece rates dropped to a level that violated their understanding of reasonable rates for the value of their time and labor and their negotiation with the employers failed. *Tihng che* (Cantonese: shutting down the machine) was a major form of open confrontation between workers and employers. Older workers in the industry recalled that tihng che was not unusual in Chinatown shops before 1982.[54]

Nevertheless, the limited autonomy workers possessed did not allow them to change the fundamental conditions in the Chinatown shops. Frustrated by the situation, a growing number of young workers began to seek opportunities in larger midtown shops run chiefly by Jews or Italians. Workers of the earlier ethnic groups might consider the conditions of these shops far from satisfactory, but with plenty of light and air, "spotless" floors, air-conditioning, and a seven-hour, five-day week, they were like paradise for the workers from the Chinatown shops. There is no denying that many Chinatown workers had romanticized the world of the garment industry outside Chinatown. However, the fact that the younger Chinese workers yearned to work outside Chinatown further demonstrates the undesirable conditions of the Chinatown shops.

Sisters and Strangers

While the conflicting yet interdependent relations between Chinese workers and their employers were largely shaped by the position of the Chinatown garment industry within the city's industry, relations among Chinese garment workers were also influenced by their backgrounds prior to immigration. New York's Chinatown underwent great changes since the late 1960s. New immigrant workers came from different places, spoke different languages and dialects, and had different social backgrounds and past experiences. Although the majority continued to come from Guangdong and Hong Kong, a significant number came from other parts of China and Southeast Asia.

New immigrant workers who came from different places tended to have different occupational backgrounds. For example, a significant number of those from Hong Kong had been homeworkers, and some had worked in the garment industry prior to immigrating. Many of those from Guangdong had been peasants, and those from major Chinese cities had been schoolteachers, nurses, doctors, and even university professors.

Their life experiences were also different, and many still carried psychological wounds resulting from a traumatic past. For example, many workers from China remembered clearly the atrocities committed by the Red Guards and how they and their families had been sent to the countryside during the ten chaotic years of the Cultural Revolution (1966–76). Those from Vietnam could not forget their narrow escape from that country: how their possessions had been looted by pirates, and how their relatives' dead bodies had been left dangling from the sides of their boats when they arrived in the country of their destination.

Workers from Burma and other Southeast Asian countries had witnessed their family businesses going bankrupt in the wave of anti-Chinese riots in the 1960s. Workers from Hong Kong worried about 1997, when the colony was to revert to China, and those from Taiwan were apprehensive about the island's possible unification with the mainland.

There were also differences among workers who spoke the same dialect but came from different places. Cantonese-speaking workers from Hong Kong, for example, do not use the same vocabulary as those from Guangzhou (Canton), and they might not be able to fully understand each other. In the early 1980s, while workers from Hong Kong talked passionately about how McDonald's hamburgers and french fries tasted better in Hong Kong than those from New York, young women from Guangzhou missed the tasty little stir-fried field snails on Xihao Street, a small lane in the city well known for its local delicacies and goodies. Workers from Hong Kong might talk enthusiastically about the Hong Kong tabloid stories about famous pop singers such as Mui Yim Fong and Lau De Hua and the well-known movie stars Chow Yung Fat and Chung Chor Hung. Those from Guangzhou, however, would bitterly criticize the stereotyping approach adopted by "the eight revolutionary model theatrical programs" during the Cultural Revolution.[55] The first group might be more interested in finding out how to buy a car or secure a mortgage. The latter group was more interested in sharing information about a cheaper way to send the so-called eight big things (radio, tape recorder, sewing machine, washing machine, bicycle, refrigerator, camera, and electric fan) to their families and relatives in China.[56] Neither group understood what the other group was talking about, nor were they interested in understanding. This was especially true in the late 1970s and early 1980s, when China was still not fully open to the outside world.

Similar differences could also be found among Mandarin-speaking workers from different places. Their accents and vocabularies easily betrayed their origins and political inclinations. A telling example was how they referred to the year 1949. While those who called it the year of "the fall" tended to come from Taiwan or pro-Taiwan overseas Chinese communities, those who referred to it as "the year of liberation" were likely to have come from China or pro-Beijing overseas Chinese communities.

Shaped by their prior social status and political inclinations, the same political event might not have the same impact on workers from the same country and at the same time. For example, while some workers from China would talk bitterly about the Cultural Revolution and how they and their families had been victimized by the excesses committed by the Red Guards, others who had been Red Guards or their sympathizers found it difficult to accept their reactions without reservation and felt nostalgic about those days. Xiao Hong, a former Red Guard and the daughter of a district military commander in China, talked about it during a lunch break with a group of close friends in the shop:

Truly, I am not proud of what I did during the Cultural Revolution. In those days, as sons and daughters of the high-ranking officials, my friends and I could do whatever we wanted. Whoever were classified by us as "bad elements" of the society, we beat them and shaved off their hairs. . . . We were so "high" at that time that my friends and I finally decided to cross the border to stage revolution. I left the country but ended up in Hong Kong. . . . I know, it was difficult to believe but it was what happened to me.

With all the privileges that I enjoyed in China gone with my separation from the family, I had a very difficult time in Hong Kong. I worked at whatever jobs I could get and, not being afraid of shaming myself in front of you, I even sold my body to a rich old man for a couple of months in order to survive. . . . Why didn't I go back to China? . . . At first I was afraid that I would be labeled as a spy or traitor for leaving the country, because the political atmosphere was so tense in China at that time, and I did not want to cause any more trouble to my family—my father was already classified as a so-called capitalist roader by that time and was locked up. And then years later I was so ashamed of myself that I did not want to go back. I simply did not know how to explain to my parents. . . . No way out, so I married a man whom I did not love to come to the United States.

Yes, looking back to those days in China, I do hate very much those in power who took advantage of our ignorance and manipulated us to obtain their personal interests. I also hate myself for my craving for vanity at that time. But putting all the bad things aside, I should say that I was very idealistic at that time. Most of the time, I truly believed that I was defending the party and our beloved Chairman Mao, who, I was taught since I was a child, were the saviors of our country. I would bet my life on defending them. . . .

Now, after going through all these years of hardship, yes, I came to see how inhumane my friends and I were during the Cultural Revolution, but I also miss those days very much. I miss the days when I could be so carefree, so wholeheartedly embrace a belief, and be so sincere in defending it. I believe we, as human beings, should have some belief to hold on to in order to make our lives meaningful, but now, look, I can't trust anyone any more. . . . I have no faith in anything. What I concern most is how much my boss is going to pay for the piece that I have sewed.[57]

Her comments generated heated responses from her friends. Such casual chats often turned the shop into an unusual place for workers to freely exchange their different viewpoints and reflect on their past experiences.

Differences could also be found among workers who came from the same places but at different times. For example, many workers who left China before 1979 said that they were dismayed to find how materialistic their compatriots had become. Young workers who came from China after the economic reforms, however, said that they were amazed to see how little the older ones had been changed by their lives in the West, so "closed-minded," "outmoded," and ingrained in their old ways of thinking.

There seems to be a certain continuity in the backgrounds of certain groups of workers. For example, many workers from Hong Kong came from the working class or small business families, and many of those from Guangdong Province in China came from or were related to the emigrant families in the districts of San Yi and Si Yi. Among workers who spoke Mandarin, those who immigrated from Taiwan had proportionately declined by the 1970s and 1980s. Replacing them were workers from the major cities of China. Many had professional backgrounds or experience working in an industrial setting. Like workers from Taiwan who came to New York in the immediate postwar era, many also experienced downward mobility in the United States.

Despite differences in their backgrounds and past experiences, women workers in the Chinatown garment shops had similar experiences in the United States. Most were disillusioned with their lives in their new country. They came with much hope but often did not find the lives that they had sought. Many began working in the garment shops a few days after they arrived in the city. Nearly all secured their first employment in the Chinatown shops with the help of relatives and friends. Except for a number of those who came from Hong Kong, working in a garment shop was a new experience. Almost all needed on-the-job training from their relatives, friends, employers, or fellow workers. Since few alternatives were available when they first came, they had to take jobs in the Chinatown garment industry, with the belief that they would find better ones after they settled in the city. However, once they settled in the garment shops, there was little room for advancement. With their energy drained gradually by the exhausting labor in the shops, the workers came to realize that they had to spend the rest of their work lives in the Chinatown garment shops.

Workers' reactions to their workplace varied according to their backgrounds and experiences prior to immigration. For example, many of those who had lived in urban areas and had professional training found the backbreaking work in the shops unbearable and their downward social mobility in the new land distressing. In contrast, many who came from rural China felt that their working conditions were improved by working indoors and in an industrial setting. As one worker commented, "What better work can we expect? Can any work be worse than toiling in the fields and under the sun for an annual income of less than ten dollars in China?"

Despite their differences, most workers agreed that working in the Chinatown garment shops was an important part of their lives. Constrained by long hours of work and heavy duties in the family, they had hardly any time to explore the world beyond their homes and their workplaces. Social contacts made and information collected at their workplace were therefore especially important for them.

Contacts among the workers began with the ways in which they addressed each other. Unlike many other places in Chinatown, where women were primarily addressed according to their positions in the family, women workers in the

Chinatown shops were identified as individuals. Titles in the shops were assigned according to the worker's age, marital status, and his or her position in the "big family" of the shops. This practice tightened the ties among them.

Workers also developed close relations by sharing each other's joys and sorrows. In many shops, workers would pool their money to buy gifts for their co-workers whenever there was a new birth, a wedding, or an engagement in their families. They also tried to comfort those who had experienced unhappiness in their lives, such as an accident or a death in the family. Those who received gifts or comfort would follow the conventional ways to express their gratitude. For example, they would invite fellow workers to the party when there was a wedding; bring the traditional red eggs and vinegar-and-ginger pork feet soup to the shop when a newborn was one month old; or simply buy everyone in the shop an afternoon tea.

As in the case with many ethnic garment shops in the city, sharing food was an important means for women workers to build their friendships.[58] Especially after the late 1960s, when workers' places of origin became increasingly varied, sharing food from their homeland and recipes for cooking became an important pastime. Major Chinese festivals were often turned into cooking contests. There were taro or turnip cakes with different ingredients and dumplings with various kinds of stuffing for Chinese New Year; pyramid-shaped glutinous rice dumplings wrapped in reed leaves with various types of stuffing for the Dragon Boat Festival; and moon cakes with different ingredients and styles for the Moon Festival. Each of these treats was from a distinct region in China. Workers enjoyed these occasions enormously. As a worker proudly put it, "we don't have to make a trip to different parts of China, we don't have to go to other parts of the world. Just here, in the shops, we can taste food from all over the world. Our shop is all of China; our shop is a United Nations!"

Friendships among workers were reinforced when they shared information and ideas at work. The topics of conversation ranged from daily issues, such as where to get the best food at the lowest possible price in Chinatown, how to use skin-care products in the most effective way, and how to obtain various kinds of social services in the city and the community, to political issues, such as their lives during the Cultural Revolution, the possible changes after 1997 in Hong Kong and after 1999 in Macao, and Taiwan's probable unification with the rest of China.

Among workers in the same social circumstance, topics could be more specific. For example, mothers of young children were more inclined to share information about day care and schools; elderly workers were more likely to talk about activities at the Chinatown Senior Center and brag about the success of their grown-up children; students tended to share information about the admissions policies of different schools or better job opportunities; and young single women workers were more likely to seek out interesting places to shop and travel. These conversations sometimes helped workers to solve major problems in their lives. An older worker reported that in the early 1970s it was through these seemingly casual talks that mothers of young children in her shop realized that they all had the same child-care problem. They decided to form a co-op and take turns staying home and caring for each other's children.

Workers also shared information about job opportunities. With a highly mobile workforce, it was not difficult for workers to obtain the most updated information about working conditions in other shops. My interviews showed that although most workers got their first employment with the help of their relatives, many landed their next job with the help or information of their fellow workers. Close friends in a shop would sometimes change jobs together or in a "chain" fashion. The movement would begin with the most skilled worker, who would then persuade her new employer to offer employment to her close friends from her former workplace after her new employer came to see her worth and she was convinced that it was a better place to work. This chain migration between shops and friendship among workers could sometimes offer even the elderly workers a better workplace.

There were, however, tensions among workers in the shops. Prejudices based on regional differences were a major problem.[59] Before 1965, when the Taishan dialect was the dominant dialect in the shops, those who did not speak this dialect were called *ngoi saang yahn* (Cantonese: people from other provinces). Their Chinese ethnic identity was questioned, and they were ostracized. However, when the workers began to come from diverse regions after 1965, regionalism, interacting with other factors, began to take a more complicated form.

Factors such as the degree of westernization of their places of origin, level of education, former class status, and their Cantonese speaking ability could all become sources of pride and prejudice among the workers. Many workers from Hong Kong, believing that they had come from a place more westernized and thus more "civilized" than the rest of China, looked down on their fellow workers, particularly those from rural China. Inheriting prejudice from their homeland, they tended to call immigrants from China *daaih luhk mui* (Cantonese: girls from the mainland) or A Chaan (the name of a movie character), and those from rural areas in particular were called *heung hah mui* (Cantonese: female bumpkins or boors).[60]

Workers from urban China, Taiwan, and other parts of Southeast Asia with middle-class or professional backgrounds prided themselves on their better education, past experience, and social background. Many considered workers from Hong Kong and rural China to be low-class, tasteless, and materialistic. Cantonese-speaking workers, who were the majority of the workforce, scoffed at those who spoke Mandarin and called them *lau sung* (Cantonese imitation of the Mandarin "big brothers"). Mandarin-speaking workers in turn called the Cantonese speakers *nan man* (southern barbarians).[61] Ethnic Chinese workers who had been born and raised in places other than China, Hong Kong, or Taiwan were considered to be without authentic roots in China. Workers from

China, Taiwan, and Hong Kong, with different past experiences and having been indoctrinated by different political ideologies, also did not see themselves sharing a common identity.

Regionalism was more obvious in the shops with workers from different places. To survive in the highly competitive work environment, workers tended to team up with those who shared the same native geographical identity. This division among workers was so intense in some Chinatown shops that to avoid uninvited conflicts, many chose to work in shops where owners and workers shared their regional identity. This further reinforced the different regional identities of many garment shops in Chinatown.

Although regionalism seems to have played a major role in dividing the workers, my interviews suggest that it was but a foil. This can be understood by an analysis of the relationships between different groups of workers. Some workers from Hong Kong told me that they did not like the "Taishan *a mouh*" (Cantonese: Taishan grannies). They scorned them for working too hard and being so money-crazy that they were even reluctant to spend money and time on *yam cha* (Cantonese: traditional Cantonese-styled brunch), the most popular recreational activity in the community.[62] Interestingly, for a similar reason the "Taishan a mouh" also blamed their fellow workers from Fuzhou. As one of them put it, "You were talking about those people? They are money-crazy, workaholic, people of no moral value! They can't tell day from night if they have work to do!" What undermined the solidarity of workers was obviously not regionalism but the competition generated among them by the structure of the industry.

The shifting categorical dislike among workers in the following years attests to the accuracy of this observation. Particularly in the early 1980s, when new immigrant workers entered the industry in large numbers, many earlier workers, regardless of their different native identities, did not seem to have any difficulty in joining the choir to blame the newcomers for breaking the basic rules in the shops and accepting work at unreasonably low rates. This in turn made it hard for the newcomers to understand them and see how easily they could have forgotten what it was like to be a new immigrant worker.

Although old and new immigrant workers had difficulty in understanding each other, they shared similar attitudes toward their undocumented fellow workers.[63] As is the case everywhere, many Chinatown employers took advantage of the undocumented status of these workers and paid them the lowest possible rates. To make ends meet these workers had to work as many hours as they could. Their long work hours bred resentment against them, which not only made their lives even harder but also further undermined workers' solidarity in the shops.

Competition among workers was also encouraged by their employers. This can be understood from the way in which many employers distributed work in the Chinatown shops. With the excuse of "letting one work according to her or his ability," many of them simply put garments of all sizes together and let workers scramble for their share. Since piece rates were generally low, not paid according to size, and smaller sizes required less time to complete, many workers would fight for the smaller sizes of work. This tended to create a tug-of-war.

The situation could be even more chaotic when employers joined the fray. To show their favoritism, some employers would sneak work of smaller sizes to the fastest hands in the shops. To make up for the disparity in their earnings, less-skilled workers had to work harder and longer hours, which inevitably escalated tensions between them and their skilled fellow workers. This kind of tension surfaced even among workers from the same native place.[64]

Although competition in the shops undermined workers' solidarity, friendship and camaraderie fostered by their mutual understanding and based on their similar experiences in the shops and shared positions in their families also had the potential to create bonds among workers. The relationship between A Ying and A Ling, who were once bitter rivals in the shop, is a case in point.[65]

A Ling was born in 1961 to a Hakka family in Zhuhai, a city formerly included in Zhongshan County and close to the Macao border. When she was only five years old, her father, who had illegally emigrated to Hong Kong and worked for a shipping company there, deserted his family in China and formed a new one in Hong Kong. From that time on, A Ling led an extremely difficult life with her mother and sister in Zhuhai. She remembered her family was so poor that her mother could not even afford to buy her candy.

China's economic reforms, which began in 1979, made life even harder for A Ling's family. They could no longer receive assistance from other villagers after collectivization was dismantled and competition was encouraged under the new economic policy. In despair, her mother decided to send one of her daughters to join the massive wave of illegal emigration to Hong Kong to try her luck. To decide which daughter she should send, her mother took A Ling and her sister to a fortune-teller, who predicted a good future for A Ling, who therefore became the pawn in her mother's scheme of family survival.

In 1980 she was put on her way to Hong Kong by her mother through a smuggling network in the village. As she recalled, she was so scared at that time that she could hardly remember any part of the ordeal. The only thing she could remember was that she seemed to have been pushed through a tunnel to sneak across the border. Once out of the tunnel, she saw an old woman beckoning to her, who turned out to be a member of the smuggling network. The old woman took her to her father's place and forced him to pay a ransom of six thousand Hong Kong dollars to secure her release. For this amount of money, A Ling promised her father to work in his family.

Almost a year after she arrived in Hong Kong, at the age of twenty, she was introduced to her future husband, Benny Lee, a young and energetic Hakka man who had emigrated to the United States and returned to look for a wife. A restaurant worker himself, he wanted a woman whom he could marry at low cost and bring back to the United States. A Ling's low status in her father's family made her an ideal choice. After the young man managed to strike a deal with the father, the young couple soon married. One year later, A Ling joined her husband in the United States and began working in a Chinatown garment shop. She tried her best to live up to her in-laws' expectations of a good wife and good daughter-in-law at home and to earn as much as possible for the family by working hard in the shop.

However, despite all her efforts A Ling still failed to please the Lee family because her first child was a baby girl. The family's desire for a son made her life miserable in the first few years after her daughter was born. As she recalled, even when her baby girl was hospitalized with diarrhea and, overworked at home and at work, she fainted while taking care of her in the hospital, none of the Lees came to see her. The only person who offered her comfort was A Ying. A Ying cooked her traditional Cantonese medical soups almost every other day, replaced her to care for the baby after work, and kept her company whenever she needed. "I just can't tell you how much I owe A Ying," she said emotionally. "We are more than *sisters*."

A Ying's sympathy for A Ling did not come out of the blue. As she explained, it arose from her own experience before and after immigrating to the United States. She learned about A Ling's difficult life only when they rode together on the same train home the night before A Ling fainted in the hospital. A Ying noted that she too had suffered tremendously as a daughter, wife, and daughter-in-law. She was born to a family who lived on a farm in Xin Jie (New Territories) in Hong Kong, near the Chinese border. She was denied love in the family from the time she was born. Although she was the only daughter and the youngest in the family, she had to take care of the thirty pigs raised on her family's farm so that her three older brothers could go to school. As she put it, in her parents' eyes she was not worth a pig. She remembered that once a pig drowned in a well due to her oversight, and her father was so furious that he would have drowned her in the same well had he not been stopped by their neighbors.

Like A Ling, she was married in Hong Kong to a returned emigrant man from the United States who was looking for a wife. She admitted that she had tried desperately to impress the young man when first introduced to him, not because she was attracted to him, but because she could not wait to leave her family. However, her life after marriage was not as easy as she thought. Like A Ling, she endured hardships. The only difference was that her first child was a son, which did not reduce her sympathy for A Ling's situation.

Although as the two fastest hands in the shops they had been bitter rivals at their workplace, they became close after sharing their life stories. As the baby girl was recovering from her illness, A Ling asked A Ying to be her *kaih ma* (Cantonese: sworn mother), which was the closest relation two married Chinese women can form.[66] From then on they held nothing back from each other. Only then did they discover their employer's manipulation behind their rivalry. Having realized this, they decided to join efforts to fight back. A year later they left the shop together and moved to a new one.

Both took part in the historic Chinese garment workers' strike in 1982. A Ling took part despite having a high fever on that day. When asked what motivated her, she said, "You don't know how bad the bosses can be. If A Ying and I kept competing against each other, the boss could drive us crazy to work for him. If we workers don't unite, no one can save us. Besides, it was A Ying who asked me to join, so I joined."

Like many workers from Hong Kong, A Ying had prejudice against workers from China. Ironically, all her closest friends, almost without exception, were from China.[67] I brought this up one day when we were having a chat. She was at a loss as to how to respond. Speechless for a while, she said, "Strange, isn't it? I never thought about it. . . . After all, there are good people and bad people everywhere, aren't there?"

The story of A Ling and A Ying may not fit neatly into the conventional interpretation of the formation of working-class consciousness. Nevertheless, it points out an important factor that is largely missing in most studies of labor that simply focus on the workplace. Unlike their male counterparts, solidarity and labor activism among women workers was not merely a reaction to economic conflicts on the shop floor. Although A Ling and A Ying did not consider themselves to be militant workers and have laughingly brushed away any such suggestions, mutual sympathy between them, fostered by their similar status in the workplace and the family, laid a foundation for solidarity between them. Under particular circumstances, this solidarity among workers could turn into labor militancy to defend their rights. Without understanding this, one cannot fully understand the dynamics of political activism among women garment workers in New York's Chinatown.

Neat Craft Sports, Inc., a union shop at 198 Canal Street, 1956. (Courtesy of the UNITE Archives, Kheel Center for Labor-Management Documentation and Archives, Cornell University, Ithaca, N.Y.)

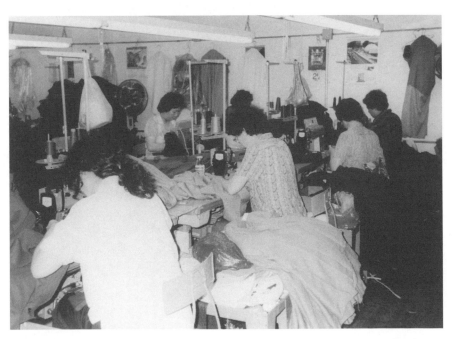

Working conditions in a Chinatown garment shop in 1992. (Photograph by Xiaolan Bao)

Chinese "ILGers" at the Labor Day Parade in 1963. (Courtesy of UNITE Local 23-25)

Chinese workers and their supporters from other ILGWU locals rallying in Columbus Park. (Photograph by Image Unlimited, courtesy of UNITE Local 23–25)

Chinese women workers on strike. The slogan in Chinese reads the same as in English. (Courtesy of UNITE Local 23-25; used by permission of the photographer, Earl Dotter)

A women striker wearing her union badge in preparation for the strike. (Courtesy of UNITE Local 23-25; used by permission of the photographer, Earl Dotter)

Shui Mak Ka speaking at the rally, with Shiree Teng serving as her interpreter. (Photograph by Image Unlimited, courtesy of UNITE Local 23-25)

Lily Moy speaking at the rally. (Photograph by Image Unlimited, courtesy of UNITE Local 23-25)

The lion dance leading the march of the workers. The slogan reads, "Where there is a union, there is strength." (Photograph by Image Unlimited, courtesy of UNITE Local 23-25)

Women workers on strike in front of a Chinatown shop in 1983. (Courtesy of UNITE Local 23-25)

Children in the Chinatown Day Care Center, officially established in 1984. (Courtesy of UNITE Local 23-25)

The Chinese CLUW at the 1988 Labor Day Parade advocating the need for quality day care. (Courtesy of UNITE Local 23-25)

New Year's celebration; the Chinese CLUW choir in 1987. (Courtesy of UNITE Local 23-25)

Local 23-25 delegates at the first national convention of the Asian-Pacific American Labor Association in 1993. (Courtesy of UNITE Local 23-25)

CHAPTER 7

Chinese Women Workers
and the ILGWU

Gender inequalities in trade unions have long been an issue in U.S. labor history. Since the mid-1970s, when Alice Kessler-Harris successfully turned the nagging question of why there are so few organized women workers around by asking how women have been kept out of unions, a wealth of studies on women and organized labor have emerged.[1] The New York women's garment industry, with an overwhelming majority of immigrant women in its workforce, and the ILGWU, the major labor organization of the industry, have become important venues for feminist scholars to investigate how class, gender, and ethnicity intersect to shape the status of women in organized labor.[2]

The picture presented in these studies is mixed. On the one hand, women fought for unionization, and unionized women workers, like their male counterparts, enjoyed union benefits and more meaningful representation in the workplace than did their unorganized sisters. On the other hand, unlike their male counterparts, women were always underrepresented in the ranks and frequently excluded from positions of leadership and power in their unions, which would in some cases fight to maintain men workers' interests at the expense of theirs. However, women's earlier experience of unionization also shows that the status of women in a union did not remain the same. Although different groups of ethnic workers shared many similar experiences, there were also differences among them, contingent on the time and the state of the union when they entered the industry. How we can explore and historicize the complexity of women's unionized experiences has become a major concern in the study of women's labor history.

Many studies have explored the record of the ILGWU in relation to women of various ethnic groups. None, however, focuses on the experience of Chinese

American women. The unionization of the Chinese garment workers reveals a complicated picture. To understand this, it is essential to review the experience of the Chinese women garment workers on the West Coast.

Unionization of the Early San Francisco Chinese Garment Industry: A Comparative Perspective

The ILGWU's first organizing efforts among Chinese workers took place on the West Coast.[3] The San Francisco Chinese began to enter clothing manufacturing in the 1860s, when the gold rush and the consequent development of the West generated great demands for clothing in the city. In 1869 Chinese men already were engaged in the production of pantaloons, vests, shirts, drawers, and overalls. By 1880 Chinese accounted for 80 percent of the shirtmakers, and Chinatown produced most of the ready-made clothing and nearly all the underclothing in the city.[4] Nevertheless, San Francisco never developed into a national garment production center.

Like workers elsewhere, the San Francisco Chinese clothes makers did not passively accept abusive working conditions. The city's *Evening Bulletin* recorded in 1895 that Chinese workers struck a Chinese sweatshop owner to demand higher wages.[5] By the end of the nineteenth century, three vertical guilds were founded to ease competition among the Chinese clothes makers. They were *Tong Ye Tang* (hall of common occupation), representing tailors as well as the ready-made clothing makers; *Juan Yi Hang* (guild of silk clothing), representing workers on shirts, ladies' apparel, and undergarments; and *Jing Yi Hang* (guild of brocaded clothing), representing makers of overalls and other clothing.[6] Admittance to these guilds required a period of apprenticeship. However, once in a guild a member was guaranteed certain basic employment rights and other benefits. Some guilds secured for their members a monthly wage much higher than the average Chinatown wage. Early Chinese clothes makers tried to join the San Francisco local of the ILGWU but were rejected due to the anti-Asian sentiments that prevailed among West Coast labor unions at the time.[7]

Early San Francisco Chinese clothes makers were all men. Chinese women did not enter the industry in significant numbers until the end of the nineteenth century, when competition with the East Coast garment industry intensified and the profit margins and wages of the San Francisco Chinatown garment industry plummeted. By the early twentieth century women had replaced men and become the majority of the workforce. However, they were consistently denied membership in the male-dominated Chinese clothing guilds and deprived of the benefits they offered.

The three Chinese clothing guilds began to decline at the end of the nineteenth century, with the numbers of male workers dwindling in the shops. By the end of the First World War they had either simply disappeared or were hardly functional. Him Mark Lai reports that a new unionist guild, the *Sanfanshi Gongyi Tongmeng* (workers' league of San Francisco), was founded by Chinese anarchosyndicalists in 1919. It began to target shirt manufacturers in the city and managed to sign agreements with thirty-two shops and win benefits for the workers. However, due to the universal opposition of employers, the guild was short-lived and practically defunct by 1927.[8] Although the garment industry became one of the major industries in San Francisco's Chinatown by the early 1930s, its workers remained largely unorganized.[9]

Working conditions, as Rose Pesotta witnessed on her visit to the Chinatown shops in 1934, were "worse than in the old tenement sweatshops on New York's East Side." She observed the following:

> Most of the workshops were situated in Chinatown, with its paradoxical swank retail stores on the street floor and unsanitary underground dwellings below, at times three cellars deep. . . . Three stories down, where daylight and fresh air never penetrated, we entered long narrow lofts with barely space enough between rows of sewing machines for one person to walk through. A wooden partition, the height of a seated operator, separated the machines. Thus workers were prevented from seeing or conversing with their neighbors. They toiled under electric lights, seldom bright enough and often unshaded.[10]

In the early 1930s the ILGWU began to organize the San Francisco Chinese workers, fearing that work would continue to leak from the union shops to Chinatown.[11] In 1934 the twenty-second convention of the ILGWU passed a resolution to endorse a campaign to organize Chinese workers in San Francisco. Pesotta, a committed unionist and the only female vice president of the ILGWU at that time, undertook the task. Despite her sincerity in carrying out her mission, she was unable to convince the Chinese workers that the ILGWU, with its anti-Asian history, would work to protect their interests. Nor could she obtain strong support within the ILGWU for accepting Chinese workers as members of the union. As a result, her organizing efforts failed.[12]

The ILGWU resumed its efforts in late 1934 and employed Ben Fee as its organizer. He was born in China, the son of an American-born Chinese interpreter, and came to the United States in 1922 at age thirteen. Like most young Chinese leftists of his time, he was committed to the Communist Revolution in China and actively joined the left-wing faction of the National Party before it split with the Communist Party in China. In early 1927, together with radical Chinese students in San Francisco, he joined the Communist Party of the United States. Anxious to put Marxist-Leninist theory into practice to improve workers' conditions, he actively participated in a series of labor activities in the Chinese community.[13] After he was hired by the ILGWU, he helped establish an independent Chinese Garment Workers' Union but the organization had little success in recruiting members due to the prevailing conservative sentiments in the community.[14]

The ILGWU's organizing efforts in San Francisco did not make any headway until 1936, when "heaven had opened up," as the ILGWU organizer Jennie Matyas put it.[15] Workers at the National Dollar Store were outraged because their employer had contracted work to other shops in an attempt to cut labor costs and, as a result, their wages dropped. This reduction in their incomes occurred when they needed money badly, both for surviving the Great Depression in the United States and supporting the Anti-Japanese War in China. Women workers were also unhappy about the gender inequalities in the shop. To redress the situation, a group of Chinese workers approached the ILGWU and expressed their eagerness to join the union.

Matyas welcomed the Chinese workers' decision enthusiastically. On November 13, 1937, she wrote to David Dubinsky, petitioning to form a Chinese charter. In the meantime, with her advice the workers managed to gather eighty signatures among workers in the shop in favor of unionization. The Chinese Ladies' Garment Workers' Union (CLGWU) was finally founded in the end of 1937, as ILGWU Local 341.

After the factory was unionized, the owner of the National Dollar Store decided to sell the store to the owner of the Golden Gate Company. The new and old owners of the factory both refused to comply with the union's demands. In response, the newly formed CLGWU decided to strike. The strike began on February 26, 1938. Lasting for 105 days, it became the longest strike in the history of the San Francisco Chinatown garment industry. The protracted strike tested the strength of the workers. Joe Shoong, the owner of the National Dollar Store, was one of the most influential and wealthy Chinese businessmen in the United States, and his store was the largest business establishment in the San Francisco Chinese community. With his prestige and reputation for philanthropic contributions to the community, Shoong was confident that he would win the battle.

The workers, however, were undaunted. As Jennie Matyas noted in 1955: "This was one strike I had in which I was able to turn almost everything over to the Chinese members themselves. They arranged their picketing schedules; they arranged who was to be on what shift. It was all very democratically done. They took turns, they lived up to it completely."[16]

Like workers in the early-twentieth-century shirtwaist workers' strikes in New York City, the San Francisco Chinese garment workers, who were also overwhelmingly women, sustained the strike with courage, determination, and devotion. They faced strong challenges in their own community, especially when tensions increased. The shop owner's wife cursed them as *ni di seui tohng yahn* (Cantonese: these damned Chinese). Although many in the community were sympathetic, they hesitated to support the workers because of the overarching influence of the shop owner. The strikers, however, persisted. They pledged to fight to the end to raise living conditions not only for themselves but also for other garment workers in Chinatown. Their commitment to the cause deeply touched Matyas:

> It was one of the most inspiring experiences I've ever had. . . . We had one girl, her name was Edna Lee. Pretty as could be. No parents, she was an orphan, and she had younger sisters or brothers. Anyhow, she was sort of the head of the family. I was told one day that she couldn't be on picket duty because she was sick, so I went to her house to see whether I could do anything. I saw the house in which she lived. It was one room somewhere on Grant Avenue, a kitchen was shared by the other tenants on the floor. When I went in to see Edna, she was in bed. I asked her how sick she was. "Oh," she said, "I'm not sick at all." "Well, why are you in bed if you're not sick at all?" "Well, you know, it's funny, but if I stay in bed I don't get hungry. And so I often stay in bed because then I don't get hungry."
> . . . The International was ready to help. I could have given Edna, this girl, some more money. I gave her a little more, but she wouldn't take it. She was very proud. She said that if that was all the others got, that's all she got.[17]

For more than fourteen weeks the strike was conducted without a turncoat. It finally ended with the employers signing a contract that met most of the workers' demands.

Subsequent events, however, were not as encouraging. Shortly after an agreement was reached, the new owner closed the shop and moved his operations to Los Angeles to avoid compliance. As a result, membership of the Chinese local shrunk from more than a hundred to fewer than forty. The remaining members voted to disband the Chinese local and join the predominantly white Local 101.[18]

Despite all the setbacks the strike was historic. It was the first time that Chinese garment workers, most of whom were women, proved their collective strength. As Sue Ko Lee, an active participant in the 1938 strike, noted, "The strike was the best thing that ever happened. It changed our lives."[19] The strike led them to see the importance of collective bargaining. Unionization not only resulted in better wages and working conditions but also, more importantly, fostered the workers' belief in labor activism and unionism. Although the Chinese local disbanded, its former members continued to take an active part in the labor movement and other political activities in the years that followed the strike.

What accounted for the ILGWU's success in organizing the San Francisco Chinese workers in the late 1930s? Some studies attribute it largely to good timing. They argue that the ILGWU's organizing efforts could not have been so successful without the convergence of the workers' strong desires to join organized labor outside Chinatown, the change in the Unites States's perception of the Chinese due to antiwar efforts in China (1937–45), and the enactment of the Wagner Act in 1935, which accorded greater legal protection to labor strikes than at any other time in the history of the U.S. labor movement.[20]

There is no denying that this assessment is valid, especially when we compare what happened in 1938 with the outcome of Rose Pesotta's organizing efforts in 1934 and that of Jennie Matyas's first three years in San Francisco.[21] However, as Sue Ko Lee has pointed out, Matyas's contribution to their struggle was also pivotal. From the beginning, when the workers expressed their intention to join the union, she lent them a sympathetic ear and warm support. She tried to understand them, respected their opinions, and helped to make their desires come true in every possible way. For example, when the workers preferred to form an all-Chinese local, she helped them translate their Chinese names into English, choosing words with positive meanings in English, such as "Fortunate," "Self-Reliant," and "Pine Tree, the Successful," in order to impress the leaders of the union and make the workers' desires more understandable and appealing to them.[22]

During the strike, when the Chinese workers were under attack from their employer in their own community, it was Matyas who tried to rally as many forces as possible in the labor movement outside Chinatown to support them. Following the strike, when the shop closed down and the newly unionized Chinese workers lost their jobs, Matyas helped every one of them to locate a job in union shops outside Chinatown. Her ability to understand the issues of Chinese women workers from their perspectives and her unfailing support made it easy for them to identify with her. As Sue Ko Lee related in an interview: "She's not Chinese but she's a woman. She's dedicated and she's honest. . . . She really wanted to help us. . . . Everyone trusted her within the group."[23]

Matyas's work at that time was not easy. She had to overcome all kinds of difficulties to support the Chinese strikers. First of all, there were problems caused by racist stereotyping in the union and society. As she recalled, "People who thought they knew Chinese tried to discourage me. They kept saying that there was no use, the Chinese were not dependable, the Chinese fought among themselves, they'd never stick to anything, they wouldn't do any picket duty. They tried to discourage me in every possible way."[24]

Conflicts also existed within the larger U.S. labor movement. For example, when Matyas began to make headway in organizing Chinese workers, the AFL organizer Ted Goldstein regarded the strike as an important opportunity to promote his own interests as well as those of his organization, and he jumped at the chance to try and reap the fruits of organizing the Chinese. The fierce competition between the two major unions in their organizing efforts created great confusion and uneasiness among the Chinese workers, who had little knowledge about organized labor beyond their own community.

Jennie Matyas also had to overcome barriers in her own mind. As she later admitted, she too was not immune to the prejudices of her time: "Let me confess that when I first worked with the Chinese, in spite of all my convictions and beliefs in non-discrimination, the Chinese were people I didn't really know. . . . I believe I was more influenced by the propaganda about smoking opium pipes than I knew. . . . I had a sort of a little shaky feeling inside when I went to Chinatown at night alone and when I came away from their homes at eleven or twelve or later and walked through Chinatown alone."[25]

The complex situation in the Chinese community was not easy for an outsider like Jennie Matyas to grasp in a short time. She was clearly confused by the political parties in the Chinese community, as illustrated in her interview with Gibbs:

> Gibbs: Was this Chinese boy [Ben Fee] a Communist in the Russian rather than the Chinese sense?
> Matyas: Yes . . . well, I didn't know enough in those days to know about the Russian sense or the Chinese sense. He was a member of the *Kuomintang*. We thought that was Communist.[26]

Nevertheless, Matyas's strong commitment to unionism propelled her forward and enabled her to do whatever was needed to obtain the union's goal. In her own words, "once I was there I'd wash dishes if necessary; it didn't matter what I was doing . . . unionism was in my blood." Like Rose Schneider, Pauline Freeman, Fannia Cohn, Rose Pesotta, and many other committed women unionists in the ILGWU, Jennie Matyas would not be content simply with the number of workers who joined the union. She believed in the importance of educating the unionized workers and felt that the strength of the union rested on its rank and file, which was reflected in her comments about organizing the Chinese workers: "My main concern for the time being was not Chinatown," she said. "It was to make the people who flocked to the union more than mere card holders, to bring unionism to them, to make them function as union members, and to make them understand what the union agreement was."[27]

Her understanding of unionism led her to see the importance of involving all members in union activities, regardless of their ethnic background. She respected the Chinese workers, tried to understand them, and followed their ways of doing things. As she put it, "When they came to me, I didn't press them. . . . I met with the Chinese in their homes a good deal, met them in restaurants after a while."[28] Her contact with the Chinese workers in turn helped her to better understand them, as she later acknowledged: "I . . . learned to have tremendous respect for their character. . . . I got to feel that if they said something, it was so. . . . They had their other characteristics, but from the point of view of dependability and integrity and all that, they were certainly as good as anybody else I know."[29]

As they began to understand each other, Matyas and the workers built up mutual trust. Not only did workers benefit and gain greater acceptance in the union, but Matyas also received crucial support from the workers in moments of crisis. For example, when Ted Goldstein of the AFL created confusion in Chinatown, Matyas was not aware. She admitted, "I didn't know about it until one day some of the workers came to me and said, 'Workers in Chinatown, him organized.' I said, 'What do you mean? "Him organized?" Well, speak up, man, what do you mean, "Workers in Chinatown, him organized?" They're not in the union.' 'No worry, no worry. Him only sign piece of paper. Nothing say, nothing say. Him only sign piece of papers.'"[30] With the information from the workers and their support, Matyas faced the challenge with confidence and successfully beat her rival. No wonder she later considered working with the Chinese workers to be one of the two most meaningful experiences in her life.

Like many committed unionists, however, Matyas also had her limits. She was cognizant of racism in the ILGWU, which she admitted years later in her reminiscences, but in public she would readily deny any such implications and defend the union's reputation at all cost.[31] Her utter commitment to the union also led her to fight against any political parties and ideologies that she believed would harm or had harmed the unity and other interests of the union.

This was reflected in her attitude toward the Communists. Like many women union members at the time, she at first felt frustrated by the union's internal fights against the Communists and left the organization. However, when she came to believe that the Communist Party had done "a very thorough job in smashing out unions," she vowed to fight them. It is only against this backdrop that one can understand why she would vigorously support the union's decision to fire the "young Chinese boy," who was sincere in the effort to improve the workers' lot, after she found out that he was a Communist, believing that his political inclination would harm the image of the union in the conservative Chinese community.[32] The irony is that Jennie Matyas, labeled an anti-Communist and an outsider of the community, managed to accomplish what a committed young Chinese Communist had tried but failed to do. Their different styles of work, the timing of their efforts, and the political inclination of the Chinese community are surely key to understanding this irony.

Matyas's contribution and the successful outcome of the 1938 strike proved that given the right timing, a committed union organizer who understood the workers, and the proper union strategies, Chinese workers could be as devoted and successful as any group of workers in staging and sustaining a struggle to defend their rights. They were able to form a cross-cultural coalition with labor forces outside Chinatown to combat the conservative antilabor forces in their own community. Regrettably, the ILGWU failed to build on this important legacy.

Matyas left San Francisco in 1939, shortly after the strike. Despite the consolidation of the ILGWU as a major labor organization and its growing influence in the 1940s and 1950s, its organizing campaigns in San Francisco's Chinatown remained lukewarm and sporadic, at best. The union's organizing efforts heated up a bit in the 1960s, when a substantial number of new Chinese immigrant women entered the industry.[33] However, it often won only a hollow victory or simply failed.

What happened as a result of the Chinese workers' strikes at a subcontracting shop of the Margaret Rubel Company in 1968 and later at the San Francisco Gold Company in 1973 provides some insight into the situation during this later period. Twelve workers in a Chinatown shop that contracted work from the Margaret Rubel Company were fired for demanding a union shop in 1968. With the ILGWU's support, they picketed the shop for four weeks. As in 1938, the owner signed the contract but closed the shop. The union could do nothing about it.

A similar situation with a similar outcome took place in 1973, when sixty Chinese workers mobilized 250 Latino, Filipino, Chinese, white, and black workers at the San Francisco Gold Company (formerly the Alvin Duskin Company) and struck. The workers won union recognition, but they were seriously demoralized after the strike because the union failed to employ effective strategies to check massive layoffs by the owner.[34]

Reasons for the union's failure to organize the San Francisco Chinese workers are many, but the union organizers' inability to develop effective strategies to organize the Chinatown shops, stemming from their lack of understanding of the Chinese community and the operation of its garment industry, is a major one. Although many Chinese workers actively participated in the strikes organized by the San Francisco local of the ILGWU, the union's repeated failure to organize successful strikes and its inability to sustain the outcome of successful strikes severely undermined workers' confidence.

To make things worse, in 1969, to make it easier for the union to organize and monitor the Chinese shops, Cornelius Wall of the ILGWU proposed an amendment to the San Francisco zoning ordinance to move the Chinese garment industry out of Chinatown. The proposal had the effect of putting a large number of Chinatown residents on welfare.[35] Although in the end the proposal was rejected by the Human Rights Commission, and the union gave in under pressure, the incident was perceived by Chinese garment workers as a lack of good faith on the part of the union, which led them to more firmly side with their community in controversies between the union and the community.

Throughout the 1980s the ILGWU's organizing effort in San Francisco's Chinatown remained unimpressive. According to Henry Shih-Shan Tsai, in 1981 there were an estimated 146 garment shops in the twenty-block rectangular area of Chinatown, employing 3,500 women workers and producing about 50 percent of San Francisco's apparel. Fewer than 40 percent of these shops were union shops, and only 20 percent of the workers were unionized.[36] Lacking institutional protection, Chinese garment workers in San Francisco continued to be subjected to labor abuses. To maximize their profit, some employers even demanded that their employees work at home, which was a gross violation of U.S. labor law.

As early as 1953 the ILGWU general executive board's annual reports began to acknowledge the union's difficulty in organizing the San Francisco Chinatown garment industry but showed no sign of improvement in the following decades.[37] The union continuously blamed the difficulty on the "language difficulties," "the distinctive way of life," the "age-old traditions of family and group loyalties," and "the complicated conditions" of the Chinese community.[38] Ironically, starting in 1971, the same union publication that had such coverage often boasted of the ILGWU's success in organizing New York's Chinatown.[39] One cannot help wondering what were the real causes of its failure in San Francisco.

Unionization of New York's Chinatown Garment Industry: A Brief History

In contrast to its efforts in San Francisco's Chinatown, from the 1960s the ILGWU's organizing efforts among Chinese garment workers in New York City appear to have been successful. Although there is no convincing historical evidence to determine the exact year when the ILGWU began organizing Chinese workers in New York's Chinatown, Wing Fong Chin, one of the earliest Chinese members of the ILGWU, recalled that the union's first organizing efforts in Chinatown in the 1950s met with resistance. Like their counterparts on the West Coast, New York Chinatown employers would hide garments in the basement and send workers home when the union organizers showed up in the area. Few Chinese workers were union members. Chin remembered that even by 1957 when she joined the union there were only about twenty union workers in the shop where she worked.[40] However, according to the local report, by the end of 1959 there were an estimated nine hundred Chinese members in ILGWU Local 23, the shirt and sportswear workers' local.[41]

Before Local 23 merged with Local 25, the blouse makers' local, at the end of 1963, most Chinese union workers affiliated with one of these two locals. Stanley Leung, the second Chinese business agent of ILGWU Local 23-25, remembered, however, that there were also some Chinese members in other locals. For example, he was a member of Local 35, the pressers' local, before he joined the union staff in 1974.[42]

The situation began to change drastically after 1965, when the garment shops mushroomed in Chinatown. With work guaranteed by the union-affiliated manufacturers, it was likely that the Chinese shop owners would be willing to come to terms with the union. In fact, in many cases the Chinese shop employers would go out of their way to offer their employees monetary or other incentives to join the union, as recounted by a longtime Chinatown worker: "I joined the union in 1958. It was because the midtown manufacturers told my boss that if his shop were not unionized, he would get no work. So, the boss came to us and said if we joined the union, we would have lots of work to do, and in addition, we would have vacation checks, and all kinds of benefits, etc. So, we joined the union. As a bonus, the boss subsidized every one of us $18 to cover our first union membership dues."[43] Her experience was typical among her contemporaries. This same process continued in much the same way for more than a decade. No wonder that the union's organizing effort in Chinatown was remarkably smooth, despite the general decline in the membership of nearly all the ILGWU affiliates in New York City. By 1968, there were already fifteen hundred Chinese ILGWU members in New York.[44]

The number of Chinese union members grew phenomenally after 1970. As early as 1971, with Chinese workers joining the union in large numbers, Local 23-25 had become the largest ILGWU local, with the largest concentration of Chinese members in the nation. Chinese women garment workers in New York City have since become the largest group of organized Chinese women workers in the United States. By 1974 Local 23-25 had a total of six thousand Chinese members.[45]

Like other union members, the Chinese workers were entitled to enjoy all benefits from the moment they joined the union. Among the most important of these were health benefits. Local 23-25 added the benefits of Blue Cross, Blue Shield, and a major medical policy to its health and welfare program as early as 1969 and a Blue Cross family plan to its benefit program in 1974, much earlier than the rest of the union.[46] Since the majority of Chinese workers joined after 1969, they readily enjoyed these benefits.

In addition, carrying on its tradition as a union of and for immigrants, ILGWU Local 23-25 also developed special programs for its Chinese members. For example, beginning in December 1957 the ILGWU began to advertise its benefit program in the *China Daily News*.[47] Thanks to the efforts of Ben Fee, who had moved from San Francisco to New York to become the first Chinese organizer in the local, the first handwritten synthesized Chinese edition of the *Local 23 News* had already appeared by 1960. Since then, a synthesized Chinese version has been published periodically and become an important source for its Chinese members to learn about the organization.[48] The early handwritten Chinese Local 23-25 news gained headline publicity in *Justice,* the ILGWU's official publication. Its May 1966 issue reprints part of an issue of the Chinese *Local 23 News* on its front page, emphasizing that "it takes two months to 'set' the paper because all lettering is by hand."[49] The Chinese editions of the *Local 23-25 News* were put in print and became more regular in the late 1970s, when the number of the union's Chinese members grew immensely.

In 1968 the union began to offer its Chinese members free English classes at the Chinese Catholic Church at 29 Mott Street. By 1974 the union reported that more than a thousand Chinese members had attended the classes, which its leaders believed to be "the most successful part of our educational program."[50] Starting from about that same year, Local 23-25 has regularly organized tours to China and Hong Kong as well as to different parts of the United States in an effort to involve its Chinese members in its activities. In 1977 the union's film, shown to all new members, was given a Cantonese soundtrack. To extend its influence and boost its membership drives among Chinese workers, the ILGWU also bought time on closed circuit radio, which still plays in every Chinatown garment shop today.[51]

How successful was the union in integrating its Chinese members? In his testimony to the U.S. Commission on Civil Rights on July 2, 1974, Shelley Appleton, the manager-secretary of Local 23-25, answered as follows: "I'd say that our success has been considerable. Our Chinese members, very uncertain and timid at the beginning, are now asserting their rights in the shop. They have become among our most active members, and this is everywhere visible in our local's affairs."[52]

The leaders of the union took credit for the local's "exemplary achievements" in integrating its Chinese members over the years. Shelley Appleton was promoted to the general secretary-treasurer of the international in 1977. Jay Mazur, the former assistant manager of the local, succeeded Appleton as the local's manager that same year. In February 1982 the New York City Central Labor Council granted Jay Mazur the Distinguished Service Award for the local's achievements under his leadership.[53]

While the local was celebrated for its remarkable achievements, the workers, labor activists, and staff members in New York's Chinatown whom I interviewed have presented a much more complicated picture. When asked about their union experience, their response was mixed. The overwhelming majority singled out the union's health insurance as the most meaningful benefit in the garment industry. Since the garment industry was the only unionized industry in the Chinese community, and the ILGWU was the only institution in New York's Chinatown that could afford to offer its members family health insurance, joining the union became indispensable for workers and their families. Workers who had benefited from special union programs and those who had received the timely support of union officials in their fight against unscrupulous employers also had positive memories.

The workers' overall response, however, was not as positive as the union leaders would like to hear. Their primary complaints stemmed from the incompetent union operation on the floor. To this date the union operation consists of two major types of functionaries: business agents and shop representatives. Business agents are full-time union officials assigned to represent the union in a number of shops. They are responsible for enforcing the union contract and handling all union business on the shop floor, which includes taking care of workers' grievances, organizing new workers, bargaining with the employers, and protecting workers from abusive management. Shop representatives, or shop stewards in the standard union language, are workers in the shops who volunteer their services to the union. They are expected to understand union contracts, serve as the union's watchdogs, and help the business agents enforce union contracts. Since they receive no compensation from the union, this position requires devotion on the part of the worker.

Workers' responses regarding the operation of union business agents in the

Chinatown shops were again mixed. They spoke highly of some business agents or some aspects of their work. Lily Moy was among the Chinese business agents praised by workers and labor activists.[54] She was the first and only Chinese woman business agent of ILGWU Local 23-25 before 1982. Only five feet tall and still in her early twenties when she began her career as a business agent, Moy never hesitated to stand up and speak for workers during her five-year service at Local 23-25. As many workers recalled, she served with her heart. Not only did she fight for their interests, but she was also mindful of promoting labor militancy on the floor. She extended her firm support to those workers who dared to stand up and fight for their rights. To redress the underrepresentation of Chinese in its ranks and on its staff, she recommended qualified workers to the union whenever she spotted them on the floor. A number of Chinese staff members currently serving in the office of ILGWU Local 23-25 were recommended by her.

Moy's commitment to workers' interests had a lot to do with her own family background and life experience. She was born to an emigrant family in Taishan, Guangdong Province. Her paternal grandfather left home at an early age and was one of the earliest laundrymen in Brooklyn. In 1966, at a very young age, her father brought her with him to join her grandparents in New York, leaving her mother and other siblings in China. Since her father lived separately from the family, she grew up with her grandparents in Brooklyn.

She noted that her early life with her grandfather aroused her interest in Chinese history and culture and fostered her attachment to New York's Chinese community. Even today she fondly recalls the wonderful time she had every Sunday, when her grandfather took her to Chinatown in her beautiful Sunday dress to meet his old friends. In addition to all the delicacies at the Chinatown restaurants, what intrigued her most were the stories about her grandfather and his friends' bitter old days, which the older generation used to talk about at their gatherings. Young as she was at that time, she already felt the urge to redress the injustices imposed on her community.

However, except for these Sunday meetings, her early life with her grandparents was not a pleasant one. Not only did she have to endure the overbearing control exerted by her grandfather, who was entrenched in traditional Chinese culture; she was also frequently caught in the conflicts between her grandparents, who themselves suffered from an unhappy traditional marriage.[55] At the age of sixteen, facing a groundless accusation by her grandfather and once again caught in the conflicts between the old couple, the young Moy could not endure the dysfunctional family life any more. Despite her record as an excellent student at her high school, she decided to end her schooling, leave the family, and stand on her own feet.

Life was indeed hard on her at first, but it has also put her strong will and talent to a good test. With a kind of fortitude unusual for her age, the young Moy managed not only to survive but also to prove her worth in society. As she worked at various jobs and even tried her hand at a management position, she also seized every opportunity to continue her education. She finally landed a position as a bookkeeper in a Chinatown garment shop. It was during these days that she was exposed to life in the Chinatown shops. She witnessed the plight of workers in the shop and felt deeply for them. "I joined the union with a purpose," she repeatedly said during our interview. "The union was not doing well. I wanted to give them the benefit of the doubt. . . . I wanted them to explain to me what was going on out there [in the union] so that I could tell the workers in the shops. . . . The workers had many difficulties. They did not know English and no one who could speak English liked to help them. . . . I believed my duty was for the workers, for my people, and for my own community."

With this clear mission in mind, she joined the union staff in 1979 and became the first and youngest Chinese woman business agent of ILGWU Local 23-25. With her knowledge of the working conditions in the shops and a command of the three major dialects in the community—Mandarin, Taishan, and Cantonese—she handled her responsibilities with confidence. Although her youthful assertiveness was often initially misunderstood by some workers as arrogance, she was able to develop a special bond with the workers shortly after she began serving them. As she fondly recalled, "Workers in the shops treated me like their daughter or granddaughter . . . . They needed my help, but they also taught me a lot. After knowing me for a while, they would say, 'hey, you silly little girl, you are, after all, not as bad as you first looked like.' . . . It is a dear memory that will live forever in my mind."

Moy's performance seems to have been unusual among the union business agents, since workers' overall comments on their work were negative. As a union researcher once commented about the business agents who served the Chinatown shops, it was "not that a few were bad and the majority were good, but that the majority were bad."[56] Workers' complaints about the agents included their infrequent visits to the shops. One worker described the situation: "The BA of my shop comes only once, or at most twice, a year. Every time he comes, he would only talk to the boss. . . . In addition, the BAs of my shop are changed so often that like the merry-go-round paper-cut figures on the Chinese lanterns, they come and go, with no relevance to me."[57]

Workers complained about the agents' close relationships with the employers. Some reported that they did not realize such behavior was problematic until they worked in a garment shop outside Chinatown. The response of one worker, who had worked in a Chinatown shop but was working in a midtown non-Asian-owned garment shop at the time of our interview, seems typical:

> I didn't realize that BAs in Chinatown and in midtown *lo fan* [Cantonese: Westerners'] shops were so different until I started working here. . . . Here, the *lo fan* BA won't go to the boss unless workers in the shop have complaints or problems with the boss, or the shop has labor violations. They avoid having contact with the

boss for no good reason. But in Chinatown, the BAs of almost all the shops where I worked enjoyed dealing with the bosses. Whenever they came to the shops, they would go to the bosses. They talked intimately and endlessly with the bosses. Some even ate their food . . . as if they were from the same family. . . . They would not come to us unless they had some new union policies to announce or union activities which requested workers' participation.[58]

This worker's response might have idealized the situation outside Chinatown. There might also be some justification to the assertions of some non-Chinese business agents that they could go to the bosses because they were the only ones in the shops who spoke English. However, this response suggests that there was little communication between agents and workers in the Chinatown shops.

To make things worse, as the workers have pointed out, some Chinatown business agents were not only friendly to employers, while tolerating violations of labor contracts in the shops, but were also unsympathetic or even antipathetic to any form of labor militancy on the shop floor. Mrs. Zheng's experience can help us to understand this:

I once worked in a shop on Canal Street. It was a typical family shop. Almost every member of the boss's family was working there. . . . So bosses were everywhere in the shop and we workers had no say in whatever matters. . . . It happened that the boss believed it would be a waste of money to let the old woman seated next to me continue to use the sewing machine. He wanted to get rid of her. To force her to leave, the boss and everyone in the family—his wife, his sisters, his nieces, his nephews—took turns cursing the elder worker from the boss's office. The office was right behind the worker, but they cursed so loudly that no one would not hear it. . . .

This had been going on for almost a week, but the old woman endured the situation quietly and stayed, because she had no other place to go and she needed the money. The curses, however, got on my nerves. I could not stand them any more. I finally blew up, "Could you people be more humane? If she was your own mother, how would you feel?" I just said this but it was enough to invite retaliation. . . . The old woman finally gave up and left, and I became the victim. I didn't want to give in, so I stayed on. Then, in addition to the barrage of curses, they turned the huge electric fan to blow to my face. . . . The wind blown out of the fan was so strong that I felt terribly dizzy by the end of the day when I got home. . . .

My son said I should go to the union because it was supposed to represent workers. In addition, he also said it would not let out the identities of the workers who made complaints about their employers. So I called the BA of my shop and told him what had happened to me. What I found totally unexpected was, the BA whom I called came to my shop the next day. He publicized my case and asked workers in the shop to submit an eyewitness account in writing to testify what I had told him—these were all done in front of the boss. Who dared to support me with the boss glaring on them like a tiger eyeing its prey? . . . Of course, I lost the case.

Realizing my hopeless and helpless position, I left the shop. For quite a long time, I was blacklisted in Chinatown. I could not stay at a job for long, because whenever the bosses found out who I was and the reason I left this shop, they did not like it. . . . I was outraged whenever I thought about my experience with this BA. I have absolutely no confidence whatsoever in the union.[59]

My interviews suggest that Mrs. Zheng's experience was not unusual among militant workers in Chinatown before 1982. Not only did a number of business agents fail to support workers and defend their rights, some even collaborated with the shop owners to dampen militancy on the floor. They confided to the employers the names of workers who had made complaints to the union, and the workers had to suffer the subsequent retaliation from their employers. Forms of retaliation ranged from insults and criticism in front of their fellow workers to constantly picking at their work, sabotaging their machines, and even talking the workers' own families into repudiating them. In the worst cases, the union business agents simply took matters into their own hands and reprimanded the workers in front of their employers for their loyalty to the union. As a militant worker recalled, this part of her experience had been so painful that afterward she could not sleep for several nights.

Given their helpless situation in the shops, workers who were determined to stand up and defend their interests had to prepare themselves to take all the dire consequences on their own. As a major organizer of the 1982 strike angrily recalled: "Every time I fought for workers' interests in the shop, I had to swallow the bitter fruits myself. Who would help me? No one. . . . At that time, if someone told me that this country had labor organizations which helped workers, I would think she or he was day-dreaming."[60]

The business agents' unresponsiveness to the workers' interests severely undermined labor activism in the Chinatown shops. Many workers were reluctant to assume the responsibilities of a shop steward. Some even changed their workplace when elected. As a result, in a number of shops those who were able to represent workers' interests and were respected by their fellow workers refused to serve, while many of those who did serve tended to be handpicked by either the unsympathetic business agents with the consent of the employers or simply by the employers themselves. This further undermined the union's operation on the floor.

Since many of these problems were also to various degrees shared by the few Chinese business agents in the Chinatown area and they could not use the language barrier to defend their case, workers were quick to develop an even stronger dislike for them. As a result, when asked whether they preferred Chinese agents in their shops, many workers showed no clear preference. Some put it vaguely: "Well, I don't know. So long as they are concerned about the interests of workers and do a good job, they are good BAs. Whether they are *louh faan* or Chinese, it doesn't matter to me." Others put it in a more explicit and straightforward way: "I like the *louh faan* BAs. They don't have that much *gam chihng*

[Cantonese: emotional ties] with the bosses. . . . The Chinese BAs talk too much with the bosses." These comments laid bare the limited advantage of ethnic commonality in the case of unsympathetic business agents.

What accounted for the problematic behavior of some business agents on the floor? The most common speculation was that they had accepted *toi dai chin* (Cantonese: money under the table) from the shop owners. The ILGWU did fire a few business agents for their criminal and other flagitious behavior.[61] However, as a number of union staff members observed, the problem was more institutional than individual. Holding to the organizational principle of the Protocol of Peace, the union's bureaucratic leadership was more concerned about the reactions of the employers than those of its rank and file. This was especially true in the late 1970s and early 1980s, when the garment industry went downhill again in New York. Facing a declining industry, the union chose to defend workers' interests by trying to keep the industry in the city, which often led to defending the employers' interests.

The union's attitude not only alienated its rank and file but created tremendous difficulties for the work of the business agents. As a Chinese business agent once complained,

> It is really difficult for us BAs to be human beings on this planet. . . . The union authorities always say that we should avoid open confrontations with the bosses and, "to a degree," tolerate contract violations in the shops. But to what degree? No one knows. They've never drawn a clear line for us. We can only rely on our own understanding or even imagination to deal with the situation. . . . What concerns the union leaders most is our cooperation with the employers. . . . Nothing but cooperation. . . . So long as we can do a good job in cooperating with the bosses, . . . or more than that, knowing their complaints about the situation and helping them to solve the problems before the situation comes to a head, our supervisors are happy, . . . Of course, the workers are not happy. They don't think much about us and even look down upon us. . . . But, what can we do, we are paid by the union.[62]

According to some union staff members, not only did the union leaders have no patience to listen to problems in the shops, they barely supervised their business agents' operations on the floor. This virtually encouraged many business agents to "play monkey" with them, in a union researcher's own words.[63] By seeing and hearing no evil in the shops and speaking no evil to their supervisors, the business agents managed to paint a mythical picture of peace for their supervisors. This picture created a comfortable world for the union leadership and the business agents. Seeing no possibility of changing the situation and content with a regular income that most of them might not have otherwise earned, many business agents were fearful of losing their comfortable jobs. The business agents' lethargic work style became so entrenched that the few who were inclined to rock the boat were ostracized by their colleagues.

The problems with the business agents stemmed not only from the attitudes of individual leaders but also from the union's "top-down" organizing policy, which can be considered an outgrowth of the Protocol of Peace signed in the early twentieth century. This policy was fully implemented in New York's Chinatown. Emphasizing the "cultural peculiarities" and the inaccessibility of the Chinese community and describing it as "a clan, a closed, secretive organization," the leaders of the union considered the top-down policy to be the easiest and most effective way to succeed.[64]

To organize the Chinatown garment shops, the union organizer would first approach the midtown manufacturers to appeal to their desire for labor stability to guarantee production. After securing manufacturers' promises to offer jobs only to unionized Chinatown shops, the union organizer would approach the Chinese contractors. Realizing that unionization could guarantee them work and union benefits for their workers at practically no cost on their part, the Chinese shop owners were more than willing to cooperate. With the consent of the owners, the union organizer would then sign up all the workers in the shops to be union members. Almost all the Chinatown shops were organized in this manner.

This top-down organizing strategy gained quick and easy success for the union but diminished its relationship with its rank-and-file members, since the union did not attempt to involve its Chinese members in its organizing efforts, nor did it offer them any meaningful follow-up education after they were in the organization. As a result, except for the family health insurance, unionization had a limited impact on most of the Chinese union workers on the shop floor. As a worker once stated, "The union doesn't really do anything, only when you get sick, maybe."[65] Her response is representative of most Chinatown workers. A scholar therefore concluded, "To many Chinese, the union is nothing more than a health-insurance company."[66]

While health benefits were the major reason for Chinese workers to join the union in the 1970s and 1980s, for those who worked to meet their family needs and hardly had the time to utilize the benefits even when they were ill, the union hardly existed. As a major organizer of the 1982 strike recalled: "I never knew that a union really existed until 1981 when the *louh faan* business agent came and asked whether I would like to join their training program. . . . Of course, I paid the dues, but I thought it was like the Social Security Tax, everyone had to pay in order to get the benefits later."[67] For the same reason, even though Chinese members were eligible to attend the union's extensive programs the moment they joined, many did not have time to enjoy them. This was especially true for new immigrant workers, who struggled to survive in their new land.

Problems in the unionization of New York's Chinatown garment industry were exacerbated by the union's election system, which was largely carried over from the mid-1920s, when the system was established. In theory, business agents, along with other officials of the local, were elected every three years by and from its rank and file, but actual practice allowed members very little democracy.[68] Again emphasizing the "uniqueness" of Chinese culture and the "inaccessibility" of Chinatown, the union leaders would prepare a list of nominees prior to the election and ask its Chinese members to "vote" for them at the time of election. To qualify for a nomination one had to be bilingual and known and accepted by the union leaders. Not many Chinese rank and file were able to meet these qualifications. Chances were even slimmer for women workers, since most of them spoke little or no English and hardly caught the union leaders' attention.

It is not surprising that the number of Chinese business agents and executive board members was small in relation to the total number of Chinese members in the union. In 1977, for example, when the estimated number of Chinese members grew to almost nine thousand, nearly half of the local's membership, only four of twelve business agents and ten of thirty-five executive board members were Chinese.[69] While Chinese staff members were greatly underrepresented, the ratio of women to men among them was even more lopsided. Despite the fact that Chinese women workers formed the majority of its members, Chinese women organizers and business agents numbered one each before the 1982 strike.

Although the gender of union officials does not necessarily prevent them from representing the interests of workers of the other gender, this was not the case in the New York Chinatown garment industry. In truth, most of the Chinese male union officials also came from the rank and file. The large number of shops each of the business agents was assigned also made it difficult for them to visit as frequently as they should. However, there were also cultural factors that kept them away from workers. Like male workers in the shops, with an anxiety to maintain their manhood in an overwhelmingly female industry, many disdained any contact with women workers, whose interests they were paid to represent. The following remark made by a Chinese male business agent in an unguarded moment is very revealing: "You are asking about them? Well, they [the workers] are all *a sim a mouh* [Taishan dialect: 'aunts and grannies']. What can you expect from them? They don't know anything. So I never bother to talk to them—you know, it is a waste of time. . . . I only talk to the bosses, they are men, they mean business."[70]

With this attitude, these men could not truly represent the interests of women workers. Nevertheless, they formed the majority of Chinese business agents. Some union leaders argued that the number of women business agents was small because the work was difficult for women to handle. Chinese women workers disagreed, however, arguing that the exemplary service rendered by Lily Moy in the earlier years and other Chinese women business agents after the strike demonstrates the inanity of this argument. What mattered most, as they contended, was not simply the gender identity of the business agents but their sincerity in defending workers' interests.

While the union's election system had perpetuated problems with its officials, the long history of sexism and racism in the leadership of the union prevented them from being corrected. As a longtime garment worker put it, "The sexist male agents in Chinatown are actually nothing. They are only the sons or little grandsons of their union bosses. Since they all have the same attitude, how can we expect the union to correct their attitude?" This worker did not have any knowledge of women's previous experience in the city's garment industry. Nor did she know the situation in any union garment shop outside Chinatown when she made this remark. She made this observation based on her own experience on the shop floor. With such a mindset, it was difficult for the Chinese women workers to identify with the union.

The union's incompetent operation on the floor undermined its ability to enforce labor regulations in the Chinatown shops. As a result, management in the Chinatown garment industry remained almost as strong as their counterparts in nonunion industries in the community. This was particularly true in the late 1970s, when competition mounted in the Chinatown garment industry. Seeing that the union had no commitment to improve their lives, the majority of women workers continued to identify themselves first and foremost as members of their family and community rather than members of the working class.

The union's failure to foster unionism among its Chinese members had a retarding impact on developing labor solidarity among its members and increasing workers' influence in the Chinese community. This has to be understood in the historical context of New York's Chinatown and the experience of immigrant workers in their original places. New York's Chinatown has never been a hotbed for the growth of unionism. Even up to the late 1970s, unionization remained irrelevant for most Chinese workers. This does not mean that there had never been any labor activism in the community. On the contrary, as Peter Kwong has argued, the history of New York's Chinatown is one of ongoing conflict between management and the working class.[71] Chinese workers in New York, like their counterparts on the West Coast, began to organize and defend their rights as early as the late nineteenth century. These efforts, however, did not have a lasting impact on transforming the community's politics. The history of unionization in the two major traditional Chinese businesses in the city, the laundry and restaurant businesses, can help us to better understand this.

As Renqiu Yu has meticulously documented, New York Chinese laundrymen began organizing among themselves in the late nineteenth century. In 1933 they founded the Chinese Hand Laundry Alliance, which vigorously challenged traditional forces inside and outside the community. Influenced by the situation in the United States and encouraged by new ideas emanating from a changing China, members of the organization tried to bring new values and practices to Chinatown.[72] The organization played an important role in supporting Chinese resistance efforts against the Japanese invasion and had a strong impact on the political life of the Chinese community in New York City in the late 1930s. The CHLA, however, began to decline in the late 1940s. The absence of support from the larger American labor movement, added to competition from the white laundry businesses, the shifts and turns of the political situation in China, and the repressive political atmosphere of American society in the immediate post-war era, contributed to its decline.[73]

Chinese restaurant workers and employers in New York City formed the Chinese Restaurant Association (CRA) in the early 1930s. The American Federation of Labor (AFL) began to recruit Chinese restaurant workers in the mid-1930s. In late 1939 it managed to recruit a number of Chinese workers and establish the Chinese Restaurant Workers Federation, a Chinese local affiliated with AFL Local 211. Encouraged by this success, the AFL decided to expand its organizing efforts to Chinatown, since most unionized Chinese workers worked in restaurants outside Chinatown.

AFL organizers came to Chinatown and called on workers to demand a minimum wage and better working conditions through collective action. Feeling threatened by the union's aggressive move, the Chinatown CRA held a meeting among Chinese workers and community leaders. Stressing ethnic commonality between Chinese restaurant workers and their employers, it decided to change its name to New York Chinese Restaurant Workers' and Merchants' Association (NYCRWMA). AFL Local 211 had little success in recruiting Chinatown workers. Even the few who had joined the local soon dropped out under pressure from the NYCRWMA and the community.[74]

Chinese restaurant workers renewed their organizing efforts in the late 1960s, when the community was further polarized along class lines by the new increment of Chinese immigration to the city.[75] In 1978, frustrated by ill treatment and the unreasonable demands of their employers, dining room employees in Uncle Tai's, a fancy Upper East Side Chinese restaurant, sought help from AFL-CIO Local 69, the Hotel Employers' and Restaurant Employees' Union (HERE). With the help of the HERE, the Chinese workers succeeded in forming a union. The unionization of Uncle Tai's restaurant set off unionizing drives among other Chinese restaurant workers in New York City. Despite management's vigorous resistance, six midtown Chinese restaurants joined the HERE in 1978.[76]

In October 1978, encouraged by the successful outcome of its uptown organizing efforts, Local 69 extended its organizing efforts to Chinatown. The Silver Palace, one of the largest restaurants in Chinatown, was its first target. Claiming that three workers in the restaurant had already applied for membership, the union pushed for unionization. The union's effort evoked strong reactions from the Chinese employers. Wu Bin, the president of the NYCRWMA, held a press conference in Chinatown, arguing that the Chinatown restaurant business had been able to thrive in the past few decades because it had not been influenced by organized labor outside the community. Emphasizing the importance of ethnic solidarity between the workers and their employers, he urged his fellow restaurant owners to improve working conditions and Chinese workers to establish a community-based Chinese union.

When the HERE escalated its organizing efforts and insisted that it represented the Chinese workers, management of the Silver Palace simply put up four workers at a Chinatown press conference to denounce the HERE and deny its legitimacy in Chinatown. In the meantime, Wu Bin also claimed to have received two letters from the HERE threatening his life and solicited police help. The union denied the charge, but its organizing efforts in Chinatown were already severely crippled.

When the HERE suffered a serious setback in Chinatown, disappointment also began to grow among unionized Chinese workers outside Chinatown. Discouraged by the union's failure to aggressively enforce labor contracts and represent their interests, these workers began to turn their attention back to their community. In 1979 they helped form a community-based labor organization, the Chinese Staff and Workers Association (CSWA).

In the summer of 1980, another labor dispute, initiated by the Chinese workers themselves, broke out at the Silver Palace. The waiters were outraged because business was good and management unreasonably asked them to contribute additional shares of their tips to the business manager and other service sectors in the restaurant. When they protested, fifteen of them were fired. In desperation, the Silver Palace waiters approached the CSWA, which soon mobilized a number of Chinese restaurant workers who worked outside Chinatown to render their support. The picket line was set up to force management into negotiation. The strike received wide-ranging support from inside and outside Chinatown and lasted for an entire year. Management finally came to terms with the strikers.

Realizing that simply getting back their jobs would not guarantee them job security in the future, the workers decided to form a union. They split, however, over the question of whether they should join the HERE or remain community-based. In the end, the workers voted to form individual-restaurant-based labor unions, independent of the HERE. This decision soon proved to be inherently impracticable. Unions based on individual restaurants could not survive, nor could they effectively help workers to protect their interests.

What is important to notice is that as workers' militancy grew, so did employers' antiunionism. The employers' attitude was the result not only of economic but also cultural factors. As Randy Wei, a former Chinese organizer and business representative of HERE Local 100, observed, "'The bosses could have paid for union benefits for ten years with the money they spent on legal fees to fight the union. The main issue wasn't economic, it was the idea of "face," . . . the boss felt he would lose face by giving in to the union. He functioned on the old feudal idea, like master and serf.'"[77] Such an attitude found a congenial climate in the 1980s. The antiunion political climate spurred by the Reagan administration and the fact that employers could use bankruptcy under Chapter 11 to evade the restrictions of labor law frustrated attempts to organize Chinatown's restaurant workers.[78]

The Chinese workers' struggle had at best a limited impact on the HERE.

Learning from its setbacks in Chinatown and impressed by the Chinese workers' determination to fight for their cause, the HERE did hire several Chinese organizers after the Silver Palace labor dispute and developed a mutually supportive relationship with the CSWA to resume its organizing drives among Chinese workers. Problems remained, however. The prevalent bureaucratic and racist influences in the union finally drove even the most committed Chinese American labor activists from its staff.[79] The Chinese restaurant and laundry workers' experiences with the major American labor unions have left some unpleasant memories not only among the workers but also in the community at large. These have provided employers with handy ammunition to fuel anti-labor sentiments in the community.

Given the racist attitude of the American labor movement outside the Chinese community and the mission of community journalism to inform and defend the interests of the community, even progressive community newspapers would emphasize the importance of ethnic solidarity and encourage the solution of problems within the community when labor disputes occurred in Chinatown. This attitude was clearly demonstrated in the matter-of-fact remarks made by a close friend of mine, who had worked for a leftist community newspaper for years: "You are asking me why I said that? How could I have said otherwise? We are the voice of the community. We have to fight for its solidarity and prosperity. . . . The American unions are too anti-Chinese, they have a history behind—Come on, you know all that. . . . How can we trust them? I have a lot of sympathy for the workers, but Chinese workers' problems can only be solved by the Chinese themselves. . . . I am not going to fool my own people."[80] This emphasis on ethnic solidarity left little room for organized labor to grow in the community, much less to form cross-cultural alliances with labor forces outside the Chinese community. As a result, the influence of labor remained weak, and employers continued to dominate the community by projecting themselves as its spokesmen.

While organized labor was historically weak in the community, the Chinese immigrant workers' perceptions of unionism and organized labor were often influenced by the political and economic situation in their native places. This posed a great challenge to the ILGWU and accentuated the importance of educating its new members. The union officials, however, seem not to have realized this.

Still holding on to the picture of the China he left in the early 1920s, the Chinese business agent Ben Fee made the following remarks to the press in 1972: "China is not an industrial society. The immigrants don't understand the meaning of strike. They are hard-working people who grab as much as they can get so as to make a dollar more. Any benefits that come their way are considered gravy."[81] His remarks fully demonstrate his ignorance of recent changes in the native places of the new immigrant workers.

Although the situation of Hong Kong and Taiwan, the two major sources of

Chinese immigrants to the United States, might not comply with some advanced industrial patterns in the West, they were by no means nonindustrial in the late 1960s and 1970s. Around the 1960s, the economies of Hong Kong and Taiwan began to take off. Producing textiles, garments, electronics, plastics, and other manufactured goods primarily for U.S. and Japanese markets, they soon developed into two of the four major economic powers in Asia.

As in many other developing regions in the world, women provided employers in Hong Kong and Taiwan with the least expensive labor force.[82] In many respects, the first generation of women workers in Hong Kong and Taiwan resembled the early-twentieth-century immigrant women workers in New York's garment industry. They came from poor families, had only a primary school education, and began working in the factories between the ages of thirteen and fifteen. Most of them worked to supplement the family income as dutiful daughters. Their earnings enabled their brothers, and sometimes a younger sister, to gain a higher education and move up the social ladder. Some continued to work in the factories in Hong Kong or in small family-run workshops in Taiwan after marriage.[83] Most worked at home.

However, unlike many of the early Eastern European garment workers in New York, many first-generation women workers in Hong Kong and Taiwan were not exposed to radical ideology.[84] Unionization had never been a major part of their lives, mainly due to the political climate. Fearing that higher wages and labor activism would drive capital out of the British colony, and in an effort to "make doing business easier," the Hong Kong government nominally adopted a "noninterference" policy in industrial relations, which in reality favored management over labor and collective bargaining.[85]

This was especially the case after the 1967 upheaval. In 1968, to ease tensions between management and labor, the Hong Kong Commissioner of Labour announced a program promising health benefits, accident compensation, labor protection, and the improvement of health and safety standards in the workplace while at the same time bringing in two advisors from England to help initiate labor tribunals, which made laws against picketing more stringent than ever. A new Trade Union Ordinance prevented workers in trades and industries from forming large, multitrade unions. All these new policies greatly sapped the vitality of labor activism in Hong Kong.

The strength of organized labor in the industrial sector was further weakened by divisions among the labor unions after the end of the Second World War and the growth in the civil service sector after the late 1960s. By 1982 the major labor unions in Hong Kong included the pro-Beijing Hong Kong Federation of Trade Unions (FTU), the pro-Taiwan Trade Union Congress (TUC), and a myriad of apolitical and nonaffiliated unions, such as the Hong Kong and Kowloon Federation of Labor Organizations and the Hong Kong Christian Industrial Committee. Although some unions, such as the FTU, addressed issues of exploitation, none of these unions was strong enough to challenge the status quo in the colony under British rule. John Young estimates that by the 1980s only 4 percent of the labor force were covered by contracts, and even these contracts were often not detailed.[86] Workers therefore had to look elsewhere to improve their lives.

Although the labor conditions and educational levels of the younger generation of working-class families in Hong Kong began to improve in the late 1970s, it was not the outcome of collective bargaining but the result of changes in government policies. Threatened by competition from cheap labor in Hong Kong, organized labor in Britain and the United States publicized the poor working conditions in Hong Kong and pressured the Hong Kong government to improve conditions in its industrial sector. In response, the Hong Kong governor, a Labor Party appointee, decided to raise the floor of compulsory education to nine years, expand postsecondary school facilities, and enact new labor protection laws, which led to the improvement in working conditions and the educational level of the younger generation of working-class families in the colony. With this experience behind them, Hong Kong workers tended to pin their hopes on government policies rather than unions.

The political climate in Taiwan, especially before the lifting of Martial Law in 1987, was repressive, to say the least. No citizens were allowed to hold meetings of any kind without police permission, and all organizations had to register and submit to central control. Class analysis was prohibited and people were taught to believe that class differences had been abolished after the 1911 Republican Revolution in China. They were encouraged to explain and justify social differences based on educational levels. Ethnic differences between the native Taiwanese and mainlanders further blurred the class lines.[87]

The prevailing authoritarian political structure also effectively shaped the pattern of industrial management in Taiwan. As several scholars have pointed out, many local investors were actually former landlords, capitalists, or military officials who fled China after the Communist success in 1949. Since foreign investors were committed to Taiwan because of its cheap labor costs and high profits, management was wary of addressing labor issues. Workers were discouraged from airing any grievances even at a rudimentary level, and strikes were outlawed.[88]

In the 1970s a series of labor laws were issued in Taiwan, and the number of registered labor unions also began to grow after the government reduced the eligible size of factories for forming unions from fifty to thirty workers.[89] However, none of the labor laws were fully enforced, and the nomination and election of union officials were strictly controlled by the local government, guided by the dominant Guomingdang Party.[90] Workers were disenfranchised from decision making in their unions, and labor unions functioned like "a backwater government bureaucracy," as Linda Gail Arrigo has described it.[91] Corruption among union leaders further undermined their reputation among people in Taiwan. All this led to cynicism about unionism on the island.[92]

The above discussion of the repressive political atmospheres in Hong Kong and Taiwan is not meant to imply that workers there had little capacity to resist exploitation and oppression. On the contrary, workers in both places had resisted in their own way. Workers in Hong Kong had a long history of labor militancy. The historic seamen's strike in 1922, which triggered the first wave of labor movements in modern Chinese history, took place in Hong Kong. Labor insurrections and political upheavals continued throughout the first half of the twentieth century. Their numbers continued to grow in the late 1960s. It was estimated that a total of 193 strikes occurred under British rule between 1960 and 1970.[93] Labor activism reached its height in late 1967, when the Hong Kong Seamen's Union, the vanguard of the 1922 strike, struck again.

Although the labor movement began to decline after the 1967 upheaval, workers continued to stage strikes. Unlike the situation in the United States, workers' spontaneous strikes on the floor, which are termed "wildcat" strikes in the United States, were not illegal in many Hong Kong industries. Janet Salaff has shown that these spontaneous strikes empowered workers and nurtured collectivism among them.[94]

Hill Gates observes that until the mid-1980s, labor activism in Taiwan took relatively ambiguous forms, whereas students and intellectuals there were more likely to turn to radicalism.[95] Linda Gail Arrigo, who did her fieldwork among women workers there, has further pointed out that workers were largely responding to repressive state policy. Since those who attempted labor organization in its true sense had been arrested, workers in Taiwan voted "'with their feet,' hopping from factory to factory for slightly better wages."[96]

Starting in the late 1970s, the number of workers from China began to increase in the Chinatown garment industry. One would expect a prolabor atmosphere in socialist China, given that the official rhetoric exalted the working class, and workers were said to be the masters of the country and the vanguards of the Communist Party. The All-China Federation of Trade Unions (ACFTU), with branches running through all administrative levels, was reestablished shortly after the founding of the People's Republic of China in 1949 and was included in consultation with the government over labor and welfare legislation.[97] Trade unions were called the "transmission-belt between the Party and the masses." However, in reality, trade unions, like other mass organizations in the country, did not enjoy autonomous power under the highly centralized political system. The Communist Party set the tone, the vocabulary, and the political discourse for people all over the country. Trade unions were no exception.

Staff management enjoyed uncontested control of production and personnel policies on the shop floor in China. Workers' wages were determined by the grades they were given after finishing their apprenticeship. Differences between grades were small, and moving up the pay ladder was based more on seniority than performance. Since the major influence in the lives of all social segments was generated from party/state policies, workers looked to them for change rather than through collective bargaining.

Despite the discrepancy between official rhetoric and reality in China, many labor organizers and union business agents in New York's Chinatown have noted that socialist education and Marxist rhetoric in China did have some positive impact on fostering the political consciousness of those workers who immigrated from China in the late 1970s and early 1980s. Under the exploitative circumstances in Chinatown garment shops, many of these workers were more inclined than others to accept the union rhetoric of class differences and translate it into militant action.

Immigrant workers' perceptions of unionism in the Chinatown shops were not only shaped by the economic and political systems of their native places but also by their social backgrounds prior to their immigration to the United States. As mentioned earlier, influenced by the emphasis on family reunification in the 1965 U.S. immigration laws, most of the Chinese immigrants who came to the United States before the late 1970s continued to come from Hong Kong and Taiwan. They came from different social classes, however. While most immigrants from Hong Kong were working-class or small business families, those from Taiwan and, later, China had more diverse social backgrounds.

These demographic profiles of the new immigrants also influenced the social backgrounds of New York's Chinatown garment workers. Many workers from Hong Kong had been exposed to the particular working-class culture in Hong Kong in one way or another. Although many of those from Taiwan, working in the garment shops either as workers or shop owners, had been small business owners or simply people with some education or moderate means, my interviews revealed that many of them were adept at detecting signs of corruption and were critical of authoritarian rule. Influenced by peoples' cynical attitudes toward the corrupted leaders of the labor unions in Taiwan and reinforced by some wrongdoings on the part of union officials in the United States, they tended to have a negative image of labor unions.

Given the anti-Asian history of the labor movement in the United States, the experience of old immigrants in New York's Chinatown, and the new immigrants' past experiences with organized labor in their native places, it was indeed not an easy task for any major labor organization in the United States to succeed in convincing members of the Chinese community of its sincerity in defending their interests or its ability to understand them. Despite the various versions of unionism in their native places and the fact that even workers from the same place might not share the same political inclination and points of view, Chinese immigrant workers were not inherently hostile to labor organization. Nor were they ignorant of any form of labor militancy on the floor, as the union officials believed. Like other ethnic women workers in the history of New York's garment industry, Chinese women workers also had an important role to play in the U.S. labor movement. Despite their diverse backgrounds, their determination to emigrate from their homeland demonstrated their strong desire for change. Given the size of the Chinese membership of ILGWU Local 23-25 and the union's position in the American labor movement, the ILGWU could have helped build a labor stronghold in the Chinese community and linked it with the larger labor movement in the society. Regrettably, this did not happen before the 1982 strike. The union failed to tap the rich human resources in its rank and file in New York's Chinatown.

PART 3

The 1982 Strike and Its Impact

The summer of 1982 witnessed a historic event in New York's Chinatown. More than twenty thousand Chinese garment workers, most of whom were women, turned out to join two union rallies. With a unified effort they succeeded in pressuring the Chinese employers to sign the union contract. Never before had so many people, especially so many women, turned out over a labor issue in Chinatown. Although the event received little coverage in the major metropolitan or national newspapers, it made headlines in almost all the community newspapers and was generally deemed a great success.

The 1982 Chinese garment workers' strike is the largest labor strike to take place in New York's Chinatown to date. It was a pivotal event not only in the history of Chinese women garment workers but also in the Chinatown community as a whole. Without understanding the significance of the strike and its impact, one cannot understand fully the dynamics of the Chinese community in New York City.

CHAPTER 8

Winds of Change:
Preconditions of the Strike

After the historic strike, the union wasted no time in claiming credit for it. The 1983 Chinatown Garment Industry Study, commissioned by ILGWU Local 23-25, notes: "Why did the ILGWU, a non-Chinese institution with a non-Chinese leadership, prevail in its conflict with the Chinatown contractors? One answer . . . is that the union so strongly identified itself with the Chinese membership that it became an effective voice for the expression of the workers' collective grievances."[1]

Hence the strike is described as a trial of strength between the union and a small group of Chinese contractors who had decided to break with the union and the outcome of the strike as a demonstration of the union's successful organizing effort among the Chinese garment workers and its Chinese members' loyalty to the union. How accurate is this interpretation? What were the real causes of the strike? What roles did the leaders of the union actually play in the strike? Who should wear the crown of laurels? To answer these questions it is necessary to understand the particular context of the early 1980s and the multiple factors that led to the strike. These factors included changes in the U.S. garment industry, which were impacted by the globalization of the industry; changes in the city's garment industry; and the special challenges the union, Chinatown employers, and workers faced during that time.

The Chinatown Garment Industry in the Early 1980s

Although New York City's garment industry maintained its leading position after 1975, problems remained. As elsewhere in the country, the city's garment industry continued to face the challenge of imports and offshore production.

While imports comprised 6.9 percent of domestic production of all women's and men's apparel in 1959, they reached 51 percent in 1980 and climbed another 16.6 percent in the next two decades.[2] Challenge also came from other parts of the nation. Although at a much slower rate, the city's share of national employment continued to decline after 1975.[3]

To meet competition from home and abroad, manufacturers who chose to retain their businesses in New York City had to strive relentlessly to cut labor costs, the major variable costs of garment production. Their hunt for cheap labor had a strong impact on the city's garment industry. However, no significant institutional force could check it, especially in the 1980s. The Reagan administration's antilabor position, demonstrated by its tax reductions in favor of corporations and its breaking of the Professional Air Traffic Controllers Organization during its 1981 strike, sent a "green light" to manufacturers.

By the late 1970s, Chinatown, as the center of the city's garment production, began to feel the pressure. There was increased coverage of issues pertaining to the garment industry in both the city's and the Chinese community's newspapers. The *China Daily News,* for example, hardly covered the Chinatown garment industry in the 1950s and 1960s, except for the publication of union benefits and the major ILGWU strike in the 1950s.[4] The number of reports, however, began to increase in the early 1970s, and by 1979 almost every other month the newspaper had such coverage.[5]

In 1979 the spokesman for the Chinese shop owners complained about their difficult situation to the community press. Describing them as merely the "middlemen" or the "foremen" of midtown manufacturers and jobbers, he said they were "barely surviving in the crevice" between various forces in the industry.[6] Considering the situation at that time, the Chinese employers' complaints were not entirely groundless. Their major problems included the capricious reduction of prices offered by midtown manufacturers, the mounting competition among the Chinese employers themselves, the skyrocketing rents in Chinatown as a result of the booming real estate market in the area, other mounting production costs, and increased attention from the press outside the community.

The reduction of prices paid by midtown manufacturers was largely an outcome of their fervent search for cheap labor in the city. The globalization of the U.S. garment industry provided them with increased leverage over garment production in the city, which had a devastating impact on its labor market. Chinatown garment production was hard hit by this trend. Chinese employers were forced to live with the whims of manufacturers, who had complete control over the allocation of their work. By pitting one contractor against another at home and abroad, manufacturers profited by lowering their labor costs. To secure enough work for their shops, Chinese contractors had to compete with each other in accepting the lowest possible prices set by the manufacturers. The competition was so intense that it was described by the Chinese shop owners as *ni si wo huo* (a life-and-death struggle).[7]

Although competition among the Chinese contractors existed from the outset of the Chinatown garment industry, it was accentuated in the 1970s. With the drastic increase in Chinese immigration into the city and the rapid growth of garment shops in the Chinatown area, Chinese shop owners had to compete not only for work from midtown manufacturers but also for skilled workers, who they believed would turn out "gold" for them at the peak seasons. To keep their skilled workers, the Chinese shop owners had to cater to their needs. To compensate for their loss in offering increased benefits to these workers, they reduced wages for the rest of the workers, which aggravated tensions not only between employers and their workers but also among workers.[8]

The rapid increase in rents and utility costs was another major difficulty the Chinese shop owners faced in the late 1970s. With the influx of Chinese immigrant capital into the city, rents in Chinatown's industrial buildings were swept upward, from one or two dollars per square foot in the mid-1970s to three or four dollars by the fall of 1981. Even at these rates landlords were unwilling to make long-term commitments. Although five-year leases had been customary in the past, three years became the limit, and many shops were actually on month-to-month leases by the early 1980s.[9]

As rents increased, utility rates also rose. Since almost all Chinatown shops submetered their utilities through the landlord's master meter, landlords could increase utility rates at will, charging much higher prices than those charged by the power company. By 1983 it was estimated that utility costs had run as high as 85 percent of the median rent.[10] No wonder Chinatown shop owners lamented, "In Chinatown, you work for the landlord."[11]

The increase in production costs did not end with rents and utilities. There was also extortion by some trucking companies.[12] Since the late 1960s, with the shift of the city's garment production center from midtown back to Chinatown and the change in the ethnic composition of the city's garment industry, the functions of trucking companies began to change. They provided midtown manufacturers with information about garment production in Chinatown, which helped the manufacturers contain the costs of changing product flow caused by the unpredictability of market demand. In the meantime they also provided Chinatown employers with information about midtown manufacturers, which helped them to get access to work. Trucking companies have thus played a crucial role in the city's garment production, well beyond the mere shipping of goods.

Although many trucking companies operated by the rules, some did not. Taking advantage of many Chinatown contractors' lack of knowledge about the midtown situation, some trucking companies began to rake in extra profits by demanding inflated freight and other charges. This situation prevailed by the late 1970s, as the unpredictability of market demand increased and competition among Chinatown employers heightened. Many trucking companies not only controlled work distribution among the Chinese contractors but also financed

and controlled the operation of some Chinatown shops. To eliminate competition among themselves, the companies even carved up territories of influence
in Chinatown. By 1981 the companies reportedly managed to rake in an estimated $9 million from the Chinatown garment shops by demanding a freight charge
of ten cents or higher per piece for transportation from Chinatown to a midtown warehouse.[13]

According to the 1981 report of the New York State Senator Franz Leichter,
many of the trucking companies operating in Chinatown were controlled by
organized crime families. Not every Chinese shop owner I interviewed agreed
with this allegation. Some even emphasized the indispensable role the trucking companies played in the growth of the Chinatown industry. None, however, denied the fact that freight charges had been exorbitantly increased since the
late 1970s. Some of them in fact paid a rate much higher than the ones quoted
in Leichter's report.[14]

In addition, there were other expenses that the Chinatown shop owners could
not keep "on the books" but could not avoid. As the manager of a Chinatown
shop told a reporter for the *China Daily News,* on top of all these expenses he
still had to spend a monthly fee of one hundred dollars to "bribe the ILGWU
officials to look the other way" and pay occasional tips of twenty-five dollars
"demanded by the fire inspectors to ignore blocked exits and the piles of flam-
mable cloth that littered the floors."[15] With a conglomeration of all these expenses, it was not easy for the Chinese shop owners to keep their businesses in
Chinatown.

Ironically, at least up to the late 1970s, few garment shop owners moved their
businesses out of Chinatown. The reason given by one shop owner was, "We
can move our shops [out of Chinatown], but we can't move our workers."[16] The
Chinese population in the city began to disperse to other boroughs in the 1950s,
but as late as the early 1980s Chinatown continued to have the largest concentration of Chinese residents in the city. Almost all residents in the area lived
within walking distance of a garment shop. This proximity between their home
and workplace provided employment opportunities to women workers "who
might otherwise have been tied to the home by their family responsibilities."[17]
Even for those who had settled elsewhere in the city, Chinatown continued to
be the center of their lives. Working in Chinatown permitted them easy access
to Chinese ethnic food, social organizations, language, and all the conveniences
they and their families needed. With workers anchored to Chinatown, the Chinese garment shops could not but stay in the area.

The shop owners, however, would not sit back and let all the difficulties over-
take them. To maximize their profits, they followed the example of midtown
manufacturers, severely lowering the prices to their workers and increasingly
taking in nonunion work. This aggravated their relationship with the workers
and the union.

Tension between the Chinese contractors and the union did not come to a
head until the late 1970s, when the union's financial situation began to deterio-

rate. The union's budget deficit began to grow in the latter half of the 1970s. By 1982 deficit spending of Local 23-25 reached a peak of $6 million.[18] This deficit spending was widely believed to have stemmed from the extensive use of the Health and Welfare Fund by its Chinese members, the union's failure to collect funds from runaway Chinese shops, and Chinese employers' failure to keep adequate records of their work. To improve its financial status, the union decided to enforce labor contracts in the Chinatown shops and increase its organizing effort in the area.

The union did not realize that times had changed, and so had the attitudes of Chinese shop owners. With the number of union-affiliated midtown firms sharply reduced over the years, the union did not carry as much weight for the Chinese shop owners as before. According to a Chinatown shop owner who had been in the industry for more than ten years, a medium-sized shop, with thirty to forty machines, needed to work for three to six jobbers, and a large shop, with over seventy machines, needed an average of ten jobbers each year to make up for short production runs and the effects of seasonal fluctuations. These numbers coincided with those given by the 1983 Chinatown Garment Industry Study.[19] Although manufacturers had courted Chinatown employers for contracting work in the late 1960s and early 1970s, this was no longer the situation in the late 1970s and early 1980s. In 1982, for example, the community newspaper reported that there were only 125 union-affiliated jobbers in the city, but the number of Chinatown shops had grown to more than five hundred. As a result, many of the Chinatown shops were left without adequate union work.[20]

The insufficient work supplies provided by the union-affiliated manufacturers undermined the union's attraction to the Chinese contractors and forced them to look elsewhere for business. More and more contractors accepted work from nonunion manufacturers and engaged in activities that violated union contracts. Although piece rates for nonunion work were often higher than those offered by union-affiliated manufacturers, they were not high enough to fully cover the Chinese owners' payments to the union's Health and Welfare Fund for accepting nonunion work required by the union. To avoid payments to the union fund, Chinese employers tended to conceal this work by resorting to off-the-books cash transactions. This practice was commonplace long before it was discovered by the union.

Eager to solve its financial problems, the ILGWU began to mount an effort to enforce labor contracts in the shops. Between 1979 and the early 1980s, many Chinatown shops were frequently investigated by government agencies as well as union officers. Constantly harassed by a union that could no longer help provide adequate work, the Chinese shop owners saw no reason to abide by its rules. Emphasizing their difficult situation, the owners described the union's contract enforcement tactics as *luo jing xia shi* (throwing stones at someone who has already fallen into a well.)[21] The "daring" ones already attempted to shake off its control.

Two incidents indicated the growing tension between the union and the

Chinese shop owners. One occurred at the Gong Hing garment factory, a non-union shop located at 82-14 Baxter Avenue in the Elmhurst district of Queens Borough, on the morning of May 15, 1979.[22] A number of union organizers came to the shop after the union had allegedly been informed that the shop owner had vowed that his workers would not join the union. A confrontation between the union organizers and the shop owner's family members soon turned violent. Guns were fired, and a forty-five-year-old passerby was hit in the stomach. Family members of the shop owner and five union organizers were also reportedly injured.

The two parties involved had different stories after the incident. The daughter of the shop owner claimed that more than twenty union organizers came to the shop, and a total of six members of her family were injured. She insisted that her brother opened fire in self-defense only after her parents were injured. The union officers, however, denied all the charges, contending that only ten union officers went to the shop; eight were set upon by the owner's relatives who brandished guns, sticks, and other weapons, and five were injured. To strengthen its case, the owner's family held a press conference in Chinatown to solicit support from the Chinese employers' organizations. Outraged by the family's story, some Chinatown employers called the ILGWU a racist Mafia-type organization that only knew how to bully Chinese owners but had no guts to curb midtown manufacturers' wrongdoings.

Another major confrontation occurred in July 1980, after a worker at a Chinatown shop had secured eight thousand dollars in back pay with the help of the union. In retaliation, the shop owner, with the acquiescence of the Chinese employers' organizations, ran an advertisement in three major Chinatown newspapers displaying the worker's picture, posting her name and social security number, and publicizing the case. This sent an unmistakable threat to all workers who dared seek help from the union. The union brought the owner to court on the worker's behalf. Although the employer apologized in the end, and the Chinese employer's organizations did not publicly defend the owner, seeds of antagonism between the union and Chinese employers were planted even deeper than before.[23]

Problems increased for the Chinese shop owners after the late 1970s, when the sweatshop phenomenon of the Chinatown garment shops drew increased attention from the media and society at large. Between the late 1970s and early 1980s, almost all major newspapers in New York City had at one point carried detailed coverage of the conditions in the Chinatown garment shops. By the end of the 1970s, the journalistic sensation generated by the "sweatshop revival in Chinatown" had rivaled almost any other major topic in the city. Chinatown once again drew attention not only as an exotic tourist attraction but as a criminal area breeding one of the most flagrant vices of the city's industrial world.

"The New Sweatshops: A Penny for Your Collar," written by Rinker Buck and published in New York in January 1979, was one of the most sensational reports.

The story begins with a gripping sentence: "It's a part of Chinatown that no outsider is meant to see." It goes on to describe the appalling conditions in the Chinatown shops: nine thousand workers toiling for ten, eleven, and sometimes even twelve hours a day under conditions that ranged from the tolerable to the squalid, while earning less than fifty dollars a week. Many of these workers, according to Buck, were illegal aliens with no identification papers, work permits, or "any indication at all of what they are and where they came from." They were "unseen, unheard of, and virtually unprotected by law." These shops, he told his readers, were "the closest thing we have in this country to a slave-labor system."[24]

How did this system manage to survive and remain intact? Buck had his own interpretation: it was because "the many tenement lofts above Chinatown are a closed system, impenetrable to all but those who work there." The nineteenth-century image of Chinatown as a mysterious ethnic enclave was thus reinforced by this twentieth-century coverage. This report aroused the curiosity and wrath of the outside world. By 1980 "sweatshops" had become such a heart-gripping and best-selling topic that to get the "inside dope" on the story, a reporter even ventured to seek employment in a midtown garment shop disguised as an illegal immigrant.[25]

Buck's article enraged shop owners in Chinatown. At a community press conference shortly after its publication, the CGMA denounced the article for defaming the Chinese community by failing to differentiate between union and nonunion shops and exaggerating the dark side of the Chinatown garment industry.[26] The article triggered a series of reports in the press and other media in the city. Realizing the infectious impact of the situation and anxious to stay "clean," not only shop owners in Chinatown but involved government agencies began to react. Reactions after the raids of the Chinatown shops launched by the U.S. Department of Labor in February 1979 give us a better understanding of the situation.

Although no one denied the abusive conditions inside the Chinatown shops, major parties disagreed about their causes. Frank Mercurio of the U.S. Labor Department attributed the increase in sweatshop operations in part to the rise in the number of undocumented workers in Chinatown, whose fear of deportation kept them from complaining about abusive conditions. Although his remarks were denounced by the Chinese community as a ludicrous exaggeration, Buck's article had the effect of urging the Immigration and Naturalization Service to tighten its grip over the city's undocumented immigrants.[27]

Union officials were also prompt to react. Rather than Chinatown, Federick Siems, the executive vice president of the ILGWU, pointed to nonunion shops in the South Bronx, Queens, and North Jersey as the major problem. Jay Mazur, the secretary-manager of Local 23-25, stressed the union's difficulty in insuring labor contracts in Chinatown because, according to him, the Chinese workers were "unfamiliar with the nature and purposes of unions."[28] Two years later, Sol Chaikin, the president of the ILGWU, simply charged the Department of Labor with making a "damn mistake" by raiding the unionized Chinatown shops.[29]

Midtown manufacturers, although widely believed to be the culprits in this matter, also pleaded innocent. Saying that they were facing a doubled-edged sword of "cheap imports on the one hand, and domestic goods made in sweat-shops with low-paid, nonunion labor on the other," spokesmen for the manu-facturers' and employers' associations chided the union for failing to "get the nonunion shops out of the city." "With the nonunion industry rampant," Alex Redein, the executive director of the American Apparel Manufacturers' Asso-ciation, said, "the union has failed the employers."[30]

The only dissident voice came from Ed Koch, the mayor of New York City. In defense of Chinatown, one of the city's most important tourist attractions, he declared that "the small factories in Chinatown and Little Italy are relatively safe and healthy places to work in." According to him, none of the 779 fire vio-lations and 364 building code violations in Chinatown, issued during the two-month inspection conducted by his office in 1979, was unusually hazardous. The press sarcastically described his attitude as "sweatshops smell like roses."[31]

The Chinese owners hedged on the union's and manufacturers' positions. While joining the union in defending the image of the Chinatown shops, they also sided with manufacturers in denouncing the union for failing to curb union-affiliated manufacturers' capricious reduction of piece rates and failing to organize the nonunion-affiliated manufacturers. According to them, the most important problem was the lack of sufficient work and the unscrupulous re-duction of piece rates by the union-affiliated manufacturers. They blamed the union for diverting public attention to issues that they believed were of no immediate relevance to the survival of the industry.[32]

The debates over sweatshops continued into the 1980s. All parties involved insisted on their innocence while trying to shift responsibility to others. Spokes-men for major government agencies pledged their commitment to examine the phenomenon in the city. "To think that we are going to tolerate the rebirth of the sweatshop is inconceivable," Frank Mercurio of the U.S. Department of Labor said in 1980, his face red with anger.[33] Raymond Donovan, the newly appointed secretary of the U.S. Department of Labor, also vowed with unflinch-ing resolution: "The Department of Labor—at least while I am in charge—will not tolerate anything that even resembles a sweatshop."[34]

With all this vowing and pledging, a number of government agencies, at least for a short period, did try to enforce labor laws in Chinatown. In 1979, during their investigations in Chinatown, U.S. Labor Department investigators visited some shops as frequently as three times a week.[35] In order to gather evidence of child labor on the floor, New York City's Department of Labor even pressured Chinatown public schools to release information about their students' after-school activities.[36] New York City's office of the Immigration and Naturaliza-tion Service and the New York Fire Department waged a series of surprise attacks on Chinatown to demonstrate the city's sincerity in cooperating with the U.S. Department of Labor to crack down on sweatshops in Chinatown. As a result, more than 35 percent of the five hundred Chinatown shops were investigated, and eighty-five separate actions charging violations of the Fair Labor Standards Act were filed by the U.S. Labor Department in 1979.

Although the raids conducted by various agencies were sporadic and short-lived, they had a devastating impact on the lives of people in Chinatown. Not only shop owners but workers, especially those without proper documents, felt intimidated and harassed. As reported in the community newspapers, women garment workers could not share the joys of their children, who were thrilled to see them returning home surprisingly early when their shops were raided. With their work constantly interrupted by the investigations, their paychecks shrank. To make ends meet, the Chinese women garment workers had to curtail their family expenditures. Anxiously waiting for this devastating period to end, they described it as "the most unpleasant season of receiving the most unwelcome guests."[37]

Although raids by governmental agencies were sporadic and did not lead to any significant improvement in Chinatown, they did have some psychological effect on a number of Chinese shop owners. The investigations alerted Chinatown employers to the power of the media and the judicial system beyond the community. Even though they continued to look for loopholes in U.S. labor legislation, they would think twice before they acted. No wonder some of them also called this period "an earthquake of magnitude 12."[38]

However, the Chinatown garment industry continued to grow, despite all the difficulties Chinese shop owners faced and all the complaints they had. The number of jobs in the Chinatown garment industry grew from 13,400 in 1975 to almost 20,000 in 1982.[39] By 1980 Chinatown contained about one-third of all the jobs in Manhattan's women's outerwear industry.[40] In spite of the growing tension between the Chinese shop owners and the union, the number of union shops also continued to grow, rising from 388 in 1979 to 430 in 1980.[41] In fact, as some newspaper coverage indicated, there were already close to five hundred garment shops in Chinatown in 1979.[42]

How can we explain this continuous growth of the Chinatown garment industry, with all the challenges it faced? The answer given by a shop owner, "I had no choice: that's why I went into business," is likely part myth and part truth.[43] As a worker put it in an interview, "No boss will go into business if he can't make money out of it."[44] The Chinese entrepreneurial immigrants chose to work in the garment industry because the industry could still provide them with opportunities to gain profit and move up the social ladder in their new land. An analysis of the disparity in average incomes of Chinese shop owners and their employees in 1982 can shed some important light on the reality.

The 1983 Chinatown Garment Industry Study reported that in 1981, after accounting for seasonal and part-time work, garment workers in ILGWU Local

23-25 earned an average of $5,500 in reported wages. In the same year Chinatown owners received an estimated $20,000 in salaries plus an average profit of $25,000.[45] Chinese shop owners were not a monolithic group, however. While some made their fortunes "through the eye of the needle," as Roger Waldinger puts it, others managed to thrive, owning more than ten shops in the same area and becoming landlords themselves.[46] However, compared with workers' situation, differences among the employers were more in degree than in kind.

The question then is, where did the owners' money come from? Many longtime workers pointed out that since the late 1970s, despite the increase in pay and benefits stipulated in every three-year union contract, piece rates in Chinatown garment shops had remained largely unchanged or had become even lower. While workers' incomes might not indicate a significant decrease in dollar amounts over the period between 1979 and 1982, their actual living standard was lowered, given the ever-rising cost of living in New York City. It is therefore not surprising to hear a worker say in an interview, "A few years ago, I could feed my family a fresh chicken every day. But now, I have to think twice if I want to buy one every other month for my family."[47] Obviously, Chinatown employers, like their predecessors in the city's garment industry, exploited their communal ties to thrive. The irony is that while they denounced midtown manufacturers for their willful reduction of piece rates to extract profits, they too were using the same tactics.

What should not be ignored, however, is the confidence Chinese shop owners gained after their remarkable progress following the growth of the garment industry in Chinatown in the late 1960s. By the late 1970s a group of ambitious Chinese shop owners began to emerge, who were ready to fight for a greater share of the city's industry at all costs. Many of them were younger and better educated. These Chinese employers were more knowledgeable about the nature of American society, better informed about the operation of the U.S. legal and political systems, and knew better how to make their voices heard and assert their interests. This group of garment shop owners constituted the most articulate members and the backbone of the Chinese garment employers' association, the CGMA, in the late 1970s.

The growing aggressiveness of these Chinese shop owners was demonstrated by their strong and immediate reaction to the media coverage on the Chinatown shops and the ensuing investigations in the late 1970s. Shortly after the publication of Buck's article and the raids, the CGMA held a community press conference, condemning the media and government agencies for defaming the Chinese community and lacking respect for its ethnic culture. Emphasizing the ethnic commonality between employers and workers in the Chinese garment shops, its spokesmen argued that the labor/management relationship was unique in Chinatown.[48]

This unique relationship between labor and management was further elaborated in many reports in the community newspapers. An article in *Gong Shang*

Zhou Bao (labor/management weekly), an organ of the Chinese shop owners, asserted that the special rules in the Chinatown shops were set by the Chinese workers and their employers together. They both welcomed piecework and the irregularly long hours in the shops because these systems could cater to the workers' need. The workers' relationship to their employers was like "Zhou Yu da Huang Gai": one liked to beat, and the other was willing to be beaten. Their relationship was their own choice and none of the business of the outside world.[49]

By the late 1970s, after sitting through a number of negotiation sessions for union contracts, Chinatown garment shop owners became cognizant of union negotiation procedures and were increasingly disappointed by the union for being out of touch with the reality of Chinatown. As some of them pointed out, as late as 1981, when a large number of union-affiliated manufacturers had left the city, and the Chinatown shops suffered severely from the lack of work, the union contract still wishfully stipulated that a union-affiliated manufacturer should place sufficient orders with five or six contractors and the contractors could agree among themselves on the prices to demand from their manufacturers.[50]

Equally disappointing for the Chinese employers was their underrepresentation in the Greater Blouse, Skirt, and Undergarment Association (GBSUA), the umbrella organization of the more than seven hundred contractors in the city, Chinese as well as non-Chinese, and its "nonresistant policy" in relation to the union. Although Chinese employers formed more than half of its membership, none of them held a decision-making position in the organization. In 1978, leaders of the CGMA, who were also members of the GBSUA, decided to form a Chinese pressure group within the GBSUA to defend their interests at the upcoming negotiations for a new contract. To increase their influence in the GBSUA and to prevent leaders of the GBSUA from pitting one group of Chinese contractors against another, they decided to join forces with the Association of Oriental Garment Manufacturers of America (AOGMA).[51] The AOGMA, comprised also of members of the GBSUA, was a dissident group of Chinese shop owners who had chosen to maintain loyalty to Taiwan when the CGMA decided to recognize the People's Republic of China as the only legitimate Chinese government in 1978, shortly before the normalization of diplomatic relations between the United States and China in 1979.

The CGMA's attempt turned out to be a failure. While the CGMA advocated the importance of ethnic solidarity, the AOGMA emphasized political uniformity as a prerequisite for any alliance between the two organizations. For the first meeting between them, the AOGMA insisted that the CGMA raise the national flag of the Republic of China (Taiwan) at the conference site, which the CGMA found difficult to accept. Members of the CGMA could not but give up their dream of forming a pressure group among all Chinese contractors. Nevertheless, the CGMA's stress on ethnic solidarity did manage to gain the sympathy of the community press.[52]

Members of the CGMA did make their voice heard at the 1979 union negotiation, even though the union, as usual, signed the contract with the midtown manufacturers without paying due attention to the Chinese employers' reactions. They expressed great dissatisfaction with the terms of the new union contract and the ways in which leaders of the GBSUA and the ILGWU had handled the negotiations. The CGMA's conflicts with the leaders of the GBSUA and the union were the prelude to the 1982 labor dispute in Chinatown.

The Growing Militancy among Chinese Women Workers

By the late 1970s, as the Chinese garment employers were becoming increasingly aggressive, workers in the shops were demonstrating a higher degree of militancy, which tended to be overlooked by the Chinatown shop owners as well as the union. Despite the growing tensions between them, they had at least one thing in common: their attitude toward women workers on the floor. While many Chinese shop owners, who were disproportionately male, considered women workers to be nothing but a group of *a sim a mouh* (Taishan dialect: grannies and aunts), union officials regarded them as culture-bound and passive, with little capacity for militancy and uninterested in unionism.

Sol Chaikin, the president of the ILGWU, was quoted in a public television documentary before the 1982 strike as saying, "'It is part of Chinese culture to work long hours. . . . women are able to sit at a sewing machine for eight, nine, ten hours—it's hard to make them understand the provision for overtime pay.'"[53] Jay Mazur, the secretary-manager of ILGWU Local 23-25, once commented that it was the culture not the language that made Chinese workers difficult to organize. "The Chinese feel more alien to this culture than other immigrant groups, and the intensity of our effort has to be greater to communicate," he said.[54] In making these judgments, the male union officials had forgotten that similar traits had also been attributed to European women garment workers in the early years, women who may well have been their mothers or grandmothers.[55]

The fact is that, like their predecessors in the city's garment industry, Chinese women workers never sat back and took things as they were. Individually or collectively, women workers fought against all kinds of injustice from the beginning of the Chinatown garment industry. Their spirit of resistance strengthened as their employers became increasingly unscrupulous. The experience of a Mrs. Liao at the Fu Li Hua garment shop in 1977 is illustrative.[56]

A militant worker who refused to give up, Mrs. Liao was always the one who rallied her fellow workers to fight against labor violations whenever they occurred in the shop. As a result, she had long been regarded by the shop owner as a "troublemaker," a thorn in his side. In February 1977 the owner created an unfounded incident and fired her. Mrs. Liao protested but to no avail. Instead, her employer haughtily reminded her that he was the boss who had the money and could fire anyone, even without any reason. Believing that the union would not fight for her case, he taunted her and told her to go to the union and file a grievance if she was dissatisfied.

Regrettably, what her employer predicted was true. The union's business agent called the situation a "conflict between relatives" and persuaded her to apply for layoff compensation and avoid further confrontation with her employer. When she refused to give up, the union business agent simply handed the case to the grievance committee and let it rule. Mrs. Liao was not treated fairly at the hearing, as she later told the community press. As a non-English speaker, she was not allowed to bring her son to serve as her interpreter. The employer, however, was allowed to bring not only one but two of his most favorable workers to testify against her. It is no surprise that she lost the case twice.

In despair, Mrs. Liao turned to the community for help. Together with her husband she distributed leaflets and held a press conference in Chinatown. Outraged by what had happened to her and impressed by her courageous efforts to fight for justice, various community organizations extended their immediate support. Under pressure from the Asian Americans for Equal Employment and other community organizations, the union finally agreed to rearbitrate the case, which ended with a penalty against her employer.

Like Mrs. Liao, many women workers learned to pressure existing institutions within the community and the industry to fight for their rights. ILGWU records show that between 1979 and 1983 the union helped Chinese workers who filed grievances gain a total of five hundred thousand dollars in back pay.[57] Although this represents only a fraction of workers' struggles in the industry, it does indicate rising labor militancy in the shops.

In addition to individual resistance, there were also instances of collective effort on the part of workers to redress their lots. The most memorable of these was the Chinese women workers' struggle to establish a day-care center in Chinatown.[58] Child care had long been one of the most serious problems in the lives of Chinese women workers. In 1981, for example, while Chinese members of the ILGWU in the Chinatown shops had an estimated one thousand preschool children, and approximately ten thousand children needed day-care services in the community, there were only about twelve day-care centers in the Chinatown neighborhood with the capacity to serve fewer than twenty-five hundred children.[59] The waiting list was so long that even though parents had put their children on a waiting list the day they were born, a majority still had not been accepted into a day-care center when they reached the age of four or five and were ready for kindergarten. Hence many women garment workers had to take their children to work.

Taking children to the shops was both illegal and dangerous. The shops not only contained dust, which was harmful to the children's health, but also other potentially fatal hazards. On February 22, 1979, in an old building with a broken elevator system, a girl of twelve fell to her death as she left her mother's workplace.[60] Frightened by the dreadful conditions in the shops, many workers decided to leave their children at home, even without adult supervision. This was equally dangerous. On the eve of Mothers' Day in 1982, while a mother was working in a Chinatown garment shop, her ten-year-old daughter, left in the care of her teen-aged sister at home, fell to her death while trying to reach an air-conditioner placed on an unstable windowsill.[61]

The first call for establishing a union day-care center for women workers was made in 1977 when an old building, which once housed PS 23, became available for public use. A group of women workers sent an open letter to their union pleading for help. They asserted that Chinese workers were entitled to this benefit because 95 percent of them were women, and Chinese workers formed more than 70 percent of the membership of ILGWU Local 23-25 and contributed $3.5 million in dues to the union each year. The letter, which was published in Chinese community newspapers, asserted:

> We are members of Local 23-25 and workers busy with their work. We find it difficult to choose between our work and our children. If we bring them to work, it is very dangerous; the union will not allow that, and it is also illegal; if we leave them at home, it is also extremely dangerous. Many members of our parents' association leave their children at home, or even bring them to work. Especially during those public holidays when we have to work, we simply don't know what to do. It is indeed very hard on us working mothers who are torn by our financial need and our children. Under these circumstances, children become victims. We are forced to leave them home without any care.[62]

The efforts of the Chinese women workers, however, received no response from the union.

A call for union day care was reissued in October 1981, when a group of fifteen women workers sat down and talked about the problems in their lives. The difficulty of finding child care again became the center of discussion. The women workers then decided to send another petition to the union. This time, to strengthen their case, they held a press conference in Chinatown. The response was strong and immediate. In support of the day-care request, the *China Daily News* carried a series of articles on the issue. Underlining family values and women's traditional roles in the family, the newspaper stressed the importance of day care in the community. The effect was striking.

The union's attitude, however, was elusive, to say the least. A Chinese community newspaper described the union as "shadow-boxing" with the Chinese workers.[63] It first demanded that the workers should present evidence to verify the need for day care. In response, Chinese women workers spent their precious lunch hours climbing up and down the narrow stairs of tenements and industrial buildings and reaching out to the majority of Chinatown women workers to gather an adequate number of signatures from workers in the Chinatown shops. When they managed to amass about twenty-five hundred signatures from the shops, the Chinese day-care activists demanded a formal meeting with the union leaders. On November 16, 1981, carrying their babies on their backs or holding them in their arms, four Chinese women, representing the day-care activists, came to the union office in midtown. The ways in which they dealt with their own child-care problems for this meeting was clear evidence of the seriousness of the problem.

According to what the activists told the community press afterward, their meeting with the union leaders lasted for two hours and was very unpleasant. Insisting that providing day care was unprecedented in the local's history and that child care was not the union's primary concern, Jay Mazur, the secretary-manager of the local, emphasized the union's financial difficulties and refused to give further consideration to the workers' request. When arguments ensued, he became so irritated and impatient that he yelled at the women and banged his fist on the table, startling a child from sleep and making her cry. The meeting did not lead to any immediate results.

The Chinese day-care activists, however, refused to give up. On March 17, 1982, at the membership meeting of ILGWU Local 23-25, they brought up the issue and petitioned to include funds for day care in the new union contract. As they told the Chinese press, Mazur again dodged the issue at the meeting by stressing the need to investigate the actual situation.[64] It is ironic to see how reluctant the union was in helping its rank and file with their problems, given that the ILGWU had taken great pride in its tradition of "social unionism."

The Chinese women workers persisted. They tried to organize meetings between themselves and their fellow workers in the shops. The women workers, overloaded by their household responsibilities, proved to be extremely difficult to organize and could not be persuaded by routine tactics used in organizing male workers. Most of the activists were also inexperienced in organizing. They had difficulty finding a meeting time that suited the schedule of all the participating workers. They also had trouble maintaining order when the meetings were eventually held. Overwhelmed by their family responsibilities, those who did come would talk about day care, about their kids, and about changing diapers "all in one sentence," as Katie Quan, one of the major organizers, later noted.[65] Nevertheless, the day-care activists continued their efforts.

Under the pressure of its rank and file, the union finally agreed to form a committee to champion the day-care cause. Although the effort did not lead to the establishment of a day-care center prior to the strike, the campaign, initiated by the women activist workers, had provided them with invaluable organizing experience. In the process of championing the cause, they learned about the political system of their host country and the language and strategy to deliver public speeches and mobilize supporters. This campaign had fostered a militant Chinese rank and file in the union who later became the spearhead of the 1982 strike.

Like the day-care activists, most of the 1982 strikers were rank-and-file workers. Although there were differences among them in terms of age, marital status, immigration, and educational and social backgrounds, they shared the same concern for workers' collective interests and were determined to fight to the end. Profiles of some activists during the strike will help us to better understand them.

Shui Mak Ka, whose life experience has been partially discussed in chapter 5, was a major organizer of the 1982 strike. She later became the first vice chair of the Chinese committee of the Coalition of Labor Union Women (CLUW) and a union staff member. She is well built and forceful but sensitive to the needs of the person she is addressing. As she related, her struggle began at home when she was a child. She was the youngest child of an emigrant family in Taishan County, Guangdong Province, and her father and uncles had all been immigrant workers in the United States. It had long been a bona fide rule in her family that boys ate first with better food and girls ate later with inferior food at family banquets. The young Ka could not tolerate it any longer when this rule was practiced again at a cousin's wedding banquet. She bravely stood up and confronted her father: "It's unfair for girls to get inferior food. We should have the same food as everyone else, or we won't eat!" Feeling that he had lost face in front of his peers and juniors, her father flew into a rage. Nevertheless, overcome by his affection for his youngest child, he finally gave in. From that time on, girls and boys were given the same food at the same time whenever there was a banquet in the family.

Shui Mak Ka's life was difficult after she came to the United States, but despite her own difficulties and her relations to the shop owners, who were mostly her own relatives, she was the watchdog of the employers' misdeeds on the floor. She was always chosen by the workers as their representative and never failed to fight for their interests. Once, in a slack season when she was away from New York, the employer, who was her cousin, attempted to close the shop and avoid payments to his employees after withholding a significant amount in back wages. Ka flew back when she was informed of the situation and reasoned with her cousin. When reasoning failed, together with her fellow workers she waged a strike in the shop.

The strike successfully helped the workers to gain their back pay, but it ended her relationship with her cousin. From then on, her reputation as one who placed righteousness above family loyalty became well known in various circles of Chinatown. When asked why she was so dedicated to workers' collective interests, she replied, "I was a worker myself, I know how their lives were like. . . . I never saw kinship as important as the interests of workers. Holding on to justice is the principle of my life."[66]

Alice Ip and Connie Ling represent a different type of labor activist whose goal was to fight for a better life. Alice Ip was in her mid-thirties when the strike broke out. Like Shui Mak Ka, she is outspoken, warm-hearted, and always ready to help. However, for a person as generous as she is, the early part of her life did not do her character justice. As noted earlier, she had an unhappy marriage and a difficult life after immigrating to the United States. Nevertheless, like Shui Mak Ka, she also tried her best to help her fellow workers wherever she worked. Left with no other institutional support, she pinned her hope on the union. The support she received from Lily Moy, the first and only Chinese woman business agent before the 1982 strike, also reinforced her trust in the union:

> I joined the union in October 1976, right after I began working in a garment shop. I had a lot of trust in the union at that time, because I could not get any help from my family, but I could get a lot of help from Lily Moy, the first Chinese woman business agent in Chinatown. She inspired me. She made me feel that the union was my true family. At one time I even had a dream, dreaming that I was talking to the president of the ILGWU about all my suffering in the family and in life. . . . At that time I was very confident because I believed that the union was for the workers, and with the union's backing I was powerful.[67]

Connie Ling was born in a family of Chinese descent in Jolo Solo in the southern part of Mindanao in the Philippines. She had received an English education in a Catholic school and completed two years of college before she and her family left the Philippines for Hong Kong to escape political turmoil in 1964. Life in Hong Kong was not easy for Connie Ling and her family, but she was resourceful in dealing with the situation:

> My family and I entered Hong Kong with tourist visas. Our visas expired after staying there for three months. We tried to avoid being deported by changing our address, but problems remained. I needed a job, but my employer could not hire me because of my illegal immigration status. I was the oldest child in the family. I had to take care of my siblings. So I decided to sacrifice myself and surrender to the Hong Kong police department. To my great surprise, the policemen were very nice to me. They said they were greatly impressed by my courage and honesty and agreed to grant me legal residency in Hong Kong after I admitted my "crime" of illegal immigration and swore not to do it again. So, after that I was able to get a job and my parents and siblings could also stay in Hong Kong.

Unlike Alice Ip, Ling had a happy marriage. She met her husband in Hong Kong in 1966; she was a salesperson at a gift shop for tourists, and he was a tourist customer from the United States. The couple fell in love and married after knowing each other for three months. In 1967 Ling came to New York to join her husband. She had a difficult life in New York's Chinatown:

> When we met in Hong Kong, my husband kept telling me how wonderful life was in the United States and that I did not have to work as hard as I did in Hong Kong. But once I arrived in Chinatown, I was dismayed to find out the living conditions there. The building we lived in was very old and our apartment could only be reached by climbing up five flights of steep narrow stairs. We had to live with my mother-in-law in the one-bedroom apartment. We had the bedroom and she

the living room. The living conditions were much worse than our place in Hong Kong.

Things were even worse when my mother-in-law took me to work in a Chinatown garment shop three weeks after I arrived in New York. She was a finisher herself and taught me to sew as a machine operator. Life was very hard in the shop, but I tried my best to learn and adapt myself to the new environment. The major comfort in my life was that I had a very loving husband and very supportive mother-in-law. My husband loved me very much, and my mother-in-law always kept me company and helped me to take care of my children when my husband was away, working long hours in the restaurant.

My husband and I had three children in a row, one in 1968, one in 1970, and one in 1973. My mother-in-law was a great help. She made every stage of my life easier for me. We have been getting along with each other very well.

The difficult life Connie Ling experienced in Chinatown made it easier for her to identify with her fellow workers. Difficult as her own life was, she never hesitated to help other workers whenever they were in need. Making the best use of her English, she took the initiative to inform workers of the union's new policies whenever there was a change and helped the union to enforce labor laws in the shop. It is not surprising that, like Shui Mak Ka and Alice Ip, she was elected as the shop representative in almost all of the shops she worked in.

It was not easy for Ling to serve her fellow workers. Because she had received no formal education in Chinese, she had difficulty communicating with the rest of the workers. The Cantonese she had picked up in Hong Kong was limited. Her family spoke Jiu Jiang dialect, a regional dialect of Guangdong not readily intelligible to everyone in the Cantonese community. However, she would not let herself be hindered by this difficulty. Working hard for her family's survival herself, she could fully understand the pain and frustration of her fellow workers. "I have a big mouth," she said. "I just can't keep my mouth shut when I see any wrongdoing by the bosses." It was this "big mouth" that made her an outspoken and competent shop representative for fifteen years before she joined the union and became its second Chinese woman business agent in 1982.[68]

Susan Yan and Nancy Leung were rank-and-file labor activists during the 1982 strike who were determined to fight for their own rights in the industry. The motivations behind their labor activism exemplified those of the majority of workers who participated in the 1982 strike. Yan was in her late fifties when I first met her in 1987. She is slimly built, calm, and succinct in her comments on issues that she believes to be unimportant, but eloquent on those she deems important. Born in Taishan but raised in Hong Kong, she came to the United States in 1956. Although she knew prior to immigrating that she would have to work in the United States, she had not imagined that life in the "Gold Mountain" could be so hard:

Shortly after I came to join my husband in New York, we had our first kid, and then another one—only a year and two months apart. My husband was in very poor health and could not find a regular job. Without a regular income, we could hardly make a living. We had to borrow money from friends and relatives. But how much could people lend you? I hated to see all those unhappy faces, trying to shy away from us. I could not stand it any more. So, I decided to work. In 1958 when my first child was only one year old and the second one still a newborn I began to work in a garment shop. With two very young children, I needed very flexible work hours. Sewing in the Chinatown shops suited my need, so I have worked there ever since.

Did she like to work in the garment shop? "No! No one would like to work there if he or she has a little English and other skills," she said. However, she said she was grateful to have a job and to be able to support her family with her earnings. She could vividly recall how thrilled she was when she received twenty-eight dollars after working in a Chinatown garment shop for the first week.

She said her children were the entire meaning of her life in the United States. With her husband working in a Chinese restaurant outside the city and coming home only once or twice a month in the later years, she was both "the mother and the father" of the family. To ensure that her children did well in school and stayed away from the gang influence in the Chinatown neighborhood where her family lived, she was a strict mother:

> Like most of my fellow workers in the shop, I would check their work at home from the phone in the shop when I figured that it was time for them to arrive home. I could be very relentless if they did not do well at school. . . . To this day, my son still remembers how he was once made to kneel on the floor with his book on his head for hours because he did poorly at school. My daughter also remembers how she was subjected to physical punishment for the same reason. Well, I know that I should not have done that, but how could I do otherwise? The environment of Chinatown was so bad that I did not want them to be a part of the gang wars there. I did this for their own good.

She held on to the belief that with a good education, her children could live a life much better than that of their parents. To protect their interests and provide them with the best education she could, she was ready to sacrifice everything and fight against any injustice that would keep her from obtaining this goal. It was from this perspective, she said, that she was concerned about the relationship between workers and employers and the role of the union. "It is not easy for both shop owners and workers to make a living in Chinatown. . . . But rice has to be shared and both sides have to be fair to each other. I only hope that we workers can be fairly treated by the bosses. It is not right for them to go so far and treat us as if we were not human beings."

To protect her rights as a worker in the shop, she was one of those Chinese workers who actively participated in union meetings even before the strike. When asked why she was so active in union activities, she responded, "I've suffered enough, and I don't want to be fooled by my bosses any more. To protect ourselves, which itself is also to protect our children and our families, we should know our rights as workers. Joining union activities is a good way for us to know our rights."[69]

A similar answer was given by Nancy Leung, one of the few young single women workers in the Chinatown shops. Leung is quiet but outspoken and straightforward once she discusses the issues in which she is interested. Slenderly built, about five feet tall, and always with a smile on her face, she was the darling baby sister of her fellow workers in the shop. Born and raised in Hong Kong, she came to the United States with her parents in 1977 under the sponsorship of her older sister. Speaking no English and without any other skills for the job market, she had to content herself with working in the garment shops.

Unlike the majority of her fellow workers, Leung did not have the pressure of family need. As a single young woman and the youngest in her family, her life was relatively carefree. The goal of her life, as she confided, was "to earn enough money to travel around the world!" Young as she was, she was well aware of the poor working conditions in the Chinatown garment shops and the tensions between workers and their employers. When asked about things in the Chinatown shops, she replied without hesitation, "Don't listen to any sweet talk by bosses. The interest of workers and bosses are always in conflict with each other. When the boss needs you, he will promise you everything, but once he doesn't need you, he will forget everything he said. I have had enough of it. So don't ever trust all those bosses. The most important thing is, you should know how to protect your own rights." How would a worker know how to protect her rights? She responded, "I don't have any big theory. I only know that we workers should unite and fight. There is no savior in this world. We ourselves should fight for our own rights. To know what rights we have in this country is the first step, and the union is the place to go and get such information. That's why I have been active in attending all union meetings and have never missed one even before the strike." Because of her history of labor activism, she was elected to the local's executive board after the strike.[70]

Betty Leung is in a category by herself. Five feet four inches tall and slimly built, Betty was one of only two bilingual Chinese staff members in the local before 1982. Born in a not-so-well-to-do family in Hong Kong, Leung had worked hard to be admitted to the Chinese University of Hong Kong (CUHK) and worked through her years in the university. She majored in public administration in the hope that one day she could serve the public. In 1974 she completed her education at CUHK and came to the United States as an exchange student to pursue a higher degree.

By her own admission she did not purposely choose to work for a labor union. It happened that in 1978, when she graduated from Long Island University, ILGWU local 23-25 was hiring a bilingual staff member to help out with its Chinese members. Since she needed a job to stay in the United States, she applied and was offered the position.

As she recalls, it was not easy to work as a bilingual Chinese staff member in the local at the time:

> Sam Wong and I were the only Chinese on the staff of the local at that time. We *yat geuk tek* [Cantonese: kick all with one foot, take care of everything]. We had to take care of everything because almost all Chinese members of the local did not speak English. At that time, we did not have so many departments providing different services to our members. We did not have the day-care center. The English school was in a church. The Chinese edition of *Local 23-25 News* was very irregular and was in handwriting. The one who took care of this seemed to like Chinese writing very much [she laughed].
>
> We had to explain union benefits and new policies to every worker who came to the local. We also had to help Chinese members with all kinds of problems in their lives, including child care, Medicare, filing immigration application forms, and purchasing daily necessities. I remember that once I even had to help a worker to get a refund from the department store because she had bought merchandise that she did not need. We had to do so many things at that time that I simply can't believe it when I look back. . . .
>
> However, I should admit that when I first came, seeing their ignorance of everything, I did look down upon them. . . . But after working with them for some time, I came to see how hard their lives were, and I also realized that there was in fact not much difference between individual human beings. The only difference is whether one has opportunities. Workers are also very talented. If they have the same education as I do, they can be as knowledgeable as I am. I, indeed, have no reason to be arrogant.

Working in the union also changed her personality. From a shy well-educated Chinese woman, she was transformed into an open and outgoing person. Witnessing the difficult lives of workers, she felt the need for a change and became active in community affairs. In addition to serving in the union as a bilingual Chinese staff member and the Chinese editor of the local and international publications, she also volunteered her time as a major editor of the *CUHK Greater New York Alumni Newsletter*. In addition, she wrote a weekly column for a community publication, commenting on and inviting comments on community affairs. She said her purpose in so doing was "to encourage people to be concerned about the community and make their voices heard."[71]

Katie Quan, another activist, represents a small group of activist workers and unionists in the Chinatown industry who were either born in America or had come to the United States at an early age. Inspired by the political climate of the 1960s, they were determined to bring about a significant change in the lot of workers by working and fighting side by side with them on the floor.

A third-generation Chinese American, Quan was an activist in the 1982 strike, a founder of the Chinese committee of the CLUW, and a full-time staff member of ILGWU Local 23-25 after the strike. She grew up in the San Francisco Bay Area. Quan is about five feet tall, clear-minded, and emotionally committed to causes in which she believes. Like many young people of her time, she was greatly affected by the anti–Vietnam War movement and the struggle for black liberation and the rights of ethnic groups in general. The influence of her family also played an important role in her growth:

> My father is a chemist, and my mother is a social worker. When the anti–Vietnam War movement took place, my parents took the entire family to march. I was particularly influenced by my father's account of his secret visit to China in 1971. What happened was, my father served in the U.S. army during the Second World War and was stationed in China. He witnessed the political chaos in China at that time. In 1971 he went back to China to visit. He was first shocked and then greatly impressed by what he saw. Life there was so different from what he saw during the Second World War. Everyone there seemed to be equal. What he saw in China convinced him that society could be changed and with great enthusiasm, he told everyone about it. I was very much influenced by his story. I was determined to make a difference and bring a good life to people in the United States, the land where I was born and raised.

American-born and speaking no Chinese, Quan did not have much knowledge of Chinese culture. To fill this educational gap, she went to the University of Hong Kong to study Chinese in her junior year at Berkeley. Subsequently, she became involved in community work in San Francisco and worked with East Bay Asians for Community Action, a youth center in Oakland's Chinatown initiated by the students at the University of California at Berkeley. In 1975, upon graduating from Berkeley, she first chose to work in a Chinese-owned garment shop in Oakland. The Chinese-owned garment shops were not strange to Quan:

> Both my grandmothers were garment workers. One was an early ILGWU member and had worked at Koret of California in San Francisco for many years. The other was a hand ironer in a small nonunion garment shop in Oakland Chinatown. I sometimes went to see them in their shops for fun when I was a child. In addition, the youth center was right next door to a nonunion garment shop. Every day on my way to the center, I saw the garment women there, about ten of them, were already bending over their machines, busily sewing. But, on my way home, usually at ten or eleven at night, they were still there, sewing. The conditions in that shop were really bad, garbage was piled up almost a foot high. That's when I began thinking about organizing. They were truly being oppressed and exploited. If they rose up, there would be a great change in our society. I had some friends who were going to work in garment factories to see if they could do some organizing so I too decided to try it.

Hearing about all the exciting things going on in New York, she and her husband decided to move there. She soon became a labor activist in New York's

Chinatown. She had been involved in labor organizing in the Chinese community before she got involved in the day-care campaign.[72] Recalling her early days in the garment industry, she said emphatically:

> Oh, it was really not easy! . . .
>
> Of course, I had motivation. Otherwise, how could I bear and overcome all these difficulties? Workers did not like to talk about politics. Most of the time, making money was their priority. So it was very difficult to do anything in the shops. To organize the workers, I began developing personal relations with individual workers. I learned Chinese from them and they laughed at my Chinese. I chatted with them at lunch time; walked them home; shopped with them after work; offered them help in English whenever needed.
>
> Gradually, things got better. The last shop I worked was a very good shop. Workers there were very united. I was the shop representative. Every afternoon, we chipped in money to buy afternoon tea and talk with each other. I developed very good relations with a highly skilled worker there and together we mobilized fellow workers in the shop to fight for our rights. It turned out to be very successful.
>
> Of course, there were also other things that I had to overcome by the time the workers were mobilized and ready to take collective action. For example, when the workers wanted to negotiate with the boss about the piece rates, I was the shop representative and had to bargain with the boss for a raise in every single penny of the piece rates. Born and having grown up in the United States, I was not used to doing this and felt very uncomfortable.
>
> In addition, it is indeed not easy to be a shop representative. The boss chided me if I helped my fellow workers, the union business agent scolded me if I was too active in organizing my fellow workers; and my fellow workers were unhappy if I did not manage to get good prices for them. I usually could not fall asleep the night before a work stoppage was scheduled to take place. I was afraid my fellow workers would change their minds. I was also worried that the boss would come up with another unexpected dirty trick.

The active part Quan played in organizing the day-care campaign demonstrates her commitment to the workers' interests. Together with other workers, she spent her lunch time gathering signatures throughout the Chinatown shops. Making the best use of her knowledge of the U.S. political system, she encouraged day-care activists to solicit social support and helped to work out their petition in English. She led the activists to hold community press conferences and formal meetings with union officials. When meetings among the workers proved to be too difficult to organize because of family responsibilities, she called them individually at home to ensure that the message got across. This took an enormous amount of time and energy.

With a reputation as a militant shop representative, Quan's life was not easy in the community. "At that time, I was young and quick at sewing, so I had no problems in getting a job after I got fired from a shop," she said. "But, very often, I would lose my job very quickly too after the boss found out from other Chinatown bosses who I was." Regrettably, as dedicated to the cause of labor as she was, she could not receive meaningful support from the union officers in Chinatown. The most painful experience she had in the Chinatown shops was the day that two Chinese business agents came to her shop and scolded her in front of her fellow workers, after they were wrongly informed by her boss that she was organizing a wildcat strike in the shops. It was not accidental that Quan was more involved in community labor organizing than in union activities before the 1982 strike.[73]

Quan is courageous and outspoken. Although discouraged by the union, she never hesitated to criticize it in public. Even after the strike she stood up to the press and pointed out that the union's lack of commitment in organizing non-union shops was a major reason why sweatshops continued in Chinatown. "They don't go into shops and shake things up," she said. The union "sits back and waits for people to write grievances."[74] Because of her uncompromising and critical attitude, Katie Quan was once considered to be a troublemaker, a nuisance by the union.

It is clear that by the end of the 1970s, changes had already taken place in the Chinatown garment industry. As the Chinese employers became increasingly self-confident and aggressive with the growth of the Chinese industry, workers responded by demonstrating a higher degree of labor militancy. Tensions between the Chinese employers and the union and between the workers and their employers were bound to erupt in a time of crisis. As Shui Mak Ka once said, "Even a ball will bounce when it is beaten, not to mention us human beings."

CHAPTER 9

The 1982 Strike

The crisis did come in the summer of 1982, when a number of Chinese garment shops balked at signing the union contract. More than twenty thousand Chinese garment workers, most of whom were women, turned out to join two union rallies. The strike took place after the second rally. With a successful joint effort with other members in their community and their union, Chinese garment workers pressured their employers to sign the contract. The strike made headlines in almost all the community newspapers. It marked the beginning of a new chapter in the history of the labor movement in the Chinese community and the city.

Although the strike was the inevitable outcome of the escalating tensions in the Chinatown garment industry, it is necessary to examine the process that led to this eruption in order to understand fully the dynamic of the strike and its impact.

The Contract Negotiations

The 1982 strike took place after the contractors' association, the GBSUA, twice turned down the union contract. The opposition was led by Chinatown contractors, who formed the majority of the GBSUA's membership. Although many of them expressed considerable unhappiness with the previous contract in 1978, neither the union nor the non-Chinese leaders of the GBSUA were prepared to fight a tough battle in the 1982 negotiations. The union continued to conduct negotiations along the previous track. Given the strategic role manufacturers played in the structure of the industry, the ILGWU negotiated first with the American Apparel Manufacturers Association. The agreement that came out of that negotiation would be passed on to be approved by the GBSUA.

The opening meeting of the negotiations was held on March 31. Leading the negotiating team were Jay Mazur and Tony Sciuto, the manager and assistant manager of ILGWU Local 23-25, Eli Elisa and Harry Mayer, the president and vice president of the New York Skirt and Sportswear Association, and Sam Blutter and William Isaacson, the president and attorney for the National Association of Blouse Manufacturers.

Local 23-25's initial demands included an increase in the minimum wage from the existing $4.40 per hour, an increase in holiday pay, and a twelfth paid personal day. It also initiated a demand for payment of wages during jury duty and paid sick leave with the number of days according to length of service. In addition it demanded an increase in employers' contributions to its health and welfare fund, retirement fund, and health services plan. The manufacturers' counterdemands included three fewer holidays; no cost-of-living adjustment; no increase in holiday pay; and no increase in their contributions to the union's funds. They further demanded an increase in the work week from thirty-five to forty hours and the union's agreement to hire new workers at the federal minimum wage, which was $3.35 per hour.

As each side insisted on its own demands, the negotiations came to a standstill in early May. Jay Mazur called the employers' demands "preposterous and unrealistic and totally unacceptable" and told the employers that the union would not permit them "to take the industry back to the 'dark ages' of seventy years ago."[1] Richard Rubin, the chief negotiator for the manufacturers' group, decided to suspend talks until the union agreed to meet their demands. In response, Jay Mazur threatened to call a strike.[2]

Negotiations began to meet with gradual success around mid-May, when both sides agreed to make concessions. The union and the manufacturers finally reached an agreement on May 28. Instead of the eighteen months that the manufacturers requested, the ILGWU agreed to a six-month freeze in exchange for a sufficient increase in wages and benefits later. The manufacturers agreed on a wage increase. The new contract stipulated that after six months, wages would be raised thirty-five cents per hour and then thirty-five cents and forty cents respectively over a three-year period, making a total wage increase of $1.10 after three years. The manufacturers' association also agreed to an increase in cost-of-living adjustment, two days of bereavement pay, a paid personal day, and an increase in holiday pay. In addition, they also agreed to increase their contributions to the union's health and welfare and other funds.

The reactions of the manufacturers to this outcome of the negotiations varied. Richard Rubin reportedly said, "Under normal circumstances, I would consider it a fair agreement, but under present economic conditions I consider it too expensive." Other manufacturers also expressed a similar dissatisfaction. Eli Elias, however, said that the contract was not as costly for manufacturers as the one signed in 1979. Howard Goldsmith, the vice president of Bromley Coast, Inc., also admitted that "as much as I complain about the union, it has become more responsible over the last few years." His opinion was reported to have reflected that of most manufacturers.[3]

The contract signed between the union and manufacturers, however, was unexpectedly challenged when it was passed on to be approved by the contractors' association. The strongest opposition came from Chinese contractors.[4] John Lam, the president of the CGMA, made it clear to reporters that they opposed not simply the terms of the new contract but also the procedure that led to this and other contracts without their participation. The Chinese contractors said that they were not kept abreast of the terms of the contract on which they were supposed to vote and that they were underrepresented on the GBSUA executive board. Leaders of the GBSUA denied the allegations. "They have received notice of exactly what the terms of the contractors are. We have eight Chinese contractors on our board of directors," the GBSUA assistant executive director Harold Siegal remarked bitterly, "if we gave them the moon they wouldn't be satisfied."[5]

The Chinese contractors' strong opposition was not surprising to people in the Chinese community, who had witnessed what they had been doing over the past few months. Humiliated by their lost battle in 1979 and outraged by the continuous neglect of their demands at the 1982 negotiations, they were determined to launch a decisive war. From the beginning of the contract negotiations, the Chinese shop owners had formulated their fifteen demands. The most important of these were: (1) workers' holiday pay be paid directly by the union's holiday funding committee rather than by the contractors; (2) overtime be instituted after a thirty-five-hour week; (3) contractors be allowed to take work from nonunion manufacturers and not be liable for payment to union funds if the union failed to provide them with work; (4) the system under which the union could audit a contractor's books be changed; the audit should not take place unless the union had due cause to do so, and any audit should be limited to three months preceding the request. In addition, they demanded that the union be responsible for its members' "misbehavior."[6] Chinese contractors had publicized their demands in all community newspapers and held a number of press conferences in the community explaining their position.

To justify their position, they relied on the "race card." At press conferences they described their difficult situation as sandwiched between the white-dominated employers' and workers' organizations and pledged to fight a decisive battle during the 1982 contract negotiations. They threatened to take counteractions if the union initiated a strike. They also threatened to secede from the GBSUA as an authoritative organization of all contractors if it continued to compromise on the union's demands at the expense of its Chinese members. According to them, the GBSUA's demands fell far short of its Chinese members' expectations and were at best "reformist" by nature.[7] The leaders of the GBSUA, however, were reported to have unsympathetically commented that the Chinese contractors' demands could not be realized "even in hundreds of years."[8]

On May 28, shortly after the ILGWU and the manufacturers' associations reached an agreement, Chinese contractors for the first time managed to unite across ideological lines. The pro-Beijing CGMA joined forces with the pro-Taiwan AOGMA and held a community press conference at the headquarters of the pro-Taiwan CCBA to protest the newly signed contract. The two groups agreed to share the expenses of future legal actions to defend their interests. They also resolved that if the union did strike, all Chinatown shops should continue to work and stop payment to those workers who chose to go along with the union. Li Wenbin, the consultant for the CGMA, emphasized that this was not a confrontation between employers and workers but an issue of whether employers could gain more benefits for their employees and whether or not one would like to live as a second-class citizen in the United States. "If we continue to let the white leaders of the GBSUA have their own way," he said, "our second generation will never be able to live with their heads held high." The president of the CCBA, Mei Boqun, extended his unswerving support to the Chinese shop owners.[9]

June 10 was the day scheduled for the agreement to be approved by all contractors. On that day, Chinese contractors demonstrated unprecedented unity. In five large casino buses, seven vans, and several dozens cars, an estimated four hundred Chinese contractors came to the GBSUA's meeting place to vote. Together, they voted down the agreement by an overwhelming majority of 372 to 72.[10] Frank Wong, a spokesman for the Chinatown contractors, announced that they were determined to stick to their original fifteen demands and fight to the end.[11] By voting down the union contract, they had formally declared war not only on the leaders of the GBSUA but also on the union.

Once the contractors and the union established themselves publicly in opposition to each other, they began a propaganda war for the allegiance of Chinese workers. Each side utilized all channels of publicity to make its voice heard. Open letters were sent to the newspapers inside and outside the Chinese community, spokesmen held press conferences, organized membership meetings, and spoke on the Chinese radio station. Their efforts converted Chinatown into a hotbed of debate over racial and labor issues. Emphasizing racial differences within the union and the GBSUA, Chinese shop owners claimed that they and the workers were in the same boat, underrepresented and looked down upon by the white-dominated leadership and the white members in their organizations and victimized by racism in the garment industry. Because of this, they believed, Chinese workers would also benefit from their battle against racism in the GBSUA.

A Chinese contractor supposedly explained on a radio program that he and his colleagues did not oppose improving workers' welfare; they only opposed certain aspects of the garment industrial system. On the same program another contractor assured his audience that Chinatown employers and employees were in the same family: "The bosses' friends and relatives are all workers; how could they exploit their own family?"[12]

Fearing that the CGMA would win the support of its Chinese members, the union leadership also bought time on Chinese radio programs, in addition to sending open letters to the community and holding press conferences. Emphasizing class differences between Chinese workers and their employers, Jay Mazur called the situation a "classic struggle between employers and employees." He described the Chinese contractors' opposition to the union contract as "the greatest challenge to the union in 50 years." Downplaying the resistance of the Chinese contractors as only the reaction of "a handful of Chinese employers," Mazur warned the workers, "don't let anyone tell you it's a racial issue."[13] However, while claiming to defend workers' interests, leaders of Local 23-25 confused people in the community by also reportedly approaching the pro-Taiwan and pro-employer CCBA for guidance. The union's problematic political position and the considerable propaganda on both sides were so confusing to people in Chinatown that "it was as though they were sunk in five miles of mist," as a Chinese newspaper commented.[14]

The Chinese contractors' strong opposition did, however, force the leaders of the union to take more concrete action. Three options were open to them: First, they could call a strike at those shops that had not signed the contract, which the union was hesitant to do for fear that it would cause "potential long-term damage to the industry"; second, they could renegotiate the contract to incorporate employers' demands, which the union also felt reluctant to pursue for fear that it would have to make further concessions if negotiations were reopened; third, it could keep working without contracts and persuade individual employers to sign contracts on an interim basis. The union found only the last option acceptable. Although it was at the expense of the workers, who had to work without a contact, this strategy could undermine the contractors' unity without jeopardizing the union's relations with the manufacturers.[15]

The interim contracts were at first widely rejected by the Chinese contractors. Despite their fear that manufacturers might look elsewhere to contract their work because of labor instability in Chinatown, Chinese contractors were confident they would win the battle because of the size of the Chinatown garment production and their belief in the ethnic solidarity between Chinese employers and employees. On June 18, four hundred Chinese contractors were reported to have attended a contractors' meeting at the CCBA headquarters in Chinatown. Some proposed a mass shutdown, and their attorneys announced that they were going to file in New York County Supreme Court to obtain the GBSUA's membership list, current financial records, and recent board meeting minutes in order to take legal action to increase the say of Chinese in the operations of the organization. The meeting lasted for three and a half hours.[16]

Their strong opposition to the interim contracts, however, enraged the union as well as the manufacturers. Eli Elias, the president of the manufacturers' organization, called the contractors' demands "impossible." "Would you send work into a burning house? Chinatown is burning!" he threatened rhetorically. "Pennsylvania and the other locals are wide open," he added, referring to the contractors there who had already ratified the union contract.[17] Sol Chaikin, the president of the ILGWU, also denounced the Chinese contractors' demands as "an attempt to create a Taiwan in the United States and turn the union clock back fifty years."[18] To undermine the Chinese contractors' resistance, the union even suggested that manufacturers should stop sending work to the dissident Chinese contractors. Paul Lau, a spokesman for the Chinatown contractors, accused the union of "trying to kill the industry in Chinatown."

Organizations in the community reacted differently. The Chinese Staff and Workers Association, whose members were primarily restaurant workers at that time, was one of the few organizations to extend its firm support to the garment workers and the union contract from the start of the negotiations. The association published an open letter in the *China Daily News:*

> Whatever sweet talks the employers have made, the fact is the fact: none of the 15 demands the Chinese employers have issued is not aimed at undermining the strength of the union and sabotaging the guarantee and benefits workers have gained. . . . For the few Chinese restaurant workers who are union members, signing every contract means having to engage in a bitter struggle. In the process, they have to face the risks of being fired, being blacklisted, and even various kinds of physical threat. Compared with the restaurant workers, the garment workers who have the protection of a union contract are much better off. However, this also led to a kind of mentality that does not treasure the union contracts. . . . Now, facing employers' challenge, this kind of situation must change. . . . In the past, the Chinatown garment workers were like a giant deep in slumber, but when this giant wakes up, it will generate enormous power.[19]

Other organizations concerned about racial issues in the labor dispute were ambivalent. Asian Americans for Equality, for example, held a press conference in Chinatown on June 23. Chen Qianwen, the spokesperson for the organization, contended that since Chinese contractors' target was not workers but midtown manufacturers and their major concerns were to fight for better piece rates and sufficient work, which eventually would also benefit workers, the union should take their needs into consideration and join forces with them in their battle against midtown manufacturers.[20]

Although the union continuously threatened to strike, up to that point it had not undertaken any militant action. According to union publications, however, before negotiations commenced at the end of March the local had organized a number of leadership training sessions among Chinese shop representatives and mapped out contingency plans for a strike. In mid-May it attempted to form the Committee to Defend the Union Contract among its Chinese members.[21] Witnessing the aggressive endeavors on the part of Chinese contractors to rally the community's support, Local 23-25 had also taken some action. For example, on June 9 leaders of the local held a press conference in Chinatown after sending an open letter to the community press and holding a membership meeting at its midtown office. At the press conference, Jay Mazur condemned "a handful" of Chinese contractors for purposely misleading the community with inaccurate information and threatened to cut off work supplies by the union-affiliated manufacturers to the Chinatown shops that refused to sign the contract.[22]

However, the local's commitment to initiating militant action remained an open question. As a union researcher pointed out later in an interview, leadership training programs among its Chinese members organized by the union shortly before the strike were geared more toward increasing its leverage at the negotiations than preparing for a strike.[23] This observation was attested to by what an ILGWU spokesman told a reporter for *Women's Wear Daily*. He admitted that such advance preparations were "necessary to orchestrate a strike and did not mean there would be one."[24] Uncertain of its Chinese members' commitment to the union and fearing that the union's financial status would not allow for strike pay, union leaders were hesitant to call on its members for any militant action.

Workers' Response: The Strike

The Chinese workers, however, did not need to wait for their union's reactions to take sides. Living in the Chinese community and witnessing all the activities of the Chinese shop owners, they knew that they were left with two very limited options: either to support the unresponsive union or the exploitative employers. Most workers knew where they should stand. Based on their experiences in the shops, they knew that their employers' rhetoric of ethnic solidarity was only an excuse for further exploitation. No matter how reluctant the union had been in protecting their interests in the past, it was the only institution to which they could turn for help under such circumstances. For many it was clear that the union contract worked more in their interest than what their employers had proposed. Katie Quan's comments reflect the view of many Chinatown workers at the time: "You're talking about—here go my medical benefits, what's my family supposed to do? I've worked nineteen years and next year I get to retire. You're saying I can't collect my pension? Forget this!"[25]

Since the opening meeting of the negotiations, Chinatown garment workers had been watching every stage of their development closely. They had been talking about the issues in the shops, on the phone, in the streets, on the trains, and at home. Katie Quan jokingly recalled that never before had the Chinese workers been so fond of reading newspapers and so concerned about the current issues of Chinatown. The situation in the Kin Yip shop is representative of workers' responses at that time. Most were in favor of a strike. Whenever negotiations came to a standstill, the workers would press a dime in Quan's hand, push her to the phone, and ask her to call the union for a strike. When Quan took time off from work to go to the union office to urge for a strike, her fellow workers would voluntarily put their finished work in her basket to compensate for work time she had lost. It is difficult to imagine that there could be any more direct support than this, given how much the finished work meant to them individually. They also asked their English-speaking sons and daughters or fellow workers to call the union for a strike.

The contract negotiations and the possibility of a strike gripped almost everyone in the community. Quan's vivid account reflects the mood of Chinatown at the time: "Everybody was talking about the strike. The whole community was talking about it. People called each other at night to talk about it on the phone. They talked about it on the subways and in the grocery stores when they were shopping."[26]

The prevailing mood among workers in Chinatown was in favor of a strike. A few, like Quan, had literally been in daily contact with union officials by phone before the strike. They not only informed them of workers' emotions in the shops but also pressured the union to act whenever it showed any sign of hesitation in keeping its own word: "Workers in my shop asked me to call Jay Mazur and tell him that we want a union contract, we want a strike, and that we don't care if we don't have strike benefits. We've got to have a union contract."[27]

The union was slow to act most of the time. Some leaders even considered workers like Quan to be troublemakers and had reportedly yelled at them when the Chinese workers came to union headquarters to ask for a strike. The union was finally forced to act in late May when the Chinese employers refused to sign the contract and negotiations reached an impasse. In an attempt to form a committee among Chinese workers to defend the contract, it sent out letters to workers asking if they wanted to be on the committee. Even after they received five thousand postcards in response, the committee was still not formed. It was again the Chinese workers who pressured the union to convene the committee meeting.[28]

Despite their union's indecisive attitude, Chinese workers responded vigorously to every move that it decided to take. For example, after the union decided to have a meeting of the Committee to Defend the Union Contract, many workers, mostly from the Kin Yip shop, went to the midtown union office and offered to help. They came up with the idea of writing leaflets and volunteered to take a few hours from their work to distribute them. The next day, when the union called upon them to speak on the closed circuit radio piped into the factories, the workers again responded enthusiastically. Fifty of them went to the station, which was located on the upper floor of a building on the Bowery. So many of them lined the stairway leading to the station that the head of the station thought they were staging a demonstration against him, an episode that to this date brings laughter to the workers.[29]

On June 15, when leaders of Local 23-25 decided to hold a membership meeting to call for a strike, Chinese workers came out in unprecedented numbers and constituted more than 90 percent of the meeting's attendance.[30] After Jay

Mazur delivered a speech, Chinese women in the union also spoke out. "When our bosses refused to sign the contract, we should not sit back," said Wing Fong Chin, the vice chair of the local's executive board and a worker herself, "we should unite and fight for their signing of the union contract!" Lily Moy, the Chinese woman business agent, also spoke passionately: "The bosses are always bosses and workers are always workers. What the bosses want is only to make big money. To improve our living, we should unite and fight."[31]

To show their support for the union contract many workers seized every opportunity to voice their opinions in the community newspapers. In mid-June, after the union membership meeting, a group of Chinese garment workers, indignant at the Chinese contractors' outrageous position, published an open letter in the *China Daily News:*

> Just think about the time when workers did not have a union. They did not have any guarantee and benefits. Only when they had a union was their livelihood guaranteed. Although for years terms in the union contract have not been as desired, members' health, wages, and benefits were, in a degree, guaranteed. . . . The Chinese employers have charged the GBSUA with being discriminating. Their charge is not ungrounded and is worth supporting. But, regrettably, they use it as an excuse to refuse signing the contract, and turn their spearheads at workers rather than manufacturers and the white contractors, attacking workers heavily and making them the real victims.
>
> In fact, none of the 15 demands the Chinese employers have proposed is in workers' interests. They said their action was to increase workers' interests, but we would like to ask, without the union contract where are workers' interests?[32]

After mid-June, when the Chinese contractors became increasingly aggressive and the union decided to organize a rally with the possibility of staging a strike thereafter, the difficult task of organizing the event again fell on the shoulders of workers. As Quan recalled, "To think about organizing twenty thousand people was not an easy task, especially if you start from ground zero. But you know, everybody was galvanized. Some people even went on wildcats. They walked out when their boss said they weren't going to sign the contract, and they came up to the union office. Meanwhile, we are preparing frantically. We were making picket signs and banners and all this."[33] In addition, a phone bank was set up. Together with Susan Cowell, the assistant to Jay Mazur at the time and later the vice president of the ILGWU, Chinese workers volunteered their time at the phone bank. Some workers, such as Quan, continued to make calls even after they returned home in the evening, passing around the information among workers.

Threatened by their workers' strong reactions, some Chinese contractors began to think about abandoning opposition and signing the interim contract. The fragile unity of Chinese contractors began to fail, with the owners of larger and more stable businesses, who could afford to retract and wait for a better chance to fight, at one end and smaller shop owners, who had more at stake and had to live out the battle, at the other. Convinced that further opposition would be risky if not futile, the group of larger shop owners, who formed the majority of the Chinese members on the GBSUA's negotiating team, decided to endorse the agreement between the union and manufacturers.

This change in attitude enabled the contract to be passed on to its members with the recommendation of signing from the GBSUA's eleven-member negotiating committee, which had been formed by the contractors' organization to mediate between its disparate groups. To justify their position, Paul Lau, a Chinese negotiator on the committee who represented the larger Chinese shop owners, said, "We believe this is the best we could do under the circumstances." Part of the problem in the past few months, according to him, was that "the contractors don't really understand the American collective bargaining system. They feel if they keep turning something down they eventually will get their way."[34] The leaders of the GBSUA thereby decided to hold another vote among all its members, which they believed could outnumber the Chinese opposition.

The larger shop owners, however, were not able to convince the majority of Chinese contractors to follow suit. Many Chinatown contractors maintained their original position. Speculating that a large-scale action in the community might break their will, the union leadership decided to mobilize workers for a union rally and possibly a strike.[35] Chinatown workers again responded to the union's decision enthusiastically. Thousands of volunteers offered to produce bilingual leaflets and banners. They also helped announce the rally in the community at subway stations or by phone on a daily basis.

The rally turned out to be a great success. On June 24, the day when the rally was scheduled, Bayard, Mulberry, and Baxter Streets were closed to traffic by the police. An estimated fifteen thousand workers, carrying signs and balloons and wearing pro-union hats, turned out to join the rally. The number greatly impressed union leaders. Sol Chaikin, the president of the ILGWU, Jay Mazur, the manager of Local 23-25, and Harry Van Arsdale, the president of the New York City Central Labor Council, attended and addressed the rally. "When you go back to the shops this afternoon, take with you the memory of this rally," said Jay Mazur. "We will succeed because like other immigrant groups before us—we are united."[36]

At the rally, many workers who had been recently involved in the union activities for the strike, such as Alice Ip and Shui Mak Ka, also spoke. Their speeches were broadcast in Chinese and translated into English on the union closed circuit and the community radio programs. In her speech, Shui Mak Ka called for the unity of the workers. Quoting from a line in a Mao Zedong poem, she said, "It is not yet spring, unless all flowers blossom." Her speech elicited thunderous applause from the workers.[37]

Although city-wide press gave it poor coverage, the first union rally did effectively turn the emotional tide of the community toward the workers. While only two community organizations extended their support to the union's position prior to the rally, more than twenty signed petitions to pressure the employers to sign the contract after the rally. This community support strengthened the union's position. The Chinese workers' enthusiastic reaction, coupled with their community support, infused confidence into the union.

While the bond between the union and its Chinese members was increasingly strengthened, unity among Chinese contractors further deteriorated. On June 29, three hundred Chinese contractors gathered in Yung Wing Elementary School to hold a meeting.[38] Heated debates prevailed during the meeting. Chinese members on the GBSUA's negotiating team were charged with betraying the Chinese employers they represented. On July 1, Chinese contractors once again voted down the agreement recommended by the negotiating team with a smaller but still overwhelming majority of 268 to 85.[39]

In response, Local 23-25 held a membership meeting on July 6, at which Jay Mazur threatened to strike. Midtown manufacturers also began to declare war on the Chinese contractors. Worrying that their sportswear shipments for the fall season would be weeks late and their almost seven million items, worth about $125 million wholesale, would be tied up in Chinatown shops, Eli Elias, the head of the New York Skirt and Sportswear Association, also threatened to strike a deal with the union and send work to shops outside New York if the Chinese contractors continued to refuse to sign the contract.[40]

The group of Chinese contractors who were determined to fight to the end refused to give up. Instead they formed a new contract negotiation committee on their own, thereby invalidating the GBSUA's negotiating team. Again projecting the labor dispute as a racial battle, this new team of Chinese employers declared its resoluteness:

> As we all know, in the past few decades, we Chinese were oppressed, fooled, and deceived in the foreign land. But today, all of us Chinese must wake up immediately. We should fight for more rights and interests in this land so that our community can be more prosperous; our living conditions more comfortable, and we can enjoy equal treatment, and our human rights can receive attention and respect.
> . . .
> This is our stand: We are not afraid of pressure from any evil force. We are not afraid of obstacles and rumors. We are even less afraid of the union that is adopting an illegal strategy to sign the contract individually, nor are we afraid of its threat to strike. . . .
> We would like to appeal to you loudly: All Chinese must unite to fight to the end for our common goal. The survival of the garment industry is the survival of us Chinese.[41]

Charging that the interim agreement had many changes that did not conform with the original one proposed by the union and the contractors, the dissident Chinese contractors announced their decision to take legal action against the

union and manufacturers. They officially filed unfair labor practice charges
against the union with the NLRB for negotiating with individual shop owners.
They also threatened to charge the sportswear manufacturers with restraining
trade and violating antitrust laws if they sent work elsewhere.[42]

In response, on July 8 the union held a press conference in its midtown office.
Mazur charged that "a certain group of Chinatown employers, led by a self-
appointed, anonymous and self-serving group known as the action committee"
had "cruelly deprived thousands of garment workers of their right to work" by
using threats. Insisting that the union would not make any concessions, he formally announced the date of a strike: July 15.[43]

In addition to the phone bank set up before the rally on June 24, the union
established a provisional office in Chinatown with seven to eight telephones
installed to prepare for a strike. The office was located on the third floor of 153
Canal Street and was set up to answer workers' questions in person and provide them with information about the latest developments of the contract negotiations. Like the phone bank, it was staffed and run by Chinese volunteer
workers in their spare time.[44] Even at this juncture the union was still hesitant
to call a strike. It continued to sign interim contracts with individual Chinese
contractors, hoping that by so doing it could solve the problem.

Surprised by the union's progress in signing the interim contracts with individual contractors and furious at their futile efforts to keep their colleagues
from signing the union contract—even with the threat of using gangsters in
retaliation—the dissident Chinese contractors resorted to a final showdown. On
July 9, before the union made any concrete strike preparations, the dissident
Chinese contractors shut down their shops two days in a row, leaving a large
number of workers on the streets. Arrogantly, they proclaimed that they had
struck the union by locking out their workers.

The lockout outraged the workers, which led them to identify with the union
even more strongly. Many flocked to air their opinions in the community newspapers. In one letter a worker named Ma Zhen told readers, "I myself work in a
garment shop. I understand very clearly union contracts guarantee my employment and the interests of my family." Another worker named Guo Yulan said,
"A few troublemakers among the Chinese employers are using illegal means to
force other shops to close down. This is against the will of the people. This small
group has no real representation whatsoever." Together, workers pressed for the
signing of the union contract.[45]

The labor dispute and the subsequent lockout also took a toll on the community. It seriously affected restaurants, grocery stores, and other businesses in
the community and the lives of most Chinese immigrant working-class families in the city. By July 10, except for the small group of dissident contractors,
no one wanted to see the situation continue in the same direction. Twelve community organizations and an independent restaurant union pledged their support to the workers and urged the employers to sign the contract.[46]

Facing widespread resentment in the community and resistance from many of their own members who were anxious to keep their businesses going, the split among Chinese shop owners grew even wider. By July 10 those in the AOGMA had already decided to renounce their stand. Urging all parties involved to handle the situation with patience, the AOGMA extended its support to the original GBSUA negotiating committee and favored the signing of the contract.[47] Three days later, members of the newly formed negotiating committee of the Chinese contractors were swayed and resigned from the committee. On July 14, without significant support from the community and their own ranks, the Chinese contractors could not but announce that they would dissolve their newly formed negotiating committee.[48]

By July 13 more than 70 percent of the Chinese employers had already signed the interim contract with the union. Leaders of the union estimated that more than 90 percent of the Chinese employers would have signed the contract by July 15, the date tentatively scheduled for the strike, but they were not certain that all of them would do so. A strike was therefore still inevitable. The leaders of the union, however, were hesitant to initiate a strike for fear that the union could not afford strike pay for its members. It was again the workers who came up with resourceful proposals that dispelled their fear.

Based on her experience in the Chinatown industry and thinking of what Mao Zedong once said—"when the enemy advances, we retreat"—Shui Mak Ka proposed that the union help those workers who had been locked out by their bosses to file claims for unemployment compensation with the Labor Department. By so doing the workers could gain financial support for their livelihood, and the union did not need to be concerned about strike pay. The proposal thereby could solve both the union's and workers' problems. Her proposal was immediately accepted by the union. Local 23-25 opened a new office at 100 East Seventeenth Street, which was aimed at helping workers claim their unemployment benefits. With full confidence, the local announced its deadline for the strike: July 15.

This time it was the Chinese owners who were taken aback. Realizing the dreadful consequence of their workers' filing unemployment claims, many more chose to sign the interim agreements with the union. Nevertheless, a small group of contractors stuck to their guns and refused to give up. Realizing that there was no way to change their position, the union prepared to strike their shops if they did not sign the contract before 8:45 A.M. on July 15.

Chinatown was already very tense by 6:30 on the morning of July 15. Union staff members and a team of volunteer workers were standing at the entrance of each Chinatown subway station reminding the garment workers of the deadline for the strike and urging them to pressure their bosses to sign the contract. A trial of strength between the Chinese employers and the workers began around 8:00, as Chinatown gradually came to life. While union staff members and volunteer workers were busy preparing, mobilizing, and organizing workers for the rally, the loudspeakers of the contractors' propaganda cars were blasting in the streets, advocating ethnic solidarity and urging Chinese shop owners not to sign the contract.

Despite the blasting announcements from the employers' propaganda cars, a steady stream of mainly women garment workers, carrying signs and balloons and wearing pro-union hats, came to Columbus Park in the heart of Chinatown to join the union rally. Most worked in the Chinatown shops, but there were also a number who worked at home or in the few Chinese garment shops scattered in other boroughs. With some carrying their young children on their backs, twenty thousand Chinese workers turned out to show their stand. Among them, the most inspirational was a ninety-six-year-old retired Chinese woman worker. In her union hat, leaning on her stick and holding the union banner, she came out of her Chinatown tenement apartment and stood in front of the rally to demonstrate her support for the strike—a powerful demonstration of the workers' will.

This time the workers' protest won community-wide support. Major community organizations, such as the Chinese Methodist Church, the Asian American Legal Defense and Education Fund, the Chinese American Planning Council, and senior citizen groups, all extended their firm support to the workers. Joining the Chinese workers and their community were workers of various ethnic groups from the other ILGWU locals. The rally grew so large that the demonstrators spilled out of the park onto the surrounding streets. They were found not only at all the side streets but also at the main streets as far north as the Canal, two blocks away from Columbus Park.

Union officials and activist workers delivered highly charged speeches at this rally:[49] "Our rallies today and on June 24 were among the biggest, most enthusiastic, and most significant gatherings in the history of American trade unionism," Jay Mazur said. "We have the complete support of Local 23-25, the members of the International Ladies' Garment Workers' Union. Moreover, we have the solid and enthusiastic support of the Chinatown community. As you go to the picket lines or return to work today, remember that you are not alone. Remember always that we stand together, for we are one! We are one!"

Sol C. Chaikin, the manager of the ILGWU, said, "If the employers don't get the message, . . . should you need help of any kind, all our members in New York City and across the country will help you defend the union contract. Our union has always helped workers who want to help themselves."

Alice Ip declared: "We cannot accept any treatment that is inferior. Chinese workers are people, too! We should receive equal treatment. . . . This is the true eternal spirit of being Chinese!" She warned the employers, "Don't misunderstand our patience as a sign of weakness. We are a solid wall, and you can't break us. We will struggle until we win. Let's celebrate our coming victory and the dignity of the workers."[50]

Shui Mak Ka evoked the metaphorical images in Mao Zedong's poems and passionately declared: "The Chinatown bosses' attempt to break our union is like a grasshopper trying to stop a car in its tracks. They are daydreaming in broad daylight and acting like a blind bat trying to knock down a tree." She admonished her listeners, "Workers are workers, and employers are employers. There must be no collaboration between the two classes."[51]

Lily Moy's speech sent a clear message to both workers and the leadership of the union: "Without the workers, there's no union. The union is only an organization. We're just the staff of this organization. It is up to you, the workers, to decide what the union should do for the workers, and for the community. . . . The union is like a boat. It can take you through the rough seas. The union leadership is like the helmsman. But the decision of the direction and destination of this boat is up to the workers themselves."

A spectacular workers' march followed the rally. A Chinese dragon, escorting union banners, danced forward. Following it were the workers and children playing drums and cymbals. With members of other ILGWU affiliates, the Chinese women workers marched through the streets of Chinatown chanting: "We don't want any treatment that is inferior!"; "Chinese are people, too!"; "We should receive equal treatment!" Their furious outcry shook the old world of Chinatown.

Frightened by the workers' militant action, the Chinese contractors rushed to sign the interim contract with their union business agents. According to the *China Daily News,* before the rally there were still more than sixty shops that had refused to sign the contract. However, once the rally began, the union's provisional office in Chinatown was bombarded with endless calls from the employers. By the time the rally ended, there were fewer than forty shops left that stuck to their opposition stand. After the march workers set up picket lines and struck these shops.

It was not a tough battle. The strike began at about 11:00, but by 11:30, with shop owners continuously rushing to meet their business agents either in the streets or on the picket line to sign the contract, there were only three shops left. All shops but one had signed the contract by 1:00 P.M.[52] About twenty women workers led by Shui Mak Ka were determined to force the owner of this last shop to sign the contract. After climbing up the stairs leading to this shop, they were greatly disappointed to find that the owner, a diehard member of the employers' opposition faction, had disappeared.

"Could we call this our final victory?" Shui Mak Ka asked. "Of course not!" the workers responded passionately, "we must dig the man out of his hole!" Two women who were former workers in the shop stepped forward to offer help. Following their directions, the militant women workers spotted the employer in his favorite restaurant, sipping tea and enjoying dim sum. Under the workers' pressure, he could not help but sign the contract. It was 1:15 P.M. The opposition of the Chinese contractors was thus put to an end. The union contract was officially put into effect in all the union garment shops in Chinatown.

The more-than-six-week Chinatown labor dispute was finally ended. Everyone was intoxicated by the final victory of the strike and celebrated it in the union's office. Only at this moment did Shui Mak Ka realize how exhausted she was after months of working almost round the clock, often with only one or two meals a day. Finding herself unable to hold on any longer, with a smile of contentment on her face, she told herself, "It is time for you to go home and take a rest!"[53]

As the labor activists were exhausted from organizing the strike, those who had participated in the strike felt exuberant. Chen Miaoying, a homeworker in Brooklyn, described it as one of the most important events in her life. She remembered that she decided to join the moment she was informed of the strike. Carrying her one-year-old daughter on her back and holding the hand of her five-year-old son, she traveled to Chinatown early that day. "Never before did I feel the sky was so blue and the day so bright," she said. "I felt I was so powerful when I was marching with the crowd." The strike has had a lasting impact on the minds of many women strikers. It marks the beginning of a new chapter in the labor history of the Chinese community in New York City.[54]

CHAPTER 10

Continuing the Struggle, 1982–92

The 1982 strike was an important event in the history of New York's Chinatown. It brought class conflict to the fore and forcefully demonstrated the power of workers, particularly women workers, in the community. Its significance, however, was soon overshadowed by the severe challenges the Chinatown garment industry faced in the years immediately following the strike. By the end of the 1980s labor violations were so widespread in the Chinatown garment shops that, with a degree of exaggeration, Hugh McDaid, the director of the New York State Apparel Industry Task Force, once commented, "It would be difficult for me to walk into any place and not come out with some violations."[1] Ironically, the strike thus became an event marking the deterioration of the Chinese garment industry in New York City.

It is no surprise that many Chinese employers blamed the strike for the decline of Chinese industry in the city. It is intriguing to see that some longtime labor activists in the community for various reasons also joined the chorus. They called the strike a complete failure. As they saw it, the strike did not bring about any significant change in the Chinese garment industry. They believed that it was because the few leading strikers who were recruited to work in the union after the strike sold out its legacy.

How do we evaluate the significance of the strike? In what ways do we define its legacy? Is it true that the strike did not have any positive impact on the community? If it did, what impact did it have? Rather than focusing on changes in the lives of a few major organizers of the strike, this chapter will trace the continuing efforts of the Chinese women garment workers and examine the various forms their struggles took in the changing context of the city's garment industry in the decade after the strike.

A Decade of Challenge, 1982–92

In the decade after the strike, forces that had plagued New York City's garment industry for decades began to pose a severe challenge to the Chinese garment industry in the city. One of the major factors, the globalization of cheap labor, intensified in the 1980s and 1990s. Countries with higher wages like the United States were in an even more disadvantageous position than before. In 1980 the average hourly wage of U.S. garment workers was almost five times that of those in Hong Kong, which by then was the largest clothing exporter to the United States. The differential grew to more than 40 times that of China in 1990, which had become the largest clothing-exporting country to the United States.[2] Imported clothing accounted for 60 percent of retail sales in the United States in 1992, a 10 percent growth from 1984.[3]

The fastest-growing among imported clothing fell under the category of Item 807. Their value alone more than quadrupled from less than $500 million in 1978 to over than $2.2 billion in 1990 and accounted for about 10 percent of all imported garments in that year.[4] This was a direct outcome of three major agreements: the Caribbean Basin Initiative, the General Agreement on Tariffs and Trade, and the North American Free Trade Agreement (NAFTA), negotiated by the Bush, Reagan, and Clinton administrations in the 1980s and early 1990s.

As imports continued to grow, employment in the U.S. garment industry declined accordingly. Between 1973 and 1992, the U.S. garment industry lost nearly 233,000 jobs, or almost one-third of the 1973 level. While the volume of domestic garment output was reduced by nearly 20 percent between 1983 and 1992, actual wages (inflation adjusted) for U.S. garment workers declined by more than 18 percent between 1968 and 1992, and the garment industry has since become the lowest-paid industry among all manufacturing industries in the nation.[5]

The decline in the earnings of U.S. garment workers was caused not only by competition at home and abroad but also by changes in the configuration of power within the U.S. garment industry. Retailers rather than manufacturers became the major players on the stage. Richard P. Appelbaum and Gary Gereffi found that by 1991, major department store chains such as Saks Fifth Avenue and Neiman-Marcus accounted for 24 percent of U.S. garment purchases.[6] By 1992 almost a quarter of the manufacturing market was controlled by garments with retailers' own labels, and even major brands had to reorganize their businesses around the prices and products of major retailers in the country in order to be competitive.[7]

Piece rates on the floor were greatly affected by the retail prices set by the retailer. Statistics released by the ILGWU Research Department show that the average markup, which was only about 70 percent in the early 1960s, grew to 114.8 percent in 1989.[8] The largest portion went to the retailer. In 1988 *Business Week* estimated that while material costs accounted for 22.5 percent of the retail price and the manufacturer's profit and overhead accounted for 12.5 percent, the retailer took out 50 percent in expenses and profit and only 15 percent went to labor, which included contractors and workers.[9] In the following years the retailer continued to extract a lion's share of the retail price. Workers were the ones to pay the price.[10]

These problems affected the garment industry over the entire country, but they were most serious in New York City. From 1975 to 1990 there was a significant decline in almost all branches of the city's garment industry, except for dresses and women's sportswear. The niche the city's garment industry had managed to carve out for itself around the mid-1970s began to backfire. Sportswear, a comparatively standardized branch, continued to account for 50 percent of all women's outerwear produced by the city in 1990. However, one-fourth of the dresses made in the United States, which had the most uncertain market in the industry, were also produced in New York City, accounting for 33 percent of the city's women's garment manufacturing.[11] As the city's garment industry increasingly gravitated toward the most unpredictable segments of the industry, garment workers found themselves coping with increasingly small lots of work, frequently changing styles, and growing demands for the fastest possible delivery.

Working conditions in New York City's garment industry further deteriorated in the 1980s and early 1990s. Influenced by competition at home and abroad and the frequently changing styles of the work they received, the hourly wages of New York's workers began to drop drastically by the late 1980s. Evelyn Blumenberg and Paul Ong have reported that the average hourly wage of New York City's garment workers dropped from a high of $10.27 in 1972 to $8.16 in 1987—actually $0.35 lower in the 1990 dollar rate than in 1950.[12] Like their counterparts in other parts of the country, New York City's garment workers learned to accept shorter periods of work each year, due to the insufficient work they received, and much longer work hours during busy weeks, due to the demand for fast delivery as an indispensable term of the contractor's bids for work.

Chinatown, as the center of garment production in New York City, felt the pains of the time. The problem of insufficient work from the union-affiliated manufacturers became even more acute after the strike. As a result of the continuing exodus of these manufacturers from the city, the number of manufacturers belonging to the New York Skirt and Sportswear Association declined from 297 in the 1960s to 189 in 1979 to 72 in 1987.[13] Like workers elsewhere in the city, Chinese garment workers found their work seasons significantly shortened and piece rates greatly reduced. As early as the mid-1980s, many workers discovered that while the cost of living rose by 40 percent in the eight years of the Reagan administration, the absolute amount of their earnings remained the same or even decreased. Workers in a number of Chinatown shops learned to accept six to seven months of work a year and more than sixty hours in a busy week.[14]

Challenges to the Chinatown garment industry came not only from import penetration and the outflow of capital from the city but also from the nonunion garment shops run by other ethnic groups in the city. Among these were Korean shops. The Chinese *Central Daily News* reported that these Korean-owned garment shops first appeared in Queens. Although they were almost invisible in the late 1970s, their number grew to 180 by 1986. Starting in the late 1980s, Korean-owned garment shops began to appear in midtown Manhattan, mostly on Eighth Avenue between Thirty-fifth and Fortieth Streets.[15] Most of these shops were nonunion. Hiring primarily Mexican and other Latino and Asian immigrant workers, many of whom were believed to be undocumented, these shops were able to reduce their labor costs to such a level that they became a major threat to the union shops in Chinatown.

Challenges also came from the Chinese community. As the piece rates offered by the midtown jobbers shrank distressingly, the surging tide of rents and utility costs in Chinatown showed no sign of receding. The average rent per square foot of space in industrial buildings skyrocketed from three to four dollars in 1981 to eight dollars in 1987 and approximately thirteen dollars in 1989.[16] These rising costs, coupled with the ever-shortened leases offered by the building proprietors, threatened the survival of the Chinese garment industry in Chinatown.

The rising crime rate in the neighborhood added to these problems. The 1983 study of the Chinatown garment industry reported that the problem of public safety had already begun to threaten the Chinatown garment industry. Break-ins and burglaries of garment shops as well as thefts from trucks were common, particularly in the East Broadway, Canal Street, and Tribeca areas, where the buildings were most vulnerable and protection was lax.[17]

The problem continued to plague the industry in the following years. According to the Chinese community newspapers, in 1991, for example, thirteen shops in a single Chinatown building were reported to have been burglarized on the same night, and there was not a single clue left for the police department.[18] Women workers were reported to have been frequently robbed and sometimes even raped on their way home.[19] Police officers at the Fifth Precinct of the Chinatown area therefore had to warn them not to go home unaccompanied. The concern for public safety further undermined Chinatown as an ideal place to develop the garment industry in the city.

"What is the future of the Chinese garment industry in New York City?" became the major theme of discussion at various forums sponsored by the community press throughout the 1980s.[20] While the union identified imports as the major problem, Chinese contractors condemned the union for failing in its responsibility to organize sufficient sources of union work for the Chinatown shops. There were also disagreements among Chinese contractors regarding the prospects of the Chinese garment industry in the city. Some suggested moving out of Chinatown and even out of New York City. Others disagreed, instead advocating the application of advanced technology and the upgrading of facilities as a crucial means of saving the industry. While heated debates were underway among the most politically active employers in the Chinatown garment industry, others were actively trying various means to meet the challenges.

Since the actions of all parties involved spoke louder than words in shaping the ensuing course of the Chinese garment industry in the city, let us look first at the reactions of the union. There were positive changes on the part of ILGWU Local 23-25 after the strike. The most significant of these from the community's point of view was the increased number of Chinese among its officers and staff. Chinese workers were also delighted to see their union's increased involvement in their community affairs.[21] For example, immediately after the strike the union organized Chinese workers to march in protest against the city's proposal to build a prison in the center of Chinatown. In addition, with financial contributions from the union and various institutions of the city's garment industry, a Chinese garment workers' day-care center was finally established in Chinatown in 1984. In the following years the union also campaigned to fight against the Simpson-Mazzoli bill, aimed in part at checking the "chain immigration" of Asian communities into the United States. In 1989 the Chinese garment workers marched in protest against the Chinese government's bloody suppression of the prodemocracy movement in Tiananmen Square. When China was hard hit by the worst flooding of the century in 1991, members of the local again responded with a relief effort that raised over fifty-three thousand dollars.

There were also major aspects of the union that remained unchanged, however. One was its disinclination to promote a leadership role among its rank-and-file Chinese members. Although the 1982 strike demonstrated the strength of Chinese workers, ILGWU Local 23-25 barely made an effort to promote labor militancy among its Chinese members. Except sporadically, there were no large-scale systematic leadership training programs provided to its active Chinese rank-and-file members. In addition, although the number of Chinese women among the union's officers and staff members visibly increased after the strike, until 1990 none of them was in a decision-making position, and the leadership of Local 23-25 continued to be dominated by men of other ethnic groups. Even as late as 1989, when the local needed a new assistant secretary manager, none of the nominees was Chinese. When a Chinese was eventually appointed to the position under the pressure of the Chinese community, a man was chosen.[22] Chinese women continued to be excluded from the top leadership of Local 23-25, despite the fact that its members were overwhelmingly Chinese women.

The major concern of Local 23-25 in the years following the strike was how to improve its financial status. This problem was not unique to this local. As union-affiliated manufacturers continued to flow out of the city, their contributions to the union's welfare fund greatly decreased. From 1989 to 1991 employer contributions went down by 9 percent and covered only 66 percent of the expenses, compared to 77 percent from 1986 to 1988, and the total expenses increased by 7 percent.

Problems with the union's health and welfare funds, which provided the most important benefits to its members, were the most severe. Beginning in 1987 their total disbursements consistently exceeded their receipts. Between 1989 and 1991 the disparity led to a shortfall of more than $220 million. The situation had become so intense that by 1992 the union declared that without a "significant increase in contribution rates in the next contract renewal and some action to constrain costs," the reserves of the funds "would most certainly diminish to a critical level."[23]

The structure of the ILGWU did not provide any mechanism to reduce its expenditures, especially with its large numbers of staff members and highly paid senior officials. To solve its financial problems, the union could only rely on its locals to impose benefit eligibility requirements on their members and on making greater efforts to retain manufacturers in the city. Although the union tried to argue that keeping the industry in the city and improving its financial status would eventually benefit its members, efforts in this direction often undermined its ability to enforce labor law on the floor and were thus carried out at the expense of workers' interests.

As the largest local of the union, Local 23-25 bore the brunt of the challenge the ILGWU faced. Its financial status largely reflected that of the international.[24] The deficit in its health and welfare funds, which already exceeded income by almost $1.5 million at the end of 1981, grew to almost $4 million in 1985.[25] To reduce its financial problems, as early as 1983 the local began to increase its membership dues and set up an eligibility requirement for union benefits.[26] The benefits eligibility requirement grew from a minimum annual income of four thousand dollars in 1984 to five thousand in 1989 and continued to grow by two hundred dollars each year between 1992 and 1994.[27] To better constrain costs, in 1986 Local 23-25 merged its health and welfare funds with those of other locals in the New York Joint Board. In 1990 it merged with Local 95-105 to further reduce expenses and enlarge sources of work for the union shops in the city.

The union blamed import penetrations and the growth of nonunion garment shops for the deteriorating labor conditions in the city. To improve its financial status and redress adverse labor conditions, it was determined to combat imports and step up its organizing efforts in Chinatown, the center of the city's garment production. However, with no Chinese on its decision-making body and lacking the patience to understand the complexity of the situation in Chinatown, the union organizers and officials often blundered. This was especially true in the first few years after the strike. Two cases are illustrative.

In 1983, misinformed that the People's Republic of China was already the major clothing exporter to the United States, a Local 23-25 spokesman held a press conference at the pro-Taiwan CCBA in an attempt to rally support from the community against the Beijing government. With the union's nativist slogan of "Buy American," he even threatened to stage a protest in front of the Chinese Consulate in New York.

He did not realize that people in the Chinese community resented outsiders taking advantage of its internal conflicts to advance their own cause. In addition, many Chinese workers could not understand why they should fight against their counterparts in other parts of the world, who worked under similar exploitative conditions. To make things even worse, it later turned out that Taiwan and not the People's Republic of China was the largest clothing exporter to the United States at that time, which further undermined the ILGWU's credibility in the Chinese community. To redeem its image, union leaders hastily dispatched a note to the Chinese press denying the position taken by its spokesman. The union also gave up its slogan of "Buy American" in the following years. But the die was cast, and the union's disagreeable reputation in the community was once again reinforced.[28]

Another example is an incident in the Xin Wang shop in 1986. According to news coverage, Xin Wang was a newly established shop that received work from firms affiliated with ILGWU Local 23-25 but primarily from Local 105. Workers in the shop could choose to register with either local. Local 23-25, however, wanted to enroll all the workers. Its organizers came to negotiate with the shop owner and allegedly assaulted him physically. This outraged the community of Chinese contractors. In another rare act of unity, the pro-Beijing New York CGMA and the pro-Taiwan AOGMA both denounced the union for its violent and even "hooligan" behavior in dealing with the Chinese shop owners.[29]

As with many locals in the union, the deteriorating financial status of Local 23-25 sapped its ability to promote labor militancy on the shop floor. Many union business agents were reported to have been too lenient with employers. As one worker commented: "When it comes to the time that they have to deal with the employer for problems on the floor, they are just like treating their own pets: combing the hairs on the back of their kitties, back and forth, back and forth—without ending and with no result."[30]

They often repressed any sign of militancy on the part of workers. The story of a woman worker told by Wing Lam, the director of the CSWA, is a case in point. The woman worker had been unfairly fired for demanding union wages. The union business agent took up her case and fought for her back pay, but he also accepted the contractor's request that the worker should look for work elsewhere after getting the money. When the worker refused to give up her reinstatement after receiving her back pay she was blacklisted by the union for refusing to comply with its decision.[31]

Although the union threatened to call a strike at the beginning of contract negotiations every three years after 1982, it tended to compromise with the employers in the end. This compromising attitude on the part of the union made its members even more vulnerable to the adverse conditions of the time. As many workers have pointed out, not only did working conditions in many Chinatown shops show no sign of improvement after the strike, but labor violations had been "institutionalized" in some of the shops. As the union failed to enforce union contracts in a growing number of Chinatown shops, workers had to defend themselves on their own.

What then were the Chinese employers' reactions after the strike? Having witnessed the strength of workers with the support of the union, many learned to adopt a more flexible attitude in contract negotiations. The strike, however, also led them to see clearly where their interests lay when conflicts occurred between the union and their own association, the GBSUA. Despite their differences with other members of the association, they were not hesitant in supporting every move it took to defend contractors' interests. A good example is what happened in 1984, when the GBSUA rejected the union's demands for a wage increase. The Chinese contractors unconditionally supported the association, even though it had once again failed to inform them of its position in advance.

The 1982 labor dispute also led the Chinese contractors to realize the importance of making their voices heard and being represented in the major institutions of the city's garment industry. Their strong protest against the Garment Industrial Development Corporation (GIDC) shortly after its founding in 1984 and the result of their uncompromising struggle within the GBSUA are illustrative. There were a number of influential figures from the Chinese community serving on its executive board when the GIDC was founded. These individuals, however, were either public officials or leaders of major social organizations in Chinatown who had no detailed knowledge of the garment industry. There is no denying that their inclusion in such projects is a clear indication of how ignorant the initiators of this project were about the situation in Chinatown. Fully realizing the importance of the project in the city's industry, the Chinese contractors were determined to fight to be represented on the leading body of the GIDC. After protesting for a month they finally achieved their goal.

Equally significant was their victory within the GBSUA. As a result of their years of struggle, John Lam, a major owner of Chinese garment operations in New York City, in 1985 became the first Chinese to chair the GBSUA, an organization long dominated by Jews and Italians. His election marked the beginning of the Chinese employers' entrance into the leadership of major institutions of power in the city's garment industry.

While the politically active Chinese contractors were increasing their influence in the city's garment industry, others were busy finding their way out of the dire situation. Like employers elsewhere in the country, the entrepreneurial Chinese contractors were eager to shake off union control, especially after its victory in 1982. By 1985 the most ambitious had already ventured into Philadelphia, but their businesses did not manage to get a foothold there.

In an attempt to protect the garment industry in the city, the city government developed a series of new policies in the 1980s. As early as 1983 it began to reduce energy costs for garment production and to prohibit the conversion of industrial buildings in the major garment manufacturing areas in the city. In 1987 the City Planning Commission proposed to designate a special garment manufacturing zone in midtown Manhattan, covering an area from Seventh to Ninth Avenues and between Thirtieth and Forty-first Streets and provided favorable terms for employers to establish their garment shops there. In the meantime it encouraged owners of the Chinatown garment shops to relocate their businesses to cheaper areas in the city by offering them tax exempt benefits or low interest loans to avoid skyrocketing rents in the Chinatown area.

Despite their initial resistance, it did not take long for a number of Chinese shop owners to respond actively to the city's policies. Even before the proposal of the City Planning Commission was passed in 1990, there were already visible clusters of Chinese-owned garment shops in the proposed special garment manufacturing zone in midtown Manhattan. The years following the strike witnessed a proliferation of Chinese-owned shops in different parts of the city. Most, however, were in the Flushing area of Queens, where rents for industrial buildings were only about three dollars per square foot in 1983, as compared to more than four dollars in Chinatown.[32]

There is no precise record of the number of Chinese shops in Queens in the early 1980s, but a survey by the *Central Daily News* reveals that in 1987, when ten shops in Chinatown closed down, thirteen shops in Queens placed help-wanted advertisements. Most were new and nonunion. There were already forty to fifty Chinese garment shops there in that year.[33] The Chinese garment shops in Brooklyn did not grow in significant numbers until the end of 1980s.

The most ambitious ventures of the Chinese contractors in the decade after the strike were those proposed by the Fashion Group, headed by the chair of the GBSUA, John Lam, in 1989 and the Metropolitan Fashion Center of Greater New York, headed by the former chair of the CGMA, Sherman Eng, in 1990. Both undertakings were applauded by the former mayor, Ed Koch, and his successor, David Dinkins.

The Fashion Group proposed to create two major establishments at College Point in Queens: an $8 million Industrial Plaza and a $57 million Fashion Plaza. It claimed that these two projects would create about fifteen hundred jobs and that once they were completed it would remove five hundred of its jobs from the Dominican Republic back to New York City so as to strengthen the operation of the proposed new establishments. The two projects never materialized.[34]

The proposed project of the Metropolitan Fashion Center of Greater New York was a 120,000-square-foot industrial park for garment manufacturing at the Army Terminal in Brooklyn. It was supposed to create 650 jobs and be completed by 1992. Although the facility was constructed and put to use as scheduled, mismanagement coupled with the lack of safety in the area and public transportation to the site as well as its distance from the workers' residential areas led to its closing in 1996.[35]

These projects did not yield any positive long-term results, but the Chinese contractors did manage to establish a second Chinese garment production center outside Chinatown, in the Sunset Park area of Brooklyn, by early 1990. A number of longtime Chinese residents in the area recalled that in 1980 there had been only one Chinese-owned garment shop, located at the corner of Eighth Avenue and Sixty-third Street. Although it was a union shop, work hours there were extremely flexible. Working mothers with young children could either work half a day in the shop and work at home after picking up their children from school in the afternoon, or they could simply work at home if their children were too young to go to day care. In either case, the employer would register them as union members to enable them to enjoy union benefits.[36]

Although the number of Chinese shops began to grow gradually after the mid-1980s, some workers recalled that even in the late 1980s there were only several dozen shops in the area.[37] The major factor that halted the growth of the Chinese garment industry in Brooklyn was the difficulty of recruiting Chinese workers there. Despite the better terms offered by the employers and the advantages of saving time and money by not having to travel to Chinatown, few workers who lived in the neighborhood would choose to work there. The reactions of Liu Ming, a longtime garment worker who lived in the Sunset Park area of Brooklyn but had been working in the Chinatown shops for years, sheds some light on the reasons:

> Of course, the bosses here [Brooklyn] had tried to talk me into working in their shops, but what was the point of doing that? In any case, I had to go to Chinatown to do grocery shopping for the family. Brooklyn at that time, you know, was not as it is now. There were hardly any Chinese grocery stores or other businesses in this neighborhood. Plus, my husband worked in an uptown Chinese restaurant . . . yes, I am talking about the late 1970s . . . and the restaurant picked up its employees from Chinatown every day around noon.
>
> I had two young kids at that time; my daughter had just started going to a day-care center, and my son was still an infant. My husband worked eleven to twelve hours a day, but he did not have to go to work until noon. So, every morning, I would drop my daughter at the day-care center at about eight o'clock and then go to work in a Chinatown shop. My husband took care of the baby at home. He would bring him to my workplace in Chinatown around noon before he left for work. After the baby came, I would put him in a cardboard box next to my sewing machine and work for three more hours. About 3:30 in the afternoon, I left the shop and returned to Brooklyn to pick up my daughter from the day-care center. Carrying the baby on my back, I would bring two bundles of work with me from the shop and do the grocery shopping on my way home.
>
> Things worked out pretty well for me at that time. I did not miss anything working in Chinatown. I had the grocery for the family and garments to sew after my kids got settled at home in the evening. I could work as long as I wished, if I needed more money. . . . So, what's the point of working in Brooklyn? Brooklyn was a dead town for us Chinese at that time. I enjoyed the life in Manhattan's Chinatown, full of life, full of conveniences and information that I needed.[38]

Many garment workers who worked in Chinatown but lived in Brooklyn would agree. It is therefore not surprising that the Chinese garment industry did not grow in Brooklyn. The city newspaper reported that as late as 1988 the average rent of an industrial building in the Sunset Park area was only four to five dollars per square foot, as compared with fifteen to twenty dollars in Chinatown.[39] Even so, it could not provide sufficient incentive for owners of the garment shops to begin their businesses there.

The number of Chinese garment shops, however, began to grow rapidly in the area after the end of the 1980s. By 1992 a community newspaper reported that there were already almost two hundred shops there. The number grew even more phenomenally in the following years. By the mid-1990s Sunset Park had fully established its reputation as the second Chinese garment production center in New York City. What accounted for its rapid growth in these years? Like the growth of the Chinatown garment industry in the late 1960s, the rise of the Chinese garment industry in Brooklyn was directly related to the characteristics of Chinese immigration to the city in the late 1980s, the intracity migration of the Chinese population, and the growth of the Chinese community there over the past decade.

U.S. immigration statistics show that between 1982 and 1989 a total of 71,881 Chinese entered New York City; over 90 percent came as family members or relatives of U.S. citizens or permanent residents.[40] As in previous decades, about 60 percent of those who were in their working years and had occupations prior to immigration were working-class. Almost 90 percent of these working-class immigrants came from China.[41] Although new immigrants to Brooklyn came from different parts of China and had various social and educational backgrounds, my interviews suggest that most Chinese immigrant families in the Sunset Park area were working-class, and many families of garment workers in the area either had originated in the former Si Yi District or directly immigrated from the area, and a number of them came with a rural background. Census data also show that in 1990, those who worked as operators and other blue-collar occupations formed almost 40 percent of the entire Chinese female workforce in Brooklyn, which was second only to that in Manhattan.[42]

The close proximity of home to workplace did not carry much weight in the lives of the Chinese garment workers in the past, but it did after the late 1980s. This had a lot to do with the changes in the Chinatown garment industry and the recent growth of the Chinese community in Brooklyn. In the past, in addition to all the conveniences in Manhattan's Chinatown, the major reason for the workers to work there was the union benefits, the family health care in particular. This advantage diminished in the decades after the strike, however, as the union continuously increased its benefit eligibility requirements.

Many union officials argued that the increased eligibility requirements could help improve the union's financial status and curb unlawful practices in the Chinatown shops. It had been a common practice among many Chinatown employers to implement various forms of payment to their workers, and some

Table 11. Characteristics of the Chinese Female Labor Force in New York City by Borough, 1990

	New York City	Bronx	Kings (Brooklyn)	New York (Manhattan)	Queens	Richmond
Labor force status						
Females age 16 and older	99,550	2,725	28,084	30,880	35,832	2,029
Percent[a]		2.74	28.21	31.02	35.99	2.04
Civilian labor force	60,875	1,591	17,424	19,015	21,650	1,195
Percent[b]	61.15	58.4	62.0	61.6	60.4	58.9
Employed	57,107	1,481	16,344	17,907	20,234	1,141
Percent[c]	93.8	93.1	93.8	94.2	93.5	95.5
Occupation						
Management/professional	13,128	374	2,986	3,906	5,499	363
Technical/sales/clerical	18,084	493	5,107	4,533	7,389	562
Services	4,545	160	1,186	1,229	1,917	53
Farming/forestry/fishing	67	—	—	67	—	—
Precision production/repair	2,465	91	613	715	1,026	20
Operators/fabricators/laborers	18,818	363	6,452	7,457	4,403	143
Machine operations/assemblers/inspectors	17,794	332	6,161	7,053	4,125	123
Employment status in 1989						
Employed females age 16 years and older	63,471	1,555	17,824	20,252	22,546	1,294
Employed 50–52 weeks	34,010	1,043	9,156	10,115	12,892	804
Employed 35 or more hours per week	50,837	1,318	14,695	15,762	18,065	997

Source: U.S. Department of Commerce, Bureau of the Census, *1990 Census of Population* (Washington, D.C.: G.P.O., 1992)), CP-2-34, sec. 1 of 3, table 161.
a. Percentage of total city Chinese females age 16 and older.
b. Percentage of all Chinese females age 16 and older in the city or county.
c. Percentage of all Chinese females in the city or county civilian labor force.

could enjoy union benefits without having to work in the shops. This practice was possible because the union did not have any specific eligibility requirement of work for its members to enjoy benefits. The practice enabled the Chinese employers to strengthen their ties with their employees by catering to their families' needs, and they could also profit by either providing their own family members with health care at no cost or illegally engaging in selling union benefits within their own social network.

However, around the mid-1980s, with its health and welfare funds drained, the local was determined to terminate these illicit practices on the floor. In addition to setting specific benefit eligibility requirements and increasing them over the years, it also demanded that employers of union shops contribute additional money to its benefit funds if they engaged in work from nonunion-affiliated sources. The outcome, however, did not turn out as intended. Some Chinatown workers described it as *neih yauh jeung leuhng gai, ngoh yauh tiu cheuhng tai* (Cantonese proverb: be evenly matched, or there is always a way to beat the smartest).[43] Owners of many Chinatown shops began to develop a rationale and strategies to deal with the situation. Since workers' benefit eligibility was based on the amount of work their employers reported to the union, many shop owners, with the assistance of accounting specialists in the community, learned to base payments made by check to their employees on the minimum requirements of the union and to pay the rest of their wages in cash. Many longtime workers recalled that the practice of partial payment by cash became widespread in the Chinatown shops around mid-1985.

Around the same time, instances in which employers retained some of their workers' wages or simply closed down their shops while still owing retained wages also began to increase, according to the recollections of many longtime workers. The practice had become so common that by the early 1990s Chinese garment workers learned to ask how long their wages would be held when they applied for a job. Although illegal, having their wages held by their employers for two or three weeks after they completed work was considered acceptable by the workers in a number of Chinatown garment shops. In this respect, the distinction between many union and nonunion shops blurred in Chinatown.

While workers in the 1970s and early 1980s considered the health care benefit to be the most important reason for them to work in a union shop, this was not necessarily the case with the new immigrant workers in the late 1980s and early 1990s. Many of them found it difficult and cumbersome to meet the benefit eligibility requirements set by the union; others, particularly those who did not have children or did not plan to have a child in the United States, simply ignored it. Since most were in the prime of their lives, health care benefits were the last thing they were concerned about as they struggled to survive in the new land.

An increasing number of immigrant workers also learned to rely on the social welfare system for health care. As they explained in interviews, so long as they kept no money in their bank accounts, they were entitled to free medical care and therefore did not need to depend on the union's health care benefits. Ignorant of how the social security system would work against them later in their lives if they did not report their income, many new immigrant workers did not understand why they should ask their employers to pay them by check, especially knowing that it would cost them up to 10 percent or more of their incomes. Workers were thus complicitous in their employers' unlawful acts.

Greatly disappointed by the deteriorating conditions in Chinatown, many longtime garment workers began to see the advantages of working closer to their homes and to appreciate the better terms offered by the Chinese garment shops in Brooklyn, particularly as the Chinese Commercial Center in Brooklyn could provide comparable services by then. As a result, a growing number of workers who lived in Brooklyn began to seek employment opportunities in their neighborhoods. With a sufficient labor supply in the area, the number of Chinese garment shops began to soar.

As in the case of Manhattan's Chinatown in the late 1960s and early 1970s, the growth of the Chinese garment industry boosted the rise of the Chinese community in the Sunset Park area. With garment workers and their families as their regular customers, the number of Chinese restaurants, grocery stores, and other services began to grow. By late 1992 the Chinese commercial center in the Sunset Park area, roughly covering a territory from Sixth to Ninth Avenues and between Fiftieth and Sixty-fourth Streets, had become New York's third Chinatown.[44] Its conveniences coupled with the deteriorating labor conditions in Manhattan's Chinatown effectively anchored the workers to the Chinese garment industry in the area.[45]

When interviewed by the Chinese press, owners of the Chinese garment shops tended to cite the following reasons for opening their businesses in Brooklyn: low rents, ample space, and easy access to the workforce. Apart from the low rents and roomy lofts available in the area, the spacious environment of the Chinese garment district in Brooklyn was a plus. Many said that it made the flow of garment transportation more efficient than in the overcrowded Manhattan Chinatown, and they did not have to worry about being ticketed for parking violations, which could cost as much as fifty dollars—almost equal to the profit they could make by having fifty garments sewn in their shops.[46] However, the most important—though rarely mentioned—reason was, perhaps, the benefit of union avoidance.

Since the influence of the ILGWU was weak in Brooklyn, garment shops there served as a safety valve for the city's Chinese employers to extract quick profit without having to worry about compliance with any labor laws. As a matter of fact, a number of Chinatown employers virtually opened branches of their businesses in Brooklyn to increase their leverage in dealing with the unionized situation in Chinatown and to avoid making additional contributions to the union's funds for working on nonunion work. As a result, cases of labor violation increased with the growth of the Chinese garment shops in Brooklyn.

Workers who had been lured by the better terms offered by Chinese shops in Brooklyn soon found themselves trapped in a highly competitive working environment that demanded sweated labor to make a living.

Competition among workers was generated not only from the increase in the Chinese working-class population in the area but also from the increasing number of undocumented immigrant workers in the industry. The undocumented immigrant workers in Brooklyn came not only from Fuzhou, Wenzhou, and various parts of China but also from Malaysia and other Southeast Asian countries. Most of them owed a large sum of money to smugglers in the United States and their native lands.[47] With the safety and even the lives of their families held hostage in their native lands, they were eager to pay back their heavy debts. For them, the benefits of being a law-abiding garment worker, such as the social security benefits every taxpayer was entitled to enjoy in later years and the health insurance provided by the union, held no meaning at all.

Since every penny the undocumented immigrant workers earned at their workplace counted toward paying back their debts, they were ready to accept any working conditions and work as many hours as they could. As in the case of almost every group of newcomers in the history of the industry, their willingness to work under the most exploitative conditions subjected them to shouldering the blame for lowering wages, extending work hours, and other poor labor records on the floor.

Gendered definitions of work on the shop floor also began to shift. Since the number of traditionally defined "men's jobs" were limited and likely to have been occupied by the earlier legal male immigrant workers, a number of undocumented male workers, eager to land a job to make money as soon as possible, began to take what had been considered "women's work." They became hemmers and other special machine operators. However, gender remained significant. Although their male identity enabled them to enjoy employment priority and work at better paying jobs than their female counterparts, gender was constructed so that the female identity of their work not only relegated them to a lower status than the rest of the male workers but also subjected them to an inferior position in the perception of all workers in the shops.

The undocumented immigrant workers became even more vulnerable after 1986, with the passing of the employer sanctions law.[48] Although the law was originally passed to protect U.S. workers, it increased the power of unscrupulous employers to exploit undocumented workers at the same time. Many such workers were driven underground after the enactment of the law. Realizing this, many Chinese employers sought to use them as bargaining chips against legal workers. The presence of undocumented workers in the industry thus not only worsened working conditions but also further undermined solidarity among the workers.

As working conditions further eroded, the Chinese garment shops in Brooklyn began to suffer from crime. In 1991 a shop owner in Brooklyn was reported to have been stripped naked by a group of Chinese gangsters in front of his fe-male employees after they did not find enough money in his cash box.[49] Ko-lin Chin noted that by 1992 "business owners in Brooklyn's Chinatown reported a higher level of attempted gang extortion than did merchants in Manhattan's Chinatown."[50] Employers often shifted their losses further by lowering their pay scales.

With employers in Brooklyn and Manhattan's Chinatown competing with each other in their unlawful pursuits, many Chinese garment shops in New York City were labeled by law enforcement agencies as "sweatshops," the most no-torious term used throughout the history of the city's garment industry. A spe-cial action undertaken by the State Apparel Industry Task Force in 1988 report-ed that 60 percent of Chinese shop owners, scattered throughout Queens, Brooklyn, Chinatown, and other parts of the city, had in one way or another violated labor laws. It also discovered that among the thirty shops officially charged with labor violations, more than six were owned by Chinese.[51]

As usual, workers were most victimized by the adverse conditions. Subject-ed to increasing competition in the workforce, they were left with even less le-verage in negotiating with their employers. An increasing number of workers became reluctant to take militant action to defend their rights for fear of losing their jobs. Employers were prompt to take advantage of the situation and stepped up their efforts to harass activist workers on the shop floor to main-tain a stable and docile workforce in their shops. In 1989 a Chinese community newspaper reported that many shop representatives in the Chinatown shops had resigned from their positions because they were frequently picked on by their employers and did not receive meaningful support from their fellow workers, who were afraid that even a close relationship with them might cost them their jobs.[52] This in turn posed a severe challenge to the operation of the union on the floor.

Although all workers, men as well as women, were subjected to increasingly abusive labor conditions in the shops, women faced additional problems in their workplaces and families. Cases in which young women were sexually harassed by male co-workers and employers were not unheard of. Undocumented young women workers were particularly vulnerable. Separated from their families and driven by the sweated labor in the shops, their vulnerability made it easier for them to fall prey to unwanted sexual advances, often under the initial disguise of emotional appeal.

Married women workers, especially working mothers, faced problems beyond their workplace, which were often pushed to the background in moments of conflict between gender, class, and ethnic interests in their own community and by feminist organizations in the society at large. The trial of Chen Donglu, who had beaten his wife to death after alleged adultery on her part in 1987, and the events following the ruling, can help us to understand their problems.

The trial took place at the Brooklyn Supreme Court two years after the murder. The court had made little effort to investigate the marital history of the couple prior to the trial, even though the husband was known by the wife's fellow workers to be abusive before the alleged adultery took place.[53] Judge Edward Pincus, however, readily accepted the testimony of Burton Pasternak, a professor of anthropology at Hunter College of the City University of New York, who specialized in Chinese social behavior and customs. Pincus concluded that cultural pressures caused by the devastating impact of his wife's adultery had provoked Chen Donglu into an "extreme mental state of 'diminished capacity' and left him with no ability to form the intent necessary for more serious charges of premeditated murder."[54] The judge sentenced Chen to only a five-year probation on a reduced charge of manslaughter.

The ruling sparked a furor in the Asian American community and in American feminist organizations. After studying several recent cases across the country, legal scholars and feminists realized that the cultural defense was often used to protect the offender in cases of men murdering or raping women. Having every reason to worry about the outcome of the new legal strategy to use expert testimony in such cases, the National Organization for Women joined forces with the Organization of Asian Women and the Committee against Anti-Asian Violence to file a complaint against Pincus with the State Commission on Judicial Conduct.[55] The Asian groups, however, pulled out on the eve of filing the petition. Lacking confidence in the sincerity of American feminist organizations to defend their interests, they feared that the petition was too broad and would disallow any cultural argument for defending the interests of the Asian community in future lawsuits. Their fear was, however, interpreted by the feminist group as an invitation to murder, even though the Asian American organizations had jointly held a press conference condemning the sentence. Ethnic differences in the history of U.S. feminist movements has thus eroded gender solidarity in coping with this case.

As a result, although the case placed domestic violence in the Chinese community in the limelight of social concern for the first time, it did not end up helping embattled Asian American women solve their problems. Instead, the ruling backfired in Asian American communities. An abusive husband commented, "If this is the kind of sentence you get for killing your wife, I could do anything to you. I have the money for a good attorney."[56] No wonder women in the Chinese community lamented the fact that the courts in the United States protected men in the same way their own culture did.

In the face of domestic violence, the most helpless immigrant women were those who came to the United States as newly married spouses of U.S. citizens or permanent residents. Although there are no precise statistical records of their number, my interviews suggest that they formed a significant percentage of recent immigrant women workers in the Chinese garment shops. They were particularly vulnerable after the Marriage Fraud Amendment was passed by the Congress in 1986, which required that immigrants who came to the United States as newly married spouses of U.S. citizens and permanent residents prove their marriages by living with their spouses for at least two years. The immigration attorney Benjamin Gim has aptly described it as a "spousal hostage act."[57]

Since many recently wed immigrant women would sponsor the immigration of their parental families after they came to the United States, the passing of the Marriage Fraud Amendment rendered their husbands the key to their legal status in the United States and the immigration of their parental families. For fear of their own deportation and of jeopardizing the future immigration of their parental families, many embattled Asian immigrant women could not but swallow their pain and allow themselves to be subjugated to their husbands' abuses. Although this amendment was repealed in 1990, it had cast a long shadow on the lives of immigrant women that would not disappear within a short period.

The bureaucratic judicial system at various levels also continued to set unexpected hurdles for Chinese immigrant women who had the courage to redress their abusive marital relations. The experience of one Chinese woman, covered by the *Central Daily News* in 1988, is illustrative in this regard.[58] The woman came to the Fifth Police Precinct in Chinatown with bruised arms to file charges against her husband for physical abuse. However, the police at the precinct refused to accept her case because they found that she was living in Brooklyn. The woman tried her best to explain to them her difficulty in communicating with the police in Brooklyn because of her lack of English, but to no avail. Reportedly, the woman later did file the case in Brooklyn but soon dropped it. Although no reason was given by the newspaper, it is not difficult to understand her final act. Her experience did not sound unfamiliar to many Chinese immigrant women garment workers who had taken similar actions to reshape their destinies in their new land.

Violence in the lives of Chinese immigrant women also came from society at large. Apart from the rising crime rate in the Chinese communities in various parts of the city, the lives of Chinese immigrant women were also threatened by the growth of anti-Asian violence in the city. In 1984, for example, a woman garment worker named Zheng Lirong was pushed to her death on the subway tracks as a train was speeding into the station. The man who committed the crime later claimed to have "oriental-phobia" as a result of his experience in the Vietnam War.[59] Amazingly, the case did not arouse much concern in the city.

In 1992, Patricia Eng, a committed Asian community activist, and her colleagues founded the Asian Women's Center to provide shelter to battered women in all the Asian communities in the city. Located in Chinatown, the center took in more than four hundred women a year, most of whom were reported to be Chinese. This facility for Asian women was the first of its kind in New York City and provided the most-needed help to battered women in Asian American communities. Staff members at the center were dedicated and tried their best to provide the most feasible assistance to the women who solicited their help. However, as was the case for their counterparts in the larger society, and hindered by the cultural challenges they had to face in their own communities, only a limited number of women would come forward to seek public assistance for their family problems. Restricted by the limited nature of its resources, the center could actually provide shelter to only a small number of women.

The immense cultural and social problems working-class Asian immigrant women faced in the city were much more extensive and complicated than a single social institution could handle. The issue of how to amass a conglomeration of social forces to address their problems posed a serious challenge to organized labor and feminist organizations in the Asian American communities and society at large. Yet it also provided them with an important opportunity to rally and interact with each other to explore the possibility of forming a cross-class and cross-ethnic coalition among women in the city.

Continuing the Struggle: The Legacy of the Strike

It is in the context of this difficult situation that I will explore the impact of the strike. People tend to focus on the changing lives of the few major organizers, many of whom were recruited and served in the union shortly after the strike. For example, Shui Mak Ka became a member of the Research Department of ILGWU Local 23-25 in 1983 and served as a liaison between the union and the Chinese community. Alice Ip, following Connie Ling, became the third Chinese woman business agent in the local. Katie Quan first served in the Research Department and then at the Organizing Department of the Greater Metropolitan Area in 1987.

The labor militancy demonstrated by the women workers in the 1982 strike also inspired other community labor activists to join the union. May Ying Chen was one of them. Chen is a longtime community activist. Like Katie Quan, she grew up in the 1960s. Her family background is different from Quan's, but, influenced by the political climate of the time, she embarked upon the same path. As she wrote:

> The 60s movement had a profound, creative political impact on the Asian American communities.
>
> As a middle class, suburban Chinese kid growing up in an East Coast white community, I was tracked for cultural and social isolation, assimilation, and the model minority trap. Then the 60s hit me and millions of others—with its student strikes, anti–Vietnam War protests, women's rights, civil rights. I learned for the first time about the World War II concentration camps. I learned that Chinese who supported Mainland China in the 50s were harassed and even deported in some cases. I was personally insulted and harassed in a Boson restaurant by white GIs who had been in Vietnam and came back thinking all Asian women were prostitutes.[60]

Determined to forge a new identity and political agenda for her own community, Chen moved to the West Coast and entered a graduate program at the University of California at Los Angeles. She soon became a student activist there.

She actively participated in the Asian American movement and especially attended to issues of concern to women. As early as 1972 she joined other young Asian American women activists in offering courses on Asian American women at UCLA and forming the "Little Friends Playgroup" in Chinatown to help working-class women in the community with child care.

Chen, like Quan, was drawn by the political climate of the New York Chinese community in the late 1970s. In 1980 she and her family returned to the East Coast and settled in New York's Chinatown. From that time on, she has been actively involved in the labor movement in the community. Greatly inspired by the 1982 Chinese garment workers' strike, she joined ILGWU Local 23-25 in 1984, serving first as a legal assistant in its new immigration program and then as its assistant educational director. Together with her colleagues in the local, she has made an effort to transform the union and the Chinese community.[61]

Like their counterparts in other ethnic groups, the Chinese women unionists channeled much of their energies into their own community in addition to participating actively in union activities. Whether representing the union or acting individually, they have played an active role in many community affairs. Important episodes include their role in protesting the city's decision to build a jail in Chinatown and their efforts in joining forces with other community organizations to obtain the goals of the Chung Pak Project.

The idea of the Chung Pak Project emerged in 1982 after the community's struggle against the city's decision to build a jail near the downtown court building in the center of Chinatown. The Chinese women unionists, together with their colleagues in the union, mobilized thousands of rank-and-file Chinese members to participate in demonstrations. They went to public hearings, lobbied politicians, and joined forces with other social groups in the community to demand that the area be used instead to provide services most needed by the community, such as senior housing and quality child-care facilities. Although the city voted in the end to build the jail, it did agree to preserve a small part of the area for community use, thanks to the strong protest of the community.

Community leaders formed the Local Development Corporation (LDC) to take legal responsibility for putting the area to good use. Shui Mak Ka, together with other union officers, served on the board. Members of the LDC decided that the site should be used initially to build low-income housing for senior citizens and then a day-care center. The project was named the Chung Pak Project (the pine project, symbolizing its long-lasting nature). The union was responsible for fundraising for the day-care center. Harris Zinn, the associate manager of the local, and Sherman Eng, the head of the CGMA, cochaired the fundraising committee. However, it was Shui Mak Ka and her colleagues in the local who did the actual work.

The project was finally completed in 1993. The day-care center, with a capacity of providing service to eighty children, was still insufficient to meet the enormous community demand. However, establishing the center was not only a major step toward this end; it was a positive sign demonstrating that leaders of the Chinese community, for the first time in its history, acknowledged and began to address the needs of working women, thanks to the unionists' efforts.

The Chinese women unionists fought collectively and individually to defend the civil rights of Chinese Americans in New York City. Shui Mak Ka's important role in the incident of Huang Kongwang exemplifies this. On January 2, 1989, the Huang family in the Sunset Park area of Brooklyn was brutally beaten by the police after an inspector for a cable TV company claimed that the family refused to let him inspect their premises. However, the family argued that they did allow the inspector to look through the window on their door, because their baby girl was sound asleep, and they were afraid the inspector would wake her. In any case, except for the baby girl, the entire family was brutally beaten by the police, including Mrs. Huang, who was pregnant at the time, and her sister, who was visiting the family.

The Chinese community was outraged. Bringing back the spirit of the 1982 strike, Shui Mak Ka, a resident of Sunset Part herself, joined with various community organizations to pressure the court to address the case. After months of struggle, the court ruled against the police department, which was forced to apologize to the family. This ruling had a great impact on the community.

In 1984, women union activists formed a Chinese chapter of the Coalition of Labor Union Women to address women's issues. Along with their counterparts in other chapters and on the national board of the CLUW, the Chinese CLUW members worked for child care, family leave, and pro-choice policies and fought against gender inequality in the union. The Chinese chapter also resourcefully aroused the collective consciousness of Chinese women workers by organizing a Chinese chorus, cooking classes, and other social activities. To promote rank-and-file Chinese unionists to leadership roles, it included a number of them on its executive board. The board held meetings regularly to discuss problems on the floor and strategies to deal with them.

Despite the unfavorable records of the union officers and staff members in the Chinese community, the new Chinese women unionists to some extent redeemed the union's reputation by their excellent performance, exemplified by the two business agents, Connie Ling and Alice Ip, in the early years after the strike. Unlike Lily Moy, Ling and Ip were already in their thirties and forties when they were first appointed and had worked in a number of Chinatown shops and served as shop representatives for years. Their experience contributed significantly to their work. The story of a Mrs. Wong attests to the efficiency of Ling's work:

> Once, the owner of my shop withheld our payments for more than four weeks. I got very nervous. You know, that meant that he was going to close the shop without paying us! This kind of thing happens very often in New York's Chinatown, you know. . . . In addition, we were not so rich as to live without pay. So I called Mrs. Ling. She was the BA of our shop at that time. . . .

I called her number at the union from home. Very soon, like the "almighty and infinitely merciful Buddha," she got back to me. After listening to what I said, she said, "Don't worry, the union is your backing, we will do everything to help you."

Next day, she came to the shop. After greeting and talking to the workers as she usually did, instead of talking to me in front of the boss about my grievances, as some of the BAs usually did—she went straight to the boss and presented my grievances with the evidence that she had gathered not only from me but also from other workers. The boss could say nothing but gave us the money. . . .

She is wonderful! Without her help, each of us would lose at least a thousand. One thousand dollars, you know, how much it meant to us! . . . Her help made me realize how important the union is in my life.[62]

Since many BAs had complained about difficulties dealing with employers and workers in the Chinatown garment shops, I asked Ling how she managed to cope with the situation in the shops. She said:

Things are always difficult for a BA, . . . even if you don't go to the bosses, they will follow you all the way around once you set your feet in their shops. . . . However, as the saying goes, "Where there is a will, there is a way." If you really care about workers, you will find a way to deal with the situation. . . . I was a worker before, I know the situation very well. . . . So, every time, on my first visit to a new shop, I will stand in the middle of the shop, face the workers, and announce at the top of my voice, "I am Mrs. Ling. I am your new BA. The union is an organization of workers, and I am more than willing to help you. If you have any problems and don't think you can tell me now, don't worry, call me at my office. You even don't have to tell me your name. Leave me your phone number and I will get back to you as soon as possible. My number is 212–929–2600. . . . After repeating the number at the top of my voice several times and making sure that everyone in the shop gets it, I leave the shop—Look, that's why every time after visiting a new shop, I have to drink tons of water, and that's how I've gotten the name "big mouth Ling" . . . .

Every day, after finishing my routine visit to a number of shops in my assigned areas, which usually takes three to four hours, I will rush back to my office and see whether there are any messages for me. Normally, if workers have personal problems, they will talk to me in the shops. Only those problems related to the situation in the shops will come to me by phone.

I usually call them at home and talk to them on the phone. After that, I will talk to other workers in the same shop to verify the case and get more evidence about it. . . . It is not difficult for me to do so, because, you know, I was a worker before and workers in Chinatown change their workplaces very often. So I have a lot of personal connections in different shops. . . . Of course, I have to do all this at home after the workers return from work, that's why my husband and kids also have a lot of "grievances" against me for being on the line for most of the night and making my work such a big part of our family life. . . .

I will go to the boss and talk to him directly after I think I have known all that I need to know. I will present my evidence, one, two, three, as clearly as a union business agent should do. . . . No more bullshit, and the boss has to surrender.[63]

Her effectiveness in carrying out her duty won her popularity among many workers in her assigned area.

Among the many programs provided by the union, one of the most frequently used by its Chinese members was the immigration project, successfully run by May Ying Chen. The project benefited many Chinese union workers in the city's garment industry. Wang Xiaoping was one of the undocumented workers who received her citizenship through the project. In an interview in 1989, she related her experience with the project as follows:

> Ten years ago, sponsored by my uncle, I came as a tourist to New York from a small town in the Zhejiang Province of China. I was very young at that time, barely twenty. I found everything in this country very interesting and exciting. I was tired of the boring life in the small town in China and decided to stay—illegally, you know that. I stayed with my uncle's family, but I had to pay him rent and everything. People were all very busy in this country and no one could take care of other people, you know. So, I began working in a garment shop.
>
> Life was very difficult for me as an undocumented immigrant worker. For self-protection, I tried not to talk with others about myself and made as few friends as I could. I would take whatever work at whatever prices offered by the boss. For more than five years, I virtually lived in solitude, friendless and helpless. I felt very depressed until the union started the immigration program and May became its legal assistant. . . .
>
> I can't tell you how grateful I am to May. She was very warm and very patient in explaining to me my rights as an undocumented resident in this country. She first introduced me to study at the union's Friday English classes and then at FIT [Fashion Institute of Technology]. Thanks to her help and the new immigration laws, I received my green card a couple of months ago. My teacher in FIT also kindly helped me to get a job in the *lao wai* [foreign, meaning American in this case] company where I am still working.
>
> I am very happy now. May has rescued me from my "hiding hole" and brought me back under the sun. I love my job very much. I am earning more than thirty thousand dollars a year as a sample maker in the company with full benefits, which is already quite a lot for me, as compared with my income in Chinatown. I think I am very lucky. I love the union, and I love this country. I am thinking about sponsoring my parents and the entire family to immigrate to this country and share the happy life with me!![64]

Wang Xiaoping is not the only one who benefited from the program. Shun Nan Young, whose story was discussed in chapter 3, and many other workers also obtained their permanent residence or the immigration status for their

families or relatives with the assistance of the program. Work on the immigration project required not only sufficient knowledge of U.S. immigration law but
also the "heart" to feel for the workers, which sometimes required one to go out
of his or her way to serve, as a Ms. Yen testified:

> In 1989 I finally received my green card to stay in the United States, but I didn't
> know at first because it was mailed to my brother's address and my brother's family
> was having problem with me and did not want me to stay. They thought I would
> be a burden to them. I did not know that I had already received my permanent
> residency in this country until May asked me about the status of my application
> and offered to take me to the immigration office to check it out.
>
> She went with me to the office twice. Since there were always a crowd waiting
> outside to have their cases taken care of before the door was opened, we had to go
> there at about five in the morning to stand the line. May never failed to show up
> at that early hour each time. I was so sorry that I had dragged her into this, and
> her husband too, who always kept her company at that early hour of the day. . . .
> May was truly more than a family member to me. What she did for me made me
> feel that the union is the big mountain that I can rely on.[65]

Community attention tended to focus on the activities of those who were
employed by the union after the strike, but they were not the entire picture. The
strike also fostered a number of active rank-and-file members in the union who
were ready to continue their struggle in the days to come. Some of them volunteered their time and energies to serve as executive board members of Local
23-25 and the Chinese chapter of the CLUW after the strike.[66] In fact, between
1983 and 1992 almost all the executive board members of the Chinese CLUW
and the Chinese executive board members of Local 23-25 who immigrated before 1982, be they union employees or volunteers, had participated in the strike.

The experience of the strike led the activist Chinese workers to see clearly not
only the important role the union could play in defending their interests but,
more importantly, the fact that only when the union leadership cared about its
rank-and-file members could it play such an important role. They were therefore determined to reform the union from within. While actively participating
in all union activities and providing it with free services, they also questioned
union decisions that they considered problematic. Ann Wong, a 1982 striker and
an executive board member of the Chinese CLUW and Local 23-25, had the
following to say about her experience as an active rank-and-file member on the
two boards:

> I have been actively participating in almost all the activities organized by the
> union, yes, almost all—you name it. . . . The union has had a lot of problems and
> I spoke out whenever I saw things were getting wrong. For example, the problems
> with the BAs. I spoke out at many executive board meetings. I said, workers don't
> trust the union because many BAs don't do a good job. They are friends of the

bosses not the workers. Many workers believe that they are taking bribes. Some workers and other members of the community saw them enjoying tea and food at the Chinatown restaurants during their work hours. How could you expect this kind of people to represent workers?!

Also, as early as the mid-1980s, I warned the union that some of the Chinatown employers were withholding their workers' pay and the union should do something about that. I have been working in the shop all these days and I know how it meant to the workers when their wages were withheld. So, very often, when I talked about things like this at the executive board meeting, I was so carried away by my own emotion that I talked fast and even cried, making it very difficult for others to understand and translate what I said into English for those non-Chinese members. I am sorry about that. . . .

I believe that labor unions are workers' own organizations. But only when they listen to the responses of their rank-and-file members and care about workers' interests can they be considered as such. I am a worker myself, I certainly wish that my union is strong. As a shop representative and an executive board member of the local, I also wish that I can be a bridge between the union and the workers. I hope I can inform the union of the expectations of workers and, at the same time, build up my fellow workers' confidence in the union.[67]

Regardless of their employers' coercion, a number of active Chinese rank-and-file members continued to advocate union contracts and help to enforce labor laws in the shop. Every three years, when the union contract was renegotiated, members of the Chinese chapter of the CLUW, union officers, and rank-and-file members formed the Committee on Union Contract Enforcement, which effectively evoked the memory of the 1982 strike and exerted pressure on the employers.

While a number of the former 1982 strikers were playing a visible role in the union and the community, others carried on their struggles in other arenas of the industry. Those who later helped form the ILGWU's Workers' Center in Sunset Park were among them. As they recalled, living far away from the hub of the Chinese garment industry in Manhattan's Chinatown or some even working at home or in nonunion shops, they felt that they had been forgotten by the union. Nevertheless, they continued to struggle for their rights and interests as workers.

The Sunday English school run by the union in the Sunset Park area, which began in 1991, finally provided them with a meeting place to come to know each other and share their feelings and experience. As one of them put it spontaneously and with good humor in the interview, "Do you know how I felt at that time? I was so excited that I felt I had finally *zhao dao le zu zhi* ['found my own organization,' a popular line in the play *The Red Lantern*, widely seen during the Cultural Revolution in China]."[68] They were so eager to join efforts with each other and the new immigrant workers to address labor issues in the area that one 1982 striker offered her own apartment as a gathering place for the group to meet after class. In early 1993, together with the new immigrant activist workers in the area, they helped Dan Yunfeng, an ILGWU organizer, create a workers' center in Brooklyn. On a volunteer basis, they joined efforts in advocating labor laws in the shops and promoting the cause of labor in the Sunset Park area.

While fighting arduously on their home front, the Chinese union activists also extended their support to the struggle of Chinese garment workers in other parts of the country. In the summer of 1986, when Chinese workers at the P and L Sportswear Company in Boston planned to strike and began bargaining with the city and the state for their rights in setting the guidelines and funding for their retraining programs, the Chinese union activists in New York met with them, exchanged experiences with them, and helped them map out strategies.

To advance the cause of Asian American workers in the United States, members of the Chinese chapter of the CLUW first formed a citywide Asian Labor Committee in 1989 and then joined efforts with the Asian American labor committees in San Francisco and Los Angeles to form the national Asian-Pacific American Labor Association (APALA). The association was the first of its kind in the history of the AFL-CIO. May Ying Chen and Katie Quan were on the steering committee and worked hard for its founding. In 1992, when the organization was finally formed, Katie Quan was elected president, and May Ying Chen was elected executive vice president.

From the outset, the APALA made its position clear: "While we are committed to defend affirmative action in the workplace, we are also committed to promote affirmative action within the labor movement." In a period when unions represented less than 15 percent of the workforce, the APALA pressured for change within established labor unions. It advocated the need for labor unions to represent the interests of the majority of workers rather than simply union members and the need to move away from the culture of business unionism toward a culture that "invites workers' activism and leadership."[69] Together with their counterparts elsewhere in the country, New York City's Chinese women unionists were determined to rebuild unionism in the United States.

As the Chinese activists were playing an increasingly visible role in the labor movement, some among them began to hold important positions in the ILGWU. Katie Quan was one of them. In January 1990 she was appointed manager of the ILGWU's San Francisco–based Pacific Northwest District Council. Once she returned to the place where she was born and raised, she wasted no time in organizing Chinese workers in the Bay Area. In February 1990 Seal 1, a Koret plant and the last union plant in the area, began to lay off workers after the company announced plans to close the plant. Workers stood firm. Led by Katie Quan, they formed the "Save Seal 1 Committee" to pressure the company for better terms. Although they could not dissuade the company from closing the plant, they did secure a solid severance pay agreement due to the efforts of the committee and pressure from a number of public officials.[70] To step up its organizing efforts in the San Francisco area, the ILGWU opened a workers' center in the heart of San Francisco's Chinatown.[71] Quan's remarkable organizing capability, demonstrated over the years, paved the way for her to become the first Chinese to hold the position of vice president of the union in 1997.

It is critical to remember that the Chinese women unionists and labor activists waged a battle against heavy odds in the decade after the strike. Like other women throughout the history of the ILGWU, they were fighting both inside and outside the union. Given the difficulties of the time, the ingrained bureaucracy and business unionism that prevailed, and the large number of Chinese union members they served, the changes they worked for were slow in coming. With the passage of time, the Chinese unionists began to face additional challenges. How could they continue to maintain their labor militancy within the union in the face of its increasingly bureaucratic institutions? How could they maintain their commitment to workers' interests, enlarge the ranks of active workers, and promote militancy on the floor in the face of the rapidly deteriorating labor conditions in the industry? How could they continue to promote rank-and-file democracy within the union and pressure for change? How could they develop effective strategies to organize the largest possible number of non-union workers when organized labor was facing unprecedented challenges? How could they prevent special interest groups, such as the Chinese chapter of the CLUW and the New York Asian Labor Committee, with their emphasis on social activities, from turning into mere social clubs? These were just some of the many questions they had to answer.

Disappointed by the lack of meaningful change in many aspects of the union's operation, a number of Chinese women garment workers, like the strikers in 1982, refused to sit back and wait for change. They began exploring alternative organizational forces to defend their rights. Some sought assistance from the community-based Chinese Staff and Workers Association, which had been established in 1979 and had served as a center of the labor movement in the community. Many longtime community labor activists, including Katie Quan and May Ying Chen, were once members. Although some members of the organization, like Quan, in the late 1970s and early 1980s concerned themselves with issues in the garment industry, and although the organization also rendered its timely support to the Chinese garment workers' strike in 1982, labor issues in the garment industry were initially not its major concern. Instead the organization focused on Chinese restaurants and other employers in the community.

In 1988, as labor violations grew in the Chinese garment industry, the CSWA decided to form a Women's Committee to address these issues. Rhoda Wong, who served as the director of the Women's Committee, recalled that most of the earliest members of the committee were wives of the male members of the organization. However, the Women's Committee soon managed to draw a number of women workers from the garment industry who had no previous experience with the organization. They came to the organization initially to seek assistance on issues about which they could not receive a prompt response from the union or for services that the union was unable to provide in Chinatown. For example, some Chinatown workers came to the CSWA for quick consultation about labor violations on the floor because it was conveniently located in the center of Chinatown, and ILGWU Local 23-25 did not have a permanent office in Chinatown before 1996, despite its large number of Chinese members. A number of workers also chose to attend the English classes offered by the CSWA because these classes were given on Sunday, which was their only day off, while those by the union were on weekday evenings.[72]

Many of the women workers who came to the CSWA soon became actively involved in the labor activities sponsored by the organization. This had a lot to do with the belief and organizing strategies of the CSWA as a new type of community-based labor organization. Unlike the traditional unions that fought on behalf of workers in relation to their employers, the CSWA emphasized the importance of empowering workers and encouraging them to take the initiative in fighting for their own rights. It believed that the strength of labor organizations lay in workers' political activism. As Rhoda Wong once put it, "'We're stronger if each woman sees herself as an organizer.'"[73] To this end, the Women's Committee held a special session every Sunday for members to get together, share their feelings and experiences, and practice public speaking.[74] It also offered English classes, monthly seminars on different topics, social events, and a newsletter on women's issues and labor law.

The efforts of the committee paid off. As early as 1990 members of the CSWA Women's Committee began performing plays in the streets that disclosed and condemned the sweating system in the garment shops. They also actively participated in mobilizing workers to join the political campaigns organized by the CSWA in the community. For example, before the demonstration "Fight for Economic Justice," sponsored by the CSWA in 1992, many of the women workers, following the example of the Chinatown day-care activists before the 1982 strike, went from shop to shop to urge workers to come out, concern themselves with political issues in the community, and join the demonstration. A member of the committee recalled her organizing experience at a Sunday meeting:

> I went to a number of shops, urging workers to come out. I said, "I am one of you. I am going to take two hours from my work to participate in the demonstration. For what? For equal employment opportunity for the Chinese community. For ourselves and for our second generation!" . . . Some workers said, "What's the point of doing that; we have been fighting for so long, but I don't see any result." . . . I said, "Yes, in this aspect, we need to learn from the African Americans. They never give up their struggle. Even if we can't get all that we want, we can get at least part of it."[75]

The newsletter of the Women's Committee, *Funu Gongzuo Fang* (women's workshop), reported that committee members had visited a total of five hundred garment shops and talked with about two thousand women workers before the demonstration. According to the report, they successfully brought more than a thousand women workers to the streets, and the participation of women workers in large numbers also changed men's manners in the demonstration. The male organizers were said to have become more amiable and easier to approach than before when they explained the cause of the demonstration and the intended outcome of the actions.[76]

Like those in the union who joined efforts with Asian labor activists in other parts of the country, members of the CSWA Women's Committee also formed close ties with other community-based Asian and ethnic American labor organizations. The San Francisco–based Asian Immigrant Women Advocate (AIWA) and the El Paso, Texas–based La Mujer Obrera were sister organizations of the CSWA Women's Committee. In 1992 members of the committee met and exchanged experiences with those from AIWA. The two Asian community-based organizations have since maintained close ties.

Although community-based labor organizations such as the AIWA and CSWA might not be able to bring about sweeping changes in a short period due to their limited resources, their base in the community and their rank-and-file orientation made them an effective form of labor organization in an era when the U.S. workforce consisted increasingly of nonunion ethnic women workers, both immigrant and native-born. They could also serve as a pressure group outside traditional unions to agitate for change. Such was the case with the CSWA in New York City. Since many of the garment workers in the CSWA were also members of ILGWU Local 23-25, they had the opportunity to use the CSWA to pressure their union to fight for their rights. As one woman worker noted: "If we have problems, we will come here [CSWA] first, then the union, and then the State Department of Labor. If the union was slow in solving the problem, we will show its officers our CSWA membership card. They will take our problems more seriously if they know that we have connections with the CSWA, which is likely to get involved if the union doesn't do anything for us."[77]

The approaches adopted by the Chinese women labor activists in New York represented two major trends in the larger U.S. labor movement in the 1980s and 1990s; both have advantages and disadvantages in organizing workers. Based on her study of the experiences of women garment workers in the AIWA and the union in San Francisco, Ruth Needleman has pointed out that established labor unions have the experience and resources to reach large and diverse workforces, to influence policy makers at various levels, to connect workers to national and even international support, and to ensure labor representation and improvements in workers' wages and working conditions. However, to enable them to work more effectively and democratically at the grassroots level, carrying out organizational change in these unions is a complicated, difficult, and slow process, given their entrenched structures, cultures, and traditions. In contrast, although it is difficult for community-based organizations to bring about a swift push to overcome the obstacles workers face, lacking the kind of resources the established labor unions possess, their emphasis on empowerment, consciousness raising, one-on-one contact, and long-term perseverance assumes a more humane and friendly face to workers. These organizations can cater to the needs of the changing workforce in a much more effective way and can provide workers with training and education at a pace well suited to their overwhelming responsibilities.[78]

The advantages and disadvantages of these two kinds of organizing were more salient in New York's Chinese community, given the union's strong influence in the city, the large size of its Chinese membership, and the limited number of Chinese on the union's staff or holding decision-making positions in the union, as well as the union's stage of development. How to build on the strength of each other while recognizing and respecting differences between them has become a major challenge to the Chinese women labor activists in their fight for the common cause of working people.

Nevertheless, regardless of their different approaches, the political activism of these two groups of Chinese women labor activists in New York City not only brought them into the front lines of the labor movement but also had important implications for cultural change in their families and the community. Some developed more egalitarian relationships with their husbands, either by participating in the same political activities or by gaining respect for their achievements in promoting the cause of labor in the community. The experience of Ann Wong is an example:

> When I first attended the executive board meetings of the local and the Chinese CLUW, my husband always said, "What good would it bring when you people kept talking about the *saam fuk peih* [Cantonese: the same three old blankets, meaning the same things]?!" I said, "Well, those 'three old blankets' may not mean anything to you, but they mean a lot to me. . . ." I have been actively involved in all the union's activities. I have also attended the English classes offered by the union to improve my English. Recently, I spoke on behalf of workers at the congressional hearing to condemn NAFTA. It was a pleasant surprise to my husband when he saw my picture in the local news. For the first time since we got married, he said, "How about this? To show you some support, I'll cook dinner for you every Monday and Wednesday night when you come home late after attending the English classes." . . . I simply couldn't help laughing.[79]

Understanding and support among friends and colleagues in the women's groups also encouraged some women activists to challenge their strained relationship with their husband and reshape their destinies. As Miriam Ching Louie notes, women workers at the Sunday sessions of the CSWA Women's Committee did more than "talk shop." They also talked about their families and gender issues in the Chinese culture.[80] This was also the case with the women in the Chinese CLUW. A number of women activists have gained the confidence to reshape their lives through sharing experiences with friends and colleagues in the women's groups. Alice Ip was one of them. With the respect she had gained from her colleagues and the support and encouragement of her children and her friends in the Chinese CLUW, she finally ended her more-than-twenty-year abusive relationship with her husband and began a new life.

There were also a few women labor activists in the Chinese CLUW who, for various reasons, chose to live a single life in defiance of the cultural constraints and the heavy family orientation of the community. Shun Nan Young continued to remain single according to the particular culture of her native town.[81] Nancy Liang, for a different reason, also chose to remain single and live with her two sisters.[82] Their alternative lifestyle might be considered an "aberration" and frowned upon by some traditionalists in the community but never among their friends and fellow workers in the Chinese CLUW. Class and gender consciousness as well as self-confidence fostered by their experience in the garment shops and labor activism in the union, coupled with the degree of economic independence they gained from working in the industry, enabled them to have more choices in their lives.

Apart from those labor activists in the ILGWU or CSWA, there were also a number of Chinese women garment workers who were struggling on their own terms to move out of the abusive labor conditions in the garment shops. Most of them were relatively young and had fewer child-care and other household responsibilities or had family members willing to assist them with their household chores. Like Wong Xiaoping and Tang Mei, they would attend vocational schools after taking the English classes offered by the union or other social organizations to pursue a completely different career or climb up the ladder of skill in the garment industry.

A Fang, whose story was covered by the community newspaper, is an example of this. In 1986 she came from Guangzhou to join her husband in New York. She was shocked to find that her living conditions in New York were much worse than those in her native land and that her work in the garment shop was much harder than that in Guangzhou. Working ten to twelve hours a day, six days a week, and making a little more than a hundred dollars per week, she said she cried almost every day when she first came to the United States. To escape the sweated labor in the Chinatown shop, she began learning English by attending the union-run English classes. Her husband taunted her as "having the ambition to become President of the United States," but she persisted. With the little English she had learned, A Fang embarked on a training program in data processing and began working in a bank upon completion of that program. Although income from working at the bank was not high, she told the reporter that she was happy with her new job because "it was not backbreaking."[83]

More workers, however, sought a way out by learning to become sample makers or fashion designers in midtown garment firms by attending classes at the Fashion Institute of Technology in the city. Their number began to grow after 1984 when the GIDC began its "Super Sewers" program, and FIT also offered open admission to the Chinese workers to many of its programs.[84]

Although how far they could advance remained a question, given the structural problems embedded in the industry and the difficulties of the time, many Chinese immigrant women garment workers continued to wage various forms of struggle to improve their situation in the city's industry. Like the women strikers in 1982, they learned to utilize and pressure the existing institutions to better their lives. Their arduous struggles in the decade after the strike should not be ignored. From their past image as *a sim a mouh*, who were pushed into the limbo of oblivion in community affairs, to the spokespersons for labor issues in the community and at the forefront of the Asian American labor movement in the nation, many Chinese immigrant women garment workers have come a long way. They have been holding and will continue to hold up more than half the sky in the Chinese garment industry and many working-class families.

CONCLUSION

This study has examined the significance of the experience of Chinese women garment workers in the historical context of the Chinese American community in New York City. By discussing the important roles of working-class women in the community and their changing perceptions of life over time, this study recovers an important part of history that has long been ignored.

One of the main concerns in the study of Chinese American history has been to challenge the image of passivity and unassimilability imposed upon the Chinese American community. Much discussion on this subject has been devoted to the condition of Chinese Americans during the Exclusion era. Previous studies have documented how the Chinese exclusion laws were implemented and how, as individuals and as a community in the United States, the Chinese have struggled to reduce the restrictions imposed on them.[1] These studies have persuasively argued that it was not that Chinese refused to be assimilated but that they were not given the opportunity.[2]

Recent studies have further challenged the myth of Chinese unassimilability by recovering historical records written by Chinese Americans who lived through that era to illustrate the arduous efforts they made to claim a place in the United States even during the hostile Exclusion era.[3] Increased attention has also been given to the variations of Chinese experience among different classes and generations in the community.[4] However, gender as a category of analysis, particularly regarding working-class women, remains underemphasized in these studies.[5]

This study complicates our understanding by discussing both the class and gender implications of this era. It argues that gender as well as class was at the center of the Chinese experience during this period. By relegating Chinese male laborers to what had traditionally been defined as women's occupations and by depriving them of a family life, from which many derived their sense of power and meaning of life, the discrimination against the Chinese not only effectively consigned Chinese male laborers to a much lower social and economic status than their white ethnic counterparts, it also exerted traumatic psychological impact that had important ramifications for the development of the Chinese American community in New York City.

Gender implications of this era were demonstrated also by the experiences of the workers' families, particularly those who were left behind in China. Although as a form of resistance to the constraints imposed on them many Chinese American families managed to hold on surprisingly well under the pressure of long-term separation during this period, as many studies have pointed out, the mechanism through which they managed to do so was not based on equality among their members. Anxious to maintain male domination in the community when an increasingly large number of its male members had emigrated from their homeland, the patriarchal institutions of the emigrant communities in China tightened their grip over the women who were left behind. This increased patriarchal control in the Chinese emigrant communities not only reveals the limited nature of the acculturation some Chinese immigrant men appeared to have attained after years of living in the United States, as some studies have suggested.[6] It has also demonstrated the transnational gender implications of the Chinese Exclusion laws for Chinese American working-class families.

However, like Chinese male laborers in the United States, women in many families, including the small number in the United States, refused to accept their predestined lot. The roles they played in their families, which hardly conformed to the traditional gender norm, and their various forms of resistance contribute significantly to our understanding of Chinese resistance during the Exclusion era. It must be pointed out that, although women and men in Chinese American working-class families both suffered tremendously during this period, women's experience differed significantly from that of men. The most outstanding difference was that they had to challenge the patriarchal culture in a transnational context.[7]

A gendered analysis of the Chinese experience also reveals that discrimination against Chinese during the Exclusion era operated not only through U.S. legal, political, and economic institutions but also through the interplay between the two cultures on both sides of the Pacific. It was the highly gendered, classed, and racialized culture of the United States interacting with the patriarchal culture of China during the time that has assigned discriminatory meaning to the Chinese experience during this period. The study of cultural intersection can help us better understand not only the nature of the Exclusion era but also the transformation of Chinese American culture in subsequent periods.

Previous studies have rightly argued that Chinese American culture is not a replica of Chinese culture but is molded by Chinese Americans in the changing political and economic context of the United States.[8] Few, however, have adequately explained why in different periods of Chinese American history some aspects of Chinese traditional culture appear to have been perpetuated while others have not.

This study examines the scope of cultural transformation in the Chinese community in each major historical period after World War II by placing working-class women's experience at the center of investigation. It reveals that although the gender imbalance of the New York Chinese community began to be redressed in the immediate postwar era, and the lives of immigrant families in the city also did not provide sufficient ground for the revival of traditional gender norms in the community, women in working-class immigrant families continued to be largely confined to their homes. This was not simply caused by their family-centered ethnic culture, as some believe. It was an outcome of the combined influence of the economic structure of the community, the particular setting of the Chinese family businesses in the city, and the lack of employment opportunities for Chinese immigrant women. The limited nature of change in the immediate postwar era was further demonstrated by the lives of those women in China who were continuously separated from their husbands in the United States. It was a result of the discriminatory quota imposed on Chinese immigration and the animosity between the United States and the new government in China.

Significant changes began to take place in the late 1960s, after the elimination of the discriminatory nationality quotas in U.S. immigration law and the growth of the garment industry in the community. Chinese immigrant women began to work outside the home in large numbers. Their role in the family also changed significantly due to the changing employment pattern of working-class men in the community. Although in articulating their goals, many married immigrant women workers continued to place the interest of the family above self interest, this strong family orientation cannot be understood simply as the continuing influence of their native culture. Given an understanding of their lives since the late 1960s, which were characterized by economic interdependence between husbands and wives, persistent racist and sexist attitudes exhibited by various institutions they encountered, and the limited nature of their opportunities in their new land, this study argues that their language of family orientation can also be regarded as a strategy to justify their ways of living in the United States and their various forms of resistance in their families and workplaces.

Only in this context can we better understand the changing perceptions of life among women workers in the Chinatown garment industry. Working in an industry with strong ties to the outside world, Chinese women workers were exposed to the world beyond their own community, with all its merits and challenges. Playing an indispensable role in the family after the transformation of the economic structure of the Chinese community, they came to recognize their worth in their families and society. Although their willingness to articulate their sense of value might not appear to have changed as significantly as some scholars would like to see, their actual deeds demonstrate a significant degree of change in their perceptions of their place in their families and society. It is in this context that one can understand the militancy demonstrated by the women workers in the 1982 strike.

The 1982 strike might be "a surprise" to outsiders, as one scholar describes it.[9] It was by no means a surprise to many members of the community, especially to those women workers who organized and actively participated in it. The strike not only provided them with a powerful outlet to express their bottled-up grievances; it was also an important event in the process of their integration in the United States. In initiating and sustaining the strike, many women workers and labor activists learned about the operation of the U.S. political system, picked up the union rhetoric, and utilized its institutional power to defend their rights. In so doing, they further identified themselves with the democratic principles of their host land and demonstrated to the outside world their enormous courage, wisdom, and collective strength, which has once again attested to Chinese women workers' potential to become a major force of organized labor in the United States.

In all certainty, the history of the New York Chinese women garment workers is no longer the classic Chinese American working-class story of discrimination and resistance, like that of the earlier Chinese laundrymen in New York. Shaped by the time and the changing conditions in their native and host lands, the women workers' experience differed markedly from that of the early male laborers. While the Chinese laundrymen in the early twentieth century suffered the kind of pain that could only be soothed by dreaming of returning to China one day, many Chinese immigrant women workers, especially those who came with their families during and after the late 1960s, made up their minds to settle in the United States the moment they decided to emigrate from their native land. Although they continued to maintain strong ties with their native land, they considered themselves a part of American society. As was the case for other ethnic-minority workers who were discriminated against in the United States, they fought for equal rights in their new land, and in the course of this struggle they also contributed significantly to changing the society that they had chosen to live in. In this sense, their story is a classic story of ethnic immigrant women workers in the United States. It is also a story of change in Chinese American history.

In truth, the experience of Chinese working-class immigrant women or, more specifically, the New York Chinese garment workers, does not tell the entire story of Chinese American history.[10] Their experience, however, points to the differing meanings of Chinese American history for different social groups in the community. These differences further reveal the dynamics of Chinese Americans in U.S. history.

The experience of Chinese American women garment workers also contributes significantly to our understanding of ethnic women workers in the United States. One major concern of feminist scholars in labor history has been the tendency to maintain the area as the preserve of men by defining class as "the central organizing conception of labor history," "the workplace as the only locus of class formulation," and women's experience as fundamentally cultural and social, with no bearing on the economic concept of class. To challenge this male-centrality and to place gender along with class at the center of study, feminist labor historians have proposed that we enlarge the scope of labor history to encompass not only the workplace but also the family, the household, and the community. They argue that gender informs not only the actions but also the ideas of men and women, and the multiple meanings of gender and class coexist in all social relationships and institutions.[11]

This study supports this contention. Nevertheless, like most studies of ethnic women workers it also argues that placing gender in relation to class is still not sufficient to understand the multiple meanings residing in labor history. Especially in a multilayered and highly gendered and racialized society like the United States, one has to treat race/ethnicity as an equally important parameter in analysis. Without understanding fully the multiple meanings of class, gender, and race/ethnicity in the lives of workers, the evolution of these meanings over time, and their intricate intersections with each other and with other categories of analysis one cannot fully understand the dynamics and constraints in the lives of workers in the United States.

One way to decode the multiple and contested meanings of gender, class, and race/ethnicity for workers is to examine in depth the multiple forces that shape their complex relationships with other social groups or institutions. This has been demonstrated by the analysis of the lives of the Chinatown women workers in this study. Although the relationship between workers and employers in the Chinatown shops was potentially oppositional, there was also a degree of interdependence in their relationship. Relegated to the same enclave and economic sector and subjected to exploitation by midtown manufacturers and unequal treatment by other institutional forces in the city's garment industry, Chinese employers had to rely on their communal ties to carve a niche for themselves, while their workers had to rely on the Chinatown industry to survive in their new land.

This interdependent relationship between workers and employers coupled with the particular form of management in the Chinatown shops, which was primarily based on the rhetoric and practices selected from the repertoire of their own ethnic culture, had the effect of accentuating the importance of ethnic commonality while, to a degree, weakening potential class conflicts on the shop floor. This weakening of potential class conflicts was further reinforced by the clustering of garment shops in the area of Chinatown, which allowed workers to share information and thus attain a degree of autonomy in selecting their workplace and to exert some influence toward curbing employers' unscrupulous operations on the shop floor.

Similar contradictions can be found in the relationships among workers. Although sharing the same position in the shops, solidarity among workers should not be taken for granted. With different social, cultural, and political backgrounds, workers in the Chinatown shops did not necessarily perceive

things in the same way. Various factors undermined solidarity. The most salient of these was competition among them in production, generated by the
highly competitive nature of the garment industry and manipulated by their
employers.

The Chinese workers' sense of class identity was also weakened by the union's
ineffective operation on the floor. As this study reveals, the experience of unionization for New York's Chinese garment workers was mixed. Unionization offered them important benefits that they and their families could not have otherwise had. However, the entrenched bureaucracy of the union and the gender
and racial biases built into its leadership and its policies made it even harder
for Chinese women to seek representation in their own organization. This undermined significantly Chinese workers' identification with the union and the
union's claim of legitimacy as a labor organization among workers in the Chinatown garment shops.

However, the complex relationships within the shops were not the only factor that shaped the Chinese women workers' workplace practices. As with their
counterparts in other ethnic groups, family formed the most important part of
their lives. Not only did their family responsibilities influence their choice of
work and their work schedule, but the financial and other determinants of their
family status also greatly influenced their attitudes toward labor/management
relations in the shops, the degree of their involvement in collective bargaining,
and their forms of resistance on the floor.

Furthermore, as this study reveals, immigrant women workers' perceptions
of life were not a simple reaction to the realities they faced at various sites and
various times in the United States. Their perceptions of their role in the family,
their family relationships, working conditions in the shops, and the meanings
of unionism as well as the language or rhetoric they used to either espouse or
denounce what they encountered in their lives or to simply justify their own
attitudes were all greatly influenced by their past experience. This constant interplay between their present and past experience added to the complexity of
the multiple and contested meanings of class, gender, race/ethnicity, and other
principles of social organization.

The interaction of multiple forces that shaped the lives of Chinese women
workers proves that workers' lives cannot be improved simply by changing one
aspect, nor can the nonimprovement of their lives be attributed to one single
factor.[12] This is fully illustrated by the mixed impact of women's wage-earning
labor outside the home on Chinese immigrant working-class families in New
York. Although it created a more egalitarian relationship in some families, it also
aggravated potential tensions in others. Nevertheless, this study argues that
changes in the Chinese community since the late 1960s did have a positive impact on building up a number of women workers' self-confidence. This was not
simply an outcome of their economic contribution to their families. Rather it
was the result of the combined influence of the intersections of their experience

at various sites of their lives, their changing role in the family, and the constant negotiations between their former perceptions of life and the realities they encountered in the United States.

A careful examination of the complexity of Chinese women workers' lives and the transformation of their subjectivities reveals that despite the multiple and contested nature of the meanings of class, gender, and race/ethnicity, these major principles of social organization help shape the self-identities of workers in the United States. As is the case for other social groups, Chinese women workers' identities are multidimensional, and every aspect plays an important role in determining their political allegiance, contingent on the particular circumstances in which they find themselves.

As demonstrated in this study, women in Chinese American working-class families and women workers in the Chinatown shops have a history of resistance to the injustice imposed on them by their highly gendered ethnic culture and other institutional forces. Although most of them launched protests individually before 1982, their shared position in their families, their community, and their workplaces fostered solidarity among them. Many studies, particularly those of women workers in economically developing countries under the global economy, have argued that open confrontation and large-scale labor organizing, prevalent in traditional industrialized democracies, should not be taken as the only viable form of labor militancy and that the significance of silent, individual, and nonconfrontational forms of resistance should not be ignored.[13]

This study acknowledges the constraints workers are under and the significance of their silent and individual protests. It nevertheless argues that the significance of workers' particular forms of resistance has to be understood in the context from which they emerged. In industrial countries that have a tradition of collective bargaining, the significance of labor organizing among immigrant women workers and the labor militancy demonstrated in their open confrontations with various institutional forces must not be underestimated. They signify the important cultural transformation of workers, who have immigrated from countries without such traditions, in their new land. Labor organizing remains the most effective way to protect workers' interests in countries where all social groups have to fight for their rights under relatively open political systems.

In short, based on the complexity of Chinese women workers' experience, one can conclude that class conflict is not the only social conflict workers encounter, nor is it always the major one. Without understanding the intersections of class conflict with other social conflicts, one cannot fully understand workers' lives. This conclusion has the potential to challenge the existing paradigm of U.S. labor history, which tends to privilege class conflict over other social conflicts. It also has important meanings for the development of the labor movement in this era of the global economy, when workers in economically developed countries are increasingly nonunion, members of minority ethnic groups, and women who are traditionally left out by labor and government institutions but whose lives are the hardest hit by the impact of the global economy. They are the Third World within the First World, as some scholars put it.[14]

How to develop effective organizing strategies to meet these new challenges is on the agenda of almost every labor institution in the contemporary United States. The experience of women garment workers in New York shows that labor organizing should be extended to include not only the workplace but also the community and other social institutions. It must be able to address the major contradictions workers encounter and meet their needs beyond the workplace. To combat the challenge of the globalization of capital, the U.S. labor movement must also develop viable strategies to form alliances with workers in other parts of the world.[15] Although community-based organizing is still in a stage of experimentation, there is no doubt that parochialism and the culture of business unionism, prevailing in many traditional trade unions, have proven to be inherently impotent in this new age.

In any case, like the Chinese women immigrant workers in this study, workers in all trades and all over the country, men as well as women, will not sit back and wait for a change in traditional trade unions. The present situation of the U.S. labor movement reminds one of the lines in a poem by Mao Zedong, which were quoted in Shui Mak Ka's inspirational speech at the union rally in 1982: "Thousands of sails pass by the shipwreck; thousands of saplings shoot up in front of the withered tree." For the traditional trade unions, the issue is no longer whether to change or not but whether the change is sufficient to meet the challenge of the times.

Unlike the case in the early part of the twentieth century, the Asian American labor movement is an integral part of the U.S. labor movement. Together with their counterparts in other parts of the country, Chinese American workers and labor activists, women as well as men, are fighting at the forefront of the labor movement. With strong convictions, they are writing a new chapter in the history of the U.S. labor movement.

EPILOGUE

Until 1998, the garment industry remained the largest manufacturing industry in New York City. Labor conditions in the industry show no sign of improvement, however. In 1995, the ILGWU merged with the Amalgamated Clothing Workers of America, the men's wear and textile union, to form the Union of Needletraders, Industrial and Textile Employees (UNITE!). However, the purported strengthening of the labor institution in the industry does not seem to have curbed the continuing deterioration of labor conditions. A survey of New York City's garment contractors, conducted by New York State's Apparel Industry Task Force in 1997, concluded that "the overall level of compliance decrease[d]." According to the report, only 3 percent of the shops investigated complied with all labor laws, and only 13 percent did not falsify bookkeeping records. The conditions of the Chinese shops surveyed were not better: 90 percent were found in violation of at least one labor law, and 71 percent were charged with monetary violations.[1]

As always, responses to social concerns about the sweating conditions in the garment shops varied in the Chinese community. The Chinese Staff and Workers Association called for further action to crack down on the sweating system in the Chinese garment industry. Emphasizing the investigators' inaccuracies in identifying union shops versus nonunion shops and the overrepresentation of union and Chinese shops in the investigation, the union spokesperson questioned the intention of the survey and the credibility of its findings. The strongest response, however, came from the Chinese employers. They denounced the state investigation for the closing of many Chinese garment shops by the end of the year due to the withdrawal of work by several major manufacturers. As they saw it, the investigation had "added salt to the wound" or dropped stones on the sinking Titanic of the Chinese garment industry by lumping all Chinese shops under the infamous epithet "sweatshop."[2]

Changes in the Chinese garment industry, however, were not all grim. There were encouraging signs of growing labor activism in the community. Contrary to the labor activists' earlier apprehension, UNITE!'s Brooklyn Workers' Center not only survived but grew into a command post for workers' struggles in the 1990s, thanks to the joint efforts of the Chinese unionists and workers.[3] According to the recollections of Joanna Cheng, the director of the center since 1997, between 1995 and May 1996 more than four hundred workers came to the center to solicit assistance for retrieving their back wages, which amounted to a total of a quarter of a million dollars.[4]

Realizing the growing problems in the Chinese garment shops in Brooklyn, the CSWA opened a workers' center in the same area, located only a few blocks from that of UNITE!. By mid-1998, despite its short history in the borough, the CSWA Workers' Center had already successfully mobilized workers in fighting several highly publicized battles to defend their rights in the shops.[5] Members of the CSWA Women's Committee have actively participated in these efforts. Their experience in relation to the community and the union has in many respects departed significantly from that of the earlier Chinese labor activists and merits a new study.

Remarkable changes have also taken place in the leadership of the union. In 1996 Kathie Quan became the first Chinese woman vice president of UNITE!.[6] In 1998 May Ying Chen was elected the first Chinese female associate manager of Local 23-25, the largest UNITE! local, and later a vice president of the union. Under her leadership the local launched several major community-based campaigns to combat deteriorating conditions in the industry. One of them is the No-Work-on-Sunday campaign. Starting in March 1998, dozens of union activists and workers volunteered their time on Sunday, distributing flyers and checking the union shops in Brooklyn and Manhattan's Chinatown to ensure that members were not working on Sunday. The battle may seem like déjà vu to those who are familiar with the history of the city's garment industry, but it holds important new meanings for the Chinese garment workers, women as well as men, at the start of the twenty-first century.

However, there are some major aspects of the Chinese garment industry in New York City that remain largely unchanged. The most outstanding of these is the coethnic nature of the shops. Despite the fact that the city's garment shops have become increasingly multiethnic, owners and workers in most of the Chinese shops, particularly those in the two major Chinese garment manufacturing centers in Manhattan and Brooklyn, continue to share the same ethnic identity. In what ways the concept of ethnicity works in these Chinese shops remains the central concern of those who intend to understand them.

GLOSSARY

Words and expressions in Taishan dialect are followed by (T) and those in Cantonese by (C).[1]

a baak (C)　　阿伯
A Chaan (C)　　阿灿
A Fang　　阿芳
a gu (C)　　阿姑
a je (C)　　阿姐
a mouh (T)　　阿姆
a mui (C)　　阿妹
Anhui　　安徽
a sam (C)　　阿婶
Asian Americans for Equal Employment　　亚洲人平等就业会
Asian Americans for Equality　　亚洲人平等会
a sim a mouh (T)　　阿婶阿姆
a sou (C)　　阿嫂
Association of Oriental Garment Manufacturers of America　　美洲中华自由制衣总会
a suk (C)　　阿叔
A Ying　　阿英

Baoan　　保安
bing fei yat ga (C)　　兵匪一家
bing xiang　　冰箱
bou go pihng ngon (C)　　报个平安

Chen　　陈
Chen, May Ying　　陈美瑛
Chen Donglu[2]　　陈东鲁
Cheng, Joanna　　郑爱贞
Chen Jianwan[3]　　陈建宛
Chen Qianwen　　陈倩雯
Chen Xue　　陈学
Chen Zhonghai　　陈中海

Chin, Wing Fong   陈泳芳
Chinese American Planning Council   华人策划会 (华策会)
Chinese Coalition of Labor Union Women   华工妇女联合会
Chinese Communist Party   中国共产党
Chinese Hand Laundry Alliance   华侨衣馆联合会
Chinese Ladies' Garment Workers' Union   华人妇女车衣工会
Chinese Staff and Workers' Association   华人职工联谊会
Chinese Workers' Mutual Aid Association   加州华工合作社
choih yuhn gwong jeun (C)   财源广进
Chow Yun Fat   周荣发
Chung Chor Hung   钟楚红
Chung Pak[4]   松柏
Continental Garment Manufacturers' Association   华人车衣商会

daaih luhk mui (C)   大陆妹
dim sum (C)   点心

Eng, Sherman   伍文遂
Enping   恩平

faat choi (C)   发菜
Fee, Ben   张明之 (张恨棠)
fo yuhn leuhn jyun (C)   货源轮转
Fujian   福建
Fu Li Hua   富丽华

gam chihng (C)   感情
gam saan haak (C)   金山客
gam saan poh (C)   金山婆
Gao Sha   高沙
Gao Ying   高英
Gong Hing[5]   更生 / 兴
gong si fang   公司房
Guangdong   广东
Guangzhou (Canton)   广州
Gujing   古井
gung hei faat choih (C)   恭喜发财
Guo Yulan   郭玉兰
gu po wu   姑婆屋

Hakka (Keja)   客家
Hengshui   横水
Heshan   鹤山
heung hah mui (C)   乡下妹
Huang Kongwang   黄孔旺
huhng baau (C)   红包

International Ladies' Garment Workers' Union   国际女服工会

Ip, Alice   叶月好(好姐)

jaang hei (C)   争气

jam jyu luhng (C)   浸猪笼

Jian   简

Jing Yi Hang   锦衣行

Jiujiang   九江

Juan Yi Hang   绢衣行

jyu faahn poh (C)   煮饭婆

jyu tauh gwat (C)   猪头骨

Ka, Shui Mak   贾麦穗

Ka, Sun Fook   贾山福

kaih ma (C)   契妈(干妈)

Kaiping   开平

Kin Yip (C)[6]   建业

Lam, John   林建中

Lan Gu (Aunt Lan)   兰姑

lao wai   老外

Lau, Paul   刘珠康

Lau De Wua   刘德华

lau sung (T)   老兄

Lee, Sue Ko[7]   萧修

Leung, Betty   梁雁

Leung, Stanley   梁广建

Liao   廖

Ling, Connie   凌坤儿

Li Wenbin   李文斌

louh faan (C)   老番

luo jing xia shi   落井下石

Mao Zedong   毛泽东

Ma Zhen   马珍

Mei Boqun   梅伯群

Moy (T)   梅

Moy, Lily   梅姿嫣

Mui Yim Fong   梅艳芳

Nanhai   南海

nan man   南蛮

National Party (Guomindang/Kuomintang)   国民党

neih yauh jeung leuhng gai, ngoh yauh tiu cheuhng tai (C)   你有张良计,我有跳墙梯

neuih nguk (C)   女屋

New York Asian Women's Center   纽约亚裔妇女中心

ngoi saang yahn (C)   外省人
ni di seui tohng yahn (C)[8]   呢 地 (这些) "衰" (坏) 唐人
ni si wo huo   你 死 我 活

Panyu   番禺
Pinyin   拼音

"Qiaofu Yuan"   <侨妇怨>
Quan, Katie   关少兰
"Que Zei Yao"   <却贼谣>

ru hu tian yi   如虎添羽

saam fuk peih (C)   三幅被
saan jai (C)   散仔
Sanfanshi Gongyi Tongmeng Zonghui   三藩市工艺同盟总会
Sanxi   三溪
San Yi   三邑
sau wuht gwa (sau sang gwa) (C)   守活寡 (守生寡)
Sha Dui   沙堆
Shanghai   上海
Shenzhen   深圳
Shunde   顺德
Shunde nu   顺德女
sih yauh gai (C)   豉油鸡
Si Yi   四邑

Taishan (formerly Xinning)   台山
tihng che (C)   停车(工)
toi dai chin (C)   台底钱
Tong Ye Tang   同业堂

Union of Needletraders, Industrial and Textile Employees   成衣纺织联合工会

wai zi   外子
Wu Peixuan   吴佩璇
Wu Zhenze   吴桢泽

"Xifu Yao"   <媳妇谣>
Xihao Street   西濠街
Xinhui   新会
Xinjie (New Territories)   新界
Xin Wang[9]   信旺

yam cha (C)   饮茶
yam lihk (C)   阴力
yan fu   严父

Yangchun　扬春
Yangjiang　扬江
yat bun maahn leih (C)　一本万利
yat geuk tek (C)　一脚踢
Yeung (C)　杨
Yeung jai (C)　杨仔
Young, Shun Nan　杨秀楠
Yung Wing　容闳

zhai tang　斋堂
zhao dao le zu zhi　找到了组织
Zhejiang　浙江
Zheng　郑
Zheng Lirong　郑丽蓉
zheng long　蒸笼
Zhongshan (formerly Xiangshan)　中山
Zhongshan University　中山大学
"Zhou Yu da Huang Gai"　"周瑜打黄盖"
Zhuhai　珠海
zi shu nu　自梳女

1. Pseudonyms are not included in this glossary.
2. The Chinese and English names of this man are quoted in a series of reports in *CDN* and newspapers in English.
3. The names of this woman are not consistent in the earlier Chinese and English newspapers. These are quoted in *CDN*, April 5, 1989, and *NYND*, November 26, 1989.
4. Qtd. in *Local 23-25 News* 40.4 (October 1991): 6.
5. The name in English is quoted in *DN*, May 15, 1979, and different names in Chinese are quoted in the Chinese community newspapers. See *CDN*, May 18 and 19, 1979.
6. This name stands as it was given in English by the shop owner in the 1980s.
7. Qtd. in Judy Yung, *Unbound Feet: A Social History of Chinese Women in San Francisco* (Berkeley: University of California Press, 1995), 211, but transliterated under a different transcription system.
8. Ibid., 218.
9. Qtd. in *CDN*, February 7, 1986.

NOTES

Abbreviations

CDN	美洲华侨日报 (*China Daily News*)
CTDN	中报 (*Central Daily News*)
DN	*New York Daily News*
EG	*Enping Gongbao* (恩平公报; Journal of Enping)
GEB Report	ILGWU, *Report of the General Executive Board and Record of the Proceedings of the Convention, 1900–1983; and General Executive Board Report, 1989–95.*
GSQ	*Guangdong Siyi Qiaobao* (广东四邑侨报; Journal of Guangdong Si Yi overseas Chinese)
GSZHZ	*Guangdong Sheng Zhi: Huaqiao Zhi* (广东省志. 华侨志.; The history of Guangdong Province: the history of its overseas Chinese)
GWZ	*Guangdong Wenshi Ziliao* (广东文史资料; Cultural and historical materials of Guangdong)
GWZX	*Guangzhou Wenshi Ziliao Xuanji* (广州文史资料选集; Cultural and historical materials of Guangzhou)
HSLJ	*Huaqiao Shi Lunwen Ji* (华侨史论文集; Essays on overseas Chinese history)
Mead Papers	The Papers of Margaret Mead and the South Pacific Ethnographic Archives at the Library of Congress. "Projects in Contemporary Culture."
1910 U.S. Census	U.S. Department of Commerce, Bureau of the Census, *Thirteenth Census of the United States Taken in the Year 1910*, bulletin *127, Chinese and Japanese in the United States* (Washington, D.C.: G.P.O., 1914).
1920 U.S. Census	U.S. Department of Commerce, Bureau of the Census, *Fourteenth Census of the United States Taken in the Year 1920*, vols. 2 and 3 (Washington, D.C.: G.P.O., 1922).
1930 U.S. Census	U.S. Department of Commerce, Bureau of the Census, *Fifteenth Census of the United States: 1930. Population*, vols. 3, 5, and 6 (supplement), (Washington, D.C.: G.P.O., 1932–33).
1940 U.S. Census	U.S. Department of Commerce, Bureau of the Census, *Sixteenth Census*

of the United States: 1940. Population (vol. 2) and *Characteristics of the Non-White Population by Race* (Washington, D.C.: G.P.O., 1943).

1950 U.S. Census   U.S. Department of Commerce, Bureau of the Census, *Census of Population: 1950,* vols. 2 and 4 (Washington, D.C.: G.P.O., 1952–53).

1960 U.S. Census   U.S. Department of Commerce, Bureau of the Census, *The Eighteenth Decennial Census of the United States. Census of Population: 1960,* vols. 1 and 2 (Washington, D.C.: G.P.O., 1961–64).

1970 U.S. Census   U.S. Department of Commerce, Bureau of the Census, *1970 Census of Population,* vols. 1 and 2 (Washington, D.C.: G.P.O., 1971–73).

1980 U.S. Census   U.S. Department of Commerce, Bureau of the Census, *1980 Census of Population,* vol. 1 (Washington, D.C.: G.P.O., 1983).

1990 U.S. Census   U.S. Department of Commerce, Bureau of the Census, *1990 Census of Population* (Washington, D.C.: G.P.O., 1992).

NYHT   *New York Herald Tribune*

NYND   *New York Newsday*

NYO   *New York Observer*

NYT   *New York Times*

STD   星岛日报 (*Sing Tao Daily*)

Study   Abeles, Schwartz, Haeckel, and Silverblatt, Inc., *The Chinatown Garment Industry Study* (New York: ILGWU Local 23-25 and the New York Skirt and Sportswear Association, 1983).

TXHZ   *Taishan Xian Huaqiao Zhi* (台山县华侨志; The history of Taishan overseas Chinese).

WJ   世界日报 (*World Journal*)

WSJ   *Wall Street Journal*

WWD   *Women's Wear Daily*

XZ   *Xinning Zhazhi* (新宁杂誌; The magazine of Xinning, later known as Taishan County)

A Note on Interviews and Transliterations

1. By "Cantonese," I refer to the lingua franca of major Cantonese settlements in the world, including those in Hong Kong and Macao. This dialect was traditionally spoken only by people residing in or around Guangzhou, the capital city of Guangdong Province. When transliterating words and expressions in this dialect, this study uses Kwan Choi Wah's *The Right Word in Cantonese* (Hong Kong: The Commercial Press, 1996) for reference. The rules applied in this study follow the Yale romanization system.

Introduction

1. The study commissioned by the International Ladies' Garment Workers' Union (ILGWU) Local 23-25 and the New York Skirt and Sportswear Association in 1983 reports that by 1983, the Chinatown garment industry had annually contributed $125 million in wages and profits to the city's economy, of which $32 million was spent in Chinatown and $14 million in the Chinese community in other parts of the city. See *Study,* 5. Garment manufacturing remained the largest manufacturing industry in the city until 1999. According to the statistics prepared by the real estate consultant Robert Paul and provided by the assistant to the

president of UNITE!, Carl Proper, the industry employed eighty-four thousand people and contributed more than $4.6 billion to the city's economy in 1997. Even in 1999, when the garment industry was replaced by the printing and publishing industries as the largest manufacturing industry in New York City, it employed a quarter of the labor force in the city's manufacturing sector. Data provided by the Division of Research and Statistics of the New York State Department of Labor.

2. *Local 23-25 News,* 1974 special issue; *Justice* 56.15 (August 1974).

3. As women, immigrants, and members of the working class, Chinese women immigrant workers suffer triple marginalization in most studies on Chinese American history. Most literature published before the 1980s gives only scant attention to women. A major contribution that has systematically explored the differences among Chinese American women on the West Coast before the end of World War II is Judy Yung's *Unbound Feet: A Social History of Chinese Women in San Francisco* (Berkeley: University of California Press, 1995), which contains an impressive chapter on the San Francisco garment workers' strike in 1938. Stacey G. H. Yap's study *Gather Your Strength, Sisters: The Emerging Role of Chinese Women Community Workers* (New York: AMS Press, 1989), which focuses on a specific group of women community workers in Boston, is a departure from the West Coast orientation in the field of Chinese American studies. For publications on men workers' experiences in New York City, see Peter Kwong, *Chinatown, New York: Labor and Politics, 1930–1950* (New York: Monthly Review Press, 1979); and Renqiu Yu, *To Save China, To Save Ourselves: The Chinese Hand Laundry Alliance of New York* (Philadelphia: Temple University Press, 1992). For publications about New York's Chinese community that contain sections on the garment industry and the women immigrant workers, see, for example, Peter Kwong, *The New Chinatown* (New York: Hill and Wang, 1987); and Min Zhou, *Chinatown: The Socioeconomic Potential of an Urban Enclave* (Philadelphia: Temple University Press, 1992).

4. *Study,* ii and 97; Zhou, *Chinatown,* 170.

5. In 1980, 86.1 percent of the Chinese women garment workers in New York City were married, and 70 percent of the new arrivals with prior occupations had worked in the blue-collar or service sectors in 1979. See Zhou, *Chinatown,* 173; and *Study,* 45.

6. Nancy Schrom Dye, *As Equals and Sisters: The Labor Movement and the Women's Trade Union League of New York* (Columbia: University of Missouri Press, 1980); Elizabeth Ewen, *Immigrant Women in the Land of Dollars: Life and Culture on the Lower East Side, 1890–1925* (New York: Monthly Review Press, 1985); Carolyn McCreesh, *Women in the Campaign to Organize Garment Workers, 1880–1917* (New York: Garland Publishing, 1985); Annelise Orleck, *Common Sense and a Little Fire: Women and Working-Class Politics in the United States, 1900–1965* (Chapel Hill: University of North Carolina Press, 1995); Barbara Wertheimer and Anne Nelson, *Trade Union Women: A Study of Their Participation in New York City Locals* (New York: Praeger, 1975). For studies that relate to New York's garment industry, see Miriam Cohen, *Workshop to Office: Two Generations of Italian Women in New York, 1900–1950* (Ithaca, N.Y.: Cornell University Press, 1992); Susan A. Glenn, *Daughters of the Shtetl: Life and Labor in the Immigrant Generation* (Ithaca, N.Y.: Cornell University Press, 1990); Nancy Green, *Ready to Wear and Ready to Work: A Century of Industry and Immigrants in Paris and New York* (Durham, N.C.: Duke University Press, 1997).

7. Peter Kwong reports that the ILGWU's organizing efforts began in 1957. Several old-time workers, however, disagree. For example, Wing Fong Chin, a Chinatown garment worker since 1955, claims that the union began to organize Chinese workers in the early 1950s. As she recalled, there were already union members in the shops who had joined the union a couple of years ago when she began working in the industry in 1955. Chin's recollection, though

conflicting with what has been quoted in Shiree Teng's essay, coincides with the ILGWU's official records. For example, on July 12, 1974, Shelley Appleton testified that Local 23-25 had members of Asian origin for more than twenty years, and nearly all of them were Chinese. In 1971, the first Chinese union member, King T. Chu, was reported to have retired and received union pension after working in the garment industry for twenty years. It is therefore safe to assume that the ILGWU began organizing Chinese workers in the early 1950s. See Kwong, *New Chinatown*, 147; interview with Wing Fong Chin by the author on April 14, 1989, and March 6, 1998; Shiree Teng, "Women, Community, and Equality: Three Garment Workers Speak Out," *East Wind* 2.1 (Spring/Summer 1983): 20; "Oral Statement to U.S. Commission on Civil Rights Presented by Shelley Appleton," International Ladies' Garment Workers' Union archives, M. P. Catherwood Library, Cornell University [hereafter ILGWU archives, Cornell]; and *GEB Report* (1971).

8. The exact time the garment shops first appeared in New York's Chinatown also remains debatable. As recorded in the transcripts of a workshop on the Chinatown garment industry organized by the New York Chinatown History Project and in Kwong's study, the first two Chinatown garment factories were set up by Chinese American ex-GIs in 1948. The same worker who had provided the information to the workshop also told me that both of the shops were located on Canal Street and were named the Shanghai Garment Shop and the Ming Fei Garment Shop; she had worked in the first one. Other longtime workers believe that Chinese-owned garment factories first appeared in the mid-1940s. Most, however, agree that by the mid-1950s there were already three or four garment shops in Chinatown. Author's interviews with a Mrs. Chan on March 6, 1988, and April 5, 1989; a Mrs. Tong on May 7, 1988; and Wing Fong Chin, April 19, 1989.

9. For discussions of the gendered and racialized concept of class, see, for example, Joan W. Scott, "On Language, Gender, and Working Class History" and "Women in the Making of the English Working Class" in *Gender and the Politics of History*, ed. Joan W. Scott (New York: Columbia University Press, 1988); and David R. Roediger, *The Wages of Whiteness: Race and the Making of the American Working Class* (New York: Verso, 1991). For a discussion of differences among women, see Joan W. Scott's introduction to *Feminism and History*, ed. Joan W. Scott (New York: Oxford University Press, 1996).

10. For the lives of New York's Chinese laundrymen and the Chinese Left's difficulties in defining their class identity, see Yu, *To Save China*, 24–30, 56–64.

11. Virginia Heyer, "Patterns of Social Organization in New York City's Chinatown" (Ph.D. diss., Columbia University, 1953), 43–44. See also Rose Hum Lee, "The Stranded Chinese in the United States," *Phylon* 19 (1956): 180–94, and *Chinese in the United States of America* (Hong Kong: Hong Kong University Press, 1960), 107; and "Interview with the Student Couple," in Mead Papers, vol. 22, chap. 491.

12. See, for example, Kwong, *New Chinatown*, 58–63.

13. Seventy percent of the students the Chinese court sent to the United States were from Guangdong Province. See Mei Jia, "Guangdongji Liumei Youtong Jianshi" (A brief account of the Guangdong children who studied in the United States), *GWZ* 48 (1986): 179–99.

14. For the lives of the earliest Chinese students in the United States, see Yung Wing, *My Life in China and America* (New York: Henry Holt, 1909).

15. There were wealthy and politically influential Chinese merchants and businessmen in Chinatown; there were also Chinese grocery store owners and restaurant and laundry workers who resided and worked in upper Manhattan. The latter shared the same social and linguistic background with the Chinatown working-class. In addition, there was a third but small Chinese concentration in a poor midtown neighborhood. For a detailed discussion of the

distribution of Chinese in Manhattan in the 1950s, see Cheng Tsu Wu, "Chinese People and Chinatown in New York City" (Ph.D. diss., Clark University, 1958), 42–53.

16. Wu, "Chinese People and Chinatown," 57–58.

17. As many longtime residents of New York's Chinatown have pointed out, the Taishan dialect became the lingua franca of the community to such a degree that a person's Chinese identity would be questioned if he or she could not speak the dialect. See Bernard P. Wong, *Chinatown: Economic Adaptation and Ethnic Identity of the Chinese* (New York: Holt, Rinehart and Winston, 1982), 9.

18. The former Si Yi District included four counties: Kaiping, Enping, Xinhui, and Taishan, to which one more county (Heshan) was recently added and the district was renamed Wu Yi District. San Yi District includes three counties: Panyu, Naihai, and Shunde. For the locations of the San Yi and Si Yi Counties in Guangdong Province, see map 1. For a good discussion of the geographical background of early Chinese immigrants in the United States, see June Mei, "Socioeconomic Origins of Emigration: Guangdong to California, 1850–1882," in *Labor Immigration under Capitalism: Asian Immigrant Workers in the United States before World War II*, ed. Edna Bonacich and Lucie Cheng (Berkeley: University of California Press, 1984), 219–47.

19. For an understanding of the dialect defined as "Cantonese," see note 1 of my note on interviews and translations. For a discussion of the linguistic and cultural differences of the emigrant communities in Guangdong, see *GSZHZ*, 142–201; and Li Xinkui, *Guangdong de Fangyen* (The dialects of Guangdong) (Guangdong: Guangdong Chuban She, 1991), 25–30, 92–139.

20. For a discussion of the conflict between Hakka and the locals, see Wan Lo, "Communal Strife in Mid-Nineteenth-Century Kwangtung: The Establishment of Ch'ih-ch'i," in *Papers on China*, vol. 19 (Cambridge, Mass.: East Asian Research Center, Harvard University Press, 1965), 85–119.

21. By "the shared Chinese ethnic identity," I intend to emphasize its importance in the self-identity of many Chinese immigrants in the United States, including not only those from China, Taiwan, and Hong Kong but also those from Southeast Asia and other parts of the world.

22. For example, I volunteered to serve as a substitute teacher and taught a number of sessions at the ILGWU Sunday English school in Brooklyn in the fall of 1994. I also participated in various forms of workers' recreational activities whenever I visited New York. In addition, I joined workers' demonstrations and a Chinatown rally to demand the end of sweatshops in 1998, when I was a resident fellow with the Sweatshop Project in New York City.

23. Many scholars have discussed tensions in the relationship between interviewer and interviewee as a result of their different social standings. I have found that social differences did not seem to be a major factor affecting my relationship with my worker friends. To this date, long after I began teaching in an institution of higher education, they call me *A Lan* (part of my first name), *Lan Jie* (sister Lan), or *Lan Lan* (a pet name given by the older workers) whenever we see each other. All these names are based on age and generational rather than social differences. Is it because my relationship with most of them began when I was only a student or their tenant? I am still struggling for an answer. Nevertheless, I am sure that social tensions between an interviewer and interviewee from different social backgrounds can be reduced significantly if the interviewer takes a proper attitude toward the interviewee and their mutual trust is built upon a long-term relationship.

24. This was caused not only by the subjective nature of the narratives but by my own subjectivity in understanding them. My experience shows that a researcher's long-term relationship with a narrator can pose new challenges to interpreting and representing his or

her narratives. How to read a narrator's changing account in the particular context from which each of the versions emerged and how to analyze the meaning of the discrepancy between these different versions are only two of the many issues that I had to face in the course of my research.

25. Virginia Yans-McLaughlin, "Metaphors of Self in History: Subjectivity, Oral Narrative, and Immigration Studies," in *Immigration Reconsidered: History, Sociology, and Politics,* ed. Virginia Yans-McLaughlin (New York: Oxford University Press, 1990), 283.

26. This is especially true with the newspapers of New York's Chinese community. This study has substantially drawn on the coverage of *CDN* because more representation of workers' viewpoints can be found in this newspaper than in any other in the community. In addition, having been inaugurated in 1939, it has the longest history among all the community newspapers prior to 1989.

This study has also drawn substantially from *CTDN* and *STD,* largely because these two newspapers were widely read by the Cantonese-speaking garment workers in the 1980s and 1990s, as they tend to transcribe vernacular Cantonese in their coverage and substantially cover Hong Kong. (*CTDN* stopped publishing in 1989.)

27. For instance, at the very beginning of this study, Aunt Yeung was so excited to hear about my decision to pursue this project that she cooked me a great meal to extend her support; Tang Wei devoted her precious day off on Mother's Day 1992 to teach me sewing in her shop after my application was repeatedly turned down by the shop owners, leaving her disappointed daughter home alone to be cared for by her father; Aunt Chen prepared me an entire sewing kit and comforted me with a good meal after my first frustrating week of sewing in the shop; Shun Nan Young not only patiently answered my endless questions and introduced me to her pool of friends and acquaintances but also volunteered to provide me with information that she believed I had left out. This list can go on and on.

Chapter 1: The Vicissitudes of New York City's Garment Industry

1. See, for example, Rosara Lucy Passero, "Ethnicity in the Men's Ready-Made Clothing Industry, 1880–1950: The Italian Experience in Philadelphia" (Ph.D. diss., University of Pennsylvania, 1978), 3–5; and Jesse Eliphalet Pope, *The Clothing Industry in New York* (New York: Burt Franklin, 1905), 2–8.

2. Egal Feldman, *Fit For Men: A Study of New York's Clothing Trade* (Washington, D.C.: Public Affairs Press, 1960), 74–75; Christine Stansell, "The Origins of the Sweatshop: Women and Early Industrialization in New York City," in *Working-Class America: Essays on Labor, Community, and American Society,* ed. Michael H. Frisch and Daniel J. Walkawitz (Urbana: University of Illinois Press, 1983), 83; Passero, "Ethnicity," 10; Glenn, *Daughters,* 91; and Roy B. Helfgott, "Women's and Children's Apparel," in *Made in New York: Case Studies in Metropolitan Manufacturing,* ed. Max Hall (Cambridge, Mass.: Harvard University Press, 1959), 47.

3. Stansell, "Origins," 83; Passero, "Ethnicity," 9.

4. Feldman, *Fit for Men,* 53; Stansell, "Origins," 84.

5. It was during this time that Levi Strauss, a merchant from New York, began to design and manufacture work clothes for prospective miners in California. See Feldman, *Fit for Men,* 64; and Passero, "Ethnicity," 12 and 42, n. 30.

6. While the first foot-treadle machine sewed eight hundred stitches per minute, by 1885 a

power-driven one could sew twenty-eight hundred. A skilled tailor could make only a hundred buttonholes a day by hand, but a woman worker with a machine could make more than three thousand. See Passero, "Ethnicity," 25–39; and Pope, *Clothing Industry,* 12–13. For a further discussion of the sewing machine's improvement in the years after its invention, see Green, *Ready to Wear,* 37–39.

7. See Robert Ernst, *Immigrant Life in New York City, 1825–1863* (New York: King's Crown Press, 1949), 215; and Feldman, *Fit for Men,* 95.

8. See, for example, Glenn, *Daughters,* 94; and Passero, "Ethnicity," 145. A number of scholars, however, believe that it began with the entrance of Eastern European Jews. See, for example, Roger Waldinger, *Through the Eye of the Needle: Immigrants and Enterprise in New York's Garment Trades* (New York: New York University, 1986), 51–52; Helfgott, "Women's and Children's Apparel," 48; and Louis Levine (Lewis L. Lorwin), *The Women's Garment Workers: A History of the International Ladies' Garment Workers' Union* (New York: B. W. Huebsch, Inc., 1924), 14–15.

9. Many of the earliest owners of the inside shops were British-born master tailors who had managed to accumulate enough capital to carry out their businesses on a large scale. They were soon replaced by German Jews, who dominated this kind of shop until the end of the nineteenth century. See Passero, "Ethnicity," 37.

10. Nancy Green, "Women and Immigrants in the Sweatshop: Categories of Labor Segmentation Revisited," *Comparative Studies in Society and History* 38.3 (July 1996): 417.

11. Waldinger, *Through the Eye,* 51.

12. For a detailed description of the women's and children's industry, which formed the largest component of the city's garment industry, see the categories under women's outerwear (SIC 23233) and women's and children's undergarments (SIC 23236) in the U.S. standard industrial classification system. U.S. Office of Management and Budget, *Standard Industrial Classification: Manual* (Washington, D.C.: National Technical Information Service, 1987).

13. Waldinger, *Through the Eye,* 51.

14. These statistics are from Stanley Vittoz, *New Deal Labor Policy and the American Industrial Economy* (Chapel Hill: University of North Carolina Press, 1987), 34; Nancy Green, "Sweatshop Migrations: The Garment Industry between Home and Shop," in *The Landscape of Modernity: Essays on New York City, 1900–1940,* ed. David Ward and Olivier Zunz (New York: Russell Sage Foundation, 1992), 214, and *Ready to Wear,* 48. Green cites the 1899 figure as 65 percent.

15. Waldinger, *Through the Eye,* 52.

16. Levine, *Women's Garment Workers,* 17.

17. According to Levine, fifty dollars was sufficient to open a shop in the 1880s. See ibid., 14; and Pope, *Clothing Industry,* 62, n. 4.

18. Vittoz, *New Deal,* 36.

19. Green, *Ready to Wear,* 148 and 333, n. 37.

20. See Cynthia R. Daniels, "Between Home and Factory: Homeworkers and the State," in *Homework: Historical and Contemporary Perspectives on Paid Labor and Home,* ed. Eileen Boris and Cynthia R. Daniels (Urbana: University of Illinois Press, 1989), 22–23.

21. Ewen, *Immigrant Women,* 246.

22. Qtd. in Daniels, "Between Home," 23.

23. Green, "Sweatshop Migrations," 221.

24. Pope, *Clothing Industry,* 169.

25. Roger Waldinger, "Another Look at the International Ladies' Garment Workers' Union:

Women, Industry Structure, and Collective Action," in *Women, Work, and Protest: A Century of U.S. Women's Labor History,* ed. Ruth Milkman (New York: Routledge and Kegan Paul, 1985), 95. For a discussion of the causes of this shift, see Green, *Ready to Wear,* 57.

26. Frederick M. Binder and David Reimers, *All the Nations under Heaven: An Ethnic and Racial History of New York City* (New York: Columbia University, 1995), 123.

27. Waldinger, "Another Look," 95; and Green, *Ready to Wear,* 57.

28. Passero, "Ethnicity," 143–50; and Pope, *Clothing Industry,* 127–37.

29. By 1925, 40 percent of the city's garment workforce who worked in Manhattan lived in Brooklyn, the Bronx, or upper Manhattan. The construction of the IRT and the BMT subway lines helped to link them to the garment district, where, by the early 1950s, approximately 65 to 80 percent of garment production in Manhattan took place. Since the IND line did not reach the Lower East Side until 1930s, it put the area in a relatively disadvantageous position in the 1920s. See Green, "Sweatshop Migrations," 223 and 219.

30. Ibid., 214.

31. Ibid., 215 and 225. See also Green, *Ready to Wear,* 57.

32. Waldinger, *Through the Eye,* 54.

33. For a more detailed discussion of the space problem in Manhattan factories, see Helfgott, "Women's and Children's Apparel," 98–104.

34. In 1975, for example, with roughly comparable productivity, the average wage for garment workers was $3.75 per hour in the United States, as compared with $0.75 in Hong Kong, $0.29 in Taiwan, and $0.22 in Korea. See Edna Bonacich and David V. Waller, "Mapping a Global Industry: Apparel Production in the Pacific Rim Triangle," in *Global Production: The Apparel Industry in the Pacific Rim,* ed. Edna Bonacich et al. (Philadelphia: Temple University Press, 1994), 22.

35. Green, "Sweatshop Migrations," 215.

36. Waldinger, *Through the Eye,* 72.

37. With the CBI, the Reagan administration extended special trade privileges to first twenty-one and then twenty-seven countries. See Andrew Ross, ed., *No Sweat: Fashion, Free Trade, and the Rights of Garment Workers* (New York: Verso, 1997), 22.

38. Waldinger, *Through the Eye,* 77.

39. *Study,* 23.

40. See Robert Laurentz, "Racial/Ethnic Conflict in the New York City Garment Industry, 1933–1980" (Ph.D. diss., State University of New York at Binghamton, 1980), 194–97.

41. Between 1960 and 1970, weekly earnings in apparel fell from 160 percent of welfare benefits to 130 percent; by 1970 the weekly welfare allowance in New York City exceeded the equivalent income from a minimum-wage job by 30 percent. Waldinger, *Through the Eye,* 111. Oral histories of these workers show that their wages in the 1960s were even lower than in the 1950s. See Altagracia Ortiz, "'*En la aguja y el pedal eche la hiel*': Puerto Rican Women in the Garment Industry of New York City, 1920–1980," in *Puerto Rican Women and Work: Bridges in Transnational Labor,* ed. Altagracia Ortiz (Philadelphia: Temple University Press, 1996), 70.

42. Altagracia Ortiz, "Puerto Rican Workers in the Garment Industry of New York City, 1920–1960," in *Labor Divided: Race and Ethnicity in United States Labor Struggle, 1835–1960,* ed. Robert Asher and Charles Stephenson (Albany: State University of New York Press, 1990), 123; and U.S. Department of Commerce, Bureau of the Census, *U.S. Census of Population,* 1950–70.

43. See *Study,* 28; and Laurentz, "Racial/Ethnic Conflict," 367; quote from Kwong, *New Chinatown,* 30.

44. Waldinger, *Through the Eye*, 89.

45. See, for example, *Study*, 40.

46. For a discussion of the spot market, see Waldinger, *Through the Eye*, 89–122; and *Study*, 34–40.

47. *Study*, 31 and 34.

48. Besides Chinese and Dominicans, the new immigrant groups who came after the end of World War II included Cubans, South and Latin Americans, Haitians, Greeks, and Koreans. See Nancy Green, "Immigrant Labor in the Garment Industries of New York and Paris: Variations on a Structure," *Comparitive Social Research* 9 (1986): 238; and Ortiz, "'*En la aguja*,'" 69.

Chapter 2: The Garment Workers

1. Glenn, *Daughters*, 130.

2. The following discussion about the early gender division of labor in the industry is primarily based on Glenn, *Daughters*, chap. 3; Stansell, "Origins," 78–103; and Egal Feldman, *Fit for Men*, 102–5.

3. For the different working conditions and products of the inside and outside shops, see Pope, *Clothing Industry*, 13; and Passero, "Ethnicity," 147–49.

4. Waldinger, "Another Look," 91. For a similar observation, see Pope, *Clothing Industry*, 15–16.

5. For the ethnic components of the garment industries in various cities in the late nineteenth century and how they shaped the geographical differences, see Glenn, *Daughters*, 109–10; and Passero, "Ethnicity," 76–83.

6. Green, "Sweatshop Migrations," 215.

7. Alice Kessler-Harris, *Women Have Always Worked: A Historical Overview* (New York: The Feminist Press, 1981), 85, and *Out to Work: A History of Wage-Earning Women in the United States* (New York: Oxford University Press, 1982), 78.

8. Vittoz, *New Deal*, 39–40.

9. Passero, *Ethnicity*, 141; and Green, *Ready to Wear*, 165–66.

10. Glenn, *Daughters*, 145. For sexual harassment in the nineteenth-century workplace, see 145–48.

11. Stansell, "Origins," 91.

12. Meredith Tax, *The Rising of the Women: Feminist Solidarity and Class Conflict, 1880–1917* (New York: Monthly Review Press, 1980), 210.

13. The statistics are from Green, *Ready to Wear*, 53; the quote is from Waldinger, "Another Look," 86.

14. Ewen, *Immigrant Women*, 254.

15. Joan M. Jensen, "Inside and Outside the Unions: 1920–1980," in *A Needle, a Bobbin, a Strike: Women Needleworkers in America*, ed. Joan M. Jensen and Sue Davidson (Philadelphia: Temple University Press, 1984), 185.

16. Although the protocols signed by different ILGWU locals varied slightly in wording, they shared the same principles and followed the one signed in 1910 by the male cloak makers. See Levine, *Women's Garment Workers*, 229–30.

17. For other benefits included in the agreements, see Levine, *Women's Garment Workers*, 229–30; Joel Seidman, *The Needle Trades: Labor in Twentieth-Century America* (New York: Farrar and Rinehart, 1942), 106–7; and Green, *Ready to Wear*, 54–55.

18. Levine, *Women's Garment Workers*, 303.

19. This was said by the president of the manufacturers' negotiating group. See Vittoz, *New Deal,* 41.

20. Levine, *Women's Garment Workers,* 225.

21. Green, *Ready to Wear,* 55 and 59. For various perspectives on the protocols, see, for example, Vittoz, *New Deal,* 41–46; Philip Foner, *Women and the American Labor Movement: From the First Trade Unions to the Present* (New York: The Free Press, 1982), 158–59; Orleck, *Common Sense,* 76.

22. See Tax, *Rising of the Women,* 239.

23. Orleck, *Common Sense,* 65.

24. Levine, *Women Garment Workers,* 224.

25. For an account of the strike, see Orleck, *Common Sense,* 76. Quotes from Levine, *Women Garment Workers,* 226.

26. For Local 25's rebellion from within, see Orleck, *Common Sense,* 75–76, 181–83; and Alice Kessler-Harris, "Problems of Coalition-Building: Women and Trade Unions in the 1920s," in *Women, Work, and Protest: A Century of U.S. Women's Labor History,* ed. Ruth Milkman (New York: Routledge and Kegan Paul, 1985), 110–38.

27. Levine, *Women's Garment Workers,* 353.

28. Orleck, *Common Sense,* 182.

29. Laurentz, "Racial/Ethnic Conflict," 64–66.

30. Orleck, *Common Sense,* 183; and Kessler-Harris, "Problems," 127–28. See table 1.

31. Kessler-Harris, "Problems," 125.

32. Ewen, *Immigrant Women,* 261.

33. Besides Orleck's study, see, for example, Alice Kessler-Harris, "Rose Schneiderman and the Limits of Women's Trade Unionism," in *Labor Leaders in America,* ed. Melvyn Dubofsky and Warren Van Tine (Urbana: University of Illinois Press, 1987), 213–32; and Gary Endelman, *Solidarity Forever: Rose Schneiderman and the Women's Trade Union League* (New York: Arno Press, 1982). See also autobiographical accounts such as Rose Pesotta, *Bread upon the Waters* (1944; Ithaca, N.Y.: ILR Press, 1976); and Rose Schneiderman, *All for One* (New York: Paul S. Eriksson, 1967).

34. Almost all of them experienced interference by male union officers in organizing difficult campaigns. See, for example, Kessler-Harris, "Rose Schneiderman," 169; Orleck, *Common Sense,* 69, 71, 108, 177, and 181; and Rose Pesotta's letter of resignation in John Laslett and Mary Tyler, *The ILGWU in Los Angeles, 1907–1988* (Inglewood, Calif.: Ten Star Press, 1989), 135–42, appendix 6.

35. Orleck, *Common Sense,* 171.

36. Kessler-Harris, "Problems," 117.

37. Besides Cohn, Pauline Newman was once the health educator for the ILGWU's Union Health Center; Rose Schneiderman supported Cohn's education effort; and Rose Pesotta and Jennie Matyas stressed the importance of educating the workers in their organizing efforts. See Orleck, *Common Sense;* Pesotta, *Bread,* 64–77; Laslett and Tyler, *ILGWU in Los Angeles,* 32–33; and "Jennie Matyas and the ILGWU," interview by Corrine L. Gibbs, 1955, 123–205, ILGWU archives, Cornell.

38. Qtd. in Orleck, *Common Sense,* 198.

39. During the 1909–10 Uprising of 20,000, about 55 percent of the female shirtwaist makers were Jewish, 35 percent Italians, and 7 percent native-born American. See Green, *Ready to Wear,* 202–3. For the differences among women workers in the shops and during the strike, see Ewen, *Immigrant Women,* 259; and Tax, *Rising of the Women,* 222–26.

40. This is only a general account of the situation. Recent studies reveal a much more complicated picture. See Green, *Ready to Wear,* 203.

41. Laurentz, "Racial/Ethnic Conflict," 83.

42. Their numbers grew from 7,500 in 1940 to 32,545 in 1950, an increase of more than 25,000. For their numbers between 1910 and 1950, see *Justice* 4.19 (May 5, 1922); Lorenzo J. Green and Carter G. Woodson, *The Negro Wage Earner* (Washington, D.C.: The Association for the Study of Negro Life and History, Inc., 1930), 305; Elaine Gale Wrong, *The Negro in the Apparel Industry* (Philadelphia: University of Pennsylvania Press, 1974), 31, 36–37; and Laurentz, "Racial/Ethnic Conflict," 187.

43. Lawrence R. Chenault, *The Puerto Rican Migrant in New York City* (1938; New York: Russell and Russell, 1970), 53.

44. Binder and Reimers, *All the Nations,* 169.

45. Laurentz, "Racial/Ethnic Conflict," 100–101; and Adalberto Lopez, "The Puerto Rican Diaspora: A Survey," in *Puerto Rico and Puerto Ricans: Studies in History and Society,* ed. Adalberto Lopez and James Petras (New York: Halsted Press, 1974), 316.

46. Chenault, *Puerto Rican Migrant,* 60.

47. This percentage was estimated by the Puerto Rican employment service in New York. See Chenault, *Puerto Rican Migrant,* 74–75. For a relevant discussion of the early Puerto Rican workers, see Roy B. Helfgott, "Puerto Rican Integration in the Skirt Industry in New York City," in *Discrimination and Low Incomes: Social and Economic Discrimination against Minority Groups in Relation to Low Income in New York State,* ed. Aaron Antonovsky and Lewis Lorwin (New York: State of New York Interdepartmental Committee on Low Incomes, 1959), 252–53; Laurentz, "Racial/Ethnic Conflict," 101–5; and Altagracia Ortiz, "Puerto Rican Workers," 105, and "'En la aguja,'" 56–68.

48. Laurentz, "Racial/Ethnic Conflict," 90.

49. Ibid., 188–89 and 244.

50. Ibid., 124–25 and 202–3.

51. Ibid., 90.

52. See ibid., 225; and Herbert Hill, "The Racial Practices of Organized Labor: The Contemporary Record," in *The Negro and the American Labor Movement,* ed. Julius Jacobson (Garden City, N.Y.: Anchor Books, 1968), 353.

53. Laurentz, "Racial/Ethnic Conflict," 94. This number remained in the early 1930s. See Wrong, *Negro in the Apparel Industry,* 57.

54. Laurentz, "Racial/Ethnic Conflict," 104–5.

55. The ILGWU membership grew from twenty-four thousand in 1931 to more than two hundred thousand in 1935. See table 1.

56. For the ILGWU's refusal to provide African American and Puerto Rican workers with a training program, see Hill, "Racial Practices," 335–36, and "Guardians of the Sweatshops: The Trade Unions, Racism, and the Garment Industry," in *Puerto Rico and Puerto Ricans: Studies in History and Society,* ed. Adalberto Lopez and James Petras (New York: Halsted Press, 1974), 400.

57. This was indicated in the 1958 workers' demonstration, which will be discussed below.

58. Laurentz, "Racial/Ethnic Conflict," 148–53.

59. For a discussion of underrepresentation of African Americans and Latinos in the ILGWU leadership, see Hill, "Guardians," 387; and Ortiz, "'En la aguja,'" 58–59, 65. For changes in the following decades, see Laurentz, "Racial/Ethnic Conflict," 335.

60. For a discussion of the ILGWU election system, see Hill, "Racial Practices," 322–23; Laurentz, "Racial/Ethnic Conflict"; and Ortiz, "'En la aguja,'" 65.

61. In 1961, for example, a housing project for the aged that the ILGWU leadership attempted to undertake was not made available to its non-Jewish members. For a discussion of the union's discriminatory practices in the 1950s and 1960s, see Hill, "Guardians," 385 and 401–2, and "Racial Practices," 341–42.

62. Qtd. in Laurentz, "Racial/Ethnic Conflict," 127.

63. See ibid., 296–97; and Hill, "Guardians," 392.

64. Laurentz, "Racial/Ethnic Conflict," 338; and Florence Rice, "It Takes a While to Realize That It Is Discrimination," in *Black Women in White America: A Documentary History,* ed. Gerda Lerner (New York: Random House, 1973), 275–81.

65. Laurentz, "Racial/Ethnic Conflict," 335–37, 411–12.

66. For the dispersal of the garment shops into these areas and their working conditions, see Laurentz, "Racial/Ethnic Conflict," 236, 253–56; and Ortiz, "'En la aguja,'" 61–62.

Chapter 3: The Growth of the Chinatown Garment Industry

1. See Yung, *Unbound Feet,* 299–302, and tables 6 and 7.

2. Previous studies show that in Chinatown there were two tailor shops for Chinese men's clothing in 1888, thirty Chinese men sewing-machine operators in 1898, and six tailor shops in 1918. See Wong Chin Foo, "The Chinese in New York," *Cosmopolitan* (March–October 1888): 308 and 311; Louis J. Beck, *New York's Chinatown: An Historical Presentation of Its People and Places* (New York: Bohemia Publishing Co., 1898), 28; Warner M. Van Norden, *Who's Who of the Chinese in New York* (New York: n.p., 1918), 90. New York State Census manuscripts show that in the same area there were nineteen Chinese men registered as "tailors" in 1905, fifteen in 1915, and only two in 1925. State of New York, *Census of Population,* manuscripts, 1905, 1915, 1925.

3. *1930 U.S. Census,* vol. 5, chap. 3, table 6. For New York City's share in the state's Chinese population, see table 2 in this study.

4. See tables 2 and 3. Many studies have discussed the various cultural and economic reasons that contributed to the small number of Chinese women in most parts of the country. However, as Sucheng Chan has argued, it was the passage of the Chinese Exclusion Acts since 1882 that denied Chinese immigrants the right to make decisions on their own. See Sucheng Chan, "The Exclusion of Chinese Women, 1870–1943," in *Entry Denied: Exclusion and the Chinese Community in America, 1882–1943,* ed. Sucheng Chan (Philadelphia: Temple University Press, 1991), 95.

5. Leong Gor Yun, *Chinatown Inside Out* (New York: Barrows Mussey, 1936), 182.

6. Guo Zhengzhi, *Huafu Cangsang: Niuyue Tangrenjie Shihua* (The vicissitudes of a Chinatown: the history of New York's Chinatown) (Hong Kong: Buo Yi Press, 1985), 56.

7. See table 4.

8. Census data show that in 1930, 4,761 of the 6,574 Chinese men who worked in the laboring service sector were in these two businesses. See *1930 U.S. Census,* vol. 5, chap. 3, table 6. The numbers of the city's Chinese laundries and restaurants in different historical periods, recorded in various studies, have been inconsistent, to say the least. However, many studies agree that by the 1930s about 80 percent of adult Chinese men worked in these two businesses. For the numbers in the late nineteenth century, see Beck, *New York's Chinatown,* 28; Arthur Bonner, *Alas! What Brought Thee Hither? The Chinese in New York, 1800–1950* (Cranbury, N.J.: Associated University Press, 1997), 68; and Wong, "Chinese in New York," 297. For the numbers in the 1930s, see Wu Jianxiong, *Haiwai Yimin yi Huaren Shehui* (Overseas Emigration and the Chinese Overseas Community) (Taibei: Yunchen Wenhua Chunbanshe,

1993), 258–61; Bonner, *What Brought,* 167; Leong, *Chinatown,* 37; and Shepard Schwartz, "Mate-Selection among New York City's Chinese Males, 1931–1938," *American Journal of Sociology* 56 (May 1951): 563.

9. Over 60 percent of the Chinese laundries in the city were one- or two-manned businesses. See Julia I. Hsuan Chen, "The Chinese Community in New York: A Study in Their Cultural Adjustment, 1920–1940" (Ph.D. diss., American University, 1941), 57; and Bonner, *What Brought,* 167. For a detailed discussion of the lives of the New York Chinese laundrymen, see Yu, *To Save China,* chap. 1. Quote from Chen Hsiang-shui and John Kuo Wei Tchen, "Towards a History of Chinese in Queens" (manuscript, Asian American Center, Queens College, City University of New York, n.d.), 4.

10. In 1930 only thirty-four women, as compared to almost 4,800 men, worked in these two businesses. See *1930 U.S. Census,* vol. 5, chap. 3, table 6.

11. This took place even in some merchant families. This was suggested in an interview with a Chinatown-born Chinese American woman, who grew up in a Chinese merchant family of seven children, all taken care of by their mother. See interviews no. 1 and 6 with informant no. 6 in Mead Papers, container no. 23, vol. 9, chap. 137, p. 7, and container no. 24, vol. 9, chap. 182, pp. 4–5.

12. Hua Liang, "Living between the Worlds: Chinese American Women and Their Experiences in San Francisco and New York City, 1848–1945" (Ph.D. diss., University of Connecticut, 1996), 196–97 and 223–24.

13. See ibid., 316–17.

14. Interview no. 4 with informant no. 6 in Mead Papers, container no. 24, vol. 9, chap. 167, pp. 11–16.

15. See Bonner, *What Brought,* 163–64.

16. State of New York, *Census of Population,* manuscripts, 1905, 1915, 1925.

17. Guo, *Huafu Cangsang,* 69.

18. *NYT,* April 11, 1937. The same information is quoted in Chen, "Chinese Community," 29; and Liang, "Living between the World," 228. There are indications that the low rate of Chinese using the city's assistance during the Depression can be credited to the participation of women in labor outside the home. See, for example, Guo, *Huafu Cangsang,* 69. For the low rate of using assistance, see Carl Glick, *Shake Hands with the Dragon* (New York: Whittlesey House, 1941), 242–43; and Bonner, *What Brought,* 175.

19. The 1950 census publications do not have such statistics. Since about 90 percent of the state's Chinese population lived in New York City, it is safe to assume that the city's rate was close to the state's. See *1940 U.S. Census,* (Non-white), tables 31 and 32; and *1950 U.S. Census,* vol. 4, P-E no. 3B, table 23.

20. See Guo, *Huafu Cangsang,* 69; and Liang, "Living between the World," 188. New York State Census manuscripts show that there were a number of female-headed families with young children in the Chinatown area between 1905 and 1925. Although all the female heads registered their occupation as "housework," it is difficult to imagine that they could support their families without engaging in any wage-earning labor. State of New York, *Census,* 1905, 1915, 1925.

21. Between 1946 and 1978 a total of 28,692 Chinese refugees were admitted to the United States. See U.S. Department of Justice, Immigration and Nationalization Service (hereafter INS), *Statistical Yearbook,* (Washington, D.C.: Government Printing Office, 1978), table 6E. For a good discussion of changes in the U.S. immigration laws in the 1940s and 1950s, see David Reimers, *Still the Golden Door: The Third World Comes to America* (New York: Columbia University Press, 1985), 21–29; Roger Daniels and Harry H. L. Kitano, *Asian Americans: Emerg-*

ing Minorities, 2d ed. (Englewood Cliffs, N.J.: Prentice Hall, 1995), 16–18; and Sucheng Chan, *Asian Americans: An Interpretive History* (Boston: Twayne Publishers, 1991), 121, 140–41.

22. See *NYT*, January 15, 1964.

23. See table 5.

24. See table 5; and INS, *Annual Report* (Washington, D.C.: Government Printing Office, 1950), table 9A.

25. This "little-noted act," passed in 1946, not only was "more immediately significant" than other postwar changes in the U.S. immigration laws, as Roger Daniels and Harry Kitano have observed, but continues to shape Chinese immigration to this date. See Daniels and Kitano, *Asian Americans*, 42.

26. See table 2.

27. For the gender ratio of the Chinese population in New York City, see table 2.

28. See, for example, *CDN*, January 10, 22, 24, February 28, March 1, 22–24, 1949.

29. Rose Hum Lee, "Chinese in the United States Today," *Survey Graphic: Magazine of Social Interpretation* 31.10 (October 1942): 419. The remaining Chinese laundries experienced a boom, caused by women's participation in the labor force. See Yu, *To Save China*, 140–41.

30. For a discussion of Chinatown's economic revival in the immediate postwar era, see Y. K. Chu (Zhu Xia), *Meiguo Huaqiao Gaishi* (A general history of Chinese Americans) (New York: China Times, 1975), 135.

31. *CDN*, December 13, 1951.

32. *CDN*, February 5–8, 1979. Her story was retold and followed up in 1982. See *CDN*, April 19 and 20, 1982.

33. For a more detailed discussion of the "separated wives" and "war wives," see Lee, *Chinese*, 200–230.

34. It is estimated that more than seven hundred thousand refugees poured into Hong Kong from China in the first six months of 1950, and by the end of 1956, Hong Kong's population had grown from 1.6 million in 1946 to 2.5 million. See John Young, "The Building Years: Maintaining a China–Hong Kong–Britain Equilibrium, 1950–1971," in *Precarious Balance: Hong Kong between China and Britain, 1842–1992*, ed. Ming K. Chan (Armonk, N.Y.: M. E. Sharpe, 1994), 131; and Helen F. Siu, "Immigrants and Social Ethos: Hong Kong in the Nineteen-Eighties," *Journal of the Hong Kong Branch of the Royal Asiatic Society* 26 (1988): 1. For the close ties between many families in Guangdong and Hong Kong, see Mary Sheridan and Janet W. Salaff, eds., *Lives: Chinese Working Women* (Bloomington: Indiana University Press, 1984), 4.

The assumption that most of the Chinese immigrants who came to the United States in the 1960s and 1970s had resided outside China can be attested to by a comparative reading of the numbers of Chinese immigrants by their places of birth and their places of last permanent residence since 1959, the year when the relevant statistics were first available. Although an overwhelming majority of the Chinese immigrants registered China/Taiwan as their place of birth, over half of them identified Hong Kong as their place of last permanent residence. In addition, only about a third of those who came before 1967 from Hong Kong were born there. Given our understanding of the massive migration from China to Hong Kong after 1949 and based on my interviews with the immigrant workers, it is no surprise that most of those who came from Hong Kong were born in China. In other words, many who registered China as their place of birth had resided in Hong Kong before they immigrated to the United States. They might also have resided in Taiwan, but there is no statistical documentation available about this because the numbers of Chinese immigrants from China and Taiwan were not divided until 1982. See INS, *Annual Report*, 1959–78, and *Statistical Yearbook*, 1979–95.

35. Janet Salaff shows that their parents were mostly migrants from China. Since they had to work outside the family at an early age, most of them only had a primary school education. In contrast, daughters in some emigrants' families in the Si Yi District were able to enjoy a higher education because of the emigrants' heavy investment in local education before 1949 and the state effort to improve literacy after 1949. See Janet W. Salaff, *Working Daughters of Hong Kong: Filial Piety or Power in the Family?* (1981; New York: Columbia University Press, 1995), 19–29; and Fang Di, "Cong Renkou Ziliao Zhong Fanying Chulai de Qiaoxiang Laonian Nuqiaoshu de Tedian" (The characteristics of elderly emigrant women in the emigrant communities reflected in the census materials), in *Huaqiao Huaren Shi Yanjiu Ji* (Collection of essays on the history of overseas Chinese and people of Chinese descent), vol. 1, ed. Zheng Min and Liang Chuming (Beijing: Haiyang Chuban She, 1989), 309.

36. *CDN*, May 8, 1951.

37. *CDN*, April 5, 1952. A tangible description of these young immigrant women's lives in the immediate postwar Chinatown of New York can be found in Louis Chu's novel, *Eat a Bowl of Tea* (1961; Seattle: University of Washington Press, 1979).

38. *CDN*, November 26, 1948; and Bonner, *What Brought*, 177. According to *CDN*, they frequented the garment and textile shops on Orchard Street between Broom and Houston Streets, which they called "the Jewish Street," where they could use their bargaining skill to bid for merchandise at lower prices. See *CDN*, December 28, 1962.

39. *CDN*, November 26, 1948.

40. There is a vivid description of this aspect of life in *NYHT*, January 31, 1965.

41. See map 2 and tables 4 and 7.

42. For housing problems in New York's Chinatown, see Chu, *Meiguo*, 173–75; Kuo Chia-ling, *Social and Political Change in New York's Chinatown: The Role of Voluntary Associations* (New York: Praeger, 1977), 47; and Joann Faung Jean Lee, *Asian Americans: Oral Histories of First- to Fourth-Generation Americans from China, the Philippines, Japan, India, the Pacific Islands, Vietnam, and Cambodia* (New York: New Press, 1992), 41–42. West Coast Chinese communities also had similar problems. See Ginger Chih, "Immigration of Chinese Women to the U.S.A., 1900–1940 (M.A. thesis, Sarah Lawrence College, 1977), 26; and Stanford M. Lyman, *Chinese Americans* (New York: Random House, 1974), 149.

43. See, for example, *CDN*, February 28 and March 1, 1949.

44. Lee, *Chinese*, 222.

45. See Wu, *Haiwai Yimin*, 267; Chu, *Meiguo*, 267; and Bonner, *What Brought*, 176.

46. The column was named "Huafu Xiaoshe" (A snapshot of Chinatown), and the three stories are covered in *CDN*, January 22, 1949.

47. See Chu, *Meiguo*, 179–81.

48. *CDN*, May 27, 1950.

49. Heyer, "Patterns," 83–85.

50. *NYHT*, January 31, 1965.

51. Guo, *Huafu Cangsang*, 62–63; and *CDN*, September 22 and 24, 1979. See also *CDN*, November 17, 1981.

52. Stuart H. Cattell, *Health, Welfare, and Social Organization in Chinatown* (Mimeograph, New York: Community Service Society of New York, 1962), ii. The community newspaper also reported that the U.S.-trained Chinese American nurses at its Chinatown center began to provide the new Chinese women immigrants with general education on prenatal hygiene and children protection in the early 1950s. See *CDN*, April 8, 1954.

53. See, for example, *CDN*, May 8 and 29, 1952; the first help-wanted advertisement appeared in *CDN*, June 27, 1952.

54. Guo, *Huafu Cangsang,* 88–90.

55. Author's interview with Nancy Ng (pseudonym), March 4, 1988, in Cantonese.

56. These workers came from urban areas north of the province of Guangdong and did not speak the Taishan dialect or Cantonese.

57. *CDN,* May 29, 1952; my translation. A good discussion of the Chinese immigrant families in this period appears in the same issue.

58. Author's interview with a Mrs. Yeung, April 30, 1989, in Cantonese.

59. Prior to 1949 and particularly before the 1930s, when the silk industry flourished in various areas of the Pearl River Delta, many young women there traded off their relations with their prospective husbands by buying substitutes to bear children for them and refused to move into their husbands' families but still retained their names in their husbands' lineage for social identity and protection. Others simply resisted being married. The latter would join a sworn sisterhood of spinsters, move into *gu po wu* (spinster houses) or *zhai tang* (vegetarian halls) to form fictive families, and care for each other for the rest of their lives. They were called *zi shu nu* (women who dress their hair on their own). Since Shunde was a major site of this culture, *Shunde nu* (women or girls of Shunde) became a synonym for these women. Scholars still cannot come to an agreement as to the origins of this local culture. Many concede that it became widespread among working-class families only after the silk industry began to grow in the nineteenth century, when many young women gained economic independence by working in the steam filatures. This regional culture has aroused great interest among scholars in China and abroad. For literature on this culture in English, see Janice E. Stockard, *The Daughters of the Canton Delta: Marriage Patterns and Economic Strategies in South China, 1860–1930* (Stanford, Calif.: Stanford University Press, 1989); Marjorie Topley, "Marriage Resistance in Rural Kwangtung," in *Women in Chinese Society,* ed. Margery Wolf and Roxane Witke (Stanford, Calif.: Stanford University Press, 1975) 67–88; Helen Siu, "Where Were the Women? Rethinking Marriage Resistance and Regional Culture in South China," *Late Imperial China* 11.2 (December 1990): 32–62; and Robert Y. Eng, "Luddism and Labor Protest among Silk Artisans and Workers in Jiangnan and Guangdong, 1860–1930," *Late Imperial China* 11.2 (December 1990): 63–101. For a glimpse of the numerous related publications in China, see Chen Yuzeng, Li Sifu, and Wu Qinshi, "Zishunu yu Buluojia" (Women who combed up their hair and their refusal to move into their husbands' homes), *GWZ* 12 (1964): 172–88; and Li Benli, "Shunde Cansiye de Lishi Gaikuang" (A general historical account of the silk industry in Shunde), *GWZ* 15 (1964): 102–31.

60. Besides the child's biological parents, his or her "sworn parents" are also expected to assume responsibility for his or her well-being. Unlike the relationship between godparent and godchild, the Chinese sworn parent/child relationship does not stem from religious faith, nor is it bound by legal terms, as in the case of adoption. This relationship is largely decided by the child's biological and sworn parents and is based on the good faith and commitment between them, particularly when the child is too young to make a decision.

61. Even to this day she cannot help laughing whenever she thinks about this part of her life.

62. *Study,* 42. A small number of the Chinatown population was involved in this industry. Stuart Cattell shows that among the Chinatown family heads who sought assistance from a social welfare organization in 1962, only 1.7 percent were employed in the garment industry. See Cattell, *Health,* 109.

63. *1960 U.S. Census,* vol. 2, PC(2)-1C, table 17.

64. *CDN,* December 31, 1962.

65. For a detailed discussion of the 1965 amendment, see Reimers, *Still the Golden Door*, 63–121; Chan, *Asian Americans*, 145–47; and Daniels and Kitano, *Asian Americans*, 18–19.

66. See table 5.

67. For a discussion of this event, see Young, "Building Years," 139–40.

68. INS, *Annual Report*, 1966–79. This number is based on those who registered Hong Kong as their last place of permanent residence.

69. Chen Hsiang-shui, *Chinatown No More: Taiwan Immigrants in Contemporary New York* (Ithaca, N.Y.: Cornell University Press, 1992), 54–55, 60–68. Their numbers greatly increased after the mid-1980s, when the Taiwanese currency appreciated. I am indebted to Linda Gail Arrigo and Ping-Chun Hsiung for reminding me of this change.

70. For a discussion of the difficulty in counting the number of these immigrants caused by the lack of ethnic specificity in census taking, see Robert W. Gardner, Bryant Robey, and Peter C. Smith, "Asian Americans: Growth, Change, and Diversity," *Population Bulletin* 40.4 (October 1985): 3–43. The 70 percent estimate is Sucheng Chan's, and the 80 percent estimate is based on *Study*. Barry Wain further estimates that more than 90 percent of the refugees who left Vietnam by boat between 1975 and 1979 were ethnic Chinese. See Chan, *Asian Americans*, 157; *Study*, 88; and Wain, *The Refused: The Agony of the Indochina Refugees* (New York: Simon and Schuster, 1981), 80. For a discussion of the refugees from Southeast Asia in general, see Chan, *Asian Americans*, 152–65; and Reimers, *Still the Golden Door*, 155–99.

71. See table 8.

72. See *Study*, 94.

73. See tables 2, 5, and 6; *Study*, 89.

74. See, for example, *NYT*, January 15, 1964.

75. For example, the Chinese American Planning Council was founded in 1964 and significantly reorganized in 1978, and the Asian Americans for Equal Employment was founded in 1974. For a detailed discussion of new social organizations in the community and their conflicts with the traditional ones in the 1970s, see Enoch Yee Nock Wan, "The Dynamics of Ethnicity: A Case Study on the Immigrant Community of New York Chinatown" (Ph.D. diss., State University of New York at Stony Brook, 1978), 242–64.

76. See *Study*, 97–98.

77. Zhou, *Chinatown*, 126, table 6-1.

78. *Study*, 98–99, table 20.

79. Many women immigrants from China had worked in the field, and many from Hong Kong had engaged in wage-earning labor at home, assembling plastic flowers, toys, wigs, and transistors. For a discussion of women's wage-earning labor at home in Hong Kong in the 1960s and 1970s, see Salaff, *Working Daughters*, 19–23 and 259.

80. My interviews have indicated this. See also, for example, *WSJ*, September 13, 1966.

81. For a discussion of the characteristics of the Chinese female immigrant labor force from 1970 to 1980, see *Study*, 95.

82. See *Study*, 99, table 20.

83. The following discussion of space availability and the general trends of Chinese distribution in the area is primarily based on *Study*, 47–48 and 107; and Waldinger, *Through the Eye*, 140–42.

84. The *Study* assesses that the rate of vacancy was 35 percent, while Roger Waldinger estimates it to have been 30 to 35 percent. See *Study*, 48; and Waldinger, *Through the Eye*, 141–42.

85. Waldinger, *Through the Eye*, 142.

86. Ibid., 138; Kwong, *New Chinatown,* 31–32; and *Study,* 54.

87. See table 9.

88. See map 3; *Study,* 49.

89. *Study,* 5.

90. *Study,* 49.

91. The city's share in the nation's garment industry declined by only 3.5 percent between 1975 and 1996, dropping from 23.6 percent to 11.9 percent, as compared to 11.7 percent between 1958 and 1974, dropping from 11.9 percent to 8.4 percent. See Waldinger, *Through the Eye,* 54; and Mark Levitan, *Opportunity at Work: The New York City Garment Industry.* (New York: Community Service Society of New York, 1998), 24.

92. Zhou, *Chinatown,* 170.

93. *Study,* 5.

94. Kowng, *New Chinatown,* 32–36. My interviews with some restaurant and grocery owners showed that by the early 1980s, the two businesses in Chinatown had become so dependent on the garment workers that during the Chinese garment workers' strike in 1982, a chain grocery store owner said that he lost almost a hundred thousand dollars of business on that single day, and a small restaurant owner complained about losing more than a thousand dollars' profit on that same day.

95. The impact of the unionization of the Chinatown garment industry and its problems will be further discussed in chapter 7.

Part 2 Introduction

1. Although this part examines the Chinese women workers' family and work lives in separate chapters, it does not intend to dichotomize these two major aspects of their lives. Rather it intends to explore the multiple forces in various aspects of their lives that interplayed to change their perceptions of life in the United States. For a collection of essays that challenge the dichotomous approach of the public and private spheres of women's lives, see Dorothy O. Helly and Susan M. Reverby, eds., *Gendered Domains: Rethinking Public and Private in Women's History* (Ithaca, N.Y.: Cornell University Press, 1992).

Chapter 4: New York's Chinese Working-Class Families during the Exclusion Era

1. My interviews and the coverage in the community newspapers indicate that there was always a number of young single women among the workers in the Chinatown garment industry, who, as daughters of their families, also contributed significantly to their family incomes. See, for example, *CDN,* June 29, 1977. However, limited by space and due to their disproportionately small numbers in the industry, this study will focus on married women workers in the industry. For the married women workers' percentage in 1980, see Zhou, *Chinatown.*

2. See for example, Francis L. K. Hsu, *The Challenge of the American Dream: The Chinese in the United States* (Belmont, Calif.: Wadsworth, 1971); and Shien Woo Kung, *Chinese in American Life: Some Aspects of Their History, Status, Problems, and Contributions* (Seattle: Washington University Press, 1962). An exception to the authors of this period is Rose Hum Lee, who was more inclined to examine various factors that shaped the characteristics of the Chinese American family and its variations. See, for example, Lee, *Chinese,* 185–251.

3. Evelyn Nakano Glenn, "Split Household, Small Producer, and Dual Wage Earner: An Analysis of Chinese-American Family Strategies," *Journal of Marriage and the Family* 45 (February 1983): 35. Similar arguments have also been made by Peter Li, based on his study of Chinese immigration in Canada. See Peter S. Li, "Immigration Laws and Family Patterns: Some Demographic Changes among Chinese Families in Canada, 1885–1971," *Canadian Ethnic Studies* 12.1 (1980): 58–59.

4. Evelyn Nakano Glenn, "Racial Ethnic Women's Labor: The Intersection of Race, Gender, and Class Oppression," *Review of Radical Political Economics* 17.3 (1985): 103.

5. Evelyn Nakano Glenn with Stacey G. H. Yap, "Chinese American Families," in *Minority Families in the United States: A Multicultural Perspective,* ed. Ronald L. Taylor (Englewood Cliffs, N.J.: Prentice-Hall, 1994), 115–45, esp. 117 and 141.

6. Merchants were not legally restricted by the Chinese Exclusion Acts and could sponsor the immigration of their families to the United States.

7. As she recalled, the border control on both sides in the early 1950s was not as tight as it was later. Since wages in Hong Kong were higher than in the mainland, people tended to cross the border to work there. Many studies have mentioned the wave of migration from China to Hong Kong after 1949. See chap. 3, n. 33.

8. See, for example, Bonner, *What Brought;* Leong, *Chinatown;* and Yu, *To Save China.*

9. See table 3 in chapter 3.

10. This estimate of about 80 percent is based on *1940 US Census* data, which show that in 1940 there were 772 married Chinese women and 5,245 married Chinese men in New York City. Since few Chinese women entered interracial marriages, and if the percentage of the Chinese interracial families still formed more than 20 percent of all the city's Chinese families in 1940 as in 1925, which was quite unlikely given Shepard Schwartz's finding of the continual decline of Chinese interracial marriages in the 1930s, one can safely assume that there were about twelve hundred Chinese and interracial Chinese families in New York City and about four thousand married Chinese men still living in the absence of their wives, which was 78 percent of all married Chinese men in the city. See *1940 US Census* (Non-white), table 28; Schwartz, "Mate-Selection," 563; State of New York, *Census,* 1925. Also see note 12 in this chapter.

11. See, for example, Wong, "Chinese in New York," 308; Stanford Lyman, *Chinese Americans,* 91; and Kung, *Chinese,* 214–15.

12. New York State Census manuscripts reveal that Chinese interracial marriages constituted more than 60 percent of Chinatown families in 1905, more than 50 percent in 1915, but only 22 percent in 1925. State of New York, *Census.* This trend of decline is coincidental with Shepard Schwartz's findings by studying the city's Chinese marriage registers from 1931 to 1938 in comparison with those in previous periods. See Schwartz, "Mate-Selection," 563.

13. See John Kuo Wei Tchen, "New York Chinese: The Nineteenth-Century Pre-Chinatown Settlement," in *Chinese America: History and Perspectives, 1990* (Brisbane, Calif.: Chinese Historical Society, 1990), 161–68; and Schwartz, "Mate-Selection," 564–68. However, by the 1930s they tended not to live in Chinatown. See Leong, *Chinatown,* 185.

14. See note 12.

15. See Fang Fuer and Zhang Manli, "Niuyue Huaqiao Xiyiguan de Bianqian" (Changes in the Chinese hand laundries in New York City), *GWZX* 23 (1981): 191.

16. This was also practiced in San Francisco and other major Chinese settlements in the country. See, for example, Victor Nee and Brett de Bary Nee, *Longtime Californ': A Documentary Study of an American Chinatown* (New York: Pantheon Books, 1972), 148; Glenn, "Split Household," 38; and Lyman, *Chinese Americans,* 110–11.

17. Similar problems are discussed in other accounts. See, for example, Xie Yingming, "Lumei Jianwen Zaji" (Random recollections of my stay in the United States), *GWZ* 39 (1983): 114–61; and Chen Ke, "Fangwen Liumei Huaqiao Chen Ke Xiansheng" (An interview with Mr. Chen Ke, a Chinese who returned from America), *HSLJ* 2 (1980): 340–54.

18. Many have noted the strained relationship between fathers and sons after their reunion. See, for example, Wong, *Chinatown,* 62; Lee, *Chinese,* 204; and Ben Loy's relations with his father in Chu, *Eat a Bowl of Tea.* The strengthening of the mother/son relationship in Chinese American "split households" was also in part due to the characteristics of the traditional Chinese family. For a discussion of the "uterine family" (the mother-centered informal family) within the traditional Chinese family, see Kay Ann Johnson, *Women, the Family, and Peasant Revolution in China* (Chicago: University of Chicago Press, 1983), 10, 18–20.

19. Wong, "Chinese in New York," 298. For a more detailed account of the lives of Chinese laundrymen in New York, see Yu, *To Save China,* chap. 1.

20. For scattered information about women in New York's laundry business, see Nancy Woloch, *Women and the American Experience* (New York: Alfred A. Knopf, 1984), 228; and Christine Stansell, *City of Women: Sex and Class in New York, 1789–1860* (Urbana: University of Illinois Press, 1986), 13.

21. This was confirmed by the author's interviews with old-timers in the community.

22. For cases of how Chinese men in New York were ruined by these vices throughout the years, see, for example, Wong, "Chinese in New York," 306 and 308–11; Leong, *Chinatown,* 186–87, 191–235; and Guo, *Huafu Cangsang,* 214–15.

23. Author's interview with Professor Yu Dingbang, who is the son of an emigrant family with generations of male members working in the United States, at Guangzhou Zhonhshan University, July 28, 1997, in Mandarin. With the point of geographical reference changed, I hereafter will use "the Chinese American emigrant family" to refer to those families in Guangdong that had members in the United States.

24. One *mu* equals 0.0667 hectares.

25. Author's interview with Wu Zhenze, in the town of Gu Jing, Xinhui County, August 8, 1997, in Taishan dialect.

26. See, for example, Chen Han-seng, *Landlord and Peasant in China: A Study of the Agrarian Crisis in South China* (New York: International Publisher, 1936), 104. He focused solely on female laborers while ignoring women's labor in the emigrant families.

27. Although lives in Si Yi were somewhat different, the description in Daniel Harrison Kulp's study of the northeastern part of the province offers a glimpse into the lives of women in rural Guangdong. See Daniel Harrison Kulp, *Country Life in South China: The Sociology of Familism* (1925; New York: Paragon Book Gallery, 1966), 96–98.

28. This folk song was recorded in many publications about the Si Yi customs and culture. See, for example, *EG* 11 (April 1985): 36.

29. *XZ,* a major publication of Taishan County, had a special column of *feiqing shijie* (The column on the information of bandits) as early as 1917. This was also a constant theme covered by the publication throughout the years before 1949.

30. It is estimated that there was a total of 2,450 watchtowers in Changsha and the other four areas of Kaiping County alone. See *GSZHZ,* 150; *TXHZ,* 173.

31. Ibid., 154.

32. The villagers told me about this woman when I visited the town in the summer of 1997.

33. *Li* is a Chinese unit of distance; it equals a half-kilometer. This folk song can also be found in many writings on the lives of the emigrant families in the Si Yi District. See, for example, *GSZHZ,* 153.

34. I came across a number of cases similar to Aunt Yeung's experience before immigration when I visited Guangdong and interviewed members of the Chinese American emigrant families in 1997.

35. *GSZHZ*, 149. There are stories of family tragedies covered by the local publications during this time. See, for example, Huang Feng, "Qiaojuan Lei" (The tears of the overseas Chinese families) *GSQ* 18 (October 15, 1948), 42–43.

36. This is based on my interviews with Liu Zhongmin, the chief editor of *TXHZ*, in Taishan, August 5, 1997, in Taishan dialect, and many individuals in Xinhui and Taishan.

37. See, for example, *XZ* 26 (1934): 52, and 8 (1935): 62–63.

38. Liu Zhongmin is such an adopted son; his father and grandfather were also adopted by the family. Author's interview with Liu in Taishan, August 5, 1997, in Taishan dialect.

39. See *XZ* 23 (1935): 66.

40. In traditional Chinese families only males could carry on the family line, and their loyalty and sense of obligation to the family were considered to be of paramount importance for maintaining the family system. Those men adopted by families other than their biological ones were therefore held in contempt by the society.

41. For studies of the lineage system in southeast China and the former Si Yi, see Maurice Freedman, *Lineage Organization in Southeastern China* (London: Athlone Press, 1958); Ta Chen, *Emigrant Communities in South China: A Study of Overseas Migration and Its Influence on Standards of Living and Social Change* (New York: Institute of Pacific Relations, 1939); Helen Siu, *Agents and Victims in South China: Accomplices in Rural Revolution* (New Haven, Conn.: Yale University Press, 1989), esp. chap. 3; and Yuen-Fong Woon, "Social Change and Continuity in South China: Overseas Chinese and the Guan Lineage of Kaiping County, 1949–87," *China Quarterly* 118 (June 1989): 324–44. For the status of women under the lineage system in the Pearl River Delta, see Rubie S. Watson, "Girls' Houses and Working Women: Expressive Culture in the Pearl River Delta, 1900–41," in *Women and Chinese Patriarchy: Submission, Servitude, and Escape*, ed. Maria Jaschok and Suzanne Miers (Atlantic Highlands, N.J.: Zed Books, 1994), 30.

42. A commentary in *XZ* well illustrates this gender bias: it denounces the wife for her lack of understanding for her husband, who had an affair with their young maid. See *XZ* 10 (1936): 50–52.

43. *XZ* 17 (1935): 67.

44. *XZ* 31 (1934): 74–76.

45. The division of remittances from abroad also often caused tension between the mother-in-law and the daughter-in-law in a family. See, for example, *XZ* 6 (1935): 64–65, and 11 (1935): 11.

46. Ta Chen's study of the Chinese emigrant communities in Guangdong, including those in San Yi and Si Yi, shows that the severity of such punishments had somewhat decreased by the 1930s and 1940s, but in some cases women still had to face the death penalty under the order of the ad hoc local leaders. See Chen, *Emigrant Communities*, 127–28.

47. This punishment was practiced in both San Yi and Si Yi but under somewhat different circumstances. While it was largely used to punish adulterers in Si Yi, it was used to punish women who had breached their promises and fallen in love with men after they decided to *shu qi* (comb up their hair, showing their determination to remain single throughout their lives) in San Yi. Although many in the former Si Yi District and some women garment workers in New York who had come from this area whom I interviewed also mentioned this form of death penalty in the area, most stories seemed to be hearsay.

48. "Hunyin Buheli Caocheng Yimu Beiju" (A tragedy caused by an unreasonable marriage), *GSQ* 18 (October 15, 1948): 20.

49. My interviews with women in Taishan suggested that no matter how much the young women would like to continue their education, an overwhelming majority of them would be summoned to return home and get married once they reached marriageable age. For comments on the strong patriarchal control over women's education in Taishan, see Fang, "Cong Renkou Ziliao," 311.

50. For an excellent discussion of Chinese American acculturation in the United States during the Exclusion era, see K. Scott Wong and Sucheng Chan, eds., *Claiming America: Constructing Chinese American Identities During the Exclusion Era* (Philadelphia: Temple University Press, 1998).

51. On August 18, 1934, six young women between the ages of eighteen and nineteen in the village of Kai in Enping County tied themselves together and drowned themselves in a deep pond. See *EG* 20 (July 1965): 55–56. Committing suicide was a powerful form of resistance used by women in traditional China. For a discussion of this, see Margery Wolf, "Women and Suicide in China," in *Women in Chinese Society,* ed. Margery Wolf and Roxanne Witke (Stanford, Calif.: Stanford University Press, 1975), 111–41.

52. For a literary representation of the Si Yi girls' houses and the bonds between members of such women's communities, see Zhang Jianren, Wen Wanfang, and Mei Yimin, *Sheng Gua* (Leading a widow's life while the husband is still alive) (Guangzhou: Huacheng Chuban She, 1994).

53. See, for example, *XZ* 15 (1939): 47; Office of Taishan County Communist Party History and Office of Taishan Women's Federation, *San Tai Jun Guo* (The women warriors in San Tai) (Taishan, Guangdong: Office of Taishan County Communist Party History and the Office of Taishan Women's Federation, 1987), esp. 4, 25–26, 55–58, and 117–19 (available at Taishan Archival Library). My interviews in Xinhui and Taishan also showed that women played an important role in the war effort. Huang Meifang, the wife of the head of the former District no. 2, was such a case. As everyone in the group whom I interviewed in Taishan on August 5, 1997, agreed, the war-resistance effort in their local areas led by her husband could not have been carried out successfully without her crucial support and resourceful cooperation.

54. *TXHZ,* 172; and Marion K. Hom, *Songs of Gold Mountain: Cantonese Rhymes from San Francisco Chinatown* (Berkeley: University of California Press, 1987), 146

55. See Madeline Yuan-Yin Hsu, "Living Abroad and Faring Well: Migration and Transnationalism in Taishan County, Guangdong, 1904–1939" (Ph.D. diss., Yale University, 1996).

Chapter 5: The Transformation of New York's Chinese Working-Class Families after World War II

1. For the observation that family life became the norm in other major Chinese American communities by the 1920s, see, for example, Glenn, "Split Household," 39.

2. For the definition and a discussion of the small producer family, see Glenn, "Split Household," 39–40.

3. Author's telephone interview with a Mrs. Tang, October 12, 1998, in Cantonese.

4. Similar cases took place in the Chinese settlements in other parts of the country. See, for example, Guo, *Huafu Cangsang,* 68–69. For a different response of the women of these families to their lives in San Francisco, see Yung, *Unbound Feet,* 80–83.

5. The following discussion is based on author's interview with Aunt Chen in her apartment in Brooklyn, April 7, 1986, in Taishan dialect.

6. See *1960 U.S. Census,* vol. 2, PC(2)-1C, table 12.

7. For the rationale behind this assumption, see chap. 3, n. 34.

8. *GSZHZ,* 149.

9. For a good discussion of the situation in Taishan during World War II and before 1949, see Hsu, "Living Abroad," 236–42.

10. For a critique of the gender relations in the People's Republic of China, see Johnson, *Women;* Margery Wolf, *Revolution Postponed: Women in Contemporary China* (Stanford, Calif.: Stanford University Press, 1985); Philis Andors, *The Unfinished Liberation of Chinese Women, 1949–1980* (Bloomington: Indiana University Press, 1983); and Judith Stacey, *Patriarchy and Socialist Revolution in China* (Berkeley: University of California Press, 1983).

11. Author's interview with Wu Peixuan in Taishan, August 6, 1997, in Taishan dialect.

12. *CDN,* January 15, 1952. For a similar report on the improvement of women's literacy in the emigrant community in China, see *EG* 1 (March 1958): 9; *EG* 3 (September 1958): 26.

13. For a discussion of this aspect of life, see *GSZHZ,* 155.

14. See Yu, *To Save China,* 186–87 and 191–92.

15. For example, in the mid-1950s the government gave overseas Chinese visitors, overseas Chinese students studying in China, and overseas Chinese dependents various forms of preferential treatment to attract remittances from abroad in an attempt to help realize the First Five Year Plan.

16. The following account is based on my interview with Mrs. Jian (pseudonym), November 18, 1994, in Cantonese.

17. Mr. Jian's biological mother was one of the concubines.

18. Under the system of collectivization, work points were given by the production team as a way to keep records of its members' labor contribution around the year. The value of a work point was calculated based on the profit the team made by the end of that year.

19. The numbers are 3,344 out of 11,051 in 1960, and 2,428 out of 20,125 in 1970. See *1960 U.S. Census,* vol. 2, PC(2)-1C, table 12; and *1970 U.S. Census,* vol. 2, PC(2)-1G, table 20.

20. The percentage of the state's Chinese adult men registered as operators in the census data, who in the Chinese case were most likely to engage in the laundry business, dropped from almost 40 percent in 1930 to 37.6 percent in 1940 and 19.5 percent in 1950. See *1930 U.S. Census,* vol. 5, chap. 3, table 6; *1940 U.S. Census,* (Non-white), table 32; and *1950 U.S. Census,* vol. 4, P-E no. 3B, table 23.

21. *1970 U.S. Census,* vol. 2, PC(2)-1G, table 29.

22. *Study,* 64.

23. Author's interview with Christine Lin (pseudonym), August 9, 1989, in English.

24. The Chen family name as well as Mark Chen are pseudonyms.

25. Eight characters are instrumental for Chinese fortune telling. They are usually in four pairs, indicating the year, month, day, and hour of a person's birth, with each pair consisting of one Heavenly Stem and one Earthy Branch. It is believed that marriage will be successful only when the eight characters of the couple match.

26. Tang Mei and Wang Weijun are pseudonyms. The literal translation of *dim sum* is "a little essence." It refers to light refreshments, such as pastries and small dishes, served with tea in the morning, at brunch, or, more commonly, at lunch or teatime. I thank Sue Fawn Chung for the above detailed description of the term. This diet is very popular in Guangdong Province, Hong Kong, and many other major Chinese communities in the world.

Numerically limited immigration preferences included: (1) unmarried sons and daughters of U.S. citizens and their children; (2) spouses and unmarried sons and daughters of permanent resident aliens; (3) members of the professions of exceptional ability and their spouses and children; (4) married sons and daughters of U.S. citizens and their spouses and children; (5) brothers and sisters of U.S. citizens (at least twenty-one years of age) and their spouses and children; and (6) workers in either skilled or unskilled occupations in which laborers are in short supply in the United States and their spouses and children. In addition to immediate relatives of U.S. citizens (i.e., spouse, minor children, and parents of U.S. citizens at least twenty-one years of age) and babies born abroad to legal permanent resident aliens who have resided continuously in the United States since January 1, 1972, special immigrants in the category of numerically exempt immigrants include certain ministers of religion, certain former employees of the U.S. government abroad, certain persons who lost U.S. citizens, and certain foreign medical graduates. (Adapted from City of New York, Department of City Planning, *The Newest New Yorkers: A Statistical Portrait* [New York, 1992], 247.)

27. A phrase used to symbolize the employment system in China at that time, which was as secure and stable as an unbreakable iron bowl.

28. A popular saying in China at the time. Thirty-eight yuan was the basic wage for all workers of his grade. Since salary increases in China at that time were based on seniority rather than work performance, employees found no incentive to work hard.

29. Author's interview with Tang Mei's family in their Brooklyn apartment, March 19, 1989, in Cantonese.

30. Although Ka's father was an old immigrant in the United States, she could not come to this country to meet him, since China and the United States did not have diplomatic relations at that time. The following account is based on author's interviews with Shui Mak Ka, March 15, 1989, in Cantonese, and with Jia San Fu, October 15, 1994, in Mandarin.

31. This was recently confirmed by the statistics provided by the New York Asian Women's Center. According to its tenth-anniversary report, 74 percent of the women it had assisted between 1982 and 1992 were Chinese. See New York Asian Women's Center, "Tenth Anniversary Report, 1982–1992," 8. Old-timers in the community believe that this number represented only a fraction of the women who needed help.

32. Staff members in the Asian American Women's Center, which was established in 1982, however, dispute this assumption and contend that domestic violence is a cross-class phenomenon.

33. The case was covered by almost all major English and Chinese newspapers in the city in September 1987, December 1988, and April 1989. See, for example, *NYT,* April 5, 1989; *NYND,* April 4 and 5, November 26, 1989; *CDN,* September 9 and 21, 1987, December 5, 7, and 23, 1988, April 1, 3, and 5, 1989; *WJ,* September 9, 1987, and April 5, 1989.

34. See INS, *Annual Report.* Out of a total of 273,770, 22,595 immigrants belonged to this category.

35. This story of Wang Ying (pseudonym) was drawn from my personal contacts and conversations with her between 1984 and 1991 in New York City. Chen Mingxin (her husband) is also a pseudonym.

36. The complete version of this folk song appears in chapter 4.

37. See, for example, *STD,* January 18, 1989.

38. *New York Times Magazine,* April 24, 1988.

39. The following discussion is based on author's interview with Alice Ip, March 2, 1989, September 13 and December 12, 1994, as well as many other occasions, in Cantonese.

40. Author's interview with Alice Ip, December 12, 1994, in Cantonese.

41. Written by Amy Tse, courtesy of Alice Ip.

Chapter 6: Women in the Chinatown Garment Industry

1. *NYHT,* January 31, 1965.
2. See, for example, *NYT,* September 13, 1966, and June 28, 1967.
3. See *NYT,* August 5, 1972.
4. See, for example, *NYT,* September 18 and October 19, 1979; *DN,* October 19 and December 20, 1979.
5. *DN,* October 19, 1979.
6. See the coverage in *NYT,* September 18, 1979; *DN,* December 20, 1979.
7. *NYT,* September 18, 1979.
8. *DN,* December 20, 1979.
9. The most influential of these is perhaps the report by Jane H. Lii. See *NYT,* March 12, 1995.
10. Levine, *Women's Garment Workers,* 18.
11. Leon Stein, introduction to *Out of the Sweatshop: The Struggle for Industrial Democracy,* ed. Leon Stein (New York: Quadrangle, 1977), xv.
12. Levitan, *Opportunity,* 40–41.
13. Green, *Ready To Wear,* 155.
14. *Study,* 49. For a more accurate description of the shops' location, see *Study,* fig. 13, or map 3 in this study.
15. *Study,* 49; see also map 3.
16. *Study,* 55.
17. The average floor space per worker was 115 square feet. See ibid., 55.
18. *CDN,* June 8, 1977.
19. For a discussion of the conditions of Chinatown shops, see *Study,* 57–58.
20. This aspect of life remained largely unchanged in the late 1980s. See *CTDN,* August 20, 1988.
21. *Faat choi* is a homonym of "making fortunate" in Cantonese. Interestingly, women workers in other ethnic garment industries have also adopted similar strategies. For example, Korean women garment workers eat boiled pork instead for the same purpose. See Kyeyoung Park, *The Korean American Dream: Immigrants and Small Business in New York City* (Ithaca, N.Y.: Cornell University Press, 1997), 67.
22. In most Chinatown shops there was only one toilet for all employees. This remains largely unchanged. For a worker's discussion of this condition in the 1970s, see *CDN,* June 8 and September 17, 1977.
23. In 1979 a girl fell to her death as she left her mother's workplace in an old building with a faulty elevator system. See *CDN,* February 22, 1979. For a discussion of unsafe elevators in the 1970s, see *CDN,* September 17, 1977.
24. Author's interview with a Mrs. Wong, February 23, 1987, in Cantonese.
25. *Gung Hei Faat Choih* is also often used on Chinese New Year among the Cantonese as New Year's greetings, especially among those from Hong Kong and other Chinese communities in Asia in the late 1970s and early 1980s.
26. This operation remains to this day. For the situation in the 1970s, see *CDN,* January 26, 1977.
27. *Yam lihk* refers to an intense, exhausting type of labor that does not require brutal strength but has an equally heavy toll on a workers' health. See JoAnn Lum and Peter Kwong,

"Surviving in America: Trials of a Chinese Immigrant Woman," *Village Voice*, October 31, 1989, 40.

28. This is based on the author's interviews and a reading of some workers' wage-record books by their courtesy. For the late 1980s figure, also see *NYT*, May 30, 1990; and *NYND*, April 8, 1990.

29. Author's interview with a Mr. Wong (pseudonym), April 16, 1990.

30. See Glenn, *Daughters*, 90–131; and Green, *Ready To Wear*, 161–87.

31. For such a case, see *NYT*, August 23, 1977.

32. *NYT*, August 23, 1977.

33. Similar groups of workers can also be found in the study by Ching-wing Hui and Thomas Lacey, "Participation of Chinese Women in the Garment Industry in New York City" (Manuscript, New School for Social Research, July 22, 1976).

34. The following discussion is based on my own observations and frequent conversations with A Ying from 1984 to 1987.

35. "Chicken in soy bean sauce" is one of the most delicious and nutritious Cantonese dishes. Here the term is used to describe the inviting nature of easy work in the garment shops. "Pork neck bones," though barely having any meat, are indispensable for making the nutritious soups that the Cantonese believe to be critical for a good health. The term is used to refer to difficult work in the shops. Although uninviting, it is also indispensable for workers to make a living. Guo Zhengzhi believes that these terms have been widely used since the garment factories first appeared in Chinatown in the early 1950s. See Guo, *Huafu Cangsang*, 194–95.

36. See tables 7 and 10

37. *Study*, 117.

38. Other homeworkers included undocumented immigrants, refugees from Southeast Asia who were receiving social welfare during the time, as well as those who could not work in the shops for physical or other reasons.

39. *Study*, 93–94.

40. Sung, *Survey*, 93–102.

41. Betty Lee Sung cited in *Study*, 93.

42. For a discussion of the single-child policy and its impact, see Judith Banister, "Population Policy and Trends in China, 1978–1983," *China Quarterly* 100 (December 1984): 717–38; and Joyce K. Kallgren, "Politics, Welfare, and Change: The Single-Child Family in China," in *The Political Economy of Reform in Post-Mao China*, ed. Elizabeth J. Perry and Christine Wong (Cambridge, Mass.: Harvard University Press, 1985), 131–56.

43. While it was 18.3 in 1970 and 10.6 in 1980, those in Queens and Brooklyn were 25.7 and 24.2 in 1970 and 1980, respectively. See *Study*, 240, table A-3.

44. Author's interview with a Ms. Lee at her apartment in Brooklyn, September 2, 1989, in Cantonese.

45. Green, *Ready To Wear*, 152.

46. Eileen Boris and Cynthia R. Daniels, introduction to *Homework: Historical and Contemporary Perspectives on Paid Labor at Home*, ed. Eileen Boris and Cynthia R. Daniels (Urbana: University of Illinois Press, 1989), 7–8.

47. Quoted in May Ying Chen, "Reaching for Their Rights: Asian Workers in New York City," Report for the Center for Labor-Management Studies, 1989, manuscript in the author's possession (courtesy of May Ying Chen).

48. For a discussion of other ethnic garment shops in New York City and other parts of the United States in various historical periods, see for example, Glenn, *Daughters*, 133–39;

Waldinger, *Through the Eye*, 149–87; and Louise Lamphere, *From Working Daughters to Working Mothers: Immigrant Women in a New England Industrial Community* (Ithaca, N.Y.: Cornell University Press, 1987), 289–325.

49. *CDN*, June 27, 1952.

50. These characteristics of the Chinese garment shops are also mentioned in Waldinger, *Through the Eye*, 157–60; and *Study*, 61.

51. Author's interview with a Mrs. Tong, May 10, 1989, in Cantonese.

52. Author's interview with a Mrs. Wong, March 19, 1989, in Cantonese.

53. See Glenn, *Daughters*, 128–29.

54. The frequency of stoppages varied according to the situations in the shops. Some workers said it happened so frequently in their shops before the 1982 strike that they simply could not recall the exact number. Others said there were only one or two such incidents in a span of five to six years.

55. These were the only theatrical programs that were allowed to be performed during the Cultural Revolution. They uniformly glorified the Chinese Communist Party and the Communist revolution.

56. People in China in the 1970s and early 1980s believed that a modern household should have these eight things.

57. Xiao Hong (pseudonym) told me about this when I worked in a Chinatown garment shop in the summer 1992.

58. See, for example, Park, *Korean American Dream*, 67; and Lamphere, *From Working Daughters*, 311–19.

59. Regionalism has historically been a major factor that undermined the unity of people in China. For a discussion of how it affected the unity and militancy of women workers in the shops, see Emily Honig, *Sisters and Strangers: Women in the Shanghai Cotton Mills, 1919–1949* (Stanford, Calif.: Stanford University Press, 1986); and Ching Kwan Lee, *Gender and the South China Miracle: Two Worlds of Factory Women* (Berkeley: University of California Press, 1999).

60. A Chaan, or "Ah Chan" as it appears in Siu's essay, is portrayed to be a vulgar, ignorant, and vulnerable young man in Hong Kong who had recently migrated from China. For a discussion of the sentiments of Hong Kong people toward the migrants from China during this period, see Siu, "Immigrants," 12.

61. This term alludes to the historical fact that Guangdong Province was one of the last places to be conquered and thus "civilized" by the Han, the Chinese ethnic majority.

62. Outsiders tend to call it "dim sum." For a description of dim sum, see chap. 5, n. 25.

63. Before the mid-1980s, their numbers were small, especially those from Taiwan. Most undocumented immigrants from the island were men, seamen who jumped ship and stayed in New York. It was not until the early 1980s that the number of undocumented women workers with tourist visas from Taiwan began to grow; because of the appreciation of the Taiwanese currency during the time, more people could afford to travel to the United States. I am indebted to Linda Gail Arrigo for helping me historicize the situation and reminding me of this change.

64. Many workers have identified work distribution as the major cause of conflicts in the shops. See *CDN*, March 16, 1977.

65. The following account is based on my conversations with both of them between 1984 and 1989.

66. For the meaning of *kaih ma*, see chap. 3, n. 59.

67. Even A Ling, who had lived in Hong Kong for only a few years, held this prejudice.

Chapter 7: Chinese Women Workers and the ILGWU

1. There are a number of review essays that offer good summaries of scholarship on women in U.S. labor history, of which the study of women in trade unions forms an indispensable part. See Mari Jo Buhle, "Gender and Labor History," in *Perspectives on American Labor History: The Problems of Synthesis,* ed. Carroll Moody and Alice Kessler-Harris (Dekalb: Northern Illinois University Press, 1990), 55–79; Ruth Milkman, "Gender and Trade Unionism in Historical Perspective," in *Women, Politics, and Change,* ed. Patricia Gurin and Louise Tilly (New York: Russell Sage Foundation, 1990), 87–107, and "New Research in Women's Labor History," *Signs* 18.2 (Winter 1993): 376–88; Ava Baron, "Gender and Labor History: Learning from the Past, Looking to the Future," in *Work Engendered: Toward a New History of American Labor,* ed. Ava Baron (Ithaca, N.Y.: Cornell University Press, 1991), 1–46, and "On Looking at Men: Masculinity and the Making of a Gendered Working-Class History," in *Feminist Revision History,* ed. Ann-Louise Shapiro (New Brunswick, N.J.: Rutgers University Press, 1994), 146–71.

2. For a list of related studies, see introduction, n. 6.

3. Information scattered throughout various publications and oral histories indicates that sewing was also a major source of income for women in Los Angeles and other West Coast Chinese Communities. However, due to the lack of sufficient sources on the garment industry in these communities, this section will only focus on the one in San Francisco's Chinatown.

4. See Dean Lan, "Chinatown Sweatshops," in *Counterpoint: Perspectives on Asian America,* ed. Emma Gee (Los Angeles: Asian American Studies Center, UCLA, 1976), 351. The numbers of the Chinese garment shops in Ping Chiu's study are somewhat different from others. See Ping Chiu, *Chinese Labor in California, 1850–1880: An Economic Study* (Madison: University of Wisconsin Press, 1963), 93 and 98. More research has yet to be done.

5. My account of this strike is drawn from Chan, *Asian Americans,* 83.

6. The names of these guilds in most of studies are in Cantonese, and the descriptions of their members' occupations differ somewhat from one another. See Morrison G. Wong, "Chinese Sweatshops in the United States: A Look at the Garment Industry," *Research in the Sociology of Work: Peripheral Workers,* vol. 2, ed. I. H. Simpson and R. L. Simpson (Greenwich, Conn.: JAI, 1983), 361; Jack Chen, *The Chinese of America* (San Francisco: Harper and Row, 1980), 112–13; and Him Mark Lai, "Chinatown Garment Industry Started a Hundred Years Ago," *East/West Chinese American Journal,* December 3, 1969, 7.

7. See Benjamin Stolberg, *Tailor's Progress: The Story of a Famous Union and the Men Who Made It* (New York: Doubleday, Doran, and Co., 1944), 50; Levine, *Women's Garment Workers,* 111; Green, *Ready to Wear,* 240; and Laurentz, "Racial/Ethnic Conflict," 39.

8. Him Mark Lai, "A Historical Survey of the Chinese Left in America," in *Counterpoint: Perspectives on Asian America,* ed. Emma Gee (Los Angeles: Asian American Studies Center, UCLA, 1976), 65.

9. According to Him Mark Lai, Chinese Marxists in the community tried and failed to establish a Chinese branch of the Needle Trade Workers' Industrial Union in San Francisco's Chinatown in the early 1930s. The *China Daily News* in New York, however, has noted that in the following years, a number of male garment workers joined the Chinese Workers' Mutual Aid Association, which was formed by the Chinese cannery workers in 1937. See *CDN,* May 14, 16, and 23, 1977. For a discussion of related Chinese labor movements, see Him Mark Lai, "To Bring Forth A New China, To Build a Better America: The Chinese Marxist Left in America to the 1960s," in *Chinese America: History and Perspectives, 1992* (San Francisco:

Chinese Historical Society of America, 1992), 20; Lai, "Historical Survey," 67–69; *CDN*, May 22–25, 27–28, 30, 1977.

10. Pesotta, *Bread,* 68 and 69.

11. Ibid., 66. Three years later Jenny Matyas presented a more diverse picture of San Francisco's Chinese garment industry. See Jennie Matyas's letter to David Dubinsky, November 13, 1937, San Francisco Joint Board Records (no. 165), box 9, folder 3, ILGWU archives, San Francisco State University. See also *CDN,* October 22, 1958, April 4, 1960.

12. See "Jennie Matyas and the ILGWU," 164; and Pesotta, *Bread,* 75–76.

13. For Ben Fee's involvement in the labor movements of the 1930s, see Chris Friday, *Organizing Asian American Labor: The Pacific Coast Canned-Salmon Industry, 1870–1942* (Philadelphia: Temple University Press, 1994), 153 and 155; and Lai, "To Bring Forth," 19–21.

14. This union is named the Chinese Lady Garment Workers' Union" in Lai, "Historical Survey," 67. For Ben Fee's extraordinary political life and the independent Chinese Ladies' Garment Workers' Union, see Lai, "To Bring Forth."

15. "Jennie Matyas and the ILGWU," 172. The following discussion of the founding of the Chinese union and the 1938 strike is based on Gibbs's interview with Matyas; Yung, *Unbound Feet,* 209–22; Angela Y. Lean, "San Francisco's 1938 National Dollar Store Strike: An Opportunity for Change" (Senior thesis, Yale University, 1993); Tamara Watts, "Women, Gender, and Trade Unions: Jennie Matyas and the San Francisco International Ladies' Garment Workers' Union, 1934–1941" (Honor's thesis, Stanford University, 1993), 70–87; and the Sue Ko Lee Collection, Labor Archives and Research Center, San Francisco State University.

16. "Jennie Matyas and the ILGWU," 183–84.

17. Ibid., 190–92.

18. The *China Daily News* has given somewhat different reasons for the discouraging outcome: (1) the Chinese local did not receive "legal recognition" from the union, (2) the employers took advantage of the traditional influence to control the workers, (3) the women workers' income was not a major source of their family income. See *CDN,* May 17, 1977.

19. Yung, *Unbound Feet,* 221.

20. See, for example, Lean, "San Francisco's," 1–2, 43; and Yung, *Unbound Feet,* 209–22.

21. Jennie Matyas came to San Francisco in 1935.

22. Matyas's letter to Dubinsky, dated November 11, 1937, San Francisco Joint Board Records (no. 165), box 9, folder 3, ILGWU archives, San Francisco State University.

23. Yung, *Unbound Feet,* 214.

24. "Jennie Matyas and the ILGWU," 180.

25. Ibid., 174–75.

26. Ibid., 127–28. *Kuomintang* employs the Wade Giles system. It is *Guomindang* in the pinyin system.

27. "Jennie Matyas and the ILGWU," 125 and 128.

28. Ibid., 174 and 175.

29. Ibid., 180–81.

30. Ibid., 185–86.

31. Ibid., 170.

32. Ibid., 127–28.

33. At the thirty-first convention of the ILGWU, a delegate from San Francisco's Local 101 reported how hard he had tried to learn Cantonese in order to organize Chinese workers. See *GEB Report* (1962), 251.

34. See Wong, "Chinese Sweatshops," 362–63. A similar outcome occurred after Chinese

workers struck at the Great Chinese American Sewing Co. in the late 1970s. See *GEB Report* (1977), 137.

35. See Lan, "Chinatown Sweatshops," 355.

36. Tsai, *Chinese Experience,* 159. According to the report of the San Francisco Chinese Community Citizens' Survey and Fact Finding Committee, however, about seven hundred of Chinatown's thirty-five hundred women garment workers were already unionized in 1969. Lan, "Chinatown Sweatshops," 355, n. 46. It is difficult to believe that there was no change over a decade later in 1981, as quoted in Tsai's study.

37. See, for example, *GEB Report* (1953, 1959, 1962, 1971, and 1977).

38. See *GEB Report* (1953, 1968, and 1971).

39. See *GEB Report* (1971).

40. Author's interview with Wing Fong Chin, April 14, 1989, in Cantonese. See also Teng, "Women," 20–23.

41. *Local 23-25 News* 3.1 (March 1960).

42. Author's telephone interview with Stanley Leong, July 21, 1995, in Cantonese.

43. Author's interview with a Ms. Ying, April 5, 1987, in Cantonese.

44. *GEB Report* (1968).

45. *Local 23-25 News,* 1971 special issue; and Shelley Appleton's 1974 testimony (full-length and abridged versions), ILGWU archives, Cornell.

46. The international did not offer these benefits to all members until 1979.

47. *CDN,* December 6, 1957.

48. *Local 23-25 News* 3.1 (March 1960).

49. *Justice* 38.10 (May 15, 1966).

50. See Appleton's 1974 testimony (full-length), ILGWU archives, Cornell.

51. *NYT,* August 23, 1977.

52. *Justice* 56.15 (August 1, 1974).

53. See *Local 23-25 News* 31.2 (April 1982).

54. The following is based on author's interview with Lily Moy at her residence in Poughkeepsie, New York, September 29, 1994, in a mixed language of English and Cantonese.

55. As is the case for most of their contemporaries, her grandparents' marriage was arranged by their respective families, not based on love.

56. Author's interview with an anonymous union researcher, who had worked for the ILGWU Local 23-25 until 1987, March 23, 1989, in English.

57. Author's interview with a Mrs. Lee, May 2, 1989, in Cantonese.

58. Author's interview with a Ms. Chen at the local's English night school in New York's Chinatown, February 29, 1989, in Mandarin.

59. Author's interview with a Mrs. Zheng at the local's English night school in Chinatown, February 29, 1989, in Cantonese.

60. Author's interview with Shui Mak Ka, March 15, 1989, in Cantonese.

61. Before 1982, for example, a Chinese BA was fired for confiding the union's confidential policy to employers, and another was fired for alcoholism.

62. Author's interview with a Mr. Chen (pseudonym), April 15, 1989, in Cantonese.

63. Author's interview with the researcher mentioned in n. 56.

64. See the comments of Max Zimny, the general counsel of the ILGWU, in Rinker Buck, "The New Sweatshops: A Penny for Your Collar," *New York* 12.5 (January 29, 1979): 46.

65. Similar criticisms of the union's work were made by the workers who participated in a forum organized by and covered in the *China Daily News.* See *CDN,* March 16, 1977.

66. Kwong, *New Chinatown,* 151. For workers' and community activists' responses, see *CDN,* March 16, 1979; and *DN,* December 20, 1979.

67. Author's interview with Shui Mak Ka, March 9, 1989, in Cantonese.

68. Other elected officials of the local include its manager, associate and assistant managers, educational director and assistant director, and financial secretary.

69. *NYT,* August 23, 1977. The total number of members of the local was 20,978 at the end of 1976. *GEB* (1977).

70. Interview with a Mr. Lee (pseudonym) on a Brooklyn-bound train, August 15, 1980, in Cantonese.

71. Peter Kwong, *Chinatown, New York: Labor and Politics, 1930–1950* (New York: Monthly Review Press, 1979), 148.

72. Yu, *To Save China.*

73. See ibid., 141 and 156–64.

74. Kwong, *Chinatown, New York,* 84, 87–90.

75. The following discussion of Chinese restaurant workers in New York City is drawn from May Ying Chen, "Reaching for Their Rights: Asian Workers in New York City," in *Union Voices: Labor's Responses to Crisis,* ed. Glenn Adler and Doris Suarez (Albany: State University of New York Press, 1993), 133–50; Alex Hing, "Organizing Asian Pacific American Workers in the AFL-CIO: New Opportunities," *Amerasia Journal* 18.1 (1992): 141–48; Kwong, *New Chinatown,* 140–47; and *CDN,* July 11, 12, 14, 24, 1980.

76. *CDN,* July 12, 1980.

77. Quoted in Chen, "Reaching for Their Rights," 145.

78. See Kwong, *New Chinatown,* 146.

79. See ibid., 147; Chen, "Reaching for Their Rights," 145; and Hing, "Organizing," 146.

80. My friend was a reporter for the *China Daily News* in 1989.

81. *NYT,* August 5, 1972.

82. Janet Salaff and Lydia Kung have estimated that during this period women formed 80 percent of the workforce in the garment industry of Hong Kong, and 85 percent and 65 percent in Taiwan's garment and electronics industries. See Salaff, *Working Daughters,* 22; and Lydia Kung, "Taiwan Garment Worker," in *Lives: Chinese Working Women,* ed. Mary Sheridan and Janet W. Salaff (Bloomington: Indiana University Press, 1984), 109.

83. See Ping-Chun Hsiung, *Living Rooms as Factories: Class, Gender, and the Satellite Factory System in Taiwan* (Philadelphia: Temple University Press, 1996); and Salaff, *Working Daughters,* xxi.

84. Susan Glenn, however, warns that the radical image of Jewish women garment workers was part fact and part rhetorical romanticism. See Glenn, *Daughters,* 192.

85. Young, "Building Years," 133; Sheridan and Salaff, eds., *Lives,* 8–9. The following discussion of Hong Kong's labor situation is largely drawn from these two sources as well as David A. Levin and Stephen Chiu, "Dependent Capitalism, a Colonial State, and Marginal Unions: The Case of Hong Kong," in *Organized Labor in the Asia-Pacific Region: A Comparative Study of Trade Unionism in Nine Countries,* ed. Stephen Frenkel (Ithaca, N.Y.: ILR Press, 1993).

86. Levin and Chui, "Dependent Capitalism," 203.

87. See Hill Gates, "Dependency and the Part-Time Proletariat in Taiwan," *Modern China* 5.3 (July 1979), 387, and *Chinese Working-Class Lives: Getting by in Taiwan* (Ithaca, N.Y.: Cornell University Press, 1987), 54–62.

88. Sheridan and Salaff, eds., *Lives,* 7; and Linda Gail Arrigo, "Economic and Political

Control of Women Workers in Multinational Electronics Factories in Taiwan: Martial Law, Coercion, and World Market Uncertainty," *Contemporary Marxism* 11 (Fall 1985): 77–95.

89. For changes in Taiwan's labor situation over the years, see Stephen Frenkel, Jon-Chao Hong, and Bih-Ling Lee, "The Resurgence and Fragility of Trade Unions in Taiwan," in *Organized Labor in the Asia-Pacific Region: A Comparitive Study of Trade Unionism in Nine Countries,* ed. Stephen Frenkel (Ithaca, N.Y.: ILR Press, 1993), 163–67.

90. Unions independent of the GMD did not emerge until 1985, shortly before the lifting of martial law in 1987. However, to this date the political party remains in control of trade unions "through the legal arrangements surrounding union elections." See Frenkel et al., "Resurgence and Fragility," 163–64.

91. Sheridan and Salaff, eds., *Lives,* 8–9; Arrigo, "Economic and Political," 89.

92. Lydia Kung, *Factory Women in Taiwan* (1983; New York: Columbia University Press, 1994), 174–75 and 177.

93. Young, "Building Years," 146.

94. See Salaff, *Working Daughters,* 101–3.

95. For example, the student movement in the 1970s, which supported Chinese control over some islands off the Vietnamese coast and was suppressed by the government. See Gates, *Chinese Working-Class,* 63.

96. Arrigo, "Economic and Political," 88.

97. It was founded in 1925 but was cracked down by the GMD after its split with the Communists in 1927. For a brief history of the ACFTU, see Malcolm Warner, "Chinese Trade Unions: Structure and Function in a Decade of Economic Reform, 1979–89," in *Organized Labor in the Asia-Pacific Region: A Comparative Study of Trade Unionism in Nine Countries,* ed. Stephen Frankel (Ithaca, N.Y.: ILR Press, 1993), 60–61.

Chapter 8: Winds of Change

1. *Study,* 79.

2. It climbed by 8.7 percent in 1981 and another 7.9 percent in 1982. See Waldinger, *Through the Eye,* 72.

3. The city's share of national employment was 23.4 percent in 1958, 11.9 percent in 1974, and 10.8 percent in 1982. The decrease between 1974 and 1982 was only 1.1 percent, as compared with the 11.7 percent from 1958 to 1974. I am indebted to the Research and Statistics Department of the New York State Department of Labor for providing me with these statistics.

4. There was some coverage on San Francisco's Chinatown garment industry and the child-care and labor disputes there, however. See, for example, *CDN,* October 10, 12–13, 1955; October 22, 1957; and April 4, 1960.

5. The number jumped from two to five annually in the first half of the 1970s to more than twenty in 1977.

6. *CDN,* August 11, 1979.

7. *CDN,* July 14, 1981.

8. See *CDN,* July 14, 1981.

9. *Study,* 50.

10. *Study,* 57.

11. *NYT,* December 29, 1981; and *NYND,* September 16, 1981. Ironically, many successful garment employers also purchased property in the area and became landlords themselves,

after accumulating enough capital running the garment shops for several years. I am indebted to May Ying Chen for reminding me of this aspect of life in Chinatown.

12. The following discussion is largely based on *Study*, 65–66.

13. For the profit rate, see *DN*, February 26–27, 1981.

14. For Leichter's discussion of the organized crime families who ran the trucking companies, see *DN*, February 27, 1981. For the Chinese contractors' responses, see *CDN*, May 23, 1979.

15. *DN*, January 30, 1979.

16. *CDN*, July 14, 1981.

17. *Study*, 53. For similar observations in the Chinese newspapers, see *CDN*, July 14, 1981.

18. *Local 23-25 News* 30.6 (December 1981).

19. Author's interview with a Mr. Zhang, March 7, 1988, in Cantonese. The 1983 study shows that a Chinatown contractor worked for an average of 4.6 jobbers. See *Study*, 69.

20. For the number of union-affiliated midtown jobbers and Chinatown garment shops estimated by the community newspapers, see *CDN*, June 3, 1982. For the number of unionized Chinatown garment shops in 1981, see table 9. Nancy Green shows that members of the manufacturers' New York Shirt and Sportswear Association dropped from 297 in the 1960s to only 189 in 1979. See Green, *Ready to Wear*, 70.

21. *CDN*, August 11, 1979.

22. The name of the shop, as it stands in the newspaper, is in Cantonese. See *DN*, May 16, 1979. The following discussion is based on *CDN*, May 18 and 19, 1979; and *DN*, May 16, 1979.

23. *Study*, 80; and *CDN*, August 2, 1980. The advertisement appeared in *CDN* and *STD*, July 21, 1980.

24. Buck, "New Sweatshops," 40.

25. *CDN*, December 17, 1980.

26. *CDN*, February 10, 1979.

27. *CDN*, February 10, 1979; *NYT*, September 18, 1979; and *DN*, December 20, 1979.

28. *NYT*, December 20, 1979.

29. *DN*, May 21, 1981.

30. *NYT*, September 18, 1979.

31. Collection on the Chinese Clothing Industry, Chatham Square New York Public Library.

32. *CDN*, April 15, 1979.

33. *DN*, December 12, 1980.

34. *DN*, May 20, 1981.

35. See A Bing, "The Winds and Clouds of the Investigation by the Labor Department," originally published in *Yichang Gongren Zhi Sheng* (Voice of garment workers) and reprinted in *CDN*, May 3, 1979.

36. PS 65 was approached for cooperation in providing a list of students who worked in the shops after school and the names and locations of the shops where they worked. The school was reported to have angrily turned down the request. See *CDN*, June 14, 1979.

37. Author's interview with a Mr. Wong in Chinatown, September 10, 1988, in Cantonese.

38. See Bing, "Winds and Clouds."

39. *Study*, i and 41.

40. *Study*, i and 44.

41. Although the number dropped slightly from 429 in 1981 to 420 in 1982, this did not necessarily mean an actual drop in the total number of Chinatown garment shops because the start-up rate of these shops was almost as high as, if not higher than, the rate of failure.

In 1981, for example, 28 percent of Chinatown shops had been in business for less than one year, and close to half had been in operation for less than two years. See *Study*, 42 and 68.

42. *NYT*, October 19, 1979; and *DN*, October 19, 1979.

43. See Waldinger, *Through the Eye*, 175.

44. Author's interview with a Mrs. Ka, in Chinatown, March 1, 1989.

45. *Study*, 81.

46. Some of the most "successful" businessmen in Chinatown had initially accumulated their wealth through running garment shops. Although many of them had entered another business when this study was written, my interviews show that workers who had worked in their garment shops would not forget how unscrupulously they had run their businesses.

47. Author's interview with a Mrs. Lee in Brooklyn, August 3, 1988. Many Chinese immigrants, particularly the Cantonese, believe that fresh chickens are much more nutritious than frozen ones. The price of a fresh chicken in Chinatown is therefore many times higher than a frozen one.

48. See, for example, *CDN*, February 10 and August 11, 1979.

49. The saying is based on a well-known story about a conspiracy between two famous generals in the-third-century China. *Gong Shang Zhou Bao* (Labor/management weekly), May 2, 1981.

50. This provision was eliminated from the union's sportswear contracts in 1982, but some dress contracts still retained a remnant of this provision in the following years.

51. The AOGMA was referred to by the Chinese as the "free garment manufacturers association."

52. *CDN*, August 22 and 30, 1978.

53. The documentary is entitled "Trouble on Fashion Avenue," quoted in *WWD*, June 17, 1982.

54. *NYT*, August 23, 1977.

55. Chaikin and Mazur have both claimed to be from garment workers' families. For similarly adverse conditions in the old garment industry and reactions and immigrant workers' experiences, see Stein, ed., *Out of the Sweatshop*.

56. The following discussion is based on *CDN*, April 1 and 11 and May 7, 1977.

57. *Study*, 79.

58. The following discussion is based on *CDN*, September 21, 1977; October 20, November 13, November 16, 1981; and January 30, February 26 and 27, March 3, 8, 15, 17, 18, 20, 1982; as well as author's interviews with Katie Quan in New York, April 27 and 29, 1989, in a mixed language of Chinese and English; Katie Quan, "Chinese Garment Workers in New York City," in *Migration World* 14.1–2 (1986): 46–49; and Ruth Milkman, "Organizing Immigrant Women in New York's Chinatown: An Interview with Katie Quan," in *Women and Unions*, ed. Dorothy Sue Cobble (Ithaca, N.Y.: ILR Press, 1993), 281–98.

59. These statistics were provided by Katie Quan. They differ from those offered by Sui Fu, a *CDN* reporter who studied the day-care facilities in Chinatown. According to Fu, there were about twelve centers in Chinatown with a capacity of servicing an estimated twnety-five hundred children, leaving at least six to seven thousand children without any day-care service. See *CDN*, February 26 and March 3, 1982; Quan, "Chinese Garment Workers," 49.

60. *CDN*, February 22, 1979.

61. *CTDN*, May 12, 1982.

62. *CDN*, September 21, 1977.

63. *CDN*, November 16, 1981.

64. The above discussion is based on *CDN*, November 16, 1981. Katie Quan's account of

the situation in 1990, almost ten years after the incident, is somewhat different. According to her, she learned later that the union was for children and that Local 23-25 had already looked into it before their effort. However, their effort did make it a pressing issue for the union. See Milkman, "Organizing Immigrant Women," 290.

65. Author's interviews with Katie Quan, April 27 and 29, 1989, in a mixed language of Cantonese and English.

66. Author's interviews with Shui Mak Ka, March 1, 9, and 17, 1989, in Cantonese interspersed with Mandarin.

67. Author's interviews with Alice Ip, March 1, 1989, September 13, 1994, and many other meetings thereafter, in Cantonese.

68. Author's interviews with Connie Ling, March 23, 1989, in a mixed language of Cantonese and English.

69. Author's interview with Susan Yan (pseudonym), April 39, 1987, in Cantonese.

70. Author's interview with Nancy Leung (pseudonym), May 30, 1989, in Cantonese.

71. Author's interview with Betty Leung, October 20, 1994, in Cantonese; *CUHK Greater New York Alumni Newsletter,* vol. 3 (Spring 1997), 31.

72. Before getting involved in the garment workers' day-care campaign, she also engaged in organizing tenants and Chinese restaurant workers in New York's Chinatown. See Milkman, "Organizing Immigrant Women," 289.

73. Author's interviews with Katie Quan, New York, April 27 and 29, 1989, in a mixed language of Cantonese and English.

74. *NYT,* October 13, 1983.

Chapter 9: The 1982 Strike

1. *Local 23-25 News* 31.2 (April 1982): 1.

2. *Local 23-25 News* 31.2 (April 1982): 1; and *WWD,* May 6, 1982.

3. *WWD,* May 28 and June 2, 1982.

4. The agreement also met with challenges from the Atlantic Apparel Contractors' Association, representing approximately 375 Pennsylvania blouse and sportswear contractors. They were, however, opposed to certain terms rather than the entire contract. See *WWD,* June 1, 1982.

5. *WWD,* June 10, 1982.

6. For all the demands of Chinese employers, see *CDN,* May 8, 1982; and *WWD,* June 15.

7. The concept of "reformism" was evoked as conservative in contrast to "revolutionary," which was preferred by the Chinese employers to be the nature of change. See *CDN,* June 3, 1982.

8. *CDN,* June 2, 1982.

9. *CDN,* May 31, 1982.

10. *CDN,* June 12, 1982.

11. *WWD,* June 15, 1982.

12. *Hua Yu Kuai Bao,* June 10, 1982, quoted in Kathy Chevigny, "The Struggle of the New York Chinatown Garment Workers in 1982" (Senior paper, Yale University, 1990), 24.

13. *WWD,* June 16, 1982.

14. *CDN,* June 18, 1982.

15. The discussion in this paragraph is based on *Local 23-25 News* 31.3 (August 1982): 1; and *Study,* 78.

16. *WWD,* June 21, 1982.

17. *WWD,* June 15, 1982.

18. *WWD,* June 16, 1982.

19. *CDN,* June 24, 1982.

20. *CDN,* June 28, 1982.

21. *Local 23-25 News* 31.3 (August 1982): 1–2.

22. *CDN,* June 10 and 11, 1982.

23. According to the the the main organizer of the workers' leadership training programs, even by the early 1980s, when the number of the Chinese members had reached almost twenty thousand and constituted the union's largest constituency, the local leadership continued to focus its organizing efforts on the Latino American workers. When informed about the size of its Chinese membership and urged to organize a separate training program for them, leaders were again reluctant. Given their knowledge about the radical Asian American Movements in the 1970s, leaders feared that separate programs for its Chinese members would provide them with a vehicle to form an autonomous political group within the union. The local did not offer special leadership training programs to its activist Chinese members until the early 1980s, when it faced a challenge from the Chinatown employers. Author's interview with an anonymous union researcher, March 23, 1989, in English.

24. *WWD,* May 21, 1982.

25. Milkman, "Organizing Immigrant Women," 291.

26. Author's interviews with Katie Quan in New York, April 27 and 29, 1989, in a mixed language of Cantonese and English.

27. Ibid.

28. Katie Quan's account of the formation of the committee differs from that given by the *Local 23-25 News,* which recorded it as mid-May, before the first time the Chinese employers refused to sign the contract. According to Quan, although the committee was formed, there was not a meeting until she forced the union to hold one after the first collective resistance of the employers. See Milkman, "Organizing Immigrant Women," 292; and *Local 23-25 News* 31.3 (August 1982): 1–2.

29. Author's interviews with Katie Quan in New York, April 27, 1989, in a mixed language of Cantonese and English.

30. *CDN,* June 17, 1982.

31. *CDN,* June 17, 1982.

32. *CDN,* June 16, 1982.

33. Milkman, "Organizing Immigrant Women," 293.

34. *WWD,* June 23, 1982.

35. I was told that this first rally was originally designed to be a strike, although the union denied it. However, due to the union's dramatic success in having the GBSUA negotiation team sign the contract a day before, the action was turned into a rally, a mere demonstration of the strength of the union to those Chinese contractors who continued to refuse to sign the contract. See *WWD,* June 21, 1982.

36. According to the *New York Daily News,* police estimated that there were only seven thousand at the rally, but organizers believed the total to be as high as twenty thousand. *DN,* June 25, 1982.

37. Author's interview with Shui Mak Ka, March 9, 1989.

38. *CDN,* July 1, 1982.

39. *CDN,* July 8, 1982; and *WWD,* July 12, 1982.

40. *CDN,* July 8, 1982; and *WWD,* July 15, 1982.

41. *CDN,* July 8, 1982.

42. *WWD*, July 8, 1982.

43. *WWD*, July 12 and 15, 1982; and *CDN*, July 10 and 11, 1982.

44. *Local 23-25 News* 31.3 (August 1982): 2; and author's interviews Shui Mak Ka, March 9, 1989; Connie Ling, March 23, 1989; Alice Ip, March 2, 1989; and Katie Quan, April 27, 1989.

45. *CDN*, July 17, 1982.

46. *CDN*, July 15 and 17, 1982.

47. *CDN*, July 10, 1982.

48. *CDN*, July 17, 1982.

49. For excerpts from these speeches, see *Local 23-25 News* 31.3 (August 1982): 4–5; and *CDN*, July 17, 1982.

50. Author's interview with Alice Ip, March 2, 1989, in Cantonese.

51. Author's interview with Shui Mak Ka, March 9, 1989.

52. *CDN*, July 17, 1982.

53. Author's interview with Shui Mak Ka, March 9, 1989.

54. Author's interview with Chen Miaoying (pseudonym), March 30, 1998.

Chapter 10: Continuing the Struggle, 1982–92

1. *NYO*, October 19, 1987.

2. For the 1980 figure, see Waldinger, *Through the Eye*, 73; for the 1990 statistics, see *GEB Report* (1992), 37.

3. It was 51 percent in 1980. See Waldinger, *Through the Eye*, 72. The 1992 figure is from *GEB Report* (1992), 25.

4. Bonacich and Waller, "Mapping," 31.

5. *GEB Report* (1992), 26–32; and Levitan, *Opportunity*, 18–19 (fig. 5) and 78 (table B1).

6. Richard P. Appelbaum and Gary Gereffi, "Power and Profits in the Apparel Commodity Chain," in *Global Production: The Apparel Industry in the Pacific Rim*, ed. Edna Bonacich et al. (Philadelphia: Temple University Press, 1994), 50.

7. See Carl Proper, "New York: Defending the Union Contract," in *No Sweat: Fashion, Free Trade, and the Rights of Garment Workers*, ed. Andrew Ross (New York: Verso, 1997), 187.

8. The average markup slightly declined to 114.2 percent in 1991. Stores could still make a profit because foreign-sewn garments accounted for about 60 percent of retail sales. See *GEB Report* (1992), 24–25.

9. Edna Bonacich, "Asians in the Los Angeles Garment Industry," in *The New Asian Immigration in Los Angeles and Global Restructuring*, ed. Paul Ong, Edna Bonacich, and Lucie Cheng (Philadelphia: Temple University Press, 1994), 157.

10. The UNITE! Research Department estimated that by 1997 the percentages of manufacturing materials and labor dropped to 18 percent and 12 percent, while those of manufacturing overhead and profit and retail markup grew to 16 percent and 54 percent. See Proper, "New York," 178, fig. 1.

11. Proper, "New York," 189; and Kurt Salmon Associates, Inc., *Keeping New York in Fashion: A Strategic Plan for the Future of the New York Fashion Apparel Industry* (New York: The Garment Industry Development Corporation, 1992), 20.

12. See Evelyn Blumenberg and Paul Ong, "Labor Squeeze and Ethnic/Racial Recomposition in the U.S. Apparel Industry," in *Global Production The Apparel Industry in the Pacific Rim*, ed. Edna Bonacich et al. (Philadelphia: Temple University Press, 1994), 314.

13. Green, *Ready to Wear*, 70. There is some disparity between these numbers and those offered by the Chinese community newspapers. Take, for example, an issue of *Central Daily*

News, according to which there were 295 such manufacturers in town in 1965. The number dropped to 175 in 1975 and less than one hundred in 1985. By 1985 there were only about twenty manufacturers affiliated with Local 23-25 in New York. See *CTDN,* April 4, 1985. See also *CDN,* June 3, 1982; *CTDN,* October 27, 1983 and January 3, 1984; and *CDN,* March 7, 1990.

14. My interviews suggest that as early as 1990, some Chinatown workers already learned to accept twenty-four to thirty-two weeks of work each year, and sixty to sixty-eight work hours in a busy week. It is difficult to estimate the exact amount of drop in workers' incomes, however, because it varied greatly according to the kinds of work they did and their work hours.

15. These estimates are drawn from *CTDN,* February 1, 1986. They are similar to those estimated by a Korean shop owner in Park, *Korean American Dream,* 55.

16. *STD,* March 24, 1989.

17. *Study,* 152–54. Ko-Lin Chin has confirmed this observation. He found that the garment shops were less likely than the restaurant and retail food stores to be targeted by gang members, however, because most of them were located on the second story or above in buildings with no elevator, which made it difficult for the offenders to climb the stairs or to leave the crime scene. See Chin, *Chinatown Gangs: Extortion, Enterprise, and Ethnicity* (New York: Oxford University Press, 1996), 49–50.

18. *STD,* May 24, 1991.

19. See *STD,* May 21, 1991; and *NYND,* June 2, 1991.

20. Between 1983 and 1989 various forums were initiated by the community newspapers to discuss the future of the Chinatown garment industry. The *Central Daily News,* for example, covered at least three such discussions in 1982, 1983, and 1985, and *Peimei Daily* also had one in 1982.

21. The discussion of the efforts made by Local 23-25 in this and the following sections is primarily based on *Local 23-25 News,* 1982–92, and the coverage of the community newspapers.

22. For the community's response, see *CDN,* July 19 and 20, 1989.

23. *GEB Report* (1992), 66.

24. In 1992, for example, Local 23-25 had a total of 28,056 members, which was almost twenty thousand more than that of Local 132-98-102, the second largest in the ILGWU. I am indebted to the ILGWU vice president Susan Cowell for providing me with the union's 1992 membership census.

25. *Local 23-25 News,* December 1981 and January 1986. There are some statistical inflations regarding the union's financial status in the Chinese community newspapers. See, for example, *CTDN,* November 20, 1984 and April 4, 1985.

26. Local 23-25 began requiring its members to earn a minimum income of $2,200 per year to be eligible for vacation checks. Dues increased from eleven to thirteen dollars a month. See *CTDN,* September 3 and 20, 1983.

27. The amount jumped to seven thousand dollars in 1996. *Local 23-25 News* 45.4 (October 1996).

28. See *CTDN,* February 25, 26, March 7, 12, 15, April 12, 27, 1983.

29. See the coverage in the city's major Chinese newspapers issued on February 7, 1986.

30. Discussion with a group of women garment workers, October 12, 1994, in Cantonese and Mandarin. Other workers I have interviewed also shared this view.

31. Kathy Chevigny, "The Struggle of the New York Chinatown Garment Workers in 1982" (Senior paper, Yale University, 1990), 33.

32. By 1983 about half of the workforce lived in Brooklyn and Queens but still commuted

to work in the Chinatown garment shops. See *Study,* 199. For the rents of these years, see *Study,* 57 and 211.

33. *CTDN,* April 30, 1987.

34. The Fashion Group employed a total of nine hundred workers at its fourteen manufacturing locations in New York City, producing primarily private-labeled clothing for major retail chains such as Macy's, J.C. Penney, Saks Fifth Avenue, the Limited, and Sears. It also had production sites in the Dominican Republic. See *CTDN,* March 2, 1989; and *DN,* April 18, 1989.

35. The Metropolitan Fashion Center of Greater New York was an organization of twenty-two Chinese garment contractors founded in the late 1980s. See *NYND,* October 11, 1990; and *STD,* October 10 and December 15, 1990. For a discussion of the problems this project faced in the following years, see *NYND,* September 4, 1994.

36. The discussion of Brooklyn's Chinatown in this and the following paragraphs is largely based on my interviews with the longtime Chinese residents in the area in 1989, 1992, 1994, and 1998, as well as the coverage in some Chinese community newspapers. See, for example, *CDN,* December 21, 1988; *STD,* October 13, 1992, and March 8, 15, and 22, 1998.

37. Longtime residents believe that the almost one hundred shops reported by the community newspaper in 1988 was an inflated number. See *CDN,* December 21, 1988.

38. Author's interview with Liu Ming (pseudonym), April 25, 1998, in Cantonese.

39. *NYT,* February 20, 1988; and *STD,* March 21, 1989. However, the *Central Daily News* reported that the rate of individual buildings in the Sunset Park area was only seventy cents per square foot. *CTDN,* November 24, 1987.

40. Compared with the Chinese immigrants from China and Hong Kong, this class of immigrants formed the smallest proportion among those from Taiwan. Even so, they still formed more than 73 percent of the total. See City of New York, *Newest New Yorkers: A Statistical Portrait,* tables 3 and 4.

41. The total number of Chinese immigrants between the ages of sixteen and sixty-four with occupations who came to New York between 1982 and 1989 is 33,927, of whom 21,958 were from the working class. Of these working-class immigrants, 19,603 came from China, which formed almost 90 percent of the total. See ibid., table 13.

42. More than 60 percent of the women emigrants to the United States were from rural areas. See Chen Yintao and Zhang Rong, "Guangdong Sheng Taishan, Shunde Liangxian Nuxing Renkou Guoji Qianyi Bijiao Yanjiu" (A comparative study of the international migration of the female population in the two counties of Taishan and Shunde), *Zhongguo Renkou Kexue* (China population science) 13 (1989): 38 and 41. For a general idea of the social and educational backgrounds of the Taishanese who married overseas Chinese and left the country in the early 1980s, see Wu Xingci and Li Zhen, "Gum San Haak in the 1980s: A Study on Chinese Emigrants Who Return to Taishan County for Marriage," *Amerasia Journal* 14.2 (1988): 21–35. For the characteristics of the female Chinese workforce in New York City, particularly Brooklyn (Kings County), see table 11 in this study.

43. In a literal transliteration this phrase says that if you have the wisdom of *jeung leuhng,* a figure believed to possess the highest wisdom, I have the ladder long enough to climb over the wall (*tiu cheuhng tai*).

44. The second Chinatown was in Queens. By 1998 Brooklyn's Chinatown had been enlarged to encompass an area between Seventh and Ninth Avenues and from Fiftieth to Sixty-fourth Streets. See *STD,* March 8, 1998, weekly special issue, 7.

45. Even in the late 1990s, when working conditions in these shops deteriorated greatly, an increasing number of workers continued to work there.

46. *STD*, October 13, 1992.

47. Take those from Fuzhou, for example. My interviews showed that between the late 1980s and mid-1990s, smugglers charged between twenty and twenty-seven thousand dollars to smuggle a single person to the United States "by land" (in most cases, through Mexico) and between thirty and thirty-five thousand dollars by air. By 1998 the costs by air had been raised to more than forty thousand dollars. See also Peter Kwong, *Forbidden Workers: Illegal Chinese Immigrants and American Labor* (New York: New Press, 1997), 37–38.

48. This law required employers to check the work eligibility status of all their employees and prohibited the hiring of immigrants who did not have a work permit in the United States.

49. *STD*, May 25, 1991.

50. Chin, *Chinatown Gangs*, 50.

51. *CTDN*, August 17, 1988.

52. *STD*, April 23, 1989.

53. Some union staff members offered a different story concerning the couple's marital relations. According to them, the couple's relationship had deteriorated even before they immigrated. For a detailed discussion of this case, see chapter 5.

54. Patricia Hurtado, "Why Judge Didn't Jail Wife Killer: Defends Probation for Chinese Immigrant," *NYND*, April 4, 1989.

55. Alex Jetter, "Fear is Legacy of Wife Killing in Chinatown: Batted Asians Shocked by Husband's Probation," *NYND*, November 26, 1991.

56. Ibid.

57. Ibid.

58. *CDN*, November 16, 1988.

59. *CDN*, December 25, 1986.

60. May Ying Chen, ". . . The Humanism and Optimism of the 60s Still Live On," *Amerasia Journal* 15.1 (1989): 150.

61. Author's interview with May Ying Chen, March 7, 1989; and interview with Chen by Karen Harper, spring 1993, oral history program, California State University at Long Beach. For the early Asian American women's movement in Southern California and the child-care center, see Susie Ling, "The Mountain Movers: Asian American Women's Movement in Los Angeles," *Amerasia Journal* 15.1 (1989): 51–67.

62. Author's interview with a Mrs. Wong, February 15, 1989, in Cantonese.

63. Author's interview with Connie Ling, March 23, 1989, in a mixed language of Cantonese and English.

64. Author's interview with Wong Xiaoping (pseudonym), March 17, 1989, in Mandarin.

65. Author's interview with a Ms. Yen (pseudonym), May 18, 1998, in Cantonese.

66. Although in 1992 Chinese were still underrepresented on the executive board of Local 23-25 in relation to their total number in the local, their number grew from 45 percent in 1986 to 63 percent in 1989. See *Local 23-25 News*, 1986–92.

67. Author's telephone interview with Ann Wong on March 22, 1998, in Cantonese.

68. This is a line delivered by the main character in the play, an underground Communist, when he finally resumes contact with the Communist Party after some time. The story takes place before the Communist success in 1949. The play was made into a movie and operas in various major Chinese dialects during the Cultural Revolution (1966–76). The story is still very much in the memory of those Chinese immigrants in their late thirties and older. Naturally, by spontaneously evoking the memory of this line with irresistibly good humor, this worker inadvertently revealed her native place and her cultural and political backgrounds. Author's interview with a Mrs. Chen, May 24, 1997, in Mandarin.

69. May Ying Chen and Kent Wong, "The Challenge of Diversity and Inclusion in the AFL-CIO," in *A New Labor Movement for the New Century,* ed. Gregory Montsios (New York: Monthly Review Press, 1998), 185–86.

70. *Justice* 72.2 (February 1990).

71. *Justice* 72.11 (December 1990).

72. These were the responses and information I received when I attended a Sunday meeting of the Women's Committee at the CSWA office in Manhattan's Chinatown on August 22, 1992. See the newsletters of the CSWA women's committee, *Funu Gongzuo Fang,* 1991–92.

73. Miriam Ching Louie, "It's a Respect Thing: Organizing Immigrant Women," *Equal Means* (Fall 1993): 22.

74. Miriam Ching Louie, "Immigrant Asian Women in Bay Area Garment Sweatshops: 'After Sewing, Laundry, Cleaning, and Cooking, I Have No Breath Left to Sing,'" *Amerasia Journal* 18.1 (1992): 20.

75. Author's interview with an anonymous committee member on August 22, 1992, in Cantonese.

76. *Funu Gongzuo Fang,* September 1992.

77. Author's interview with an anonymous committee member on August 22, 1992, in Cantonese.

78. See Ruth Needleman, "Building Relationships for the Long Haul: Unions and Community-Based Groups Working Together to Organize Low-Wage Workers," in *Organizing to Win: New Research on Union Strategies,* ed. Kate Bronfenbrenner, et al. (Itacha, N.Y.: Cornell University Press, 1998), 75–85.

79. Author's telephone interview with Ann Wong (pseudonym), March 22, 1998, in Cantonese.

80. Louie, "Immigrant Asian Women," 20.

81. For her life history see chap. 3.

82. Nancy Liang is a pseudonym.

83. See *CTDN,* August 16, 1988.

84. This information was provided by A Ying and several students in my classes when I taught at a Chinatown Sunday English School from 1987 to 1988. Many of them were part-time students at FIT. According to them, there were few Chinese women garment workers there prior to the late 1980s, but the number grew so rapidly in the following years that they had to preregister for required courses to get into the classes.

Conclusion

1. For major works on this subject, see Ronald Takaki, *Strangers from a Different Shore: A History of Asian Americans* (New York: Penguin, 1990); Roger Daniels, *Asian America: Chinese and Japanese in the United States since 1850* (Seattle: University of Washington Press, 1988); Sucheng Chan, ed., *Entry Denied: Exclusion and the Chinese Community in America, 1882–1943* (Philadelphia: Temple University Press, 1991); Chan, *Asian Americans;* and Yu, *To Save China.*

2. See Chan's powerful argument in *Asian Americans,* xiv.

3. See the excellent essays in Wong and Chan, eds., *Claiming America.*

4. See, for example, Yu, *To Save China;* and various essays in Wong and Chan, eds., *Claiming America.*

5. Given the dearth of conventional historical sources, most studies on gender differences

in this era are still focused on the second generation or the prominent elite or well-educated Chinese American or immigrant women. See, for example, the essays by Sucheng Chan and Henry Yu in Wong and Chan, eds., *Claiming America;* and Hua Liang, "Fighting for a New Life: Social and Patriotic Activism of Chinese American Women in New York City, 1900 to 1945," *Journal of American Ethnic History* 17.2 (Winter 1998): 22–38.

6. See the essays in Wong and Chan, eds., *Claiming America.*

7. I also include the small number of working-class Chinese women who were in the United States before World War II.

8. See, for example, Chan, *Asian Americans,* xiv.

9. See Green, *Ready to Wear,* 239.

10. For example, as indicated earlier, their experience is surely different from that of second-generation Chinese American women or members of other social groups with different class, gender, sexual, and other social identities.

11. For a feminist critique of the current state of labor history, see Alice Kessler-Harris, "Treating the Male as 'Other': Re-defining the Parameters of Labor History," *Labor History* 34.2–3 (Spring-Summer 1993): 190–204 (quote on 192). See also the review essays mentioned in chap. 7, n. 1.

12. This study supports many previous studies in arguing that women's work outside the home does not necessarily change their perceptions of life and their positions in their families. Nevertheless, it calls attention to the need to further explore the complex meanings of women workers' responses to their realities by broadening the scope of study to encompass the multiple social, economic, and cultural constraints they and their families face. For an early influential work in this area, see Lousie Tilly and Joan W. Scott, *Women, Work, and Family* (New York: Holt, Rinehart, and Winston, 1978).

13. See, for example, James C. Scott, *Weapons of the Weak: Everyday Forms of Peasant Resistance* (New Haven, Conn.: Yale University Press, 1985); Aihwa Ong, *Spirits of Resistance and Capitalist Discipline: Factory Women in Malaysia* (Albany: State University of New York Press, 1987); Diane Lauren Wolf, *Factory Daughters: Gender, Household Dynamics, and Rural Industrialization in Java* (Berkeley: University of California Press, 1992); and Lee, *Gender.* The most explicit challenge to the traditional approach to labor activism is posed by Scott in *Weapons of the Weak,* 297–98.

14. See Edna Bonacich, Lucie Cheng, Norma Chinchilla, Nora Hamilton, and Paul Ong, eds., *Global Production: The Apparel Industry in the Pacific Rim* (Philadelphia: Temple University Press, 1994), 7.

15. For example, in addition to labor organizing based on trade, perhaps labor unions of industries that have become increasingly globalized, such as the garment industry, can think about forming international alliances along ethnic lines. Recent studies show that Chinese, migrants as well as immigrants, work in the garment industry throughout the world. In addition to those in the Special Economic Zones in China as well as those on the Northern Marinas Islands, who recently caught the attention of the *New York Times* reporters, Chinese also work as garment workers in Paris, London, Toronto, Vancouver, and many other parts of the world. For the conditions of these Chinese women workers, see, for example, Green, *Ready to Wear;* Annie Phizacklea, "The Production of Women's Outerwear in the UK," in *Ethnic Minorities and Industrial Change in Europe and North America,* ed. Malcolm Cross (Cambridge: Cambridge University Press, 1992), 94–110; and Michele Landsberg, "One Woman's Work," *Our Time: Independent Canadian Labor Magazine* 11.3 (June 1992): 26.

Epilogue

1. "1997 New York City Garment Contracting Survey," released by the New York State Apparel Industry Task Force to UNITE!.

2. *WJ*, January 6 and 20, 1998.

3. Unfortunately, the center had closed by early 2001.

4. The exact amount was $243,920. See *WJ*, July 30, 1996.

5. The case of Hua Great Protech, Inc. in the Sunset Park area, one of the most highly publicized cases in the community in recent years, was handled by the CSWA.

6. She resigned from the position in 1998, however, and began working at the Center for Labor Relations at the University of California at Berkeley.

BIBLIOGRAPHY

Chinese-Language Sources

Newspapers Consulted

Central Daily News (中报), 1982–89
China Daily News (美洲华侨日报), 1940–89
Sing Tao Daily (星岛日报), 1978–98
United Journal (联合日报), 1978–91
World Journal (世界日报), individual issues

Guangdong Local Histories, Gazettes, and Other Historical Publications

[Key to location of copies: (1) The East Asian Library at Columbia University; (2) The Hoover Institute at Stanford University; (3) East Asian Institute at the University of California at Berkeley; (4) The Zhongshan Archival Section of the Guangdong Provincial Library, Guangzhou, China; (5) Taishan County's Archival Library, Taishan, Guangdong, China; and (6) The Office of Overseas Chinese Affairs at the provincial or county level.]

Enping Gongbao (恩平公报; Journal of Enping), 1958–66, 1984–87 (4).

Enping Wenshi (恩平文史; Culture and history of Enping), 1983–94 (4).

Foshan Shihua (佛山史话; Foshan's history), Guangzhou: Zhongshan University, 1988 (1).

Guangdong Sheng Zhi: Huaqiao Zhi (广东省志.华侨志; History of Guangdong Province: history of its overseas Chinese), 1996 (6).

Guangdong Siyi Qiaobao (广东四邑侨报; Journal of Guangdong Si Yi overseas Chinese), individual issues of the 1940s (2).

Guangdong Wenshi Ziliao (广东文史资料; Selection of cultural and historical materials of Guangdong), vols. 1–2, 9, 11–13, and 15–63, 1959–88 (1, 4).

Guangzhou Wenshi Ziliao Xuanji (广州文史资料选集; Cultural and historical materials of Guangzhou), vols. 14–37, 1965–87 (1, 4).

Huaqiao Shi Lunwen Ji (华侨史论文集; Essays on overseas Chinese history), Guangzhou: Jinan University, 1980 and 1981 (6).

Kaiping Wenshi (开平文史; Culture and history of Kaiping), 1981–89 (4).

Shunde Wenshi (顺德文史; Culture and history of Shunde), 1983 and 1986 (1, 4).

Taishan Xian Huaqiao Zhi (台山县华侨志; Overseas Chinese history of Taishan County), 1996 (6).

Xinhui Wenshi Ziliao Xuanji (新会资料选集; Selection of cultural and historical materials of Xinhui), 1981–94 (4).

Xinning Zazhi (新宁杂誌; The magazine of Xinning, the former name of Taishan County), 1909–97 (4, 5).

Periodicals, Newsletters, Pamphlets, and Directories of the New York City Chinese Community

Association of Oriental Garment Manufacturers in America (美洲自由车衣业总商会). 1978 special issue and 1988 tenth anniversary issue.

Chinese Business Directory Inc. *Da Meidong Ban Dian Hua Bu* (大美东版电话簿; New York Chinese business directory), bilingual, 1986, 1989, 1992, 1996, 1998.

Chinese Staff and Workers Association (华人职工联谊会). *Funu Gongzuo Fang* (妇女工作坊; Women's workshop), 1991–92. Individual issues.

The Continental Garment Manufacturers' Association of Greater New York (纽约华人车衣商会). *Yi Chang Zhi Sheng* (衣厂之声; Voice of garment makers), 1978, individual issues.

———. Special issues on the fifteenth anniversary (1977) and the thirty-fourth anniversary (1996).

Greater Blouse, Skirt, and Undergarment Association (纽约制衣业总商会). *Shanghui Zhi Sheng* (商会之声; Greater voice), bilingual, 1992–94, individual issues.

ILGWU/UNITE! Garment Workers' Center at Sunset Park, Brooklyn (布碌仑工人中心). *Cheyi Gongren Zhi Sheng* (车衣工人之声; Garment workers' voice), 1993-98.

Books and Articles

All China Women's Federation (中国全国妇女联合会). *Guangdong Nuying Liezhuan* (广东女英烈专; Biographies of Guangdong women revolutionary martyrs). Vols. 1–4. Guangzhou: Guangdong Renmin Chuban She, 1988.

———. *Zhongguo Funu Yundong Shi* (中国妇女运动史; The history of the Chinese women's movement). Beijing: Funu Chuban She, 1989.

Chen Ke (陈科). "Fangwen Liumei Huaqiao Chen Ke Xiansheng" (访问留美华侨陈科先生; An interview with Mr. Chen Ke, a Chinese who returned from America). *Huaqiao Shi Lunwen Ji* 2 (1981): 340-54.

Chen Yintao (陈印陶) and Zhang Rong (张蓉). "Guangdong Sheng Taishan Shunde Liang-xian Nuxing Renkou Guoji Qianyi Bijiao Yanjiu" (广东省台山顺德两县女性人口国际迁移比较研究; A comparative study of the international migration of the female population in the two counties of Taishan and Shunde). *Zhongguo Renkou Kexue* (中国人口科学; China population science) 13 (1989): 36–42.

Chen Yuzeng (陈迁曾), Li Sifu (黎思复), and Wu Qingshi (邬庆时). "Zishunu yu Buluo-jia" ("自梳女"与"不落家"; Women who combed up their hair and their refusal to move into their husbands' homes). *Guangdong Wenshi Ziliao* 12 (1964): 172-88.

Chen Zhongmei (陈中美). *Taishan Difangzhi* (台山地方志, Annals of Taishan local history). Taishan: Taishan Huaqiao Shushe, 1989.

Chu, Y. K. (Zhu Xia, 朱夏). *Meiguo Huaqiao Gaishi* (美国华侨概史; A general history of Chinese in America). New York: China Times, 1975.

Fang Di (方地). "Cong Renkou Ziliao zhong Fanying Chulai de Qiaoxiang Laonian Nu-qiaoshu de Tedian" (从人口资料中反应出来的侨乡老年女侨属的特点; The characteristics of elderly women in the emigrant communities reflected in the census materials). In *Huaqiao Huaren Shi Yanjiu Ji* (华侨华人 史研究集; Collection of studies on the history of overseas Chinese and people of Chinese descent). Vol. 1. Ed. Zheng Min and Liang Chuming. Beijing: Haiyang Chuban She, 1989. 304–20.

Fang Fuer (方福尔) and Zhang Manli (张满利). "Niuyue Huaqiao Xiyiguan de Bianqian" (纽约华侨洗衣馆的变迁; Changes in the Chinese hand laundries in New York City). *Guangzhou Wenshi Ziliao Xuanji* 23 (1981): 186–203.

Guo Zhengzhi (郭征之). *Huafu Cangsang: Niuyue Tangrenjie Shihua* (华阜沧桑: 纽约唐人 街史话; The vicissitudes of a Chinatown: A history of New York's Chinatown). Hong Kong: Buo Yi Press, 1985.

Huang Feng (黄峰). "Qiaojuan Lei" (侨眷泪; The tears of the overseas Chinese families). *Guangdong Siyi Qiaobao* 10–11 (December 1, 1947): 42–43.

Liang Yingyuan (梁应沅) and Luo Yongan (罗永安). "Shunde Nuzi `Zishu' Fengqi de Xingqi" (顺德女子"自梳"风气的兴起; The rise of Shunde women's custom of combing up their hair). *Shunde Wenshi* 8 (1986): 64–67.

Li Benli (李本立). "Shunde Cansiye de Lishi Gaikuang" (顺德蚕丝业的历史概况; A general historical account of the silk industry in Shunde). *Guangdong Wenshi Ziliao* 15 (1964): 102–31.

Li Chunhui (李春辉) and Yang Shengmao (杨生茂). *Meizhou Huaqiao Huaren Shi* (美洲 华侨华人 史; A history of Chinese and people of Chinese descent in America). Beijing: Dongfang Chubanshe, 1990.

Liu Boji (刘伯冀). *Meiguo Huajiao Shi* (美国华侨史; The history of overseas Chinese in the United States). Taipei: Liming Publishing Co., 1976.

Li Xinkui (李新魁). *Guangdong de Fangyen* (广东的方言; The dialects of Guangdong). Guangdong: Guangdong Renmin Chuban She, 1991.

Mei Jia (梅嘉). "Guangdongji Liumei Youtong Jianshu" (广东籍留美幼童简述; A brief account of the children who studied in the United States). *Guangdong Wenshi Ziliao* 48 (1986): 179–99.

Office of Taishan County Communist Party History and Office of Taishan Women's Federation. *San Tai Jin Guo* (三台巾帼; The women warriors in San Tai). Taishan, Guangdong: Office of Taishan Communist Party History and Office of Taishan Women's Federation, 1987.

Wu Jianxiong (吴键雄). *Haiwai Yimin yu Huaren Shehui* (海外移民与华人 社会; Overseas emigration and the overseas Chinese community). Taipei: Yunchen Wenhua Chubanshe, 1993.

Wu Xingci (吴行赐) and Li Zhen (李真). "'Jinshan Ke' hui Tangshan Zeou Chengqin Xianxiang Paoxi" ('金山客'回唐山择偶成亲现象剖析; An analysis of the "guests from Gold Mountain's" return to China to find mates and marry). *Guangzhou Yanjiu* (广州研 究; The study of Guangzhou) 10.2 (1985): 36–39.

Xianggang Funu Laogong Xiehui (香港妇女劳工协会; Hong Kong women workers' association). "Xianggang Waifa Nugong Qingkuang Diaocha" (香港外发女工情况调查; An investigation of women homeworkers in Hong Kong). In *Zhongguo Funu Fencheng Yanjiu* (中国妇女分层研究; A study of the stratification among Chinese women). Ed. Li Xiaojiang and Tan Shen. Zhengzhou: Henan Renmin Chubanshe, 1991. 131–42.

Xie Yingming (谢英明). "Lumei Jianwen Zayi" (旅美见闻杂忆; Random recollections of my stay in the United States). *Guangdong Wenshi Ziliao* 39 (1983): 114–61.

Ye Di (叶地). *Guangdongsheng Diming Tanyuan* (广东省地名探源; An exploration of the origins of the names of places in Guangdong Province). Guangzhou: Guangdongsheng Ditu Chuban She, 1986.

Zhang Jianren (张建人), Wen Wanfang (温婉芳), and Mei Yimin (梅逸民). *Sheng Gua.*

(生寡; Leading a widow's life while the husband is still alive). Guangzhou: Huacheng Chuban She, 1994.

Zhang Xuyu (张絮雨). "Yi Qun Ku Ming de Tai Kai Funu" (一 群苦 命 的台 开妇女; A group of bad-luck Taishan and Kaiping women). *Guangdong Siyi Qiaobao* 10–11 (December 1, 1947): 53–54.

Zheng Dehua (郑 德 华) and Wu Xingci (吴行赐). "Yipi You Jiazhi de Huaqiao Shi Ziliao" (一 批有价值的华侨史资料; A group of valuable materials about overseas Chinese history). In *Huaqiao Huaren Lishi Luncong* (华侨华人历史论丛; Collection of essays about the history of overseas Chinese and people of Chinese descent). Guangdong, China: Zhongshan Daxue Chubanshe, 1985. 204–38.

"'Zishunu' de Xinsuan Lei" ("自梳女" 的 心酸泪; The bitter tears of "the women who combed up their hair"). In *Foshan Shihua*, 106–8.

English-Language Sources

Archival Collections

Collection on the Chinese Clothing Industry. The Chatham Square New York Public Library.

Collection of the Oral History Program, California State University at Long Beach.

    Interview with May Ying Chen by Karen Harper (Spring 1993)

International Ladies' Garment Workers' Union (ILGWU) Archives. M. P. Catherwood Library, Labor-Management Documentation Center (now known as the Kheel Center for Labor-Management Documentation and Archives), New York State School of Industrial and Labor Relations, Cornell University.

    "Jennie Matyas and the ILGWU," interview by Corrine L. Gibbs, 1955.

    Local 23-25 minutes, vols. 1–13 (December 1963–72).

    Local 23-25 Education Department records (1952–80).

    Local 23-25 Regional Department records, southeast region (1937–70).

International Ladies' Garment Workers' Union (ILGWU) Archives. Labor Archives and Research Center, San Francisco State University.

    San Francisco Joint Board Records.

    Sue Ko Lee Collection.

New York Chinatown History Project Archives (now known as the Museum of Chinese in the Americas).

    Transcripts of the workshops on the Chinatown garment industry, 1984.

    Oral history project of the Chinese women garment workers, 1989.

The Papers of Margaret Mead and the South Pacific Ethnographic Archives. Library of Congress.

    "Projects in Contemporary Culture."

Robert F. Wagner Labor Archives. Tamiment Library, New York University.

    Oral History Collections. NS 18: "Asian Garment Workers in New York City."

Newspapers Consulted

New York Daily News, 1979–98 and individual issues

New York Herald Tribune, individual issues

New York Newsday, 1978–98 and individual issues

New York Observer, 1978–98 and individual issues

New York Times, 1937–98

Wall Street Journal, individual issues

Women's Wear Daily, 1982 and individual issues

Books, Reports, Essays, and Other Publications

Abeles, Schwartz, Haeckel, and Silverblatt, Inc. *The Chinatown Garment Industry Study.* New York: ILGWU Local 23-25 and the New York Skirt and Sportswear Association, 1983.

Andors, Philis. *The Unfinished Liberation of Chinese Women, 1949–1980.* Bloomington: Indiana University Press, 1983.

Appelbaum, Richard P., and Gary Gereffi. "Power and Profits in the Apparel Commodity Chain." In *Global Production: The Apparel Industry in the Pacific Rim.* Ed. Edna Bonacich et al. Philadelphia: Temple University Press, 1994. 42–62.

Arrigo, Linda Gail. "Economic and Political Control of Women Workers in Multinational Electronics Factories in Taiwan: Martial Law Coercion and World Market Uncertainty." *Contemporary Marxism* 11 (Fall 1985): 77–95.

———. "The Industrial Work Force of Young Women in Taiwan." *Bulletin of Concerned Asian Scholars* 12.2 (April–June 1980): 25–38.

———. "Taiwan Electronics Workers." In *Lives: Chinese Working Women.* Ed. Mary Sheridan and Janet W. Salaff. Bloomington: Indiana University Press, 1984. 123–45.

Asian American Studies Center, University of California at Los Angeles. *Linking Our Lives: Chinese American Women of Los Angeles.* Los Angeles: Chinese Historical Society of Southern California, 1984.

Banister, Judith. "Population Policy and Trends in China, 1978–1983." *China Quarterly* 100 (December 1984): 717–38.

Bao, Xiaolan. "Chinese Mothers in New York City's New Sweatshops." In *The Politics of Motherhood: Activist Voices from Left to Right.* Ed. Alexis Jetter, Annelise Orleck, and Diana Taylor. Hanover, N.H.: University Press of New England, 1997. 127–37.

———. "Sweatshops in Sunset Park: A Variation of the Late-Twentieth-Century Chinese Garment Shops in New York City." Report submitted to the Sweatshop Project, cosponsored by the New York Lower East Side Tenement Museum and the Union of Needletraders, Industrial and Textile Employees, September 1998.

———. "When Women Arrived: The Transformation of New York's Chinatown." In *Not June Cleaver: Women and Gender in Postwar America, 1945–1960.* Ed. Joanne Meyerowitz. Philadelphia: Temple University Press, 1994. 19–36.

Baron, Ava. "Gender and Labor History: Learning from the Past, Looking to the Future." In *Work Engendered: Toward a New History of American Labor.* Ed. Ava Baron. Ithaca, N.Y.: Cornell University Press, 1991. 1–46.

———. "On Looking at Men: Masculinity and the Making of a Gendered Working-Class History." In *Feminists Revision History.* Ed. Ann-Louise Shapiro. New Brunswick, N.J.: Rutgers University Press, 1994. 146–71.

Barringer, Herbert R., Robert W. Gardner, and Michael J. Levin. *Asians and Pacific Islanders in the United States.* New York: Russell Sage Foundation, 1993.

Barth, Gunther. *Bitter Strength: A History of the Chinese in the United States, 1850–1870.* Cambridge, Mass.: Harvard University Press, 1964.

Beck, Louis J. *New York's Chinatown: An Historical Presentation of Its People and Places.* New York: Bohemia Publishing Co., 1898.

Binder, Frederick M., and David M. Reimers. *All the Nations under Heaven: An Ethnic and Racial History of New York City.* New York: Columbia University Press, 1995.

Blumenberg, Evelyn, and Paul Ong. "Labor Squeeze and Ethnic/Racial Recomposition in the U.S. Apparel Industry." In *Global Production: The Apparel Industry in the Pacific Rim.* Ed. Edna Bonacich et al. Philadelphia: Temple University Press, 1994. 309–27.

Bonacich, Edna. "Alienation among Asian and Latino Immigrants in the Los Angeles Garment Industry: The Need for New Forms of Class Struggle in the Late Twentieth Century." In *Alienation, Society, and the Individual: Continuity and Change in Theory and Research.* Ed. Felix Geyer and Walter R. Heinz. New Brunswick, N.J.: Transaction Publishers, 1992. 165–80.

———. "Asian and Latino Immigrants in the Los Angeles Garment Industry: An Exploration of the Relationship between Capitalism and Racial Oppression." In *Immigration and Entrepreneurship: Culture, Capital, and Ethnic Networks.* Ed. Ivan Light and Parminder Bhachu. New Brunswick, N.J.: Transaction Publishers, 1993. 51–73.

———. "Asians in the Los Angeles Garment Industry." In *The New Asian Immigration in Los Angeles and Global Restructuring.* Ed. Paul Ong, Edna Bonacich, and Lucie Cheng. Philadelphia: Temple University Press, 1994. 137–63.

Bonacich, Edna, and Lucie Cheng, eds. *Labor Immigration under Capitalism: Asian Immigrant Workers in the United States before World War II.* Berkeley: University of California Press, 1984.

Bonacich, Edna, Lucie Cheng, Norma Chinchilla, Nora Hamilton, and Paul Ong, eds. *Global Production: The Apparel Industry in the Pacific Rim.* Philadelphia: Temple University Press, 1994.

Bonacich, Edna, and David V. Waller. "Mapping a Global Industry: Apparel Production in the Pacific Rim Triangle." In *Global Production: The Apparel Industry in the Pacific Rim.* Ed. Edna Bonacich et al. Philadelphia: Temple University Press, 1994. 21–41.

———. "The Role of U.S. Apparel Manufacturers in the Globalization of the Industry in the Pacific Rim." In *Global Production: The Apparel Industry in the Pacific Rim.* Ed. Edna Bonacich et al. Philadelphia: Temple University Press, 1994. 80–102.

Bonner, Arthur. *Alas! What Brought Thee Hither? The Chinese in New York, 1800–1950.* Cranbury, N.J.: Associated University Press, 1997.

Boris, Eileen. *Home to Work: Motherhood and the Politics of Industrial Homework in the United States.* Cambridge: Cambridge University Press, 1994.

———. "Organization or Prohibition? A Historical Perspective on Trade Unions and Homework." In *Women and Union.* Ed. Dorothy Sue Cobble. Ithaca, N.Y.: ILR Press, 1993. 207–25.

Boris, Eileen, and Cynthia R. Daniels. Introduction to *Homework: Historical and Contemporary Perspectives on Paid Labor at Home.* Ed. Eileen Boris and Cynthia R. Daniels. Urbana: University of Illinois Press, 1989. 1–9.

Buck, Rinker. "The New Sweatshops: A Penny for Your Collar." *New York* 12.5 (January 29, 1979): 40, 43–46.

Buhle, Mari Jo. "Gender and Labor History." In *Perspectives on American Labor History: The Problems of Synthesis.* Ed. Carroll Moody and Alice Kessler-Harris. DeKalb: Northern Illinois University Press, 1990. 55–79.

Cantor, Milton, and Bruce Laurie, eds. *Class, Sex, and the Woman Worker.* Westport, Conn.: Greenwood Press, 1977.

Cattell, Stuart H. "Health, Welfare, and Social Organization in Chinatown." Mimeograph. New York: Community Service Society of New York, 1962.

Chan, Ming K., ed. *Precarious Balance: Hong Kong between China and Britain, 1842–1992.* Armonk, N.Y.: M. E. Sharpe, 1994.

Chan, Sucheng. *Asian Americans: An Interpretive History.* Boston: Twayne Publishers, 1991.

———, ed. *Entry Denied: Exclusion and the Chinese Community in America, 1882–1943.* Philadelphia: Temple University Press, 1991.

———. "The Exclusion of Chinese Women, 1870–1943." In *Entry Denied: Exclusion and the Chinese Community in America, 1882–1943*. Ed. Sucheng Chan. Philadelphia: Temple University Press, 1991. 94–146.

Chen, David Yeesui. "Needs and Services Utilization Patterns of Older Chinese Americans Residing in New York City's Chinatown." Ph.D. dissertation, Columbia University, 1981.

Chen, Jack. *The Chinese of America*. San Francisco: Harper and Row, 1980.

Chen, Julia I. Hsuan. "The Chinese Community in New York: A Study in Their Cultural Adjustment, 1920–1940." Ph.D. dissertation, American University, 1941.

Chen, May Ying. ". . . The Humanism and Optimism of the 60s Still Live On." *Amerasia Journal* 15.1 (1989): 150.

———. "Reaching for Their Rights: Asian Workers in New York City." Report for the Center for Labor-Management Policy Studies, 1989. In the author's possession.

———. "Reaching for Their Rights: Asian Workers in New York City." In *Union Voices: Labor's Responses to Crisis*. Ed. Glenn Adler and Doris Suarez. Albany: State University of New York Press, 1993. 133–50.

Chen, May Ying, and Kent Wong. "The Challenge of Diversity and Inclusion in the AFL-CIO." In *A New Labor Movement for the New Century*. Ed. Gregory Montsios. New York: Monthly Review Press, 1998. 185–201.

Chen, Ta. *Emigrant Communities in South China: A Study of Overseas Migration and Its Influence on Standards of Living and Social Change*. New York: Institute of Pacific Relations, 1940.

Chenault, Lawrence R. *The Puerto Rican Migrant in New York City*. 1938. New York: Russell and Russell, 1970.

Cheng, Lucie, and Liu Yuzun with Zheng Dehua. "Chinese Emigration, the Sunning Railway, and the Development of Toisan." *Amerasia Journal* 9.1 (1982): 59–74.

Chen Han-seng. *Landlord and Peasant in China: A Study of the Agrarian Crisis in South China*. New York: International Publisher, 1936.

Chen Hsiang-shui. *Chinatown No More: Taiwan Immigrants in Contemporary New York*. Ithaca, N.Y.: Cornell University Press, 1992.

Chen Hsiang-shui and John Kuo Wei Tchen. "Towards a History of Chinese in Queens." Manuscript. Asian American Center, Queens College, City University of New York, n.d.

Chevigny, Kathy. "The Struggle of the New York Chinatown Garment Workers in 1982." Senior paper, Yale University, 1990.

Chih, Ginger. "Immigration of Chinese Women to the U.S.A, 1850–1940." M.A. thesis, Sarah Lawrence College, 1977.

Chin, Ko-Lin. *Chinatown Gangs: Extortion, Enterprise, and Ethnicity*. New York: Oxford University Press, 1996.

Chinatown Study Group. "Chinatown Study Group Report, 1969." Manuscript. Columbia University, 1969.

Chinn, Thomas W. et al., eds. *A History of the Chinese in California: A Syllabus*. San Francisco: Chinese Historical Society of America, 1969.

Chiu, Ping. *Chinese Labor in California, 1850–1880: An Economic Study*. Madison: University of Wisconsin Press, 1963.

Chow, Chunshing. "Immigration and Immigrant Settlement: The Chinese in New York City." Ph.D. dissertation, University of Hawaii, 1984.

Chu, Louis. *Eat a Bowl of Tea*. 1961. Seattle: University of Washington Press, 1979.

City of New York, Department of City Planning. *Annual Report, 1993*.

———. "Asians in New York City: A Demographic Summary—A Report Prepared for the

Mayor's Task Force on the Year 2000: Asian American Issues." New York: Office of Immigrant Affairs and Population Analysis Division, 1986.

———. *The Newest New Yorkers: A Statistical Portrait.* New York, 1992.

———. *The Newest New Yorkers, 1990–1994: An Analysis of Immigration to NYC in the Early 1990s.* New York, 1996.

Clark, Helen. "The Chinese of New York." *Century Magazine* 53 (1896): 104–13.

Cobble, Dorothy Sue, ed. *Women and Unions: Forging a Partnership.* Ithaca, N.Y.: ILR Press, 1993.

Cohen, Miriam. *Workshop to Office: Two Generations of Italian Women in New York, 1900–1950.* Ithaca, N.Y.: Cornell University Press, 1992.

Coolidge, Mary Roberts. *Chinese Immigration.* New York: Holt and Co., 1909.

Cowell, Susan. "Family Policy: A Union Approach." In *Women and Unions: Forging a Partnership.* Ed. Dorothy Sue Cobble. Ithaca, N.Y.: ILR Press, 1993. 115–28.

Dagg, Alexandra, and Judy Fudge. "Sewing Pains: Homeworkers in the Garment Trade." *Our Time: Independent Canadian Labor Magazine* 11.3 (June 1992): 22–25.

Daniels, Cynthia R. "Between Home and Factory: Homeworkers and the State." In *Homework: Historical and Contemporary Perspectives on Paid Labor at Home.* Ed. Eileen Boris and Cynthia R. Daniels. Urbana: University of Illinois Press, 1989. 13–32.

Daniels, Roger. *Asian America: Chinese and Japanese in the United States since 1850.* Seattle: University of Washington Press, 1988.

Daniels, Roger, and Harry H. L. Kitano. *Asian Americans: Emerging Minorities.* 2d ed. Englewood Cliffs, N.J.: Prentice Hall, 1995.

Diamond, Norma. "The Middle-Class Family Model in Taiwan: Women's Place Is in the Home." *Asian Survey* 8.9 (September 1973): 853–72.

———. "The Status of Women in Taiwan: One Step Forward, Two Steps Back." In *Women and China: Studies in Social Change and Feminism.* Ed. Marilyn B. Young. Ann Arbor: University of Michigan Press, 1973. 211–42.

———. "Women and Industry in Taiwan." *Modern China* 5.3 (July 1979): 275–82.

———. "Women under Kuomintang Rule: Variations on the Feminine Mystique." *Modern China* 1.1 (January 1975): 3–45.

Diner, Hasia R. *Erin's Daughters in America: Irish Immigrant Women in the Nineteenth Century.* Baltimore: Johns Hopkins University Press, 1983.

Dye, Nancy Schrom. *As Equals and Sisters: The Labor Movement and the Women's Trade Union League of New York* (Columbia: University of Missouri Press, 1980).

Eaton, Edith Maud (Sui Sin Far). "The Story of One White Woman Who Married a Chinese." In *The Big Aiiieeee! An Anthology of Chinese American and Japanese American Literature.* Ed. Jeffery Paul Chan, Frank Chin, Lawson Fusao Inada, and Shawn Wong. New York: Meridian Books, 1991. 123–38.

Endelman, Gary. *Solidarity Forever: Rose Schneiderman and the Women's Trade Union League.* New York: Arno Press, 1982.

Eng, Robert Y. "Luddism and Labor Protest among Silk Artisans and Workers in Jiangnan and Guangdong, 1860–1930." *Late Imperial China* 11.2 (December 1990): 63–101.

England, Joe, and John Rear. *Industrial Relations and Law in Hong Kong: An Extensively Rewritten Version of Chinese Labour under British Rule.* Hong Kong: Oxford University Press, 1981.

Ernst, Robert. *Immigrant Life in New York City, 1825–1863.* New York: King's Crown Press, 1949.

Ewen, Elizabeth. *Immigrant Women in the Land of Dollars: Life and Culture on the Lower East Side, 1890–1925.* New York: Monthly Review Press, 1985.

Feldman, Egal. *Fit for Men: A Survey of New York's Clothing Trade.* Washington, D.C.: Public Affairs Press, 1960.

Feng, Therese, and Shirley Mark Yuen. "Through Strength and Struggle: A Victory for Garment Workers in Boston." *East Wind* 2.1 (Spring/Summer 1983): 20–23.

Fessler, Loren W. *Chinese in America: Stereotyped Past, Changing Present.* New York: Vantage Press, 1983.

Foner, Nancy. *New Immigrants in New York.* New York: Columbia University Press, 1987.

Foner, Philip. *Women and the American Labor Movement: From the First Trade Unions to the Present.* New York: Free Press, 1982.

Franck, Harry A. *Roving through Southern China.* London: Adelphi Terrace, 1926.

Freedman, Maurice. *Lineage Organization in Southeastern China.* London: Athlone Press, 1958.

Frenkel, Stephen, ed. *Organized Labor in the Asia-Pacific Region: A Comparative Study of Trade Unionism in Nine Countries.* Ithaca, N.Y.: ILR Press, 1993.

Frenkel, Stephen, Jon-Chao Hong, and Bih-Ling Lee. "The Resurgence and Fragility of Trade Unions in Taiwan." In *Organized Labor in the Asia-Pacific Region: A Comparative Study of Trade Unionism in Nine Countries.* Ed. Stephen Frenkel. Ithaca, N.Y.: ILR Press, 1993. 162–86.

Friday, Chris. *Organizing Asian American Labor: The Pacific Coast Canned-Salmon Industry, 1870–1942.* Philadelphia: Temple University Press, 1994.

Gardner, Robert W., Bryant Robey, and Peter C. Smith. "Asian Americans: Growth, Change, and Diversity." *Population Bulletin* 40.4 (October 1985): 3–43.

Gardner, Robert W., Herbert Barringer, and Michael Levin. *Asians and Pacific Islanders in the United States.* New York: Russell Sage Foundation, 1993.

Gates, Hill. *Chinese Working-Class Lives: Getting By in Taiwan.* Ithaca, N.Y.: Cornell University Press, 1987.

———. "Dependency and the Part-Time Proletariat in Taiwan." *Modern China* 5.3 (July 1979): 381–408.

Gee, Emma, ed. *Counterpoint: Perspectives on Asian America.* Los Angeles: Asian American Studies Center, UCLA, 1976.

Getting Together: Chinese American Workers, Past and Present (An anthology of *Getting Together*). New York: Getting Together, 1972.

Glenn, Evelyn Nakano. *Issei, Nisei, War Bride: Three Generations of Japanese American Women in the Domestic Service.* Philadelphia: Temple University Press, 1986.

———. "Racial Ethnic Women's Labor: The Intersection of Race, Gender, and Class Oppression." *Review of Radical Political Economics* 17.3 (1985): 86–108.

———. "Split Household, Small Producer, and Dual Wage Earner: An Analysis of Chinese-American Family Strategies." *Journal of Marriage and the Family* 45 (February 1983): 35–46.

Glenn, Evelyn Nakano, with Stacey G. H. Yap. "Chinese American Families." In *Minority Families in the United States: A Multicultural Perspective.* Ed. Ronald L. Taylor. Englewood Cliffs, N.J.: Prentice-Hall, 1994. 115–45.

Glenn, Susan A. *Daughters of the Shtetl: Life and Labor in the Immigrant Generation.* Ithaca, N.Y.: Cornell University Press, 1990.

Glick, Carl. *Shake Hands with the Dragon.* New York: Whittlesey House, 1941.

Gluck, Sherna Berger, and Daphne Patai. *Women's Words: The Feminist Practice of Oral History.* New York: Routledge, Chapman and Hall, 1991.

Gong, Eng Ying, and Bruce Grant. *Tong War!* New York: Nicholas L. Brown, 1930.

Green, Lorenzo J., and Carter G. Woodson. *The Negro Wage Earner*. Washington, D.C.: Association for the Study of Negro Life and History, 1930.

Green, Nancy. "Immigrant Labor in the Garment Industries of New York and Paris: Variations on a Structure." *Comparative Social Research* 9 (1986): 231–43.

———. *Ready to Wear and Ready to Work: A Century of Industry and Immigrants in Paris and New York*. Durham, N.C.: Duke University Press, 1997.

———. "Sweatshop Migrations: The Garment Industry between Home and Shop." In *The Landscape of Modernity: Essays on New York City, 1900–1940*. Ed. David Ward and Olivier Zunz. New York: Russell Sage Foundation, 1992. 213–32.

———. "Women and Immigrants in the Sweatshop: Categories of Labor Segmentation Revisited." *Comparative Studies in Society and History* 38.3 (July 1996): 411–33.

Groneman, Carol, and Mary Beth Norton. *"To Toil the Livelong Day": America's Women at Work, 1780–1980*. Ithaca, N.Y.: Cornell University Press, 1987.

Hartman, Heidi. "The Family as a Locus of Gender, Class, and Political Struggle: The Example of Household." *Signs: Journal of Women in Culture and Society* 6 (1981): 366–96.

Hayner, Norman S., and Charles N. Reynolds. "Chinese Family Life in America." *American Sociological Review* 2 (October 1937): 630–37.

Helfgott, Roy B. "Puerto Rican Integration in the Skirt Industry in New York City." In *Discrimination and Low Incomes: Social and Economic Discrimination against Minority Groups in Relation to Low Income in New York State*. Ed. Aaron Antonovsky and Lewis Lorwin. New York: State of New York Interdepartmental Committee on Low Incomes, 1959. 249–79.

———. "Women's and Children's Apparel." In *Made in New York: Case Studies in Metropolitan Manufacturing*. Ed. Max Hall. Cambridge, Mass.: Harvard University Press, 1959. 19–134.

Helly, Dorothy O., and Susan M. Reverby, eds. *Gendered Domains: Rethinking Public and Private in Women's History*. Ithaca, N.Y.: Cornell University Press, 1992.

Heyer, Virginia. "Patterns of Social Organization in New York City's Chinatown." Ph.D. dissertation, Columbia University, 1953.

Hill, Herbert. "Guardians of the Sweatshops: The Trade Unions, Racism, and the Garment Industry." In *Puerto Rico and Puerto Ricans: Studies in History and Society*. Ed. Adalberto Lopez and James Petras. New York: Halsted Press, 1974. 384–416.

———. "The Racial Practices of Organized Labor: The Contemporary Record." In *The Negro and the American Labor Movement*. Ed. Julius Jacobson. Garden City, N.Y.: Anchor Books, 1968. 320–54.

Hing, Alex. "Organizing Asian Pacific American Workers in the AFL-CIO: New Opportunities." *Amerasia Journal* 15.1 (1989): 141–48.

Hom, Marion K. *Songs of Gold Mountain: Cantonese Rhymes from San Francisco Chinatown*. Berkeley: University of California Press, 1987.

Honig, Emily. *Sisters and Strangers: Women in the Shanghai Cotton Mills, 1919–1949*. Stanford, Calif.: Stanford University Press, 1986.

———. "Striking Lives: Oral History and the Politics of Memory." (With a response from Irene Ledesna, "Confronting Class: Comments on Honig.") *Journal of Women's History* 9.1 (Spring 1997): 139–63.

Hsiung, Ping-Chun. *Living Rooms as Factories: Class, Gender, and the Satellite Factory System in Taiwan*. Philadelphia: Temple University Press, 1996.

Hsiung Ping-Chen. "Constructed Emotions: The Bond between Mothers and Sons in Late Imperial China." *Late Imperial China* 15.1 (June 1994): 87–117.

Hsu, Francis L. K. *The Challenge of the American Dream: The Chinese in the United States.* Belmont, Calif.: Wadsworth, 1971.

Hsu, Madeline Yuan-Yin. "Living Abroad and Faring Well: Migration and Transnationalism in Taishan County, Guangdong, 1904–1939." Ph.D. dissertation, Yale University, 1996.

Huang, Tsen-ming. *The Legal Status of the Chinese Abroad.* Taipei: China Cultural Services, 1954.

Hui, Ching-wing, and Thomas Lacey. "Participation of Chinese Women in the Garment Industry in New York City." Manuscript. New School for Social Research, July 22, 1976.

International Ladies' Garment Workers' Union. *General Executive Board Report.* From the 40th Convention (1989) through the 42nd Convention (1995).

———. *Report of the General Executive Board and Record of the Proceedings of the Convention.* From the 1st Convention (1900) through the 39th Convention (1983).

———. *We Are One.* Documentary video (1982).

Jensen, Joan M. "Inside and Outside the Unions: 1920–1980." In *A Needle, a Bobbin, a Strike: Women Needleworkers in America.* Ed. Joan M. Jensen and Sue Davidson. Philadelphia: Temple University Press, 1984. 185–94.

Johnson, Graham E. "Family Strategies and Economic Transformation in Rural China: Some Evidence from the Pearl River Delta." In *Chinese Families in the Post-Mao Era.* Ed. Deborah Davis and Stevan Harrell. Berkeley: University of California Press, 1993. 103–36.

Johnson, Kay Ann. *Women, the Family, and Peasant Revolution in China.* Chicago: University of Chicago Press, 1983.

Joyce, Patrick. *Vision of the People: Industrial England and the Question of Class, 1848–1914.* Cambridge: Cambridge University Press, 1991.

Kallgren, Joyce K. "Politics, Welfare, and Change: The Single-Child Family in China." In *The Political Economy of Reform in Post-Mao China.* Ed. Elizabeth J. Perry and Christine Wong. Cambridge, Mass.: Harvard University Press, 1985. 131–56.

Kaye, Harvey J., and Keith McClelland, ed. *E. P. Thompson: Critical Perspectives.* Philadelphia: Temple University Press, 1990.

Kessler-Harris, Alice. "Organizing the Unorganizable: Three Jewish Women and Their Union." In *Class, Sex, and the Woman Worker.* Ed. Milton Cantor and Bruce Laurie. Westport, Conn.: Greenwood, 1977. 144–65.

———. *Out to Work: A History of Wage-Earning Women in the United States.* New York: Oxford University Press, 1982.

———. "Problems of Coalition-Building: Women and Trade Unions in the 1920s." In *Women, Work, and Protest: A Century of U.S. Women's Labor History.* Ed. Ruth Milkman. New York: Routledge and Kegan Paul, 1985. 110–38.

———. "Rose Schneiderman and the Limits of Women's Trade Unionism." In *Labor Leaders in America.* Ed. Melvyn Dubofsky and Warren Van Tine. Urbana: University of Illinois Press, 1986. 160–84.

———. "Treating the Male as 'Other': Re-defining the Parameters of Labor History." *Labor History* 34.2–3 (Spring–Summer 1993): 190–204.

———. *Women Have Always Worked: A Historical Overview.* New York: Feminist Press, 1981.

Kingston, Maxine Hong. *The Woman Warrior: Memoirs of a Girlhood among Ghosts.* New York: Alfred A. Knopf, 1976.

Kinkead, Gwen. *Chinatown: A Portrait of a Closed Society.* New York: HarperCollins, 1992.

———. "A Report at Large (Chinatown, Part I)." *New Yorker,* June 10, 1991, 45–48, 50, 63–68, 71–83.

——. "A Report at Large (Chinatown, Part II)." *New Yorker,* June 17, 1991, 56, 61–62, 64–84.

Korrol, Virginia E. Sanchez. *From Colonia to Community: The History of Puerto Ricans in New York City.* Berkeley: University of California Press, 1994.

Kulp, Daniel Harrison. *Country Life in South China: The Sociology of Familism.* 1925. New York: Paragon Book Gallery, 1966.

Kung, Lydia. *Factory Women in Taiwan.* 1983. New York: Columbia University Press, 1994.

——. "Taiwan Garment Worker." In *Lives: Chinese Working Women.* Ed. Mary Sheridan and Janet W. Salaff. Bloomington: Indiana University Press, 1984. 109–22.

Kung, Shien Woo. *Chinese in American Life: Some Aspects of Their History, Status, Problems, and Contributions.* Seattle: University of Washington Press, 1962.

Kuo Chia-ling. *Social and Political Change in New York's Chinatown: The Role of Voluntary Associations.* New York: Praeger, 1977.

Kurt Salmon Associates, Inc. *Keeping New York in Fashion: A Strategic Plan for the Future of the New York Fashion Apparel Industry.* Report prepared for the Garment Industry Development Corporation, New York, 1992.

Kwan Choi Wah. *The Right Word in Cantonese.* Hong Kong: Commercial Press, 1996.

Kwong, Peter. *Chinatown, New York: Labor and Politics, 1930–1950.* New York: Monthly Review Press, 1979.

——. *Forbidden Workers: Illegal Chinese Immigrants and American Labor.* New York: New Press, 1997.

——. *The New Chinatown.* New York: Hill and Wang, 1987.

——. "The Wages of Fear: Undocumented and Unwanted, Fuzhounese Immigrants Are Changing the Face of Chinatown." *Village Voice,* April 26, 1994, 25–29.

Kwong, Peter, and JoAnn Lum. "How the Other Half Lives Now." *The Nation,* June 18, 1988, 858–60.

Lai, Him Mark. "Chinatown Garment Industry Started a Hundred Years Ago." *East/West Chinese American Journal,* December 3, 1969, 7.

——. "A Historical Survey of the Chinese Left in America." In *Counterpoint: Perspectives on Asian America.* Ed. Emma Gee. Los Angeles: Asian American Studies Center, UCLA, 1976. 63–80.

——. "To Bring Forth a New China, to Build a Better America: The Chinese Marxist Left in America to the 1960s." In *Chinese America: History and Perspectives, 1992.* San Francisco: Chinese Historical Society of America, Asian American Studies, San Francisco State University, 1992. 3–82.

Lam, Margarita C. "Chinese Immigrant Women in the Garment Industry in Boston, Massachusetts, 1965–1985." Manuscript. Harvard College, March 1991.

Lamphere, Louise. *From Working Daughters to Working Mothers: Immigrant Women in a New England Industrial Community.* Ithaca, N.Y.: Cornell University Press, 1987.

Lan, Dean. "Chinatown Sweatshops." In *Counterpoint: Perspectives on Asian America.* Ed. Emma Gee. Los Angeles: Asian American Studies Center, UCLA, 1976. 347–58.

——. "The Chinatown Sweatshops: Oppression and an Alternative." *Amerasia Journal* 1.3 (November 1971): 40–57.

Landsberg, Michele. "One Woman's Work." *Our Time: Independent Canadian Labor Magazine* 11.3 (June 1992): 26.

Laslett, John, and Mary Tyler. *The ILGWU in Los Angeles, 1907–1988.* Inglewood, Calif.: Ten Star Press, 1989.

Laurentz, Robert. "Racial/Ethnic Conflict in the New York City Garment Industry, 1930–1980." Ph.D. dissertation, State University of New York at Binghamton, 1980.

Lean, Angela Y. "San Francisco's 1938 National Dollar Store Strike: An Opportunity for Change." Senior thesis, Yale University, 1993.

Lee, Calvin. *Chinatown, U.S.A.* New York: Doubleday, 1965.

Lee, Chew. "The Biography of a Chinaman." *Independent* 55 (February 19, 1903): 417–23. Reprinted in *The Life Stories of Undistinguished Americans, as Told by Themselves.* Ed. Hamilton Holt. New York: Routledge, 1990. 174–85.

Lee, Ching Kwan. *Gender and the South China Miracle: Two Worlds of Factory Women.* Berkeley: University of California Press, 1998.

Lee, Joann Faung Jean. *Asian Americans: Oral Histories of First- to Fourth-Generation Americans from China, the Philippines, Japan, India, the Pacific Islands, Vietnam, and Cambodia.* New York: New Press, 1992.

Lee, Rose Hum. *The Chinese in the United States of America.* Hong Kong: Hong Kong University Press, 1960.

———. "Chinese in the United States Today." *Survey Graphic: Magazine of Social Interpretation* 31.10 (October 1942): 419, 444.

———. "The Recent Immigrant Chinese Families of the San Francisco–Oakland Area." *Marriage and Family Living* 18.1 (1956): 14–24.

———. "The Stranded Chinese Students in the United States." *Phylon* 19 (1956): 180–94.

Leichter, Franz S. "The Return of the Sweatshop: An Investigation of the Garment Sweatshop Problem in North Manhattan." Albany: New York State Department of Labor, 1981.

Leong Gor Yun. *Chinatown Inside Out.* New York: Barrows Mussey, 1936.

Levin, David A., and Stephen Chiu. "Dependent Capitalism, a Colonial State, and Marginal Unions: The Case of Hong Kong." In *Organized Labor in the Asia-Pacific Region: A Comparative Study of Trade Unionism in Nine Countries.* Ed. Stephen Frenkel. Ithaca, N.Y.: ILR Press, 1993. 187–222.

Levine, Louis (Lewis L. Lorwin). *The Women's Garment Workers: A History of the International Ladies' Garment Workers' Union.* New York: B. W. Huebsch, 1924.

Levitan, Mark. *Opportunity at Work: The New York City Garment Industry.* New York: Community Service Society of New York, 1998.

Li, Peggy, Buck Wong, and Fong Kwan. *Garment Industry in Los Angeles Chinatown.* Working Paper on Asian American Studies. Los Angeles: Asian American Studies Center, UCLA, 1973–74.

Li, Peter S. "Immigration Laws and Family Patterns: Some Demographic Changes among Chinese Families in Canada, 1885–1971." *Canadian Ethnic Studies* 12.1 (1980): 58–73.

Liang, Hua. "Fighting for a New Life: Social and Patriotic Activism of Chinese American Women in New York City, 1900 to 1945." *Journal of American Ethnic History* 17.2 (Winter 1998): 22–38.

———. "Living between the World: Chinese American Women and Their Experience in San Francisco and New York City, 1848–1945." Ph.D. dissertation, University of Connecticut, 1996.

Ling, Huping. "A History of Chinese Female Students in the United States, 1880s–1990s." *Journal of American Ethnic History* 16.3 (Spring 1997): 81–109.

———. *Surviving on the Gold Mountain: A History of Chinese American Women and Their Lives.* Albany: State University of New York Press, 1998.

Ling, Susie. "The Mountain Movers: Asian American Women's Movement in Los Angeles." *Amerasia Journal* 15.1 (1989): 51–67.

Lo, Wan. "Communal Strife in Mid-Nineteenth-Century Kwangtung: The Establishment of Ch'ih-ch'i." In *Papers on China,* vol. 19. Cambridge: East Asian Research Center, Harvard University Press, 1965. 85–119.

Lopez, Adalberto. "The Puerto Rican Diaspora: A Survey." In *Puerto Rico and Puerto Ricans: Studies in History and Society.* Ed Adalberto Lopez and James Petras. New York: Halsted Press, 1974. 316–46.

Louie, Miriam Ching. "Immigrant Asian Women in Bay Area Garment Sweatshops: 'After Sewing, Laundry, Cleaning, and Cooking, I Have No Breath Left to Sing.'" *Amerasia Journal* 18.1 (1992): 1–26.

———. "It's a Respect Thing: Organizing Immigrant Women." *Equal Means,* Fall 1993, 21–13.

Lum, JoAnn, and Peter Kwong. "Surviving in America: Trials of a Chinese Immigrant Woman." *Village Voice,* October 31, 1989, 39–41.

Lyman, Stanford M. *Chinese Americans.* New York: Random House, 1974.

———. "Marriage and the Family among Chinese Immigrants to America, 1850–1960." *Phylon* 29.4 (Winter 1969): 321–30.

Mark, Diane Mei Lin, and Ginger Chih. *A Place Called Chinese America.* Dubuque, Iowa: Kendall/Hunt, 1982.

McCreesh, Carolyn. *Women in the Campaign to Organize Garment Workers, 1880–1917.* New York: Garland Publishing, 1985.

Mei, June. "Socioeconomic Origins of Emigration: Guangdong to California, 1850–1882." In *Labor Immigration under Capitalism: Asian Immigrant Workers in the United States before World War II.* Ed. Edna Bonacich and Lucie Cheng. Berkeley: University of California Press, 1984. 219–45.

Milkman, Ruth, ed. "Gender and Trade Unionism in Historical Perspective." In *Women, Politics, and Change.* Ed. Patricia Gurin and Louise Tilly. New York: Russell Sage Foundation, 1990. 87–107.

———. "New Research in Women's Labor History." *Signs: Journal of Women in Culture and Society* 18.2 (Winter 1993): 376–88.

———. "Organizing Immigrant Women in New York's Chinatown: An Interview with Katie Quan." In *Women and Unions.* Ed. Dorothy Sue Cobble. Ithaca, N.Y.: ILR Press, 1993. 281–98.

———."Union Responses to Workforce Feminization in the United States." In *North American Labor: Divergent Trajectories.* Ed. Jane Jenson and Rianne Mahon. Philadelphia: Temple University Press, 1994. 226–50.

———, ed. *Women, Work, and Protest: A Century of U.S. Women's Labor History.* New York: Routledge and Kegan Paul, 1985.

———. "Women Workers, Feminism, and the Labor Movement since the 1960s." In *Women, Work, and Protest: A Century of U.S. Women's Labor History.* Ed. Ruth Milkman. New York: Routledge and Kegan Paul, 1985. 300–322.

Moss, Mitchell L. "Made in New York: The Future of Manufacturing in the City of New York." Report published by the Robert F. Wagner Graduate School of Public Service of the Urban Research Center at New York University, 1994.

Nee, Victor, and Brett de Bary Nee. *Longtime Californ': A Documentary Study of an American Chinatown.* New York: Pantheon Books, 1972.

Needleman, Ruth. "Building Relationships for the Long Haul: Unions and Community-Based Groups Working Together to Organize Low-Wage Workers." In *Organizing to Win: New*

Research on Union Strategies. Ed. Kate Bronfenbrenner et al. Ithaca, N.Y.: Cornell University Press, 1998. 71–86.

———. "Women Workers: Strategies for Inclusion and Rebuilding." In *A New Labor Movement for the New Century.* Ed. Gregory Mantsios. New York: Monthly Review Press, 1998. 151–70.

New York Asian Women's Center. *Tenth Anniversary Report, 1982–92.*

New York Garment Industry Development Corporation. "A Child Care Study of the New York City Garment Industry." Study prepared for the New York City Department of Business Services, 1991.

Ng, Franklin. "The Sojourner, Return Migration, and Immigration History." In *Chinese America: History and Perspectives, 1987.* San Francisco: Chinese Historical Society of America, 1987. 53–71.

Northrup, Herbert R. *Organized Labor and the Negro.* New York: Harper and Bros., 1944.

O'Hare, William P., and Judy C. Felt. *Asian Americans: Americans' Fastest Growing Minority Group.* Washington, D.C.: Population Reference Bureau, 1991.

Omatsu, Glenn. "Asian Pacific American Workers and the Expansion of Democracy." *Amerasia Journal* 18.1 (1992): v–xix.

———. "The 'Four Prisons' and the Movement of Liberation: Asian American Activism from the 1960s to the 1990s." In *The State of Asian America: Activism and Resistance in the 1990s.* Ed. Karin Aguilar–San Juan. Boston: South End Press, 1994. 19–69.

Ong, Aihwa. *Spirits of Resistance and Capitalist Discipline: Factory Women in Malaysia.* Albany: State University of New York Press, 1987.

Ono, Kazuko. *Chinese Women in a Century of Revolution, 1850–1950.* Stanford, Calif.: Stanford University Press, 1989.

Orleck, Annelise. *Common Sense and a Little Fire: Women and Working-Class Politics in the United States, 1900–1965.* Chapel Hill: University of North Carolina Press, 1995.

Ortiz, Altagracia. "*'En la aguja y el pedal eche la hiel':* Puerto Rican Workers in the Garment Industry of New York City, 1920–1980." In *Puerto Rican Women and Work: Bridges in Transnational Labor.* Ed. Altagracia Ortiz. Philadelphia: Temple University Press, 1996. 55–81.

———. "Puerto Rican Workers in the Garment Industry of New York City, 1920–1960." In *Labor Divided: Race and Ethnicity in United States Labor Struggle, 1835–1960.* Ed. Robert Asher and Charles Stephenson. Albany: State University of New York Press, 1990. 105–25.

Park, Kyeyoung. *The Korean American Dream: Immigrants and Small Business in New York City.* Ithaca, N.Y.: Cornell University Press, 1997.

Passero, Rosara Lucy. "Ethnicity in the Men's Ready-Made Clothing Industry, 1880–1950: The Italian Experience in Philadelphia." Ph.D. dissertation, University of Pennsylvania, 1978.

Pesotta, Rose. *Bread upon the Waters.* 1944. Ithaca, N.Y.: ILR Press, 1976.

Pessar, Patricia R. "The Dominicans: Women in the Household and the Garment Industry." In *New Immigrants in New York.* Ed. Nancy Foner. New York: Columbia University Press, 1987. 103–29.

———. "Sweatshop Workers and Domestic Ideologies: Dominican Women in New York's Apparel Industry." *International Journal of Urban and Regional Research* 18.1 (1994): 127–42.

Phizacklea, Annie. "Jobs for the Girls: The Production of Women's Outerwear in the UK." In *Ethnic Minorities and Industrial Change in Europe and North America.* Ed. Malcolm Cross. Cambridge: Cambridge University Press, 1992. 94–110.

Pope, Jesse Eliphalet. *The Clothing Industry in New York.* New York: Burt Franklin, 1905.

Proper, Carl. "New York: Defending the Union Contract." In *No Sweat: Fashion, Free Trade, and the Rights of Garment Workers.* Ed. Andrew Ross. New York: Verso, 1997. 173–92.

Quan, Katie. "Chinese Garment Workers in New York City." *Migration World* 14.1–2 (1986): 46–49.

Reimers, David. *Still the Golden Door: The Third World Comes to America.* New York: Columbia University Press, 1985.

Rice, Florence. "It Takes a While to Realize That It Is Discrimination." In *Black Women in White America: A Documentary History.* Ed. Gerda Lerner. New York: Random House, 1973. 275–81.

Riis, Jacob A. *How the Other Half Lives: Studies among the Tenements of New York.* 1890. New York: Hill and Wang, 1957.

Roediger, David R. *The Wages of Whiteness: Race and the Making of the American Working Class.* New York: Verso, 1991.

Ross, Andrew, ed. *No Sweat: Fashion, Free Trade, and the Rights of Garment Workers.* New York: Verso, 1997.

Safa, Helen I. "Runaway Shops and Female Employment: The Search for Cheap Labor." *Signs: Journal of Women in Culture and Society* 7.2 (1981): 418–33.

Salaff, Janet W. "Wage Earners in Hong Kong." In *Lives: Chinese Working Women.* Ed. Mary Sheridan and Janet W. Salaff. Bloomington: Indiana University Press, 1984. 146–71.

———. *Working Daughters of Hong Kong: Filial Piety or Power in the Family?* 1981. New York: Columbia University Press, 1995.

Sankar, Andrea. "Spinster Sisterhoods." In *Lives: Chinese Working Women.* Ed. Mary Sheridan and Janet W. Salaff. Bloomington: Indiana University Press, 1984. 51–75.

Saxton, Alexander. *The Indispensable Enemy: Labor and the Anti-Chinese Movement in California.* Berkeley: University of California Press, 1971.

Schneiderman, Rose. *All for One.* New York: Paul S. Ericksson, 1967.

Schwartz, Shepard. "Mate-Selection among New York City's Chinese Males, 1931–1938." *American Journal of Sociology* 56 (May 1951): 562–68.

Scott, James C. *Weapons of the Weak: Everyday Forms of Peasant Resistance.* New Haven, Conn.: Yale University Press, 1985.

Scott, Joan W. "Experience." In *Feminists Theorize the Political.* Ed. Judith Butler and Joan W. Scott. New York: Routledge, 1992. 22–40.

———, ed. *Feminism and History.* New York: Oxford University Press, 1996.

———, ed. *Gender and the Politics of History.* New York: Columbia University Press, 1988.

———. "On Language, Gender, and Working Class History." In *Gender and the Politics of History.* Ed. Joan W. Scott. New York: Columbia University Press, 1988. 53–67.

———. "Women in the Making of the English Working Class." In *Gender and the Politics of History.* Ed. Joan W. Scott. New York: Columbia University Press, 1988. 68–90.

Seidman, Joel. *The Needle Trades: Labor in Twentieth-Century America.* New York: Farrar and Rinehart, 1942.

Shapiro, Ann-Louise, ed. *Feminists Revision History.* New Brunswick, N.J.: Rutgers University Press, 1994.

Sheridan, Mary, and Janet W. Salaff, eds. *Lives: Chinese Working Women.* Bloomington: Indiana University Press, 1984.

Siu, C. P. Paul. *The Chinese Laundryman: A Study of Social Isolation.* New York: New York University Press, 1987.

Siu, Helen F. *Agents and Victims in South China: Accomplices in Rural Revolution.* New Haven, Conn.: Yale University Press, 1989.

———. "Immigrants and Social Ethos: Hong Kong in the Nineteen-Eighties." *Journal of the Hong Kong Branch of the Royal Asiatic Society* 26 (1988): 1–16.

———. "Where Were the Women? Rethinking Marriage Resistance and Regional Culture in South China." *Late Imperial China* 11.2 (December 1990): 32–62.

Stacey, Judith. *Patriarchy and Socialist Revolution in China.* Berkeley: University of California Press, 1983.

Stansell, Christine. *City of Women: Sex and Class in New York, 1789–1860.* Urbana: University of Illinois Press, 1986.

———. "The Origins of the Sweatshop: Women and Early Industrialization in New York City." In *Working-Class America: Essays on Labor, Community, and American Society.* Ed. Michael H. Frisch and Daniel J. Walkawitz. Urbana: University of Illinois Press, 1983. 78–103.

State of New York. *Census of Population.* Manuscripts. 1905, 1915, 1925.

Stein, Leon. Introduction to *Out of the Sweatshop: The Struggle for Industrial Democracy.* Ed. Leon Stein. New York: Quadrangle Books, 1977. xv–xvi.

———, ed. *Out of the Sweatshop: The Struggle for Industrial Democracy.* New York: Quadrangle Books, 1977.

Stockard, Janice E. *Daughters of the Canton Delta: Marriage Patterns and Economic Strategies in South China, 1860–1930.* Stanford, Calif.: Stanford University Press, 1989.

Stolberg, Benjamin. *Tailor's Progress: The Story of a Famous Union and the Men Who Made It.* New York: Doubleday, Doran and Co., 1944.

Sung, Betty Lee. *The Adjustment Experience of Chinese Immigrant Children in New York City.* Staten Island, N.Y.: Center for Migration Studies, 1987.

———. *Chinese Population in Lower Manhattan.* Report for the Employment and Training Administration, U.S. Department of Labor, 1978.

———. *Mountain of Gold: The Story of the Chinese in America.* New York: Macmillan, 1967.

———. *A Survey of Chinese-American Manpower and Employment.* New York: Praeger, 1976.

Takaki, Ronald. *A Different Mirror: A History of Multicultural America.* Boston: Little, Brown and Co., 1993.

———. *Strangers from a Different Shore: A History of Asian Americans.* New York: Penguin, 1990.

———. "They Also Came: The Migration of Chinese and Japanese Women to Hawaii and the Continental United States." In *Chinese America: History and Perspectives, 1990.* Brisbane, Calif.: Chinese Historical Society, 1990.

Tax, Meredith. *The Rising of the Women: Feminist Solidarity and Class Conflict, 1880–1917.* New York: Monthly Review Press, 1980.

Tchen, John Kuo Wei. "New York Chinese: The Nineteenth-Century Pre-Chinatown Settlement." In *Chinese America: History and Perspectives, 1990.* San Francisco: Chinese Historical Society of America, 1990. 157–92.

Teng, Shiree. "Women, Community and Equality: Three Garment Workers Speak Out." *East Wind* 2.1 (Spring/Summer 1983): 20–23.

Thomas, R. D. *A Trip on the West River.* Canton: China Baptist Publication Society, 1903.

Tienda, Marta. "Immigrant, Gender, and the Process of Occupational Change in the U.S." *International Migration* 18.4 (1984): 1021–44.

Tilly, Louise, and Joan W. Scott. *Women, Work, and Family.* New York: Holt, Rinehart and Winston, 1978.

Topley, Marjorie. "Marriage Resistance in Rural Kwangtung." In *Women in Chinese Society.*

Ed. Margery Wolf and Roxanne Witke. Stanford, Calif.: Stanford University Press, 1975. 67–88.

Tsai, Henry Shih-shan. *The Chinese Experience in America.* Bloomington: Indiana University Press, 1986.

Tung, William L. *The Chinese in America, 1820–1973: A Chronology and Fact Book.* Dobbs Ferry, N.Y.: Oceana Publications, 1974.

Tyler, Gus. "Contemporary Labor's Attitude toward the Negro." In *The Negro and the American Labor Movement.* Ed. Julius Jacobson. Garden City, N.Y.: Anchor Books, 1968. 358–79.

———. *Look for the Union Label: A History of the International Ladies' Garment Workers' Union.* Armonk, N.Y.: M. E. Sharpe, 1995.

U.S. Department of Commerce. Bureau of the Census. *Census of Population.* 1910–90.

———. *Census of Manufactures.* 1992.

———. *Statistical Abstract of the United States.* 1970–95.

U.S. Department of Justice. Bureau of Immigration and Naturalization Service. *Annual Report.* Washington, D.C: Government Printing Office, 1945–78.

———. *Statistical Yearbook.* Washington, D.C.: Government Printing Office, 1979–95.

U.S. Office of Management and Budget. *Standard Industrial Classification: Manual.* Washington, D.C.: National Technical Information Service, 1987.

Van Norden, Warner M. *Who's Who of the Chinese in New York.* New York: n.p., 1918.

Vittoz, Stanley. *New Deal Labor Policy and the American Industrial Economy.* Chapel Hill: University of North Carolina Press, 1987.

Vogel, Ezra. *Canton under Communism: Programs and Politics in a Provincial Capital, 1949–1968.* Cambridge, Mass.: Harvard University Press, 1969.

Wain, Barry. *The Refused: The Agony of the Indochina Refugees.* New York: Simon and Schuster, 1981.

Waldinger, Roger. "Another Look at the International Ladies' Garment Workers' Union: Women, Industry Structure, and Collective Action." In *Women, Work, and Protest: A Century of U.S. Women's Labor History.* Ed. Ruth Milkman. New York: Routledge and Kegan Paul, 1985. 86–109.

———. "Immigrant Enterprises in the New York Garment Industry." *Social Problems* 32.1 (October 1984): 60–71.

———. *Through the Eye of the Needle: Immigrants and Enterprise in New York's Garment Trades.* New York: New York University Press, 1986.

Waldinger, Roger, and Yenfeng Tseng. "Diverse Diaspora: The Chinese Communities of New York and Los Angeles Compared." *Revue Europeenne des Migrations Internationales* 8.3 (1992): 91–111.

Wan, Enoch Yee Nock. "The Dynamics of Ethnicity: A Case Study on the Immigrant Community of New York Chinatown." Ph.D. dissertation, State University of New York at Stony Brook, 1978.

Warner, Malcolm. "Chinese Trade Unions: Structure and Function in a Decade of Economic Reform, 1979–89." In *Organized Labor in the Asia-Pacific Region: A Comparative Study of Trade Unionism in Nine Countries.* Ed. Stephen Frenkel. Ithaca, N.Y.: ILR Press, 1993. 59–81.

Watson, James L. *Emigration and the Chinese Lineage: The Mans in Hong Kong and London.* Berkeley: University of California Press, 1975.

Watson, Rubie S. "Girls' Houses and Working Women: Expressive Culture in the Pearl River

Delta, 1900–41." In *Women and Chinese Patriarchy: Submission, Servitude, and Escape*. Ed. Maria Jaschok and Suzanne Miers. Atlantic Highlands, N.J.: Zed Books, 1994. 25–44.

Watts, Tamara. "Women, Gender, and Trade Unions: Jennie Matyas and the San Francisco International Ladies' Garment Workers' Union, 1934–1941." Honor's thesis, Stanford University, 1993.

Wei Min She Labor Committee. *Chinese Working People in America: A Pictorial History*. San Francisco: United Front Press, 1974.

Weiner, Elizabeth, and Hardy Green. "A Stitch in Our Time: New York's Hispanic Garment Workers in the 1980s." In *A Needle, a Bobbin, and a Strike*. Ed. Jane Jenson and Sue Davidson. Philadelphia: Temple University Press, 1984. 278–96.

Wertheimer, Barbara, and Anne Nelson. *Trade Union Women: A Study of their Participation in New York City Locals*. New York: Praeger, 1975.

Wolf, Diane Lauren. *Factory Daughters: Gender, Household Dynamics, and Rural Industrialization in Java*. Berkeley: University of California Press, 1992.

Wolf, Margery. "Chinese Women: Old Skills in a New Context." In *Women, Culture, and Society*. Ed. Michelle Zimbalist Rosaldo and Louis Lamphere. Stanford, Calif.: Stanford University Press, 1974. 157–72.

———. *Revolution Postponed: Women in Contemporary China*. Stanford, Calif.: Stanford University Press, 1985.

———. "Women and Suicide in China." In *Women in Chinese Society*. Ed. Margery Wolf and Roxanne Witke. Stanford, Calif.: Stanford University Press, 1975. 111–41.

Wolf, Margery, and Roxanne Witke, eds. *Women in Chinese Society*. Stanford, Calif.: Stanford University Press, 1975.

Woloch, Nancy. *Women and the American Experience*. New York: Alfred A. Knopf, 1984.

Wong, Bernard P. *Chinatown: Economic Adaptation and Ethnic Identity of the Chinese*. New York: Holt, Rinehart and Winston, 1982.

———. "The Chinese: New Immigrants in New York's Chinatown." In *New Immigrants in New York*. Ed. Nancy Foner. New York: Columbia University Press, 1987. 243–71.

———. *Patronage, Brokerage, Enterpreneurship, and the Chinese Community of New York*. New York: AMS Press, 1988.

———. "The Role of Ethnicity in Enclave Enterprises: A Study of the Chinese Garment Factories in New York City." *Human Organization* 46.2 (1987): 120–29.

Wong, Morrison G. "Chinese Sweatshops in the United States: A Look at the Garment Industry." *Research in the Sociology of Work: Peripheral Workers*. Vol. 2. Ed. I. H. Simpson and R. L. Simpson Greenwich, Conn.: JAI Press, 1983. 357–79.

Wong, K. Scott, and Sucheng Chan, eds. *Claiming America: Constructing Chinese American Identities during the Exclusion Era*. Philadelphia: Temple University Press, 1998.

Woon, Yuen-Fong. *The Excluded Wife*. Montreal: McGill–Queen's University Press, 1998.

———. "International Links and the Socioeconomic Development of Rural China: An Emigrant Community in Guangdong." *Modern China* 16.2 (April 1990): 139–72.

———. "Social Change and Continuity in South China: Overseas Chinese and the Guan Lineage of Kaiping County, 1949–87." *China Quarterly* 118 (June 1989): 324–44.

Wong Chin Foo. "The Chinese in New York." *Cosmopolitan* 5 (March–October 1888): 297–311.

———. "The Chinese in the United States." *The Chautauquan* 9 (October 1888–July 1889): 215–17.

Wrong, Elaine Gale. *The Negro in the Apparel Industry*. Philadelphia: University of Pennsylvania Press, 1974.

Wu, Cheng-Tsu. "Chinese People and Chinatown in New York City." Ph.D. dissertation, Clark University, 1958.

Wu Xingci, and Li Zhen. "Gum San Haak in the 1980s: A Study on Chinese Emigrants Who Return to Taishan County for Marriage." *Amerasia Journal* 14.2 (1988): 21–35.

Yans-McLaughlin, Virginia. "Italian Women and Work: Experience and Perception." In *Class, Sex, and the Woman Worker*. Ed. Milton Cantor and Bruce Laurie. Westport, Conn.: Greenwood, 1977. 101–19.

————. "Metaphors of Self in History: Subjectivity, Oral Narrative, and Immigration Studies." In *Immigration Reconsidered: History, Sociology, and Politics*. Ed. Virginia Yans-McLaughlin. New York: Oxford University Press, 1990. 254–90.

Yap, Stacey G. H. *Gather Your Strength, Sisters: The Emerging Role of Chinese Women Community Workers*. New York: AMS Press, 1989.

Young, John. "The Building Years: Maintaining a China–Hong Kong–Britain Equilibrium, 1950–1971." In *Precarious Balance: Hong Kong between China and Britain, 1842–1992*. Ed. Ming K. Chan. Armonk, N.Y.: M. E. Sharpe, 1994. 131–47.

Yu, Renqiu. "Chinese American Contributions to the Educational Development of Toisan, 1910–1940." *Amerasia Journal* 10.1 (1983): 47–72.

————. *To Save China, to Save Ourselves: The Chinese Hand Laundry Alliance of New York*. Philadelphia: Temple University Press, 1992.

Yung, Judy. *Chinese Women of America: A Pictorial History*. Seattle: University of Washington Press, 1986.

————. "Giving Voice to Chinese American Women." *Frontiers: A Journal of Women Studies* 19.3 (1998): 130–49.

————. *Unbound Feet: A Social History of Chinese Women in San Francisco*. Berkeley: University of California Press, 1995.

Yung Wing. *My Life in China and America*. New York: Henry Holt, 1909.

Zhou, Min. *Chinatown: The Socioeconomic Potential of an Urban Enclave*. Philadelphia: Temple University Press, 1992.

Zo, Kil Young. *Chinese Emigration into the United States, 1850–1880*. New York: Arno Press, 1978.

Zurawshy, Christopher. "Battling the Bosses: The Chinese Staff and Workers Association Confronts the Exploitation of Immigrants in the Garment Industry." *City Limits*, April 1993, 6–8.

INDEX

AAMA. *See* American Apparel Manufacturers' Association
ACFTU. *See* All-China Federation of Trades
A Fang, 243
AIWA. *See* Asian Immigrant Women Advocate
A Ling, 140–42
All-China Federation of Trades (ACFTU), 168
American Apparel Manufacturers' Association (AAMA), 180, 197
AOGMA. *See* Association of Oriental Garment Manufacturers of America
APALA. *See* Asian-Pacific American Labor Association
Appelbaum, Richard P., 214
Appleton, Shelly, 154
Arrigo, Linda Gail, 167–68
Asian American Legal Defense and Education Fund, 210
Asian Americans for Equal Employment. *See* Asian Americans for Equality
Asian Americans for Equality, 185, 202
Asian Immigrant Women Advocate (AIWA), 241
Asian Labor Committee, 238–39
Asian-Pacific American Labor Association (APALA), 238
Asian Women's Center, 230–31
Association of Oriental Garment Manufacturers of America (AOGMA), 183–84, 209, 219
A Ying, 99, 105, 119–21, 140–42

Barbash, Jack, 36
Beekman Hospital, 58
Blutter, Sam, 198
Bonner, Arthur, 47, 57

Boris, Eileen, 128
Buck, Rinker, 178–79, 182
Burshy, Yetta, 31

Cantonese dialect, 7, 262n.1
Caribbean Basin Initiative (CBI), 24
CBI. *See* Caribbean Basin Initiative
CCBA. *See* Chinese Consolidated Benevolence Association
CCP. *See* Chinese Communist Party
CGMA. *See* Continental Garment Makers' Association
Chaikin, Sol, 179–80, 184, 202, 206, 210
Chen, Aunt, 93
Chen, Mark, 98–99, 104–5
Chen, May Ying, 231–32, 235–36, 238–39, 254
Chen Donglu, 103, 228–29, 300n.53
Chen family, 98–99, 104–5
Cheng, Joanna, 254
Chen Hsiang-shui, 62
Chen Jianwan, 103
Chen Miaoying, 212
Chen Mingxin, 104
Chen Qianwen, 202
Chen Xue, 86
Chen Zhonghai, 57
Chin, Ko-lin, 298n.17
Chin, Wing Fong, 152, 205, 263–64n.7
China: immigrants from, 53–54, 63, 106, 133–39, 223, 227; post-1949, 94–97; state of labor in, 168–69; state policy toward overseas Chinese, 95–96; women's status in, 94. *See also* Guangdong, emigrant communities in
Chinatown (Brooklyn, N.Y.), 226–27, 299n.44; Huang Kongwang incident in, 233. *See also* Garment industry, Chinese

13; types of, 114–15; worker-employer relationships in, 128–33; workers' relationships in, 133–42; work hours in, 119–22

—employers in, 118–19, 139–40, 174–84, 219, 225–26, 228, 253; compared with New York City's early contractors, 66–67, 127, 187; differences among, 127–33, 182, 294n.46; and the ILGWU, 23–25, 152–53, 176–78, 181; women among, 118–19

—unionization of, 1–2, 152–62, 169–70, 263–64n.7; and benefits for union members, 153–54; changes (or lack of) after 1982, 217–19; and Chinese on union staff, 217; and gender of union staff, 161–62; impact of the union's financial problem on, 219, 223, 225; workers' responses to, 154–55, 156

—workers in, 26; compared with New York City's early women workers, 66, 71, 73; gender differences among, 133–36, 138–40; women among, 1–2, 58–61, 66, 68, 71, 73, 105–9, 184–98

Garment industry, New York City: and the AAMA, 197; African-American workers in, 24–25, 37–42; contracting system in, 16–20, 28, 31; contracting system in, impact on women, 31; Dominican workers in, 26, 42; and the Fashion Institute of Technology, 243; and the GBSUA, 183–84, 197, 199–201, 206–7, 209, 220; and the GIDC, 220; and homeworkers, 42; and imports/offshore production, 23–24, 173–74, 214–15; Korean workers in, 216; as the largest manufacturing industry, 253; and men's clothing, 17; and men's clothing, women workers in, 28–29; and the National Association of Blouse Manufacturers, 198; and the New York Skirt and Sportswear Association, 198, 215; and the NTWIU, 39; Puerto Rican workers in, 24–25, 37–42; role of retailers in, 214–15, 297n.10; sexual harassment in, 30, 40; wages in, 23, 214–15, 268n.41; and women's clothing, women workers in, 29. *See also* Garment industry, Chinese; Garment workers, Chinese women; International Ladies Garment Workers' Union

—division of labor by gender, 20, 27–31; shifting rationale for, 30; skill scales and wages, 27–30

—early years of: "inside shops," 17, 28, 31; "outside shops," 17, 28; slop work, 15, 28; spot market, 21, 25; task system, 20; use of sewing machines, 16–17; and women, 30–31

—women workers in: ethnic/racial tension among, 37–39; solidarity among, 37, "Uprising of 20,000," 31

Garment workers, Chinese women: backgrounds of, 59–61, 66, 73, 169, 277n.79; campaign for daycare centers, 123–25, 186–87, 286n.43; childcare problems of, 185–86; compared with early European women workers, 2–3, 66, 73, 127–28, 133, 137; compared with organized Asian women workers in the U.S., 1, 153; contradictions in the lives of, 249–51; differences and similarities among, 7–8, 133–42; forms of resistance among, 132–33, 184–85, 248; and homeworkers, 121–28; and homeworkers, compared with ethnic counterparts, 127–28; impact of strike (1982) on, 231–44; marital status of, 2, 73, 278n.1; single women among, 278n.1; strike (1982) by, 203–12; unionists among, 231–39. *See also* Asian Immigrant Women Advocate; Asian-Pacific American Labor Association; Chinese Staff and Workers' Association; Coalition of Labor Union Women; Garment industry, Chinese; Garment industry, New York City; *names of Chinese women garment workers*

Gates, Hill, 168

GATT. *See* General Agreement on Tariffs and Trade

GBSUA. *See* Greater Blouse, Skirt and Undergarment Association

General Agreement on Tariffs and Trade (GATT), 214

Gereffi, Gary, 214

GIDC. *See* Garment Industrial Development Corporation

Gim, Benjamin, 230

Glenn, Evelyn Nakano, 73–74

Glenn, Susan, 27, 118

GMD. *See* Chinese National Party

Goldstein, Ted, 148, 149

Gong Hing Shop, incident at, 178

Greater Blouse, Skirt and Undergarment Association (GBSUA), 183–84, 197, 199–201, 206–7, 209, 220

Green, Nancy, 17, 21, 32, 111, 118, 128

Guangdong, emigrant communities in, 81–88, 93–97; and *jam jun luhng*, 86, 281n.47; patriarchal control in, 85–87; women's education in, 53, 97; women's resistance in, 87–88, 96–97

Guo Yulan, 208

Guo Zhengzhi, 43, 47, 58–59

HERE. *See* Hotel Employees' and Restaurant Employees' Union

Heyer, Virginia, 4, 58

Hong Kong: immigrants from, 48, 53–54, 62,

XIAOLAN BAO is an associate professor of history at California State University at Long Beach.

The Asian American Experience

Typeset in 10.5/11.5 Minion
with Fenice display
Composed by Jim Proefrock
at the University of Illinois Press
Manufactured by Thomson-Shore, Inc.

University of Illinois Press
1325 South Oak Street
Champaign, IL 61820-6903
www.press.uillinois.edu